Y0-CDD-530

STREET LAW

A COURSE IN PRACTICAL LAW

third edition

**With
New York State
Supplement**

From The National Institute for Citizen Education in the Law
and West Publishing Company

STREET LAW

LAW

A COURSE IN PRACTICAL LAW

third edition

**With
New York State
Supplement**

Edward T. McMahon, M.Ed., J.D.
Adjunct Professor of Law
Georgetown University Law Center

Lee P. Arbetman, M.Ed., J.D.
Adjunct Professor of Law
Georgetown University Law Center

Edward L. O'Brien, J.D.
Adjunct Professor of Law
Georgetown University Law Center

A Publication of the National Institute
for Citizen Education in the Law

West Publishing Company
St. Paul   New York   Los Angeles   San Francisco

Photo credits on p. 443
National Advisory Committee p. 445

Cover design: Theresa Jensen/Delor Erickson
Copy editor: Joan Torkildson
Compositor: Metro Graphic Arts, Inc.

Copyright © 1975, 1980 by WEST PUBLISHING COMPANY
Copyright © 1987 by WEST PUBLISHING COMPANY
                50 W. Kellogg Boulevard
                P.O. Box 64526
                St. Paul, MN 55164–1003

All rights reserved
Printed in the United States of America

96 95 94 93 92 91 90 89   8 7 6 5 4 3 2 1

Library of Congress Cataloging-in-Publication Data

McMahon, Edward T. (Edward Tracy), 1947-Street law.

   Rev. ed. of: Street law / Lee Arbetman. 2nd. ed. 1980.
   Includes index.
   Summary: A law textbook for students, designed to give them
practical advice, knowledge, and skills to survive in our "law-
saturated" society.
   1. Law—United States—Popular works. [1. Law. 2. Life skills.
3. Consumer education] I. Arbetman, Lee. II. O'Brien, Edward L. III.
Arbetman, Lee. Street law. IV. Title.

KF387.A73   1986   349.73'0712   85–26560
                        347.300712

ISBN 0–314–38243–7

CONTENTS

one

INTRODUCTION TO LAW AND THE LEGAL SYSTEM · 2

CRIMINAL AND JUVENILE JUSTICE ·38

CONSUMER LAW • 118

FAMILY LAW • 192

HOUSING LAW · 256

six INDIVIDUAL RIGHTS AND LIBERTIES • 308

PREFACE

This third edition of *Street Law: A Course in Practical Law* builds upon the success and popularity of the earlier editions. Incorporating the best features of the original text, this third edition provides new information, practical advice, and competency building activities designed to provide students with the ability to analyze, evaluate, and in some situations resolve legal disputes. The text reflects the changes in law and legal procedure that have taken place at the national level since the appearance of the second edition. However, law varies — in some instances significantly — from state to state. A textbook is not a substitute for the legal advice that can be provided only by an attorney.

Street Law's approach to law-related education is to provide practical information and problem-solving opportunities that develop in students the knowledge and skills necessary for survival in our law saturated society. The curriculum includes case studies, mock trials, role plays, small group exercises, opinion polls, and visual analysis activities. For optimal use, *Street Law* requires the use of community resource people such as lawyers and police officers. It also requires community experiences such as court tours and police ride-alongs. This educational methodology allows students to be active participants in their own learning. In this way, we hope to promote in students a willingness and capability to participate effectively in the legal and political system.

THE NATIONAL INSTITUTE FOR CITIZEN EDUCATION IN THE LAW

The National Institute for Citizen Education in the Law is an outgrowth of a Georgetown University program started in 1971 in which law students teach law courses in District of Columbia high schools, in juvenile and adult correctional institutions, and in a number of community based programs.

The Institute was created to promote increased opportunities for citizen education in law. It is involved in course development, teacher training, and program replication. Other Institute activities include providing technical assistance and curriculum materials to law schools, school systems, departments of corrections, juvenile justice agencies, bar associations, legal service organizations, community groups, state and local government, and others interested in establishing law-related education programs.

Other publications of the National Institute include the following:

Great Trials in American History (1985)
Excel in Civics (1985)
Current Legal Issues Filmstrip Series (1985)
Family Law: Competencies in Law and Citizenship (1984)
Street Law: Mock Trial Kit (1984)
Current Legal Issues Filmstrip Series (1984)
Consumer Law: Competencies in Law and Citizenship (1983)
Street Law Filmstrip Series (1983)
Law and the Consumer (1982)
Practical Law for Correctional Personnel (1981)

For further information or assistance, please contact the
National Institute for Citizen Education in the Law
25 E Street, N.W.
Suite 400
Washington, D.C. 20001
(202) 662–9220

ACKNOWLEDGMENTS

Development of this third edition of *Street Law* was funded in part under a grant (#79-JN-AX-0004) from the Office of Juvenile Justice and Delinquency Prevention, U.S. Department of Justice. Points of view or opinions in this publication are those of the authors and do not necessarily represent the official position or policies of the U.S. Department of Justice.

The authors also gratefully acknowledge the many teachers, law students, and attorneys who have assisted in the development of our curriculum materials. Over the years, many people have provided valuable research, editorial assistance, encouragement, and support. We appreciate all those who have assisted our efforts, and we particularly wish to thank the following people who worked with us on the third edition of *Street Law* : Paul Bergman, Marilyn Cover, Elisabeth Dreyfuss, Karen Egbert, Margaret Fisher, Jeanett Gringo, Rebecca Habbert, Bob Hayman, John Hicks, Allen Hile, Rochelle Heard, Jeff Carp, Cindy Kelly, Joe Libertelli, Melinda Smith, Nancy Switkes, and Sandra Wilmore.

We are also grateful for the assistance provided to us by our friends and colleagues at the National Institute for Citizen Education in the Law: Michael Green, Mary Curd-Larkin, Vivian Mills, Jason Newman, and Richard Roe all provided valuable ideas and encouragement. A special thanks to Cathy Holloman and Linda Jones, who spent countless hours typing the manuscript. While these acknowledgments do not list all who worked on earlier editions of *Street Law*, we very much appreciate their contributions.

Over the years, many individuals and organizations have helped make the work of the National Institute for Citizen Education in the Law possible. We appreciate their support and acknowledge their assistance. We particularly wish to thank the following organizations for their recent contributions:

Allstate Insurance Company
American Telephone and Telegraph Foundation
Exxon Corporation
Georgetown University Law Center
Hechinger Company Foundation
Holland and Knight Foundation
International Paper Company Foundation
Knight-Ridder Newspapers
Lazard Freres and Company
Mobil Foundation
Olin Corporate Charitable Trust
Publix Super Markets (through George W. Jenkins Foundation)
Satellite Business Systems
Texaco Philanthropic Foundation
Times Publishing Company
U.S. Trust Company
West Publishing Company

Allstate Insurance Company
American Telephone and Telegraph Company
Best Products Foundation
Eugene and Agnes Meyer Foundation
Exxon Corporation
Field Foundation
General Mills Foundation
Georgetown University Law Center
Hattie M. Strong Foundation
Hechinger Company Foundation
Holland and Knight
International Paper Company
Knight-Ridder Newspapers
Lazard Freres & Co.
Mead Data Central
Mobil Foundation
National Home Library Foundation
New World Foundation
Olin Corporate Charitable Trust
Publix Super Markets (through George W. Jenkins Foundation)
Robert F. Kennedy Memorial
Satellite Business Systems
Texaco Philanthropic Foundation
The Phillip M. Stern Family Fund
Times Publishing Company
U.S. Trust Company
West Publishing Company
Weyerhaeuser Foundation, Inc.

Jason Newman, Director
Edward O'Brien, Co-Director
Lee Arbetman
Edward McMahon

Washington, D.C.
March 1986

STREET LAW

A COURSE IN PRACTICAL LAW

third edition

**With
New York State
Supplement**

one
INTRODUCTION TO LAW AND THE LEGAL SYSTEM

Street law is the concept of educating people about law that is of practical use in everyday life (on the streets). Every purchase, lease, contract, marriage, divorce, crime, or traffic violation places the citizen face-to-face with the law. *Street Law* is designed to provide you with an understanding of your legal rights and responsibilities, a knowledge of everyday legal problems, and the ability to analyze, evaluate, and, in some situations, resolve legal disputes.

Many people believe that only those with power and money can win in our legal system. They see the law as a body of confusing, technical rules that work against them. Some people don't believe, for example, that a tenant can get a landlord to fix up a rundown apartment, or that a consumer can convince a merchant to repair, replace, or give a refund for poor quality merchandise. True, these things don't always happen, but they are possible, especially when you are aware of your rights and take action to exercise those rights.

Street Law addresses general problems in the areas of criminal, consumer, family, housing, and individual rights law. The text also discusses situations such as what to do if you are the victim of

3

crime, when and how to select an attorney, the legal rights and responsibilities of parents and children, how to register to vote, and what to do about discrimination or other violations of your constitutional rights. These and all of the topics covered in *Street Law* are designed to help you survive on the street.

WHAT IS LAW?

The question "What is law?" has troubled people for many years. An entire field of study known as **jurisprudence** is devoted to answering this question. Many definitions of law exist, but for our purposes, law can be defined as that set of rules or regulations by which a government regulates the conduct of people within a society. Even with this explanation, many other questions arise. Where do laws come from? Do we need laws? Are all laws written? Can laws change? If so, how? Are all laws fair? What is the difference between laws and morals?

To understand the law, we must consider the relationship of law to morals. Our legal system is influenced by traditional ideas of right and wrong. Thus, most people would condemn murder, regardless of what the law said. However, everything that is considered immoral is not necessarily illegal. For example, lying to a friend may be immoral but is rarely illegal.

One thing is certain: Every society that has ever existed has recognized the need for law. These laws may have been unwritten, but even primitive people had rules to regulate the conduct of the group. Without laws, there would be confusion, fear, and disorder. This does not mean that all laws are fair or even good, but imagine how people might take advantage of one another without some set of rules.

PROBLEM 1

Make a list of all your daily activities (e.g., waking up, eating, going to school). Next to each item on the list indicate whether there are any laws affecting that activity. Are these laws federal, state, or local? What is the purpose of each law that you have identified? Would you change any of these laws? Why?

KINDS OF LAWS

Laws fall into two major groups: criminal and civil. Criminal laws regulate public conduct and set out duties owed to society. A criminal case is a legal action by the government against a person charged with committing a crime. Criminal laws have penalties requiring that offenders be imprisoned, fined, placed under super-

THE CASE OF THE SHIPWRECKED SAILORS

Three sailors on an ocean-going freighter were cast adrift in a life raft after their ship sank during a storm in the Atlantic Ocean. The ship went down so suddenly that there was no time to send out an S.O.S. As far as the three sailors knew, they were the only survivors. In the raft they had no food or water. They had no fishing gear or other equipment that might be used to get food from the ocean.

After recovering from the shock of the shipwreck, the three sailors began to discuss their situation. Dudley, the ship's navigator, figured that they were at least one thousand miles from land and that the storm had blown them far from where any ships would normally pass. Stephens, the ship's doctor, indicated that without food they could not live longer than thirty days. The only nourishment they could expect was from any rain that might fall from time to time. He noted, however, that if one of the three died before the others, the other two could live awhile longer by eating the body of the third.

On the twenty-fifth day, the third sailor, Brooks, who by this time was extremely weak, suggested that they all draw lots and that the loser be killed and eaten by the other two. Both Dudley and Stephens agreed. The next day lots were drawn and Brooks lost. At this point, Brooks objected and refused to consent. However, Dudley and Stephens decided that Brooks would die soon anyway, so they might as well get it over with. After thus agreeing, they killed and ate Brooks.

Five days later, Dudley and Stephens were rescued by a passing ship and brought to port. After recovering from their ordeal, they were placed on trial for murder.

The state in which they were tried had the following law: Any person who deliberately takes the life of another is guilty of murder.

PROBLEM 2

a. Should Dudley and Stephens be tried for murder?
b. As an attorney for Dudley and Stephens, what arguments would you make on their behalf? As an attorney for the state, what arguments would you make on the state's behalf?
c. If they are convicted, what should their punishment be?
d. What purpose would be served by convicting Dudley and Stephens?
e. What is the relationship between law and morality in this case? Was it morally wrong for Dudley and Stephens to kill Brooks? Explain your answer.
f. Can an act be legal but immoral? Can an act be morally right but unlawful?

vision, or punished in some other way. Criminal offenses are divided into **felonies and misdemeanors.** The maximum penalty for a felony is a term of more than one year in prison. For a misdemeanor the penalty is a prison term of one year or less.

Civil laws regulate relations between individuals or groups of individuals. A **civil action** (lawsuit) can be brought when one person feels wronged or injured by another person. Courts may award the injured person money for his or her loss, or it may order the person who committed the wrong to make amends in some other way. An example of a civil action is a lawsuit for recovery of damages suffered in an automobile accident. Civil laws regulate many everyday situations such as marriage, divorce, contracts, real estate, insurance, consumer protection, and negligence.

Sometimes one action can violate both civil and criminal law. For example, if Joe beats up Bob, he may have to pay Bob's medical bills under civil law and may be charged with the crime of assault under criminal law.

PROBLEM 3

Matt and Luther decide to skip school. They take Luther's brother's car without telling him and drive to a local shopping center. Ignoring the sign Parking for Handicapped Persons Only, they leave the car and enter a radio and TV shop.

After looking around they buy a portable AM-FM radio. Then they buy some sandwiches from a street vendor and walk to a nearby park. While eating they discover that the radio does not work. In their hurry to return it, they leave their trash on the park bench.

When Matt and Luther get back to the shopping center, they notice a large dent in one side of their car. The dent appears to be the result of a driver's carelessly backing out of the next space. They also notice that the car has been broken into and that the tape deck has been removed.

They call the police to report the accident and theft. When the police arrive, they seize a small clear bag containing illegal drugs from behind the car's back seat. Matt and Luther are arrested.

a. What laws are involved in this story?

b. Which of these are criminal laws? Which are civil laws?

WHO MAKES LAWS?

Three different lawmaking groups exist in the United States: (1) legislatures, (2) agencies, and (3) courts. Legislatures pass laws directly, agencies develop laws that help put legislative rulings into effect, and courts establish laws as a result of case decisions.

Legislatures

The U.S. Constitution divides the power for making laws between the federal government and the state governments. The United States government has the power to pass federal laws. These laws are binding on the citizens of every state. In addition, every state has the power to pass laws that apply within that particular state.

The lawmaking authority of Congress is exercised by passing laws called federal **statutes.** Federal statutes affect every citizen and concern such issues as national defense, environmental quality, labor relations, veterans' affairs, public health, civil rights, economic development, postal services, and federal taxes.

America is a nation of states. Every state has a constitution, which spells out the basic structure of state government, including an executive, legislative, and judicial branch. The lawmaking

Every state in the United States has a bicameral legislature except Nebraska.

powers of the state are vested in the state legislature, which can pass state laws. Except for Nebraska, every state has a two-house legislature. In most states the legislature meets on an annual basis to pass laws affecting the state. In a few states, the legislatures meet every two years.

Besides the U.S. Congress and the state legislatures, there are other legislative or lawmaking bodies, which are found on the local level in cities, towns, and counties. Local governments pass laws known as **ordinances** or **regulations.** These laws apply only within a particular city or town.

Although legislatures have the power to pass laws affecting many aspects of our daily lives, all lawmaking—federal, state and local—is limited by the U.S. Constitution. The Constitution sets out the structure of our government and establishes the basic rights of all Americans. If a legislature passes a law that violates a basic right, such as the freedom of speech, citizens can go to court and ask that that law be overruled. The process by which courts decide whether the laws passed by Congress or by state or local legislatures are constitutional is known as **judicial review.**

PROBLEM 4

Consider each of the following laws. Is it a federal, state, or local law? After doing this, give an example, not listed in the following, of a federal law, a state law, and a local law.

a. "No parking on the east side of Main Street between 4:00 and 6:00 p.m."

b. "All persons between the ages of six and sixteen must attend school."

c. "Whoever enters a bank for purposes of taking by force or violence the property or money in custody of such bank shall be fined not more than $5,000 or imprisioned not more than twenty years or both."

d. "In order to sell any product on a public street, the seller must first apply for and receive a vendor's permit."

e. "No employer of more than fifteen persons may discriminate on the basis of race, color, religion, sex or national origin."

f. "All persons traveling on interstate airline carriers are subject to search before entering the airplane departure area."

In addition to judicial review, citizens have other ways in which they can influence the lawmaking process. These methods include voting and lobbying.

Voting Voting is a basic right provided by the U.S. Constitution. Citizens of the United States may vote for the president, vice-president, members of the U.S. Senate and House of Representatives, and numerous state and local government officials. Eligible voters may also cast their ballots on **referenda.** These deal with special issues affecting a community. For example, many states have asked voters to decide whether to raise taxes or to ban throwaway bottles.

To qualify to vote, a person must be a U.S. citizen and at least eighteen years old on or before the date of the election. In addition, all states require voters to be residents of the place in which they vote. At one time many states required voters to live in a state for a year or more before being eligible to register. The *Voting Rights Act of 1970* changed this. Eligible persons are now able to vote in all federal elections after living in a state for only thirty days. Residency requirements for state and local elections, however, vary from place to place and may be longer than thirty days.

Registering to vote is easy. Applicants can usually register by completing an application form, in person or by mail. Registering to vote has not always been so easy. Until 1965 some states had literacy and character tests, which kept millions of people from voting. These laws are no longer in effect, but almost all states still bar mentally ill persons and prison inmates from voting. In addition, in almost every state persons convicted of certain types of crimes lose their right to vote.

WHERE YOU LIVE

Where and how do you register to vote in your community? Is there a residency requirement for state and local elections? If so, how long? Where do people in your area go to vote?

PROBLEM 5

In recent years the percentage of eligible voters choosing to vote has gone down (see Figure 1). If you are eligible to vote but have

Why is it important for citizens to register to vote?

FIGURE 1   Voter Turnout in Presidential Elections

National average of voting age population voting: 1960—62.8; 1964—61.9; 1968—60.6; 1972—55.5; 1976—54.3; 1980—53.9. The sharp drop in 1972 reflects the expansion of eligibility with the enfranchisement of eighteen-to twenty-one-year-olds.

State	1980 Registered voters voting	1980 Voting age population voting	1976 Voting age population voting
Ala.	62.9%	49.7%	47.2%
Alas.	60.7	61.3	48.3
Ariz.	78.0	49.1	46.6
Ark.	70.6	53.6	52.2
Cal.	75.6	50.6	51.3
Col.	82.6	57.6	60.4
Conn.	82.4	60.6	62.4
Del.	78.4	56.1	58.4
D.C.	60.2	36.6	33.3
Fla.	76.7	53.6	51.5
Ga.	n/a[1]	43.6	43.3
Ha.	75.3	46.2	48.1
Ida.	75.3	69.0	61.6
Ill.	76.2	59.0	60.6
Ind.	n/a	58.2	61.6
Ia.	76.7	63.0	63.7
Kan.	75.9	55.8	58.4
Ky.	71.0	51.2	49.1
La.	76.8	55.7	49.8
Me.	68.8	66.2	65.0
Md.	74.6	50.7	49.9
Mass.	80.1	58.7	61.6
Mich.	68.3	59.6	58.7
Minn.	86.9	69.2	71.4
Miss.	60.2	54.1	49.5
Mo.	73.9	58.8	57.7
Mon.	73.3	65.0	63.7
Neb.	74.7	56.2	56.1
Nev.	81.7	45.7	47.5
N.H.	73.5	58.4	58.8
N.J.	79.0	55.1	58.1
N.M.	69.9	52.5	54.6
N.Y.	n/a	48.1	50.8
N.C.	66.9	45.8	44.1
N.D.	n/a	64.3	67.2
Oh.	72.8	55.6	55.4
Okla.	76.2	54.0	55.6
Ore.	75.3	61.9	62.1
Pa.	79.3	52.7	54.7
R.I.	78.4	60.5	61.5
S.C.	71.9	42.9	41.7
S.D.	73.2	67.6	63.8
Tenn.	75.3	50.5	49.6
Tex.	68.4	47.1	47.3
Ut.	77.3	67.1	69.4
Vt.	68.4	59.4	56.9
Va.	81.0	48.9	47.7
Wash.	79.8	62.3	61.1
W.Va.	71.0	54.4	58.1
Wis.	n/a	66.0	65.9
Wy.	80.5	52.8	58.1

Source: Committee for the Study of the American Electorate.

n/a = not available.

not registered, explain why. If you are registered but don't vote, explain why. What reasons can you suggest for the decline in voter participation? Should anything be done to change the situation?

Lobbying   The lawmaking process can be affected in other ways besides voting. One common method for influencing government and expressing public opinion is **lobbying.** Lobbying includes all those activities directed at public officials and designed to influence government policies and laws.

Today, interest groups and organizations lobby on behalf of every imaginable cause and issue. Many of these groups hire professional lobbyists, who maintain offices in the District of Columbia or the various state capitals. Although not everyone goes to Washington or their state captial, anyone who wants to express an opinion can be a lobbyist.

Elected representatives are influenced by pressure from their **constituents.** People, either in groups or as individuals, can sometimes affect the way an official votes by expressing their opinion in either a letter or a phone call.

WHERE YOU LIVE

What special interest, pressure, or lobbying groups exist in your state? On behalf of what issues or causes do these groups lobby? What techniques do they use?

PROBLEM 6

Select a current issue that concerns you. Write a letter about it to your state legislator, federal representative, or senator.

Agencies

Many of the laws that affect you are made by government agencies. Once Congress or a state legislature passes a law, they often authorize an administrative agency to develop regulations (rules) implementing the law. These regulations influence almost every aspect of our daily lives and are, in effect, laws. For example, Congress passed a law requiring safe working conditions in places of employment. To implement the law, Congress established the Occupational Safety and Health Administration (OSHA). This agency has the power to develop regulations governing safety and health standards for places of employment. OSHA regulations fill many volumes and cover such specifics as fire exits, employee clothing, and the height of guardrails in factories. Other federal agencies make laws in a similar manner. For example, the Internal Revenue Service (IRS) issues regulations and enforces federal tax laws. The Federal Trade Commission (FTC) issues regulations that, among other things, control advertising across the nation. For a list of the major federal agencies, see Figure 2.

> **ADVICE ON WRITING A PUBLIC OFFICIAL**
>
> Write in your own words. Personal letters are far more effective than form letters or petitions. Tell how the issue will affect you, your friends, family, or job.
>
> Keep your letter short and to the point. Deal with only one issue per letter. If you are writing about some proposed bill or legislation, identify it by name (e.g., the National Consumer Protection Act) and by number if you know it (e.g. H.R. 343 or S. 675).
>
> Begin by telling the official why you are writing. Ask the official to state his or her own position on the issue. Always request a reply, and ask the official to take some kind of definite action (e.g., vote for or against the bill).
>
> Always put your return address on the letter, sign and date it, and keep a copy, if possible. Your letter doesn't have to be typed, but it should be legible. Perhaps most importantly it should reach the official before the issue is voted on.

State and local governments also have agencies that implement the laws passed by legislatures and other governmental bodies. For example, city zoning commissions have the power to decide where different types of buildings, such as factories, homes, or office buildings, can be built. Many states have Alcoholic Beverage Control (ABC) boards, which make rules regarding the sale and drinking of alcoholic beverages in restaurants, liquor stores, nightclubs, and other public places. In addition to their regulatory (lawmaking) function, agencies also administer government programs and provide many services.

Courts

Law is also made by courts. This law is called case law or **common law.** There are two types of courts in the United States: trial and appeals.

Trial courts listen to testimony, consider evidence, and decide the facts in disputed situations. Once a trial court has made a decision, the losing party may be able to **appeal** the decision to an appellate court.

In an **appeals court,** one party presents arguments asking the court to change the decision of the trial court. The other party presents arguments supporting the decision of the trial court. Not everyone who loses a trial can appeal. Usually an appeal is possible only when there is a claim that the trial court has committed an **error of law.** An error of law occurs when the judge makes a mistake as to the law applicable in the case (e.g., give the wrong

FIGURE 2   The Government of the United States

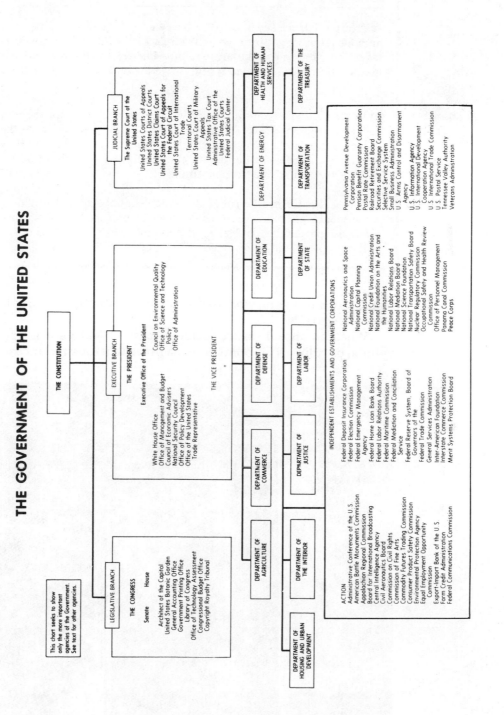

Source: United States Government Manual 1985.

WHERE
YOU
LIVE

What are the major departments or agencies of your state government? How are they organized and what do they do?

THE CASE OF TAKING A CAR BY MISTAKE

Joe Harper left the key in his 1985 blue Camaro. When he came back an hour later, he got into someone else's 1985 blue Camaro by mistake. This car also had the key in it, but Harper, who did not notice it was a different car, started it and drove away. He was arrested for auto theft.

At the trial, the judge told the jury it was not necessary for them to consider whether Harper intended to steal the car. Instead, the judge instructed the jury that to find Harper guilty of auto theft they only had to decide whether he was caught driving a car that was not his. The jury found Joe Harper guilty.

This case illustrates an error of law which could be appealed. This is because auto theft law requires that the accused person must have intended to steal the car. Harper did not intend to steal the car. The guilty verdict could be reversed.

instructions to the jury or permits evidence that should not have been allowed).

When an appeals court decides a case, it will issue a written opinion or ruling. This opinion sets a **precedent** for similar cases in

The Internal Revenue Service collects most of the tax monies that flow into the federal treasury.

the future. When an appellate court rules on a matter, all lower courts in the place where the decision is made must follow the precedent set in the opinion. This is what is meant by courts "making law." However, a higher court or a court in another area can disagree with this precedent. The most important precedents are those established by the U.S. Supreme Court, where nine justices hear each case and a majority rules. All courts in the United States must follow U.S. Supreme Court decisions.

The Supreme Court does not consider all appeals that are brought to it. Instead it rules on only the most important cases. Of more than four thousand cases appealed to the Supreme Court each year, the justices rule on about two hundred. Many laws have been changed by the Supreme Court. For example, the Supreme Court has outlawed prayer in public schools, upheld all-male draft registration, and ended segregation in public schools.

These appellate precedents are very important to our whole system of law. Other courts must follow the law announced in these cases, and prior decisions are looked to when courts decide subsequent cases.

THE CASE OF GIDEON v. WAINWRIGHT

In 1963 a case called *Gideon v. Wainwright* came before the U.S. Supreme Court. In this case a Florida man named Gideon was charged with unlawful breaking and entering into a poolroom. Gideon asked the trial court to provide him with a free lawyer because he was too poor to hire one himself. The state court refused to provide him with an attorney. It said that state law provided free attorneys only to defendants charged with capital offenses (i.e., those crimes that carried the death penalty or life imprisonment).

The Fourteenth Amendment to the Constitution says that no state may deprive a person of life, liberty, or property without **due process of law.** Gideon argued that to try a **defendant** for a felony without providing him with a lawyer violated his right to due process of law. The Supreme Court agreed with Gideon.

PROBLEM 7

a. In the case of *Gideon v. Wainwright*, what was the precedent that the Supreme Court set? Who has to follow this precedent?
b. Who would have to follow the precedent if the case had been decided by a judge in a state appeals court?
c. Does the *Gideon* case apply if you are charged with a misdemeanor? Does it apply if you are sued in a civil case?
d. Do you know of other precedents established by the U.S. Supreme Court? What are they?

The Supreme Court in 1986. Front row, from left: Thurgood Marshall, William Brennan, Chief Justice Warren Burger, Byron White, Harry Blackmun. Back row: John Paul Stevens, Lewis Powell, William Rehnquist, Sandra Day O'Connor.

Court Systems   Figure 3 illustrates the two separate court systems in the United States — federal and state. Federal courts hear criminal and civil cases involving federal law. They also hear cases involving **parties** from different states when the amount in dispute is more than $10,000. Federal trial courts are known as U.S. District Courts. If you lose a trial in the U.S. District Court, you may be able to appeal to the U.S. Circuit Court of Appeals in your region. The United States has thirteen circuit courts (see figure 4). The court of final appeal is the U.S. Supreme Court.

Most state court systems resemble the federal courts in structure and procedure. All states have trial courts. These are called superior courts, county courts, district courts, or municipal courts, depending on the state. State courts are often specialized to deal with specific areas of law, such as family law, traffic, criminal, probate, and small claims.

Family or domestic relations courts hear all actions involving divorce, separation, and child custody. Juvenile cases and intra-family offenses (fights within families) are also heard. Sometimes cases involving juveniles are heard in a special juvenile court. Traffic courts hear all actions involving violations while driving a motor vehicle. Criminal courts hear all cases involving violations of laws for which a person could go to jail. Frequently criminal court is divided between felony and misdemeanor cases. Probate courts handle all cases involving wills and claims against the estates of persons who die with or without a will. Small claims courts hear cases involving small amounts of money (e.g., $200, $500, or $1,000, depending on the state). Individuals may bring

FIGURE 3   Federal and State Court Systems

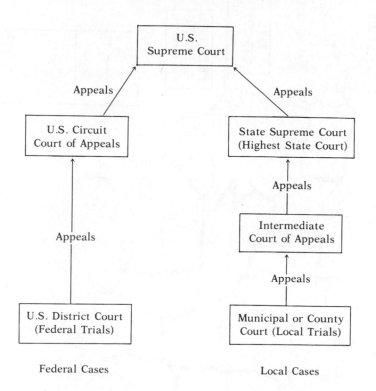

WHERE YOU LIVE

What courts exist in your community? What kind of cases do they handle? How are appeals handled in your state? What is the highest state court and where is it located?

cases here without lawyers — though it is sometimes advised that lawyers be present — and the court fees are low.

If you lose your case in the trial court, you may appeal to an intermediate court of appeals. In some states, the appeal goes directly to the state supreme court. If a state supreme court decision involves only state law, it can be appealed no further. But if it involves some federal law or constitutional issue, it can then be appealed to the U.S. Supreme Court.

PROBLEM 8

Consider the following cases. In each situation decide whether it will be tried in a federal or state court. To what court could each case be appealed? Then give an example, not listed in the following, of a case that could be heard in a state court; in a federal court.

a. A state sues a neighboring state for dumping waste in a river that borders the two states.

b. A wife sues her husband for divorce.

c. A person is prosecuted for assaulting a neighbor.

FIGURE 4   The Thirteen Federal Judicial Circuits

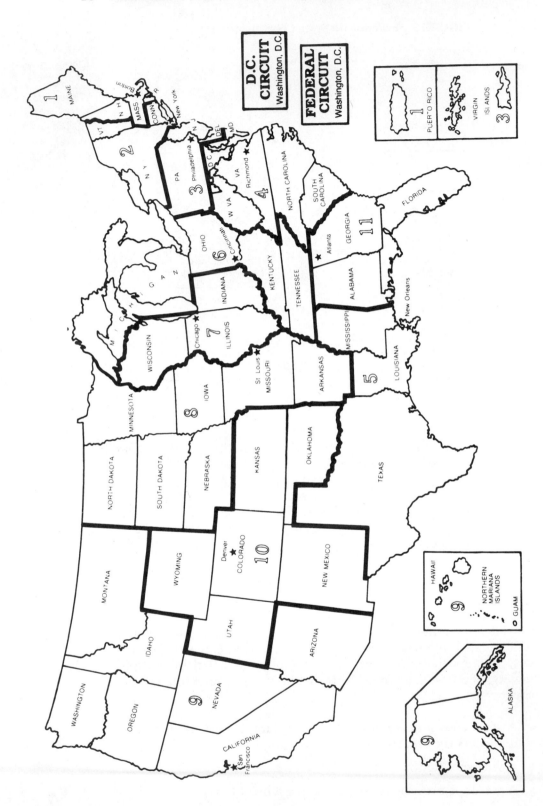

d. Two cars collide. One driver sues the other for hospital bills and auto repairs.

e. A group of parents sues the local school board, asking that their school be desegregated.

SAMPLE CIVIL CASE

Mike goes to Frank's house for a party. Mike has too much to drink and falls on top of Frank's $500 stereo. It costs Frank $150 to fix the stereo. Mike breaks his arm in the fall.

Frank files a complaint in small claims court for $150 in **damages** against Mike. Mike files an answer, denying it was his fault, and **counterclaims** against Frank for $300, claiming that he fell because Frank's floor was slippery and that he suffered damages, including medical bills, loss of a week's wages and pain and suffering.

Both attorneys make motions for pretrial discovery, which includes written and oral questions of the other person's witnesses. A trial is held six weeks after the complaint is filed.

The judge finds that the accident was Mike's fault, since he had had too much to drink and was clumsy in falling. The damages are set at $150, and the judge orders Mike to pay this to Frank. If Mike doesn't pay, Frank can go to court and file a writ of **garnishment** against Mike's wages. This means that Mike's employer will have to pay Frank 25 percent of Mike's wages until the $150 is paid off.

Criminal and Civil Process   The general steps followed in criminal and civil cases are listed below. You should note that criminal and civil cases are tried separately and can never be combined.

Criminal

1. Arrest — Police take person into custody. **Booking** (information recorded about the person) and fingerprinting takes place.

2. Initial appearance: misdemeanor case — Defendant is given a copy of the complaint and asked to enter a plea. A trial date is set, and the judge either imposes bail or releases the de-

Civil

1. Complaint filed by **plaintiff** — Plaintiff files papers claiming a civil wrong done by the defendant. See sample complaint on page 20.

2. Answer by defendant — Defendant files papers denying plaintiff's claim and stating the defense in the case. See sample answer on page 21.

Criminal	Civil
fendant. Initial appearance: felony case — Defendant is informed of the charge and is advised of his or her rights to a preliminary examination or presentation of the case to a grand jury (or both). No plea is entered.	
3. **Indictment** or **information** — **Prosecutor** (government's attorney) either takes evidence before **grand jury** to get an indictment or has sufficient evidence from police that an information may be filed.	3. Pretrial proceedings — **Motions** (requests by the parties to the court) are filed requesting **discovery** (an exchange of information between the parties).

UNITED STATES DISTRICT COURT FOR THE SOUTHERN
DISTRICT OF NEW YORK

Civil Action, File Number 000000

John Doe, Plaintiff   )
)
        v.   )   COMPLAINT
)
Richard Roe Co., Inc., Defendant   )

1. Jurisdiction is founded on diversity of citizenship and amount. Plaintiff is a citizen of the State of Connecticut and defendant is a corporation incorporated under the laws of the State of New York. The matter in controversy exceeds, exclusive of interest and costs, the sum of $10,000 (ten thousand dollars).

2. Defendant owes plaintiff $12,000 (twelve thousand dollars) for ready-to-wear women's dresses sold and delivered by plaintiff to defendant between June 1, 1980 and December 1, 1980.

   WHEREFORE plaintiff demands judgment against defendant for the sum of $12,000 (twelve thousand dollars), interest, and costs.

Signed: _____
                 Attorney for Plaintiff

Address: _____

A sample complaint

UNITED STATES DISTRICT COURT FOR THE SOUTHERN
DISTRICT OF NEW YORK

Civil Action, File Number 000000

John Doe, Plaintiff	)	
	)	
v.	)	ANSWER
	)	
Richard Roe Co., Inc., Defendant	)	

First Defense

The complaint fails to state a claim against defendant upon which relief can be granted.

Second Defense

If defendant is indebted to plaintiff for the goods mentioned in the complaint as having been sold and delivered by plaintiff to defendant, defendant owes plaintiff less than $10,000 (ten thousand dollars).

Third Defense

Defendant admits that it is a corporation incorporated under the laws of the State of New York; alleges that it is without knowledge or information sufficient to form a belief as to the truth of the allegation concerning the place of plaintiff's citizenship; and denies each and every other allegation contained in the complaint.

Fourth Defense

The right of action set forth in the complaint did not accrue within six years prior to the commencement of this action.

Counterclaim

After March 19, 1977, and continuously since that time, the plaintiff has been inducing suppliers not to sell ready-to-wear women's dresses to defendant and has otherwise been engaging in unfair trade practices and unfair competition against plaintiff to defendant's irreparable damage and has diverted business worth at least $100,000 away from defendant.

WHEREFORE, defendant demands judgment against plaintiff for the sum of $100,000 (one hundred thousand dollars), interest, and costs.

Signed: _____
Attorney for Defendant

Address: _____

A sample answer

4. Pretrial proceedings — Hearings may be held on motions to dismiss the case, to have evidence ruled inadmissible, or to permit discovery. Defendant may enter a plea of guilty with the hope of receiving a lesser sentence.

4. Trial — Presentation of evidence by plaintiff and defendant.

5. Trial — Presentation of evidence by **prosecution** and defense.

5. Decision — **Verdict** by trier of fact, which may be jury or judge.

6. Decision — Verdict is made by trier of fact, which may be jury or judge.

6. Judgment — Pronounced by the judge in favor of plaintiff or defendant.

7. Sentence — Imposition of a penalty, which may be a prison term, probation, fine or other punishment.

7. Enforcement of judgment — Court forces the person against whom a judgment was pronounced to pay or do something.

SETTLING DISPUTES OUTSIDE OF COURT

Many everyday problems can be settled without going to court. Sometimes there are disadvantages in taking a case to court. Because of backlogged cases and complicated rules and procedures, courts are often quite slow. Furthermore, the total cost of an attorney, pretrial discovery, witness fees, and other court expenses may be more than the case is worth.

Most people solve problems on their own without going to court. If a neighbor's dog barks all night — keeping you awake — you should probably complain to the dog owner before even considering going to court. It would be difficult for society to function if people had to hire attorneys and go to court every time they had a problem or a dispute.

Going to court sometimes makes the problem worse. For example, in divorces and child custody disputes, going to court often causes extraordinary anger and bitterness. As a result, many people believe that problems such as these are better handled by nonjudicial means.

Courts have an important role in our legal system, but there are other ways to settle disputes. Among the most common methods for solving disputes outside of court are **negotiation, mediation, and arbitration.**

Negotiation simply means that the parties to a dispute talk to each other about their problem and try to reach a solution acceptable to all. Sometimes people cannot settle a dispute on their own. They hire attorneys to negotiate for them. For example, people involved in auto accidents sometimes hire attorneys to negotiate with the insurance company over payments for injuries or damages to their car. People who hire attorneys to negotiate for them must approve any agreement before it becomes final. In some situations, attorneys will file a case in court and then attempt to work out a **settlement** before the case goes to trial. A large number of civil cases are settled this way, saving both time and money.

Another method for resolving disputes is mediation. This takes place when a third person helps the disputing parties talk about their problem and then settle their differences. Mediators do not impose a decision on the parties. Rather, they act as a neutral middle person. The mediator's job is to listen to both sides and then help the parties understand each other's position. Since the mediator is in the middle, he or she can often see both sides more clearly than can either of the disputing parties.

Mediation is used to solve a wide variety of disputes. Community mediation programs help settle disputes between husbands and wives, landlords and tenants, and consumers and businesses. For example, in many communities, the Better Business Bureau (BBB) mediates disputes between shoppers and store owners. In other places, neighborhood justice centers help settle disputes between community residents. Even government agencies and some universities have people known as ombudsmen, who investigate complaints and then help the parties reach some agreement. To locate a mediation program in your community, contact your local court, district attorney's office, or social service agency.

A third method for settling disputes outside of court is arbitration. In arbitration, both parties to a dispute agree to have a third party listen to their arguments and then make a decision for them. Arbitration differs from mediation. In mediation, a third person helps the parties reach their own agreement. In arbitration, a third person imposes a decision on the parties.

An arbitrator is in some ways like a judge. He or she has the sole authority to make a final decision on the issues presented. However, arbitration does not involve the complex procedures or legal formalities of a trial. Moreover, the decision of an arbitrator is usually binding and cannot be appealed.

Arbitration is commonly used in contract and labor-management disputes and in some cases of international law. For

example, many agreements between labor unions and employers often include an arbitration clause. This means both the union and the employer agree, in advance, to submit certain disputes to arbitration and to be bound by the arbitrator's award. To learn more about arbitration, contact any of the groups listed in Appendix B.

PROBLEM 9

Read the following situations and list all the methods that could be used to settle each dispute. Then decide the best method for solving each problem. Consider negotiation, arbitration, mediation, court, or other methods. Discuss the reasons for your answer.

a. Two sisters share a room. However, they disagree over how the room should be arranged and decorated.

b. A new stereo breaks after two weeks and the salesperson refuses to fix it.

c. A landlord will not make needed repairs, because he believes the tenant caused them.

d. A labor union and an employer disagree over the wages and conditions of employment.

e. A married couple wants a divorce.

f. The Internal Revenue Service sends you a letter claiming that you owe another $200 in taxes. You disagree.

STEPS IN A TYPICAL MEDIATION SESSION

Step 1. Introduction
The mediator sets the parties at ease and explains the ground rules. The mediator's role is not to make a decision but to help the parties reach a mutual agreement. The mediator explains that he or she will not take sides.

Step 2. Telling the Story
Each party tells what happened. The person bringing the complaint tells his or her side of the story first. No interruptions are allowed. Then the other party explains his or her version of the facts.

Step 3. Identifying Facts and Issues
The mediator attempts to identify agreed-upon facts and issues. This is done by listening to each side, summarizing each party's views, and asking if these are the facts and issues as each party understands them.

Step 4. Identifying Alternative Solutions
Everyone thinks of possible solutions to the problem. The mediator makes a list and asks each party to explain his or her feelings about each possible solution.

Step 5. Revising and Discussing Solutions
Based on the expressed feelings of the parties, the mediator revises possible solutions and attempts to identify a solution that both parties can agree to.

Step 6. Reaching Agreement
The mediator helps the parties reach an agreement that both can live with. The agreement should be written down. The parties should also discuss what will happen if either of them breaks the agreement.

In an effort to resolve a dispute, a mediator meets with opposing sides in a mediation session.

PROBLEM 10

Read the following situation and then roleplay a mediation session. Select a person to play the roles of each party and the mediator. Follow the steps outlined in the box on page 25.

Ken Lopez took a $100 sport coat to Ace Dry Cleaners to have it cleaned. The coat was new and had been worn only a few times. When Ken picked it up, he found a large cigarette burn on the lapel. Ken said the burn was not there when he brought it in and that he didn't smoke. Ken asked the cleaners to pay him $100. Ace denied that they were responsible for the burn and refused to pay. Ace also argued that the coat was used clothing and as such, was no longer worth $100. Ken countered that he would have to pay at least $100 for a new coat.

THE ADVERSARY SYSTEM

The trial system in the United States is an adversary process. This means it is a contest between opposing sides. The theory of this process is that the trier of fact (judge or jury) will be able to determine the truth if the opposing parties present their best arguments and show the weaknesses in the other side's case.

If a criminal case goes to trial, the prosecution has the burden of proving the defendant guilty **beyond a reasonable doubt.** In a civil case the burden is on the plaintiff to prove his or her case by a **preponderance of the evidence** (greater weight of evidence). The standard of proof is more difficult in a criminal case. This is because of a belief that more evidence should be required to take away a person's freedom.

The adversary process is not the only method for handling legal disputes. Many countries have systems differing from our own. Moreover, the adversary process is sometimes criticized as not providing the best setting for the discovery of truth with respect to the facts of a specific case. Critics compare the adversary process to a battle in which lawyers act as enemies, making every effort *not* to present *all* the evidence. In this view the goal of trial is "victory, not truth or justice."

On the other hand, the adversary process has long served as the cornerstone of the American legal system. Most attorneys believe that approaching the same set of facts from totally different perspectives will uncover more truth than would other methods.

PROBLEM 11

a. Which of the viewpoints concerning the adversary process do you favor? Why?

b. Do you agree or disagree with the following statement: "It is better that ten guilty persons go free than that one innocent person suffer conviction." Explain you answer.

c. In a criminal case, should a lawyer defend a client whom he or she knows is guilty? Discuss.

Steps in a Trial

The following is a short explanation of the steps in either a criminal or a civil trial.

1. Opening Statement by Plaintiff or Prosecutor — Plaintiff's attorney (in civil cases) or prosecutor (in criminal cases) explains to the trier of fact the evidence to be presented as proof of the **allegations** (unproven statements) in the indictment or complaint.

2. Opening Statement by Defense — Defendant's attorney explains evidence to be presented to deny the allegations made by the plaintiff or prosecutor.

3. Direct Examination by Plaintiff or Prosecutor — Each witness for the plaintiff or prosecution is questioned. Other evidence (e.g., documents, physical evidence) in favor of the plaintiff or prosecution is presented.

4. Cross-Examination by Defense — The defense has the opportunity to question each witness. Questioning is designed to break down the story or to discredit the witness in the eyes of the jury.

5. Motions — If the prosecution/plaintiff's basic case has not been established from the evidence introduced, the judge can end the case by granting the defendant's motion to dismiss (in civil cases) or by entering a directed verdict (in criminal cases).

6. Direct Examination by Defense — Each defense witness is questioned.

7. Cross-Examination by Plaintiff — Each defense witness is cross-examined.

8. Closing Statement by Plaintiff — Prosecutor or plaintiff's attorney reviews all the evidence presented (noting uncontradicted facts), states how the evidence has satisfied the elements of the charge, and asks for a finding of guilty (in criminal cases) or for the plaintiff (in civil cases).

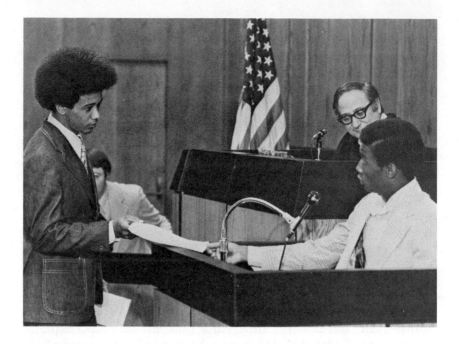

9. Closing Statement by Defense — Same as closing statement by prosecution/plaintiff. The defense asks for a finding of not guilty (in criminal cases) or for the defendant (in civil cases).

10. Rebuttal Argument — Prosecutor or plaintiff has the right to make additional closing arguments.

11. Jury Instructions — Judge instructs jury as to the law that applies in the case.

12. Verdict — In most states, a unanimous decision is required one way or the other. If the jury cannot reach a unanimous decision, it is said to be a **hung jury,** and the case may be tried again.

Judges and Juries

Judges and juries are essential parts of our legal system. The judge presides over the trial and has the duty of protecting the rights of those involved. Judges also make sure that attorneys follow the rules of evidence and trial procedure. In nonjury trials, the judge has the function of determining the facts of the case and rendering a judgment. In jury trials, the judge is required to instruct the jury as to the law involved in the case. Finally, in criminal trials, judges are required to sentence individuals convicted of committing a crime.

The right to trial by jury is guaranteed by the Sixth and Seventh Amendments of the Constitution. This right applies in both federal and state courts. However, a jury is not required in every case. Juries are not used as often as one might think. In civil cases, either the plaintiff or the defendant may request a jury trial. In criminal cases, the defendant decides whether there will be a jury. Many civil cases result in out-of-court settlements or trials by a judge. In criminal cases, most cases are never brought to trial. Instead, they are disposed of by **plea bargaining.**

If a jury trial is requested, a jury is selected and charged with the task of determining the facts and applying the law in the particular case. To serve on a jury, you must be a citizen of the United States, at least eighteen years of age, and a resident of the state. Persons commonly excused from jury duty include clergy, attorneys, physicians, police officers, fire fighters, convicted felons, and persons who are physically or mentally ill.

Once selected, jurors are assigned to specific cases after being screened through a process known as **voir dire** examination. In this process, opposing lawyers question each prospective juror to discover any prejudices or preconceived opinions concerning the case. After questioning each juror, the opposing attorneys may request the removal of any juror who does not appear capable of rendering a fair and impartial verdict. This is called **removal for cause.** In addition, each attorney is allowed a limited number of **peremptory challenges.** This means they can have prospective jurors removed without stating a cause.

| WHERE |
| YOU |
| LIVE |

How are jurors selected by the courts in your community? How many persons are on the jury in a civil trial? In a criminal trial? Is a unanimous verdict required in a civil trial? In a criminal trial?

To be a juror, you must meet your state's qualifications of age, citizenship, and good character.

PROBLEM 12

a. Why would someone choose not to have a jury trial in a civil case? In a criminal case?

b. What reasons can you give for the exclusion from jury duty of attorneys, physicians, police officers, and convicted felons? Can you think of any other group that should be exempt from jury duty?

c. If you were a defense attorney questioning jurors at the voir dire in a murder trial, what questions would you ask to determine whether the jurors could render a fair and impartial verdict?

d. Can you think of any reasons why an attorney might use a peremptory challenge?

LAWYERS

There are over 600,000 lawyers in the United States. Almost 500,000 of these are in active practice. Lawyers in private practice account for about 65 percent of the attorneys in the United States. Around 15 percent are government lawyers who work for federal, state, or local agencies. Another 15 percent work for corporations, unions, or trade associations. A small number of lawyers work for public interest or legal aid organizations. An even smaller number are law professors, judges, or elected officials.

Contrary to popular belief, most lawyers rarely go to court. The practice of law usually involves giving advice, drafting legal opinions, negotiating settlements, or otherwise providing out-of-court legal assistance.

Some lawyers do, however, go to court. In civil cases, lawyers act as advocates for their clients' position. Likewise, in a criminal case the lawyer for the defendant has a duty to do everything possible (without violating a code of professional ethics) to secure the release and acquittal of his or her client.

When Do You Need a Lawyer?

An important thing you need to know is when to see a lawyer. Many people think of seeing an attorney only after they get into trouble, but perhaps the best time to consult an attorney is before the problem arises.

Preventive advice is an important service that a lawyer can provide. You should consider consulting an attorney about a number of common situations. These include:

■ buying or selling a home or other real estate.

■ organizing a business or making a major purchase.

■ changing your family status (e.g., by divorce or adoption).

■ making a will or planning an estate.

■ signing a large or important contract.

■ handling accidents involving personal injury or property damage.

■ defending a criminal charge or bringing a civil suit.

The services a lawyer can provide are limited. If your problem is one that requires a business or economic decision, a good businessperson may be a better advisor than a lawyer. For other problems a teacher, doctor, or a friend may be a better source of advice.

PROBLEM 13

The following examples involve situations in which an attorney may or may not be needed. For each situation, discuss the reasons why you may or may not need an attorney.

a. You run into another car in a parking lot. Your insurance agent indicates the company will pay costs for bodily injuries and property damages.

b. You borrow a friend's car without his knowledge, and he reports it to the police as stolen.

c. You buy a new stereo for $300. At a party one month later, the receiver and speakers blow out. You return to the store, and they tell you they are sorry but their stereos have only a two-week guarantee.

d. You decide to trade in your old car and buy a new one.

e. Your friends are caught robbing a local store, and they name you as one who helped plan the robbery.

f. The principal suspends you from school for two days because of an article you wrote for the student paper, criticizing the school dress code.

g. You apply for a job and are turned down. You think you are rejected because of your sex.

h. You do not want your family to inherit the $10,000 you have saved. Told you will die within a year, you want the money to be used for cancer research.

Some lawyers work alone. Others work together as partners in a law firm.

i. You and your mate find you can no longer get along. You want a divorce.

j. You earn $5,000 working in a restaurant during the year. You want to file your federal income tax return.

How Do You Find a Lawyer?

If you need a lawyer, how do you find one who is right for you and your particular problem? Perhaps the best way to find an experienced lawyer is through the recommendation of someone who had a similar legal problem, which was resolved to his or her satisfaction. You might also ask your employer, members of the clergy, businesspeople, or other professionals for the name of a lawyer they know and trust.

You can always find a lawyer by looking under "Lawyers" in the Yellow Pages of your phone book. In addition, *Martindale-Hubbell Law Directory*, available in your public library, lists most lawyers in the United States. It provides some general information about their education, professional honors, and the type of cases they handle. Lawyers are also permitted to advertise their services. In many places, advertisements for lawyers may be found in newspapers, magazines, or on radio and television.

To get legal advice, poor people can go to a legal aid office.

WHERE YOU LIVE

What legal resources exist in your community? Is there a bar association? If so, what services does it offer? Are there legal aid organizations in your community? If so, where are they located and what do they do?

Another way to find a lawyer is to contact a lawyer referral service in your community. Most communities have **bar associations** which maintain a list of lawyers who specialize in certain areas. Many of these lawyers are willing to consult and advise clients at a special rate. Anyone who calls the referral service will be told the amount of the initial consultation fee and will be given the name of a lawyer for an appointment. If additional legal service is needed, the fee is subject to agreement between the lawyer and the client.

If you are unable to afford the services of a lawyer, you may be eligible for free legal assistance at a legal aid, legal service, or public defender's office. These offices are usually listed in the Yellow Pages under "Legal Services." You may also contact the Legal Services Corporation (address in Appendix B) or a local bar association or law school for the address of the legal aid office nearest you.

ADVICE ON WHAT TO ASK YOUR LAWYER

Once you have found a lawyer who seems interested in your problem, you should get answers to the following questions:

■ What is the lawyer's fee? Is the client required to pay a flat fee or by the hour? Is a **retainer** (down payment) required? What about a contingent fee in which the lawyer gets paid only if he or she wins your case?
■ Has the lawyer ever handled cases like this before? If so, with what results?
■ Will the lawyer provide you with copies of all correspondence and documents prepared on your behalf?
■ Will the lawyer keep you informed of any new developments in your case, and talk to you in "plain English?"
■ How much personal attention will you get? if the lawyer is a member of a law firm, is he or she the person who will actually do your legal work?

If you are not satisfied with the answers you get, do not hesitate to shop around.

Another thing to consider before choosing a lawyer is whether your problem is one that may be of interest to such organizations as the American Civil Liberties Union (ACLU), Environmental Defense Fund (EDF), National Association for the Advancement of Colored People (NAACP), American Conservative Union (ACU), or other public interest groups. These organizations are usually listed in the phone book and may provide free representation.

THE CAR CRASH CASE

On April 1, Al Sundance and his friend Marie Davis were driving along Sixth Street, returning home from a party. Al had stopped at a red light at the corner of Sixth Street and Florida Avenue, when a 1983 Buick hit his car in the rear.

Al's 1985 Volvo was smashed in as far as the back seat. Al suffered a severe neck injury, four broken ribs, and many cuts and bruises. As a result, Al spent three weeks in the hospital. Al's passenger, Marie, was also severely injured. She suffered a fractured skull, facial cuts, a broken right arm and hip, numerous cuts, and internal bleeding. Marie, an accountant making $25,000 a year, spent six weeks in the hospital and returned to work after twelve weeks.

The driver of the Buick, Fred Ortego, suffered minor cuts on his face and arm and was released from the hospital after twenty-four hours. As a result of the accident, Fred was given a ticket for speeding and reckless driving.

Fred's insurance company called Marie and offered her a $4,500 settlement. Marie is uncertain whether she should accept and decides to consult an attorney. After checking with a lawyer referral service, she is referred to a local attorney.

PROBLEM 14

Roleplay the initial attorney-client interview between Marie and the attorney. Persons roleplaying the attorney should attempt to ask all the questions an attorney should ask at this point. Persons roleplaying the client should provide the attorney with all necessary information and ask all those questions that are relevant to Marie's case and that relate to whether she should retain the attorney.

Working with Your Attorney

Trust is the foundation of the attorney-client relationship. You must be able to trust your attorney. To help you, however, your attorney needs to know everything about your problem. To encourage clients to speak freely to their lawyers, the law grants an attorney-client **privilege.** This means that whatever you tell your attorney about your case is secret and confidential. Without your permission, this information cannot be disclosed to anyone.

Working with an attorney also means making decisions. A good attorney will give you advice, but you must make the final decision (e.g., to sue or not to sue, or to accept or reject the settlement).

If you are not satisfied, your lawyer may be discharged at anytime. Once the case is in court, however, a judge may only permit this change for a very good reason. A client who has a serious complaint that can't be worked out with the attorney can report this either to the local court or to the bar association, which has the power to reprimand, suspend, or even disbar an attorney for serious misconduct.

two
CRIMINAL
AND
JUVENILE
JUSTICE

A crime is something one does or fails to do in violation of a law. It can also be defined as behavior for which the state has set a penalty.

Crime wears many faces. It may be the teenager snatching a woman's purse or the career criminal planning a kidnapping. It may be the youth who steals a car for a joyride or the car theft ring that takes it for later sale. It may be the professional criminal who profits from organized gambling, extortion, or narcotics traffic, or the politician who takes a bribe. Crime may be committed by the professional person who cheats on tax returns, the businessperson who secretly agrees to fix prices, or the burglar who ransacks homes while the owners are at work.

Criminal law designates certain conduct "criminal" and other conduct "noncriminal." Decisions as to what constitutes a crime are made by legislatures, which try to protect the public based on what most people believe is right and necessary for the orderly conduct of our society. Certain acts are prohibited or commanded to protect life and property, to preserve individual freedoms, to maintain our system of government, and to uphold the morality of society. Ideally, the goal of law is to regulate human conduct so that people can live in harmony.

PROBLEM 1

A commission is established to evaluate laws. You are a member. Consider the following acts and in each case decide whether the act should be treated as a crime. Rank the offenses from most serious to least serious. Give reasons for your decisions.

a. Robert is a narcotics addict who pushes heroin to anyone who will buy.

b. John and Tom are homosexuals who live together as though they were married.

c. Liz pickpockets an individual's wallet containing $50.

d. Reuben refuses to pay his income tax because he does not support government policies.

e. Susan is caught with a pound of marijuana.

f. Ted robs a liquor store at gunpoint.

g. Ellen leaves a store with change for a $10 bill after she realizes that she gave the cashier a $5 bill.

h. Lilly approaches a man for purposes of prostitution.

i. Ming refuses to wear a helmet while riding a motorcycle.

j. A company pollutes a river with waste from its automobile factory.

k. Marge gets drunk and hits a child while speeding through a school zone.

l. Burt observes his best friend shoplifting but does not turn him in.

PROBLEM 2

a. According to Figure 5, what is the most commonly committed crime?

b. Make a list of crimes that are not included in Figure 5.

c. Which crimes listed in Figure 5 have increased most since 1974? How might you explain this increase?

NATURE AND CAUSES OF CRIME

Unfortunately, preventing crime is not an easy task. Crime has long been a major problem in the United States. In 1983 more than 12 million serious crimes were reported to the police. This is an increase of over 17 percent since 1974. Recent reports suggest that

FIGURE 5 National Crime Rate and Percentage of Change

Offense	Estimated crime 1983		Percentage of change over 1982		Percentage of change over 1979		Percentage of change over 1974	
	Number	Rate per 100,000 inhabitants	Number	Rate per 100,000 inhabitants	Number	Rate per 100,000 inhabitants	Number	Rate per 100,000 inhabitants
Crime Index total[1]	12,070,200	5,158.6	−6.7	−7.7	−1.2	−7.0	+17.7	+6.4
Modified Crime Index total								
Violent crime	1,237,980	529.1	−4.9	−5.9	+4.7	−2.1	+27.0	+14.7
Property crime	10,832,200	4,629.5	−6.9	−7.9	−1.7	−7.6	+16.7	+5.5
Murder	19,310	8.3	−8.1	−8.8	−10.0	−14.4	−6.8	−15.3
Forcible rape	78,920	33.7	—	−1.2	+3.1	−3.2	+42.5	+28.6
Robbery	500,220	213.8	−8.4	−9.4	+5.4	−.9	+13.1	+2.2
Aggravated assault	639,530	273.3	−2.4	−3.4	+3.8	−2.4	+40.2	+26.6
Burglary	3,120,800	1,333.8	−9.2	−10.2	−5.9	−11.5	+2.7	−7.2
Larceny-theft	6,707,000	2,866.5	−6.0	−7.0	+1.7	−4.3	+27.4	+15.1
Motor vehicle theft	1,004,400	429.3	−5.1	−6.1	−9.4	−14.8	+2.8	−7.1

[1]Because of rounding, offenses may not add to totals.
Source: Uniform Crime Reports, 1984.

**WHERE
YOU
LIVE**

What is the major
crime problem in your
community? What
crimes have increased
most over the last three
years? Have any crime
rates decreased during
this period? Where can
you get this
information?

the crime rate is leveling off. In some areas the crime rate is
declining. Nevertheless, in 1985 there was more crime in the
United States than there was five years earlier.

Crime rates are generally higher in large cities and in urban
areas. But during the last few years crime has grown fastest in
suburbs and in rural areas. Crime is not confined to any particular
group, but youths between the ages of 15 and 24 commit more
violent crimes than people in any other age group. Males commit
six times as many crimes as females, but in recent years the crime
rate has grown fastest among women.

One way in which crime affects us all is that it costs everyone
money. The cost of lost or damaged lives, or of fear and suffering,
cannot be measured solely in dollars and cents, but the total cost of
crime in this country has been estimated at over $100 billion
dollars per year.

FIGURE 6   Crime Rate by Area, 1983

[Rate per 100,000 inhabitants]

Offense	Total United States	Metropolitan area	Rural counties	Small cities
Crime Index total .... Modified Crime Index total ..	5,158.6	5,852.3	1,881.0	4,629.4
Violent crime.............	529.1	627.2	161.2	315.3
Property crime	4,629.5	5,225.1	1,719.8	4,314.1
Murder	8.3	9.1	5.8	5.0
Forcible rape	33.7	38.9	15.1	21.1
Robbery	213.8	272.9	16.6	49.4
Aggravated assault..........	273.3	306.2	123.7	239.8
Burglary	1,333.8	1,501.5	655.9	1,039.5
Larceny-theft..............	2,866.5	3,200.3	963.8	3,085.5
Motor vehicle theft.........	429.3	523.4	100.1	189.1
Arson				

Source: Uniform Crime Reports, 1984.

PROBLEM 3

According to Figure 6, which area has the highest crime rate: big
cities, small cities, or rural counties? Which area has the lowest
crime rate? Can you think of any reason for the difference?

Most authorities agree that crime is a major problem. However, much disagreement exists over the causes of crime and what
can be done about it. Among the reasons suggested for the high
crime rate in America are poverty, permissive courts, unemployment, lack of education, abuse of alcohol or drugs, inadequate
police protection, rising population, lack of parental guidance, a
breakdown in morals, an ineffective correctional system, little
chance of being caught or punished, and the influence of television.

PROBLEM 4

a. Can you suggest causes of crime not mentioned in the text?

b. Rank the causes of crime from the most important to the least important. Discuss your ranking.

WHERE YOU LIVE

Does your community have any crime prevention programs? Does it have any victim assistance programs? What services do these programs provide?

The lack of agreement on the causes of crime indicates that they are many and complex. Evidence suggests that poor social and economic circumstances are somehow related to crime. However, crime cannot be totally explained in terms of poverty, particularly if one considers that crime rose fastest in this country at a time when the number of people living in poverty was declining. And in recent years crime rates have risen fastest in suburbs and in other affluent areas. Furthermore, if poverty were the sole cause of crime, one could not explain why countries much poorer than the United States have far less crime.

Some people explain increasing crime in terms of rising population. They say there are more people, particularly young people, so there is more crime. While this is true to a degree, the crime rate has risen faster than the population rate.

Will tougher penalties curb crime? Many people think so, but the United States already has some of the toughest criminal laws of any Western nation. Tough penalties may deter some people from crime, but compared with the number of crimes, only a small number of people ever go to prison. Thus, some experts say that longer prison terms are not the answer. They say the certainty of punishment is more important than the length of sentence. Adequate police protection obviously has something to do with the crime rate, but studies show that simply increasing the number of police officers does not necessarily reduce the overall crime rate. Finally, some experts point to peer group pressure, family background, and declining morality as causes of crime. Still others blame crime on the use of hard drugs, such as heroin. Undoubtedly, family influences, a decline in moral standards, and drugs play a role in crime, but these factors are probably not a total cause either.

Thinking about crime requires us to go beyond slogans and stereotypes. We should carefully consider each of the suggested causes and the possible solutions to the problem. Perhaps the best that can be said is that disagreement exists over the causes of crime and that the solution to the crime problem is not simple.

VICTIMS OF CRIME

Crime affects us all, but victims suffer most. Victims of crime can be found among all segments of society, young and old, black and white, rich and poor. Each year, millions of people are victimized

What qualities should a good police officer have?

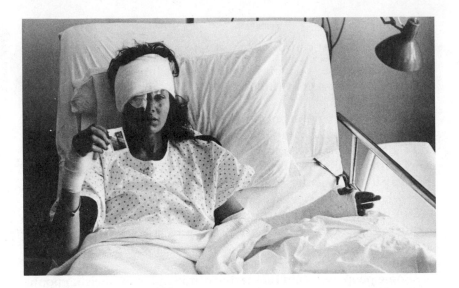

by crime. Chances are great that you may someday be a victim of crime.

In recent years, public interest in aiding the victim has grown. Most states now have victim assistance programs. These programs provide victims with counseling, medical care, and other rights and benefits. Most states also have victim compensation laws. These laws provide financial help for victims — paying medical bills, making up lost salary, and in some cases paying funeral costs and death benefits to victims' families. In addition, courts sometimes order **restitution.** This means requiring criminals to pay back or otherwise compensate the victim of their crime. To learn more about victim assistance programs, contact your local police, district attorney, or U.S. attorney's office.

Crime Prevention

Purse snatching! Home burglary! Consumer fraud! Crime is something almost everyone worries about. As a good citizen, you can help fight crime. You can do this by learning how to protect yourself. This means knowing how to prevent crime and what to do if you are ever a victim of crime. To reduce the risk of crime, follow these rules:

■ Report suspicious activity to the police. The police can't help if you don't call them.

■ Lock your doors and windows! Many homes burglaries occur because someone didn't lock up. Police suggest a deadbolt lock with a one-inch bolt on each outside door.

■ Beware of high crime areas. Dark, deserted streets, parking lots, garages, and bus stops are all high crime areas.

■ Whenever possible, have someone with you at night and in high-risk areas.

■ Don't flash money in public.

■ When on vacation, cancel the newspaper. Have a neighbor collect the mail. Consider using a timer to turn lights on at night.

■ Women living alone should list only their last name and first initial on their mailbox and in the phone book.

If You Become a Victim

If you are ever a victim of a crime, remember that your safety comes first. Most burglars and robbers will flee if they can, so don't try to stop them.

More important, don't resist. You might get injured or killed. If you are held up on the street, scream, make noise, or carry a whistle and blow it. If you can't run away, sit down so you won't get knocked down. Most important, call the police immediately. Don't wait! The longer you wait, the more likely it is that the criminal will get away.

Most burglaries occur when no one is at home. But if you ever arrive at home and suspect a burglar is inside, don't go in. Go to a neighbor's home and call the police immediately!

How To Report a Crime

If you are ever a victim of or a witness to a crime, you should do the following:

■ Stay calm.

■ Call the police immediately!

■ Always report a crime. If you don't report it, the police can't help. Someone else may become a victim.

■ Tell the police who you are, where you are, and what happened.

■ If anyone is hurt, ask for an ambulance.

■ When the police arrive tell them exactly what you saw. If possible, write the following information down before the police arrive. Try to remember what the suspect looked like; age, height, clothing, facial description. Was the suspect driving a car? If so, try to remember the make, model, color, license number, and direction of travel.

■ You may be asked to make a **complaint** or to **testify** in court. Remember, if you don't help the police, the criminal might hurt someone else.

PROBLEM 5

a. Do you know anyone who has been the victim of a crime? What was the crime? How did it affect the person?

b. List and discuss at least four things you can do to protect yourself from crime.

c. One afternoon about 2:30 p.m., you see a blue van pull up in front of a neighbor's house. Two strange men get out of the van and walk to the rear of the house. You are suspicious because you know your neighbors are on vacation. What would you do?

d. If you call the police about the previous incident, what would you say? Roleplay a phone call between yourself and the police.

e. Have you ever witnessed a crime? What happened? What did you do?

GENERAL CONSIDERATIONS

Every crime is made up of certain **elements.** Elements are the conditions that make an act a crime. A crime cannot be committed unless all its elements are fulfilled. For example, **robbery** is defined as the unlawful taking of goods or money from someone's person by force or intimidation. Thus, the elements of robbery are (1) the taking of goods or money, (2) the use of force or intimidation, and (3) the lack of consent of the person from whom the goods or money are taken.

If someone picks your pocket without your knowing it, the person cannot be convicted of robbery. This is because the person did not use force or intimidation — one of the elements of robbery. However, the person could be convicted of **larceny,** because the elements of larceny do not include the use of force or violence.

Almost all crimes require an **act** and an **intent.** Criminal intent means that the person intended or meant to commit a crime. Criminal intent involves knowing and willful action. If a person acts because of a mistake or some other innocent reason, there is no criminal intent. For example, suppose a hunter accidentally shoots another hunter whom he mistakes for a deer. No crime is committed because there was no criminal intent.

A few crimes are **strict liability** offenses. These crimes do not require criminal intent. Strict liability offenses make the act itself a crime regardless of the knowledge of the person committing the act. For example, the law makes it illegal to sell alcoholic beverages to minors. This is true regardless of whether the seller knew the buyer was under age.

Intent is different from **motive.** The motive is the reason a person commits a crime. For example, in murder, the motive is the reason a person kills someone — for revenge, to obtain money, and so on. A good motive can never justify a criminal act. Robin Hood had a good motive. He stole from the rich to give to the poor, but his actions were still unlawful.

A single act can be both a criminal and a civil wrong. For example, if Paul purposely sets fire to Floyd's store, the state may file criminal charges against Paul for arson. Floyd may also bring a separate civil action against Paul to recover for the damage to his store.

The U.S. Constitution (Article I, Section 10) forbids states from passing any **ex post facto laws.** This means that an act is not a crime unless, at the time it was committed, a law was in effect stating that the offense was a crime.

PROBLEM 6

Joe is a bully. One night while dining at a local drive-in, he notices Derek selecting a tune on the jukebox. To impress his girlfriend, Joe orders Derek to sing along with the record. When Derek refuses, Joe punches him in the face, breaking Derek's jaw. As a result of the injury, Derek misses several weeks of work and has to pay both medical and dental bills.

a. Has Joe violated civil laws, criminal laws, or both?

b. Who would decide whether Joe would be charged criminally? Sued in a civil action?

c. If Joe is charged with a crime and sued in a civil action, would these actions be tried in one case? Why or why not?

d. Would procedures in a criminal trial be the same as those in a civil trial? Why or why not?

State and Federal Crimes

There are both state and federal criminal laws. Some acts, such as simple assault, disorderly conduct, drunken driving, or shoplifting, can be prosecuted only in state court. Other acts, such as not paying federal taxes, mail fraud, espionage, or international

Shoplifting can be either a felony or a misdemeanor depending on the value of the article stolen.

GOOD SAMARITAN LAWS

Are witnesses to a crime under any obligation to come to the aid of victims? Until recently, the legal as opposed to the moral answer was no. Most states have "Good Samaritan" laws that relieve bystanders from most civil liability when they help people in danger. But now, several new state laws *require* witnesses to offer whatever help they can reasonably provide without endangering themselves. In the case of a violent crime, this simply means reporting the crime to the police.

smuggling, can be prosecuted only in federal court. Certain crimes, such as illegal possession of dangerous drugs and bank robbery, can violate both state and federal law and can be prosecuted either in state or federal court.

Classes of Crimes

A **felony** is a crime for which the maximum penalty is imprisonment for more than one year. Felonies are usually the more serious crimes. A **misdemeanor** is any crime for which the penalty is imprisonment for one year or less. **Treason** is a third class of crime. Treason is the act of a U.S. citizen helping a foreign government to overthrow, make war against, or seriously injure the United States as a nation. Minor traffic violations are not considered crimes, although they are punishable by law. This chapter deals primarily with felonies and major misdemeanors.

Parties to Crimes

The person who commits a crime is called the **principal** (e.g., the person who fires the gun in a murder). An **accomplice** is someone who helps another person commit a crime (e.g., the person who drives the getaway car during a bank robbery). An accomplice may be charged with the same crime as the principal. A person who orders a crime or who helps the principal commit the crime but who is not present (e.g., the underworld leader who hires a professional killer) is known as an **accessory before the fact.** This person can usually be charged with the same crime, and can receive the same punishment as the principal. An **accessory after the fact** is a person who, knowing a crime has been committed, helps the principal avoid capture or escape. This person is not charged with the original crime but may be charged with harboring a fugitive, aiding the escape, or obstructing justice (sometimes called aiding and abetting).

PROBLEM 7

Joe and Mary decide to burglarize Superior Jewelers. Their friend Carl, an employee at Superior, helps by telling them the location of the store vault. Mary drives a van to the store and keeps a lookout while Joe goes inside and cracks the safe. Joe later meets a friend, Fred, who was not involved beforehand, but who helps Joe get a train out of town after being told about the burglary. David, a former classmate of Joe and Mary's, witnesses the crime but doesn't tell the police, even though he recognizes both Joe and Mary. How will each be charged?

Crimes of Omission

Most crimes occur when a person does something or performs some act in violation of a law. However, in a few cases, a person may be criminally liable for an omission or a failure to act. For example, it is a crime for a taxpayer to fail to file a tax return or for a motorist to fail to stop after involvement in an automobile accident. A person is guilty of a crime of omission if there is a failure to act when there is a legal duty to do so, and if that person is physically able to perform the required act.

THE CASE OF THE DROWNING GIRL

Allen, Betty, Chin, and Doris see a girl drowning in a lake, but none of them takes steps to save her. Allen is the girl's father. Betty had deliberately pushed the girl into the lake by shoving Chin against her. Doris, a medal-winning swimmer, just stands and watches. Would any of the four be criminally liable for the girl's drowning? Should they be? Explain your answer.

PRELIMINARY CRIMES

Certain types of behavior take place before the commission of a crime but are nevertheless complete crimes in themselves. These offenses — **solicitation, attempt,** and **conspiracy** — give the police the opportunity to prevent the intended crime. Each offense can be punished even if the harm intended never occurred.

Solicitation

A number of states make it a crime for a person to solicit (i.e., ask command, urge, advise) another person to commit a crime. For example, Danny wishes to kill his wife, Jean. Lacking the nerve to do the job himself, he asks Wally to kill her. Even if Wally refuses, Danny has committed the crime of solicitation.

Attempt

In most states, an attempt to commit a crime is in itself a crime. To be guilty of the crime of attempt, the accused must have both intended to commit a crime and taken some substantial step toward committing the crime. Mere preparation to commit a crime is not enough. The difficult problem with the crime of attempt is determining whether the actions of the accused were a step toward the actual commission of a crime or mere acts of preparation. A common example of attempt is the situation in which a person decides to shoot and kill someone but, being a poor shot, misses the intended victim. The person doing the shooting would be liable for attempted murder.

PROBLEM 8

Read the following situations and decide whether any of the individuals involved would be liable for the crime of attempt:

a. Howard, a bank teller, figures out a foolproof method of stealing money from the bank. It takes him some time to get up the nerve to steal any money. Finally, he makes up his mind and tells his girlfriend, Donna, that starting tomorrow he will steal the money. Donna goes to the police, and Howard is arrested an hour later.

b. Gilbert, an accomplished thief, is caught while trying to pickpocket Lewis. He pleads not guilty and says he can't possibly be convicted, because Lewis was broke and didn't have a penny on him.

c. Stuart and Johnson decide to rob a liquor store. They meet at a pub and talk over their plans. Stuart leaves to buy a revolver, and Johnson leaves to steal a car for use in their getaway. Stuart is arrested as he walks out of the gun shop with his new revolver. Johnson is arrested while trying to hot-wire a car.

d. Amy decides to burn down her store to collect on the insurance money. She spreads gasoline around the building. She is arrested while leaving the store to get a book of matches.

Conspiracy

A **conspiracy** is an agreement between two or more persons to commit a crime. The crime of conspiracy is designed as a means of preventing other crimes and striking against criminal activity by groups. However, it is sometimes criticized as a threat to freedom of speech and association. For example, during the Vietnam War, the government charged several people with conspiracy for speaking publicly to young men on how to avoid the draft. Many critics of conspiracy said the accused were being denied the freedom of speech.

An example of criminal conspiracy is the situation in which Danny wants his wife, Jean, killed and asks Wally to commit the murder. If Wally agrees to Danny's request and then takes some step to commit the crime, both are guilty of conspiracy to commit murder, even if the murder is never attempted or accomplished.

In most states and in federal law, an **overt** act is required for conviction on a conspiracy charge. In the example of the draft evasion cases, speeches made at an antidraft rally were cited as the overt acts on which conspiracy charges were based.

CRIMES AGAINST THE PERSON

Crimes against the person include **homicide, assault, battery,** and **rape.** All of those crimes are serious offenses. A defendant found guilty of one of them may receive a harsh sentence. However, the law also protects the defendant by defining the various levels of these crimes and by considering the circumstances of each offense.

Homicide

Homicide — the killing of one human being by another — is the most serious of all crimes. The major categories of homicide are noncriminal homicide, criminal homicide (which is either murder or manslaughter), and negligent homicide.

Noncriminal Homicide   Some homicides are not crimes at all. Noncriminal homicide is a killing that is justifiable or excusable and for which the killer is deemed faultless. Examples of non-criminal homicide include killing an enemy soldier in wartime; the killing of a condemned criminal by an executioner; the killing by a police officer of a person who is committing a serious crime and who poses a threat of death or serious harm; and killing in self-defense.

Criminal Homicide   Murder, the most serious form of criminal homicide, is a killing that is **deliberate** and done with **malice.** Malice means having the intent to kill or seriously harm. At one time, there were no degrees of murder. Any homicide done with malice was considered to be murder and punishable by death. To reduce the punishment for less grievous homicides, most states now have statutes that classify murder according to the killer's state of mind or the circumstances surrounding the crime.

First degree murder is a killing that is premeditated (thought about beforehand), deliberate, and done with malice (i.e., with intent to kill).

Second degree murder is a killing that is deliberate and done with malice but without premeditation (i.e., the intent to kill did not exist until just before the murder itself).

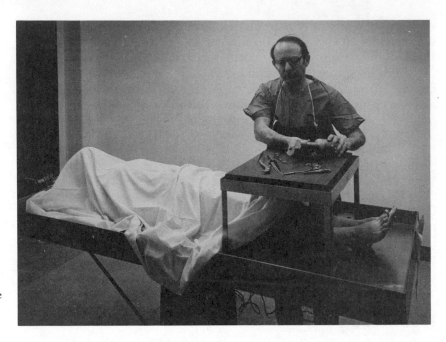

Half of all homicides are
committed with
handguns.

Felony murder is a killing that takes place during the commission of certain felonies, such as arson, rape, robbery, or burglary. It is not necessary to prove intent to kill, because felony murder includes most killing committed during a felony, even if accidental.

Voluntary manslaughter is an intentional killing committed under circumstances that mitigate (lessen), but do not justify or excuse, the killing. Manslaughter is based on the idea that even "the reasonable person" may lose self-control and act rashly if sufficiently provoked.

Involuntary manslaughter is an unintentional killing that results from conduct that is so reckless that it involves extreme danger of death or bodily injury. An example would be a killing that results from playing with a gun known to be loaded.

Negligent Homicide   Negligent homicide is the causing of death through criminal negligence. **Negligence** is the failure to exercise a reasonable or ordinary amount of care in a situation that causes harm to someone. Some states classify death by gross negligence as involuntary manslaughter. The most common form of negligent homicide is vehicular, or automobile, homicide. This is a killing that results from operating a motor vehicle in a reckless and grossly negligent manner. Any death that results from careless driving may lead to a civil suit for damages, but it is usually not considered a crime unless the death results from gross or extreme negligence.

PROBLEM 9

Candy is a member of a cult that passes poisonous snakes around during ceremonies. The group believes that God will protect all true believers from harm and they handle the snakes as a test of faith.

One day Candy convinces her friend Gary to attend a ceremony. Gary agrees to go, assuming he will be a mere observer. However, when they arrive for the ceremony, Candy tells Gary that everyone must take part. Gary tries to leave but agrees to stay when Candy assures him the snakes have never bitten anyone and are harmless anyway. Candy knows this is untrue but believes that those bitten in the past were unbelievers. The first snake passed around bites Gary and he dies before reaching the hospital.

a. Is Candy guilty of any crime? If so, what and for what reason?

b. Would it make a difference if no cult member had ever been bitten?

c. Would it make a difference if Candy knew Gary was an unbeliever?

PROBLEM 10

Walt decides to shoot Clifford, whom he blames for all his troubles. As he is driving to Clifford's home to carry out the murder, Walt hits a jogger who darts out from behind a tree. Stopping immediately, Walt rushes to help the jogger, who is already dead. Walt is upset until he discovers that the dead jogger is Clifford. Assuming Walt was driving at a safe speed and that the collision was unavoidable, is Walt guilty of murder?

PROBLEM 11

Belva is cheated when she buys a car from Fast Eddie's Car Mart. She attempts to return the car, but Eddie just laughs and tells her to go away. Every time Belva has to make a repair on the car, she gets angry. Finally she decides to wreck Eddie's car to get even. Following Eddie home from work one evening, Belva tries to ram his car, hoping to bend the axle or frame. Instead of bending the frame, the collision smashes Eddie's gas tank, causes an explosion, and kills Eddie.

a. Is Belva guilty of any degree of homicide? If so, which degree and for what reason?

b. What was Belva's motive in acting as she did? Should the motive be considered at any stage in the criminal justice process? Why or why not?

FIGURE 7

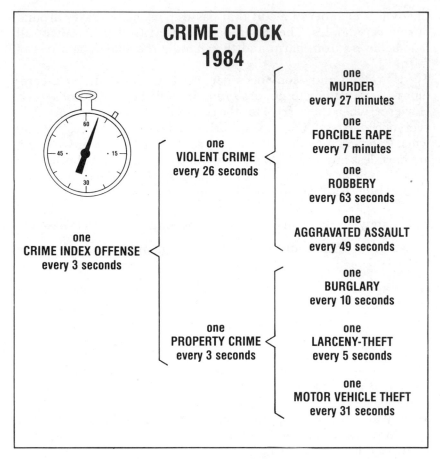

According to the crime clock, which crimes are the most frequently committed?

Assault and Battery

Assault is any attempt or threat to carry out a physical attack upon another person. To constitute a crime, the threatened person must reasonably believe that he or she is in real danger. For example, if John points an unloaded gun at Martha, this would be an assault if Martha believes the gun is loaded. **Battery** is any unlawful, unconsented to physical contact by one person upon another. Actual injury is not necessary. The only requirement is that the person intended to do bodily harm.

Just as there are degrees of murder, there are also different classifications for assault and battery. Aggravated assault and battery is an assault or battery with intent to murder, rob, rape, or do serious bodily harm. For example, if John knocks Martha down while trying to snatch her purse, he is guilty of aggravated assault. Many states impose greater punishment when the assault is made with a deadly weapon. This means a weapon that could cause death as used in the particular case. Many states also impose greater punishment for assaults on police, prison guards, or other law enforcement officers.

Assaults typically result from arguments between people who know each other and in which rage — often stimulated by alcohol or jealously — leads to violence. Whether the violence leads to serious injury or death often depends on the presence of a weapon. In a recent year, 64 percent of all homicides were committed with firearms. Almost 80 percent of these killings were committed with handguns.

The ease with which firearms can be acquired has resulted in many proposals to regulate the sale and possession of guns. Some groups oppose these proposals, citing the Second Amendment to the U.S. Constitution: "A well regulated militia, being necessary to the security of a free state, the right of the people to keep and bear arms, shall not be infringed." The U.S. Supreme Court has interpreted this amendment on several occasions, so have many lower courts. All have ruled that the Second Amendment guarantees a state's right to maintain a militia. In 1983, the Supreme Court refused to overturn a handgun law in Morton Grove, Illinois. The Supreme Court let stand a court of appeals ruling, which stated, "possession of handguns by individuals is not part of the right to keep and bear arms."

The gun lobby also argues that "if guns are outlawed, only outlaws will have guns." Handgun control advocates respond by saying that "handgun laws will make it easier to keep weapons away from felons, fugitives, drug addicts, and mental incompetents." They also say that handguns will still be available to

Are there any laws in your community that regulate the sale or possession of firearms?

responsible citizens. At a minimum, handgun control advocates say that citizens should have to get a license and undergo a background check before being allowed to own a handgun.

PROBLEM 12

a. Should the government require the registration of all handguns, rifles, and shotguns? Why or why not?

b. Should the government prohibit the sale and possession of all handguns? What about rifles?

c. Should the government prohibit certain people, such as drug addicts, mentally disturbed people, and felons, from buying, owning, or possessing firearms? Why or why not?

Rape

Traditionally the law has recognized two types of **rape.** Forcible rape is the act of unlawful sexual intercourse committed by a man with a woman by force and without her consent. Statutory rape is sexual intercourse by a male with a female who has not yet reached the legal age of consent.

Under the common-law definition, a rape occurred only when there was sexual penetration of the female by the male. To constitute forcible rape, the intercourse must have occurred without the consent of the female. There is no consent if a woman submits as a result of force or threats of bodily harm. Likewise, there is no consent if a woman is unconscious, mentally incompetent, or insensible from drugs or liquor.

A number of states have recently rewritten their rape laws. The new laws classify the offense as sexual assault and make it applicable to both men and women. States that have not adopted new sexual assault laws continue to use the common-law definition.

In statutory rape cases, consent is not an issue. Sexual intercourse with an underage female is rape *whether she consents or not.* A mistake by a male as to the female's age is not a defense even if the male reasonably believes she is over the age of consent.

Some state sexual assault laws have replaced statutory rape with the crime of sexual conduct with a minor. These laws do not limit the sex of the victim to females.

Nonchastity of a woman is *not* a defense to rape. This means anyone, including a prostitute, can be raped. However, some states allow evidence of prior unchastity to be considered on the issue of consent. Moreover, to convict a person of rape, some states require independent proof that the act took place. This means confirmation or support for the story of the victim, including testimony of a witness, a doctor's report that sexual intercourse took place, or a prompt report to the police.

PROBLEM 13

a. Statistics reveal that only a small proportion of rape cases are reported to the police. Why is this so? What can be done to encourage more women to report this crime?

b. Should the defense in a rape case be allowed to question the victim about past sexual relations with other people? Why or why not?

c. What is statutory rape? Why is it a crime?

CRIMES AGAINST PROPERTY

The category of crimes against property includes crimes in which property is destroyed (such as **arson** and **vandalism**) and crimes in which property is stolen or otherwise taken against the will of the owner (such as **robbery** and **embezzlement**).

Arson

Arson is the willful and malicious burning of another person's property. In most states, it is a crime to burn any building or structure whether owned by the accused or not. Moreover, any property that is burned with the intent to defraud an insurance company is usually a separate crime, regardless of the type of property burned and regardless of whom the property belonged to.

Vandalism

Vandalism, also known as malicious mischief, is the willful destruction of or damage to the property of another. Vandalism causes millions of dollars in damage each year. It includes such things as breaking windows, ripping down fences, flooding basements, and breaking off car aerials. Depending on the extent of the damage, vandalism can be either a felony or a misdemeanor.

PROBLEM 14

a. Why do young people sometimes commit acts of vandalism?

b. What, if anything, can be done to reduce vandalism?

c. Should parents be held liable for willful damage caused by their children? Why or why not?

d. If you saw two youths throwing rocks through the windows of a school at night, would you report the youths to the police? Why or why not? Suppose you saw two friends throwing rocks through the windows of a neighbor's home. Would you report your friends to the police? Why or why not? Did you answer both questions the same way? If not, explain why.

Larceny

Larceny is the unlawful taking and carrying away of the property of another with intent to steal it. In most states, larceny is divided into two classes: grand and petty, depending on the value of the stolen item. Grand larceny involves the theft of anything above a certain value (often $100 or more) and is a felony. Petty larceny is the theft of anything of small value (usually less than $100) and is a misdemeanor.

The crime of larceny also includes keeping lost property when a reasonable method exists for finding the owner. For example, if you find a wallet with the identification of its owner but nevertheless decide to keep it, you have committed larceny. Likewise, you may be guilty of larceny if you keep property delivered to you by mistake.

Embezzlement

Embezzlement is the unlawful taking of property by someone to whom it was entrusted. For example, the bank teller who takes money from the cash drawer or the stockbroker who takes money that should have been invested are both guilty of embezzlement. In recent years, a number of states have merged the crimes of larceny, false pretenses, and embezzlement into the statutory crime of theft.

Robbery

Robbery is the unlawful taking of property from a person's immediate possession by force or intimidation. Robbery, unlike other theft offenses, involves two harms: theft of property and actual or potential physical harm to the person. In many states, the element of force is the difference between robbery and larceny. Hence a pickpocket who, unnoticed, takes your wallet is liable for the crime of larceny. A mugger who knocks you down and takes your wallet by force is liable for the crime of robbery. Robbery is almost always a felony, but many states impose stricter penalties for armed robberies — that is, thefts committed with a gun or other weapon.

Extortion

Extortion, popularly called blackmail, is the use of threats to obtain the property of another. Extortion statutes generally cover threats to do future physical harm; threats to destroy property (e.g., "I'll burn down your barn unless you pay me $500"); or threats to injure someone's character or reputation.

Burglary

Burglary was originally defined as the breaking and entering of the dwelling house of another during the night with intent to commit a felony. Modern laws have broadened the definition to include the unauthorized entry into any structure with the intent to commit a crime, regardless of the time of day. Many states have stiffer penalties for burglaries committed at night, burglaries of inhabited dwellings, or burglaries committed with weapons.

These four photos are not in any special order. Place them in any order you want, and make up a story to go along with the photos.

Forgery

Forgery is a crime in which a person alters a writing or document with intent to defraud. This usually means signing, without permission, the name of another person to a check or some other document. It can also mean altering or erasing part of a previously signed document. **Uttering,** which in many states is a separate crime, is offering to someone as genuine a document (such as a check) known to be a fake.

Receiving Stolen Property

If you receive or buy property that you know or have reason to believe is stolen, you have committed the crime of **receiving stolen property.** Knowledge that the property is stolen may be implied by the circumstances. In most states, this is a felony if the value of the property received is more than $100, and a misdemeanor if the value is $100 or less.

Unauthorized Use of a Motor Vehicle

The crime of unauthorized use of a motor vehicle is committed when a person takes, operates, or removes a motor vehicle without consent of the owner. This would include joyriding. A passenger in a stolen car may also be guilty if that person had reason to believe the car was stolen.

Undercover sting operations are one method police use to recover stolen merchandise.

PROBLEM 15

Fred finds a valuable Afghan hound wandering in the park near his home. The dog's collar includes the address and phone number of the owner. Fred keeps the dog for several days and then offers to sell the dog to Phil for $20. Phil is eager to buy the hound but is short of cash. He decides to write Fred a check, even though he knows that the check is drawn on a bank where he does not have an account. When the bank later refuses to honor the check, Fred returns to Phil and threatens to go to the police unless Phil gives him $20 plus another $500 in cash. Has Fred or Phil committed any crimes? If so, which ones?

> **WHERE YOU LIVE**
>
> In your community, what are the penalties for possession/sale (or both) of marijuana? Cocaine? Heroin?

PROBLEM 16

Sue steals a watch from Jason. She later sells the watch to Wally, who has no reason to believe the watch is stolen. Sue leaves town, but later Jason claims his watch when he sees Wally wearing it. Wally refuses to give the watch to Jason, claiming it belongs to him because he paid for it.

a. Who would settle the dispute between Wally and Jason: a civil court or a criminal court? In what ways might this dispute be settled without going to court?

b. What additional information would help settle this dispute? How should the dispute be resolved?

CONTROVERSIAL CRIMES

Controversial crimes are those offenses considered to be crimes against society in general. They often involve issues of personal conduct, public health, or social welfare. These offenses are sometimes called victimless crimes. However, considerable controversy exists over whether they are truly victimless.

Drug Offenses

Possession, distribution, or sale of certain drugs is a crime that may violate federal law, state law, or both. Some drugs, such as heroin, are physically addictive and can cause severe disruption to the personal life of the addict. The federal drug law, known as the *Controlled Substance Act*, classifies drugs into five groups, depending on medical use (if any), potential for abuse, and capability to create physical or psychological dependence. The penalties and criminal sanctions are different for each of the five groups.

**WHERE
YOU
LIVE**

What is your community doing to fight drunk driving? What should be done with people who drink and drive?

Penalties for individuals who manufacture, distribute, or sell controlled drugs are up to 15 years in prison and fines up to $25,000. For second and subsequent offenses, penalties are double the original penalty. Simple possession of any controlled substance is a misdemeanor for the first offense under the federal law, but some states treat simple possession as a felony.

Legislation has been proposed in Congress that would decriminalize but not legalize possession of small amounts of marijuana. Violators of this proposed law would receive tickets and pay fines in much the same way that traffic violators are treated.

PROBLEM 17

a. What would be the difference between decriminalization and outright legalization of marijuana? What effect, if any, would each of these measures have on the use of marijuana?

b. Mike knows that he can be arrested for drunken driving but says that he can't be arrested for driving while under the influence of drugs. Is he right or wrong?

c. A presidential commission on crime and law enforcement concluded that it does no good to put drunks in jail. What would you recommend be done with those who abuse alcohol? Cocaine? Marijuana? Heroin?

d. Do you think any relationship exists between drug abuse, including alcohol, and crime? Explain your answer.

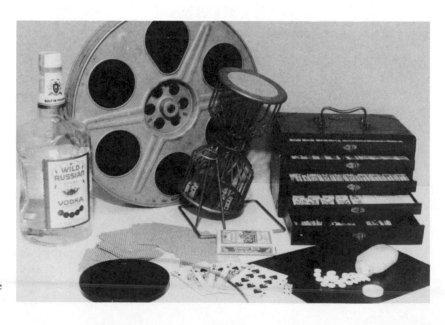

What laws could be violated using each of these items or substances?

Sex Offenses

Crimes such as rape or child molestation are regarded primarily as offenses against another person. Other sex crimes, however, are deemed illegal as offenses against public morality or decency. These offenses include **bigamy, adultery, homosexual acts,** and **prostitution.** These acts usually occur in private between consulting adults. As a result, laws against these offenses are difficult to enforce.

Bigamy is the offense of marrying a person while you are still married to someone else. Statutes making this a crime are based on the belief that the family is the basic unit of society. Bigamy is punishable as a felony in almost every state.

Adultery is the act of sexual intercourse between a married person and someone other than that person's spouse. It is a ground for divorce in almost every state. It is also punishable as a crime in many states, although this law is almost never enforced.

Homosexuality is the condition of being sexually and emotionally oriented toward people of the same sex. It is a status or condition of being and is not a crime. However, despite changing standards, many states consider specific sexual acts between people of the same sex to be crimes.

Prostitution is the performance of sexual acts for money. It is a crime in every state except for a few counties in Nevada. Prostitution almost always takes place between consenting individuals, but it is nevertheless outlawed as a violation of cultural norms and an offense against public decency.

PROBLEM 18

a. Although the acts generally occur in private, what would be the public consequences, if any, if society repealed laws against adulterous or homosexual conduct?

b. In prostitution cases, the police often arrest and charge the prostitute but let the customer go free. Should prostitution laws be enforced equally against both the customer and the prostitute? Why or why not?

c. What are arguments in favor of or against legalized prostitution?

d. Why do you think we have laws, which are generally unenforced, regulating sexual conduct?

Suicide and Euthanasia

Suicide is the deliberate taking of one's own life. In earlier times, suicide was treated as a felony punishable by burial in an unmarked grave and forfeiture of the dead person's belongings to the state. Today, criminal penalties for successful suicides have been abolished, but there are still criminal laws against attempted suicide and criminal penalties for aiding another in a successful suicide. However, as a practical matter, these laws are rarely enforced. Instead, people who attempt suicide are generally referred for counseling or other appropriate treatment.

Euthanasia, often referred to as mercy killing, is an act or method of putting to death people who are terminally ill. Some people advocate euthanasia as a humane way of dealing with victims of incurable diseases. However, many people believe that euthanasia is simply a form of murder. In any event, it is a highly controversial moral and religious issue. Euthanasia is illegal in every state and may be prosecuted as a homicide.

DEFENSES

For a conviction to occur in a criminal case, the prosecutor must establish beyond a reasonable doubt that the defendant committed the act in question. The defendant is not required to present a defense but can instead simply force the government to prove its case. However, a number of possible defenses are available in a criminal case.

No Crime Has Been Committed

The defendant may establish innocence by showing either that no crime has been committed (e.g., the defendant was carrying a gun but had a valid license; the defendant did not commit rape, because the woman was of legal age and consented) or that there was no criminal intent (e.g., the defendant mistakenly took another person's coat when leaving a restaurant). The defendant is innocent of a charge of larceny if it was an honest and reasonable mistake.

Defendant Did Not Commit the Crime

Oftentimes, no doubt exists that a crime has been committed. In such cases, the question is, who committed it? In this situation, the defendant could establish innocence by showing a mistake in identity or by an **alibi,** which is evidence that the defendant was somewhere else at the time the crime was committed.

Defendant Committed a Criminal Act but the Act was Excusable or Justified

Defenses in this category include self-defense, defense of property and others, and **duress** and **necessity.**

Self-Defense and Defense of Property and Others   The law recognizes the right of a person unlawfully attacked to use reasonable force in self-defense. It also recognizes the right of one person to use reasonable force to defend another person from imminent attack. There are, however, a number of limitations to these defenses.

A person who *reasonably* believes there is imminent danger of bodily harm can use a reasonable amount of force in self-defense. However, a person cannot use more force than necessary. If after stopping an attacker, the defender continues to use force, the roles reverse and the defender can no longer claim self-defense. Deadly force can be used only if one reasonably believes that there is imminent danger of death or serious bodily harm. A person is allowed to use nondeadly force to defend a third person if the person defended is entitled to claim self-defense. Reasonable nondeadly force may also be used to protect property.

PROBLEM 19

a. Mr. Roe kept a pistol in his home as protection against intruders. One evening, he heard a noise in his den and went to investigate. Upon entering the room he saw a man stealing his television. The burglar, seeing the gun, ran for the window, but Mr. Roe fired and killed him before he could escape. In a trial for manslaughter, Mr. Roe pleads self-defense. Would you find him guilty? Why or why not?

b. Suppose you see two men struggling with a casual friend. Thinking they are muggers, you rush to the rescue. It turns out that your friend is wanted for a crime and the men are plainclothes police officers attempting to make an arrest. You are charged with assault. Do you have a defense?

c. The owner of a jewelry store spots a shoplifter stealing an expensive necklace. Can the owner use force to prevent the crime? If so, how much?

Duress and Necessity   The defenses of duress and necessity involve situations in which an individual violates a criminal law to avoid a greater harm. In the case of duress, a criminal act may be excused by showing that the accused was not acting in free will. A successful defense must show that the accused or some member of the accused's immediate family was threatened with death or serious bodily harm. For example, Joe kidnaps Bill's child and threatens to kill her unless Bill steals money from his employer. Bill may claim the defense of duress.

Necessity may be a defense to a crime when the defendant acts in the reasonable belief that no alternative is available. For example, Sally steals a boat to escape an onrushing flood. This defense is available only when no other way exists to avoid the threatened harm. Mere economic necessity (need for money) is not sufficient to excuse a criminal act. Also, neither duress nor necessity is a defense to a crime of homicide.

Defendant Committed a Criminal Act but Is Not Criminally Responsible for His or Her Actions

In this category are the defenses of infancy, intoxication, insanity, and **entrapment**.

Infancy Traditionally, children of a very young age, usually under seven, were considered legally incapable of committing a crime. Children between the ages of 7 and 14 were generally presumed incapable of committing a crime, but this presumption could be shown to be wrong. Under modern laws, most states simply provide that children under a specified age shall not be tried for their crimes but shall be turned over to the juvenile court.

Intoxication Defendants sometimes claim that at the time of a crime, they were so drunk on alcohol or high on drugs that they didn't know what they were doing. As a general rule, voluntary intoxication is *not* a defense to a crime. However, some crimes require proof of a specific mental state. For example, when Grady is charged with assault with intent to kill, he claims he was drunk. If he can prove this, intoxication is a valid defense because it negates the specific mental state (i.e., intent to kill) required to prove the crime. Grady can still be charged with assault, however, because specific intent is not required to prove that crime. If Grady decided to kill someone before he got drunk, or if he got drunk to get up enough nerve to commit the crime, then intoxication would not be a defense. This is because the required mental state (i.e., intent to kill) existed before the drunkenness.

Insanity Over the centuries, the **insanity defense** has evolved as an important legal concept. Ancient Greeks and Romans believed that insane people were not responsible for their actions and should not be punished like ordinary criminals. Since the 14th century, English courts have excused offenders who were mentally unable to control their conduct. The modern standard grew out of an 1843 case involving the attempted murder of the British prime minister.

The basic idea is that people who have a mental disease or defect should not be convicted if they don't know what they are doing or if they don't know the difference between right and wrong. About half the states and the federal government use this standard. The other states hold that the accused must be acquitted if he or she lacked the "substantial capacity" to appreciate the nature of the act or to conform his or her conduct to the requirements of law.

During criminal proceedings, the accused's mental state can be an issue in determining (1) whether the defendant is competent to stand trial, (2) whether the defendant was sane at the time of the criminal act, and (3) whether the defendant is sane after the trial. The insanity defense applies only if the accused was insane at the time of the crime. Insanity at the time of trial may delay the proceedings until the accused can understand what is taking place. But insanity during or after the trial does not affect criminal liability.

In most states, there are three possible verdicts: guilty, innocent, or not guilty by reason of insanity. The last verdict results in automatic commitment to a mental institution in some states. In others, the judge or jury exercises discretion, sometimes in a separate hearing, to determine commitment of the accused. In recent years, a number of states have come up with a new verdict: **guilty but mentally ill.** Defendants found guilty but mentally ill can be sent to a hospital and later transferred to a prison after they've recovered.

To prove insanity, the defense must produce evidence of a mental disease or defect. Psychiatrists usually give testimony in this regard. Both the defense and the prosecution may have psychiatrists examine the defendant, and their testimony is often in conflict. The decision as to whether insanity is a valid defense rests with whomever — judge or jury — decides the facts of the case.

PROBLEM 20

a. What is the insanity defense? How does it work?

b. Should the insanity defense be kept as is, changed in some way, or abolished? Explain your answer.

c. Some of our most infamous criminals have tried to use the insanity defense. Do you know what happened in the trials of John Hinckley? Jack Ruby? Sirhan Sirhan? David (Son of Sam) Berkowitz?

**WHERE
YOU
LIVE**

How does your state's
criminal justice system
compare to the system
shown in Figure 8?

Entrapment   The entrapment defense applies when the defendant admits comitting a criminal act but claims that he or she was induced or persuaded to commit the crime by a law enforcement officer. There is no entrapment when a police officer merely provides the defendant with an opportunity to commit a crime; rather, it must be shown that the defendant would not have committed the crime *but for* the inducement of the police. Entrapment is difficult to prove and cannot be claimed as a defense to crimes involving serious physical injury, such as rape or murder.

PROBLEM 21

Can entrapment be claimed as a valid defense in either of the following cases? Explain your answer.

a. Mary, an undercover police officer masquerading as a prostitute, approaches John and tells him that she'll have sex with him in exchange for $50. John hands over the money.

b. Marvin, a drug dealer, offers to sell drugs to Walter, a police officer disguised as a drug addict. Walter buys the drugs, and Marvin is arrested.

THE CRIMINAL JUSTICE PROCESS

The criminal justice process includes everything that happens to a person from arrest through conviction to release from the control of the state. Freedom may be gained almost immediately — at the station house — or after serving time in a correctional institution. Freedom may also come at any stage in between. Figure 8 on pages 70 and 71 shows a typical state criminal justice system through which an adult passes when charged with a felony. Note that there are various places in which a person can exit the system without completing it. The juvenile justice process discussed at the end of this chapter is somewhat different. You may find it useful to refer to Figure 8 as you study each step of the process.

ARREST

An **arrest** means that a person suspected of a crime is taken into custody. A person can be taken into custody in one of two ways: by an arrest **warrant** or by a warrantless arrest based on probable cause. A person, once taken into custody and not free to leave, is considered to be under arrest, whether told that or not.

An arrest warrant is a court order that commands that the person named in it be taken into custody. A warrant is obtained by

Police officers making an arrest.

filing a complaint before a judge or magistrate. The person filing the complaint is generally a police officer but may also be a victim or a witness. The person making the complaint must set out and swear to the facts and circumstances of the alleged crime. If, on the basis of the information provided, the judge finds **probable cause** to believe that an offense has been committed and that the accused committed it, a warrant will be issued.

On many occasions, police don't have time to get a warrant. In these cases, they may make a warrantless arrest based on probable cause. Probable cause is defined as a reasonable belief that a person has committed a crime. This reasonable belief may be based on less evidence than is necessary to prove a person guilty at trial. For example, suppose the police receive a radio report of a bank robbery. An officer sees a man, matching the description of the bank robber, waving a gun and running away from the bank. The officer would have probable cause to stop and arrest the man.

There is no exact formula for determining probable cause. Police must use their own judgment as to what is reasonable under the circumstances of each case. In all cases, probable cause requires more than mere suspicion or a hunch. Some facts must be present that indicate that the person arrested has committed a crime.

Police may establish probable cause from information provided by citizens in the community. Information from victims or witnesses can be used to obtain an arrest warrant. Police also receive information from informants. Police may use informants' tips to establish probable cause, so long as they can convince a judge that the information is reliable. In determining the reliability of an informant's tip, a judge will consider all the cir-

FIGURE 8   A General View of the Criminal Justice System

This chart presents a simple yet comprehensive view of how cases move through the criminal justice system. Procedures in individual jurisdictions may vary from the pattern shown here. The differing weights of line indicate the relative volumes of cases disposed of at various points in the system, but this is only suggestive since no nationwide data of this sort exists.

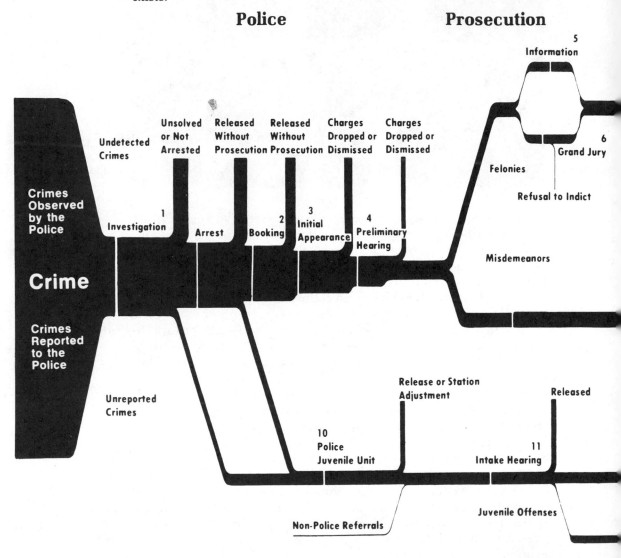

1. May continue until trial.

2. Administrative record of arrest. First step at which temporary release on bail may be available.

3. Before magistrate, commissioner, or justice of peace. Formal notice of charge, advice of rights. Bail set. Summary trials for petty offenses usually conducted here without further processing.

4. Preliminary testing of evidence against defendant. Charge may be reduced. No separate preliminary hearing for misdemeanors in some systems.

5. Charge filed by prosecutor on basis of information submitted by police or citizens. Alternative to grand jury indictment.

6. Reviews whether Government evidence sufficient to justify trial. Some States have no grand jury system; others seldom use it.

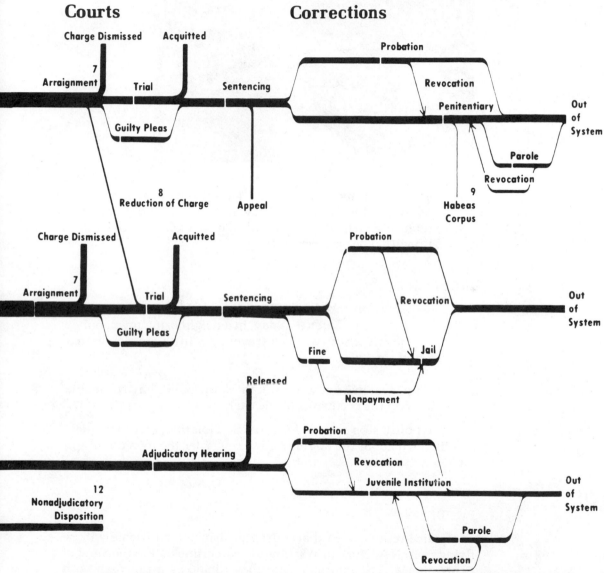

Courts

Corrections

7. Appearance for plea; defendant elects trial by judge or jury (if available).

8. Charge may be reduced at any time prior to trial in return for plea of guilty or for other reasons.

9. Challenge on constitutional grounds to legality of detention. May be sought at any point in process.

10. Police often hold informal hearings, dismiss or adjust many cases without further processing.

11. Probation officer decides desirability of further court action.

12. Welfare agency, social services, counseling, medical care, etc., for cases where adjudicatory handling not needed.

This is a modified version of a chart published in the President's Commission Report, *The Challenge of Crime in a Free Society*, note 11, p. 39 *supra*, at pp. 8–9. Modification from *Introduction to the Criminal Justice System*, Second Edition, by Hazel B. Kerper as revised by Jerold H. Israel, West Publishing Company, © 1979. Reprinted by permission of the publisher.

What is the best thing to do
if stopped by the police?

cumstances. These include whether the informant has provided
accurate information in the past; how the informant obtained the
information; and whether the police can corroborate the informant's tip with other information.

PROBLEM 22

Witnesses see two masked men flee from a holdup in an unidentified light-colored car. Later that day, in a neighboring town, police
alerted to the crime see two men traveling a little too slowly in a
light-colored car.

a. Based on what you know, do you think the police have probable
cause to arrest the occupants of the car?

b. If the police stop the car for a traffic violation, can they question the men about the holdup? Can they order the men out of the
car?

PROBLEM 23

The police receive a tip that a drug pusher named Richie will be
flying from New York to Washington sometime on the morning of
September 8. The informer describes Richie as a tall man with
reddish hair and a beard. He also tells police that Richie has a
habit of walking fast and that he will be carrying illegal drugs in a
brown leather bag.
    On the morning of September 8, the police watch all passen-
gers arriving from New York. When they see a man who fits the

description—carrying a brown leather bag and walking fast—they arrest him. A search of the bag reveals a large quantity of heroin.

a. Based on what you know, do you think the police had probable cause to arrest Richie? Why or why not?

b. Should the police have obtained a warrant before arresting Richie? Why or why not?

The police do not need probable cause to stop and question individuals whom they reasonably suspect are involved in criminal activity. In such cases, the police may ask for identification and for an explanation of the suspicious behavior. If asked specific questions about a crime with which you may be involved, you do not have to answer. However, a refusal to cooperate may result in further detention. In some cases, it may provide sufficient additional evidence to result in a valid arrest. For example, suppose a police officer has reason to suspect someone of a crime, and the person refuses to answer the police officer's questions or attempts to flee when being approached by the officer. This conduct, when considered together with other factors, might provide the probable cause necessary to arrest. In addition, if a police officer, based on his or her experience, thinks a person is behaving suspiciously and is likely to be armed, the officer may **stop and frisk** (pat down) the suspect for weapons.

Police officers may search a suspect incident to (at the time of making) a lawful arrest.

A police officer may use as much physical force as is reasonably necessary to make an arrest. However, most police departments limit the use of deadly force to incidents involving dangerous or threatening suspects. In 1985 the U.S. Supreme Court was asked to decide whether it was lawful for police to shoot an "unarmed fleeing felony suspect." In deciding the case, the court ruled that deadly force "may not be used unless it is necessary to prevent the escape, *and* the officer has probable cause to believe the suspect poses a significant threat of death or serious physical harm to the officer or others."

If a police officer uses too much force or makes an unlawful arrest, the accused may bring a civil action for damages or possibly a criminal action for violation of civil rights. In addition, many police departments have procedures for handling citizen

THE CASE OF THE UNLUCKY COUPLE

After an evening at the movies, Lonnie Howard and his girlfriend, Susan, decide to park in the empty lot behind Briarwood Elementary School. Several beers later, they are startled by the sound of breaking glass from the rear of the school.

Unnoticed in their darkened car, Lonnie and Susan observe two men loading office equipment from the school into the back of a van. Quickly concluding that the men must be burglars, Lonnie revs up his engine and roars out of the parking lot onto Main Street.

Meanwhile, unknown to Lonnie and Susan, a silent alarm has also alerted the police to the break-in at the school. Responding to the alarm, Officer Ramos heads for the school and turns onto Main Street just in time to see Lonnie's car speeding away.

PROBLEM 24

a. If you were Officer Ramos, what would you do in this situation? If you were Lonnie, what would you do?

b. If Officer Ramos chases after Lonnie, would he have probable cause to stop and arrest him?

c. How do you think Officer Ramos would act once he stopped Lonnie? How do you think Lonnie and Susan would act?

d. Roleplay this situation. As Officer Ramos, decide what you would say and how you would act toward the occupants of the car. As Lonnie and Susan, decide what you would say and how you would act toward the police.

e. What could Lonnie and Susan do if they were mistakenly arrested for the burglary? What could they do if they where abused or mistreated by Officer Ramos?

complaints about police misconduct. You should know, however, that a police officer is never liable for false arrest simply because the person arrested did not commit the crime. Rather, it must be shown that the officer acted maliciously or had no reasonable grounds for suspicion of guilt.

SEARCH AND SEIZURE

The right of the people to be secure in their persons, houses, papers, and effects, against unreasonable searches and seizures, shall not be violated, and no warrants shall issue, but upon probable cause, supported by oath or affirmation, and particularly describing the place to be searched, and the person or things to be seized.

— Fourth Amendment to the U.S. Constitution

Americans have always valued their privacy. They expect to be left alone, to be free from unwarranted snooping or spying, and to be secure in their own homes. This expectation of privacy is important and is protected by the U.S. Constitution. The Fourth Amendment sets out the right to be free from "unreasonable searches and seizures" and establishes conditions under which search warrants may be issued.

Balanced against the individual's right to privacy is the government's need to gather information. In the case of the police, this is the need to collect evidence against criminals and to protect society against crime.

The Fourth Amendment does not give citizens an absolute right to privacy, and it does not prohibit all searches — only those that are unreasonable. In deciding if a search is reasonable, the courts look to the facts and circumstances of each case. As a general rule, courts have held that searches and seizures are unreasonable unless authorized by a valid warrant.

The language of the Fourth Amendment is relatively simple, but search and seizure law is complex. Courts look at the law on a case-by-case basis, and there are many exceptions to the basic rules. Once an individual is arrested, it is up to the courts to decide whether any evidence found in a search was legally obtained. If a court finds that the search was unreasonable, then evidence found in the search cannot be used at the trial against the defendant. This principle, called the **exclusionary rule,** does not mean that a defendant cannot be tried or convicted, but it does mean that evidence seized in an unlawful search cannot be used at trial. (For a further discussion of the exclusionary rule, see the heading "The Exclusionary Rule.")

ADVICE ON WHAT TO DO IF ARRESTED

■ *Don't struggle with the police.* Be polite. Avoid fighting or swearing, even if you think the police have made a mistake. Resisting arrest and assaulting a police officer are usually separate crimes that you can be charged with even if you've done nothing else wrong.

■ Give your name, address, and phone number to the police. Otherwise, *keep quiet.* Don't discuss your case with anyone at this point, and don't sign any statements about your case.

■ You may be searched, photographed, and fingerprinted. Notice carefully what is done but don't resist. If any personal property is taken from you, ask for a written receipt.

■ As soon as possible after you get to the police station, call *a trusted relative or friend.* Tell this person where you are, what you've been charged with, and what your bail or bond is (if you know).

■ *When you're arrested on a minor offense,* you may, in some places, be released without having to put up any money (this is called an unsecured bond or a citation release). If you don't qualify for a citation release, you may have to put up some money before release (this is called posting a cash bond or collateral). Ask for a receipt for the money.

■ *When you're arrested for a serious misdemeanor or felony,* you won't be released immediately. Ask the friend or relative you have called to get a lawyer for you. If you can't afford a lawyer, the court will appoint one for you at the initial appearance.

■ Before you leave the police station, be sure to find out when you're due in court. *Never be late or miss a court appearance.* If you don't show up in court at the assigned time, a warrant will be issued for your rearrest.

■ *Don't talk about your case with anyone except your lawyer.* Be honest with your lawyer, or he or she will have trouble helping you. Ask that your lawyer be present at all lineups and interrogation sessions.

Searches with a Warrant

A **search warrant** is a court order. It is obtained from a judge who is convinced that there is a real need to search a person or place. Before a judge issues a warrant, someone, usually a police officer, must appear in court and testify under oath concerning the facts that provide the probable cause to believe that a search is justified.

This sworn statement of facts and circumstances is known as an **affidavit.** If a judge issues a search warrant, the warrant must specifically describe the person or place to be searched and the particular things to be seized.

Once issued, the search warrant must be executed within a limited period of time, such as 10 days. Also, in many states, a search warrant must be executed only in the daytime unless the warrant expressly states otherwise. Finally, a search warrant does not necessarily authorize a general search of everything in the specified place. For example, if the police have a warrant to search a house for stolen televisions or other large items, it would be unreasonable for them to look in desk drawers, envelopes, or other small places where a television could not possibly be hidden.

PROBLEM 25

a. Examine Figure 9, an affidavit for a search warrant. Who is requesting the warrant? What are the searchers looking for? Which people or places are sought to be searched? What facts and circumstances are given to justify the search?

b. Examine Figure 10, a search warrant. Who authorized the search? When may the search be conducted? Considering the affidavit, do you think the judge had sufficent grounds to authorize the warrant? Is there anything missing from the warrant?

c. As a general rule, why do you think the Fourth Amendment requires police to obtain a warrant before conducting a search?

FIGURE 9   Affidavit for Search Warrant

Form A.O. 106 (Rev. Apr. 1973)

Affidavit for
Search Warrant

United States District Court
FOR THE
Eastern District of Missouri

Docket No. A_____

Case No. 11246

UNITED STATES OF AMERICA

vs.

John Doe

**AFFIDAVIT FOR
SEARCH WARRANT**

BEFORE Michael J. Thiel, Federal Courthouse, St. Louis, Missouri
Name of Judge¹ or Federal Magistrate   Address of Judge¹ or Federal Magistrate

The undersigned being duly sworn deposes and says:

That he has reason to believe that (on the person of) Occupants, and (on the premises known as) 935 Bay Street, St. Louis, Missouri, described as a two story, residential dwelling, white in color and of wood frame construction.....

in the Eastern District of Missouri

there is now being concealed certain property, namely

here describe property

Counterfeit bank notes, money orders, and securities, and plates, stones, and other paraphernalia used in counterfeiting and forgery,

which are
here give alleged grounds for search and seizure²
in violation of 18 U.S. Code ¶471-474

And that the facts tending to establish the foregoing grounds for issuance of a Search Warrant are as follows: (1) Pursuant to my employment with the Federal Bureau of Investigation, I received information from a reliable informant that a group of persons were conducting an illegal counterfeiting operation out of a house at 935 Bay Street, St. Louis, Missouri. (2) Acting on this information agents of the FBI placed the house at 935 Bay Street under around the clock surveillance. During the course of this surveilance officers observed a number of facts tending to establsh the existence of an illegal counterfeiting operation. These include: observation of torn & defective counterfeit notes discarded in the trash in the alley behind the house at 935 Bay Street, and pick-up & delivery of parcels at irregular hours of the night by persons known to the FBI as having records for distribution of counterfeit money.

Barry T. Cunningham Special Agent
Signature of Affiant.

Federal Bureau of Investigation
Official Title, if any.

Sworn to before me, and subscribed in my presence, December 3rd , 19 78

Michael J. Thiel
Judge¹ or Federal Magistrate.

FIGURE 10   **Search Warrant**

Form A. O. 93 (Rev. Nov. 1972)   Search Warrant

United States District Court

FOR THE

Eastern District of Missouri

UNITED STATES OF AMERICA   Docket No.   A

vs.   Case No.   11246

John Doe

SEARCH WARRANT

To Any sheriff, constable, marshall, police officer, or investigative
    officer of the United States of America.
    Affidavit(s) having been made before me by
    Special Agent, Barry I. Cunningham

that he has reason to believe that { on the person of
                                    on the premises known as }

    on the occupants of, and
    on the premises known as 935 Bay Street, St. Louis, Missouri
        described as a two story, residential dwelling, white in
        color and of wood frame construction .....

                    in the Eastern   District of Missouri

there is now being concealed certain property, namely
    Counterfeit bank notes, money orders, and securities, and
    Plates, stones, and other paraphernalia used in counterfeiting and
        forgery

and as I am satisfied that there is probable cause to believe that the property so described is being
concealed on the person or premises above described and that the foregoing grounds for application for
issuance of the search warrant exist.

    You are hereby commanded to search within a period of ___10____ (not to exceed 10
days) the person or place named for the property specified, serving this warrant and making the
search { ~~in the daytime (6:00 a.m. to 10:00 p.m.)~~ } and if the property be found there to seize it,
         at anytime in the day or night[1]
leaving a copy of this warrant and a receipt for the property taken, and prepare a written inventory of
the property seized and promptly return this warrant and bring the property before me as required
by law.

    Dated this 3rd   day of December   , 19 78

                                            Michael J. Thiel
                                            _____,
                                            Judge or Federal Magistrate.

---

[1] The Federal Rules of Criminal Procedure provide: "The warrant shall be served in the daytime, unless the issuing authority, by appropriate
provision in the warrant, and for reasonable cause shown, authorizes its execution at times other than daytime." (Rule 41(C))

Why do you think there is a general requirement that searches be conducted during daylight hours?

d. Under what conditions do you think police should be allowed to search without a warrant?

Searches without a Warrant

While the police are generally required to get a search warrant, the courts have recognized a number of situations in which searches may be legally conducted without a warrant.

■ *Search Incident to a Lawful Arrest.* This is the most common exception to the warrant requirement. It allows the police to search a lawfully arrested person and the area immediately around that person for hidden weapons or for evidence that might be destroyed.

■ *Stop and Frisk.* A police officer who reasonably thinks a person is behaving suspiciously and is likely to be armed may stop and frisk the suspect for weapons. This exception to the warrant requirement was created to protect the safety of officers and bystanders who might be injured by a person carrying a concealed weapon.

■ *Consent.* When a person voluntarily agrees, the police may conduct a search without a warrant and without probable cause. Normally, a person may grant permission to search only his or her own belongings or property. In some situations, however, one person may legally allow the police to conduct a search of another person's property (e.g., parent-child).

■ *Plain View.* If an object connected with a crime is in plain view and can be seen by an officer from a place where he or she has a right to be, it can be seized without a warrant. For example, if a police officer issuing a routine traffic ticket observes a gun on the seat of the car, the officer may seize the gun without a warrant.

■ *Hot Pursuit.* Police in hot pursuit of a suspect are not required to get a search warrant before entering a building that they have seen the suspect enter. It is also lawful to seize evidence found during a search conducted while in hot pursuit of a felon.

■ *Vehicle Searches.* A police officer who has reasonable cause to believe that a vehicle contains **contraband** may conduct a search of the vehicle without a warrant. This does not mean that the police have a right to stop and search any vehicle on the streets. The right to stop and search must be based on probable cause.

■ *Emergency Situations.* In certain emergencies, the police are not required to get a search warrant. These situations include

Is an airport-luggage search a violation of the Fourth Amendment?

searching a building after a telephoned bomb threat, entering a house after smelling smoke or hearing screams, and other situations in which the police don't have time to get a warrant.

■ *Border and Airport Searches.*   Customs agents are authorized to search without warrants and without probable cause. They may examine the baggage, vehicle, purse, wallet, or similar belongings of people entering the country. Body searches or searches conducted away from the border are allowed only on reasonable suspicion. In view of the danger of airplane hijacking, courts have also held it reasonable for airlines to search all carryon luggage and to search all passengers by means of a metal detector.

PROBLEM 26

Examine each of the following situations. Decide whether the search and seizure violates the Fourth Amendment and whether the evidence seized can be used in court. Explain your reasons.

Do school authorities have the right to search student lockers?

a. Jill's former boyfriend breaks into her apartment and looks through her desk for love letters. Instead he finds drugs, which he turns over to the police.

b. After Joe checks out of a hotel, the police ask the maid to turn over the contents of the wastebasket, where they find notes planning a murder.

c. A student informs the principal that Bob, another student, is selling drugs on school grounds. The principal opens Bob's locker with a master key, finds drugs, and calls the police.

d. The police see Dell — a known drug pusher — standing at a bus stop on a downtown street. They stop and search him and find drugs in his pocket.

e. Susan is arrested for reckless driving. After stopping her, the police search her purse and find a pistol.

f. Larry is observed shoplifting items in a store. Police chase Larry into his apartment building and arrest him outside the door of his apartment. A search of the apartment reveals a large quantity of stolen merchandise.

g. The police receive a tip from a reliable informant that Rudy has counterfeit money in his office. Acting on this information, they get a search warrant and find the money just where the informant told them it would be.

h. Sandy is suspected of receiving stolen goods. The police go to her apartment and ask Claire, her roommate, if they can search the apartment. Claire says it's OK, and the police find stolen items in Sandy's dresser.

THE CASE OF FINGERS McGEE

Officers Smith and Jones receive a radio report of a robbery at the Dixie Liquor Store. The report indicates only that the suspect is male, about six feet tall, and wearing old clothes. Five minutes earlier, Fingers McGee saw the owner of the Dixie Liquor Store chasing a man carrying a sack and what appeared to be a knife down the street. McGee thinks the man looks like Bill Johnson, a drug addict who lives in a house at 22 Elm Street. Officers Smith and Jones encounter McGee on a street corner.

PROBLEM 27

a. Roleplay this encounter. As the officers, decide what questions to ask McGee. As McGee, decide what to tell the officers.
b. Assuming McGee tells the police what he knows, what should the police do then?
c. Should the police get a search warrant before going to Johnson's house? If they go to Johnson's house without a warrant, do they have probable cause to arrest him? Why or why not?
d. If the police decide to enter Johnson's house, what should they do? Should they knock and announce themselves, or should they break in unannounced?
e. If the police enter the house, decide whether Johnson can be arrested, where the police can search, and what, if anything, can be seized. Roleplay the scene at the house.

INTERROGATIONS AND CONFESSIONS

After an arrest is made, it is standard police practice to question or interrogate the accused. These interrogations often result in confessions or admissions, which are later used as evidence at trial.

Balanced against the police's need to question suspects are the constitutional rights of people accused of a crime. The Fifth Amendment to the U.S. Constitution provides citizens with a privilege against **self-incrimination.** This means that a suspect has a right to remain silent and cannot be forced to testify against him or herself. Under the Sixth Amendment, a person accused of a crime has the right to the assistance of an attorney.

For many years, the Supreme Court held that a confession was not admissable as evidence if it was not voluntary and trustworthy. This meant that using physical force, torture, threats, or other techniques that could force an innocent person to confess were prohibited. Later, in the case of *Escobedo* v. *Illinois*, the Supreme Court said that even a voluntary confession was inadmissible as evidence if it was obtained after denying the defendant's request to talk with an attorney. Although some defendants might ask for an attorney, other people might not be aware of their right to remain silent or of their right to a have a lawyer present during questioning. In 1966, the Supreme Court was presented with such a situation in the case of *Miranda* v. *Arizona*.

In its decision, the Supreme Court ruled that Miranda's confession could not be used at trial, because it was obtained without informing Miranda of his constitutional rights. As a result of this case, police are now required to inform people accused of a crime of the following Miranda rights *before questioning begins:*

MIRANDA WARNINGS

You have the right to remain silent. Anything you say can be used against you in court.

You have the right to a lawyer and to have one present while you are being questioned.

If you cannot afford a lawyer, one will be appointed for you before any questioning begins.

THE CASE OF MIRANDA v. ARIZONA

Ernesto Miranda was accused of kidnapping and raping an 18-year-old girl near Phoenix, Arizona. The girl claimed she was on her way home from work when a man grabbed her, threw her into the back seat of a car, and raped her. Ten days later Miranda was arrested, placed in a lineup, and identified by the girl as her attacker. The police then took Miranda into an interrogation room and questioned him for two hours. At the end of the two hours, the officers emerged with a written and signed confession. This confession was used as evidence at trial, and Miranda was found guilty.

Miranda later appealed his case to the U.S. Supreme Court, arguing that he had not been warned of his right to remain silent, and that he had been deprived of his right to counsel. Miranda did not suggest that his confession was false or brought about by coercion, but rather that he would not have confessed if he had been advised of his right to remain silent and of his right to an attorney.

PROBLEM 28

a. What happened in the Miranda case? On what grounds did Miranda appeal his conviction?
b. Do you think Miranda's confession should have been used as evidence against him at trial? Why or why not?
c. Do you think police should be required to tell suspects their rights before questioning them?
d. Do you think anyone would confess after being warned of their rights?

THE CASE OF HARRIS v. NEW YORK

Fred Harris was arrested and charged with selling drugs to an undercover officer. At the time of his arrest, Harris made several statements indicating that he was indeed selling heroin. These statements, however, were made before he was warned of his right to remain silent.

During his trial, Harris took the stand and denied selling drugs to the officer. At this point, the prosecutor introduced Harris's earlier statements to contradict his testimony at trial. The defense attorney objected, but the judge allowed the use of the earlier statements, and Harris was convicted.

Harris appealed his case to the U.S. Supreme Court, arguing that according to the Miranda rule, no confession or statements of a defendant made prior to being warned of his or her rights could be used at trial.

PROBLEM 29

a. If you were the judge at Harris's trial, would you have allowed his earlier statements to be used as evidence? If so, how do you justify this in view of the Supreme Court's ruling in the *Miranda* case?
b. Which statements do you consider more reliable: those made at trial or those made immediately after arrest?
c. *Harris* v. *New York* was decided by the U.S. Supreme Court in October 1971. The following are the paraphrased opinions of two of the justices on the court. Which of these opinions do you agree with and why?

Opinion 1
Evidence obtained before giving the Miranda warnings should not be allowed at trial. It would be wrong for the courts to aid law-breaking police officers. Allowing the use of illegally obtained statements to impeach or contradict testimony at trial would discourage defendants from taking the stand in their own defense.

Opinion 2
Defendants cannot be forced to testify, but if they do, they give up their right against self-incrimination and can be cross-examined like any other witness. Since Harris took the stand and told a story different from the one he had given the police, the prosecutor was entitled to introduce the earlier statement for the sole purpose of cross-examining the defendant and impeaching his testimony.

Suspects sometimes complain that they were not read their Miranda rights and that the entire case should therefore be dropped and charges dismissed. Failure to give Miranda warnings however, does not affect the validity of an arrest. The police have to give Miranda warnings only if they want to use statements from the accused at the trial. In fact, in his second trial, Miranda was convicted on other evidence.

The *Miranda* case has been controversial. It illustrates the delicate balance between the protection guaranteed the accused and the protection provided society from crime. This balance is constantly changing, and the effect of the *Miranda* case has been somewhat altered by more recent cases. In one case, the Court ruled that if a suspect confesses before police warn the suspect of his or her rights, the confession can be used if the suspect later repeats it after a warning. In another case, the Court created a "public safety" exception to the Miranda rule. It did this by holding that police may ask questions related to public safety before advising suspects of their rights. In this case, a police officer who was arresting a rape suspect in a grocery store asked the suspect where his gun was before advising him of his rights. The suspect then pointed to a nearby grocery counter, where the gun was found.

PROCEEDINGS BEFORE TRIAL

Before a case reaches the courtroom, several preliminary proceedings take place. Some of these proceedings are standard for every case. Others may result in the charges being dropped or in a plea of guilty by the defendant.

Booking and Initial Appearance

After an arrest, the accused is normally taken to a police station for **booking.** This is the formal process of making a police record of the arrest. Following this, the accused will usually be fingerprinted and photographed. In certain circumstances, the police are allowed to take fingernail clippings, handwriting specimens, or blood samples.

Within a limited period of time following the arrest and booking, the accused must appear before a judicial officer. At this initial appearance, the judge will explain the defendant's rights and advise him or her of the exact nature of the charges. The defendant will also be appointed an attorney or given the opportunity to obtain one. In a misdemeanor case, the defendant will be asked to enter a plea of guilty or not guilty. The judge may also set **bail** at this time. In a felony case, the initial appearance is known as the **presentment.** As in a misdemeanor case, the defendant will be informed of the charges and advised of his or her rights, but a plea is not entered until a later stage in the criminal process, known as the felony **arraignment.**

The most important part of the initial appearance is deciding whether the defendant will be released from custody and, if so, under what conditions.

COMPREHENSIVE CRIME CONTROL ACT OF 1984

■ Establishes new federal bail provisions and allows preventive detention.
■ Permits federal courts to consider danger to the community in setting bail conditions and to deny bail altogether when a defendant poses a grave danger to others.
■ Tightens the criteria for postconviction release pending sentencing and appeal.
■ Provides for revocation of release and increased penalties for crimes committed while on release.

Bail and Pretrial Release

An arrested person can usually be released after putting up an amount of money known as **bail.** The purpose of bail is to assure the court that the defendant will return for trial. The right to bail has been recognized in all but the most serious cases, such as murder.

BAIL HEARING

The following five people have been arrested and charged with a variety of crimes. In each case, decide whether the person should be released and, if so, under what conditions. Choose from one of the following options and discuss your decision: (1) money bond — set an amount; (2) personal recognizance — no money required; (3) conditional release — set the conditions; and (4) pretrial detention.

Case 1

Name: Jerry Davis   Age: 26
Charge: Possession of narcotics
Residence: 619 30th Street, lives alone, no family or references
Employment: Unemployed
Education: 11th grade
Criminal record: As a juvenile had five arrests, mostly mis-
    demeanors. As an adult had two arrests for petty larceny and a
    conviction for possession of dangerous drugs (probation was suc-
    cessfully completed).
Comment: Defendant arrested while leaving a pharmacy, carrying a
    large quantity of morphine. Urine test indicates defendant pre-
    sently using narcotics.

Case 2

Name: Gloria Hardy   Age: 23
Charge: Prostitution
Residence: 130 Riverside Drive, Apt. 10
Employment: Royal Massage Parlor; reportedly earns $1,500 per
    week
Education: Completed high school
Criminal record: Five arrests for prostitution, two convictions; cur-
    rently on probation.
Comment: Vice detective alleges defendant involved in prostitution
    catering to wealthy clients.

Case 3

Name: Stanley A. Wexler   Age: 42
Charge: Possession and sale of narcotics
Residence: 3814 Sunset Drive, lives with wife and two children
Employment: Self-employed owner of a drugstore chain, net worth
    $250,000

Bail may be paid directly to the court. Either the entire amount will be required or, in some places, the defendant will be released after paying a portion of the total amount (e.g., 10 percent). If the defendant doesn't have the money, a bonding company may put up the cash in exchange for a fee. For example, a defendant with a bond of $2,000 might be released after paying $200

Education: Completed college, advanced degrees in pharmacy and business administration
Criminal record: None
Comment: Arrested at his store by undercover police after attempting to sell a large quantity of unregistered morphine. Alleged to be a big-time dealer. No indication of drug usage.

Case 4
Name: Michael D. McKenna   Age 19
Charge: Armed robbery
Residence: 412 Pine Street, lives with parents
Employment: Waiter, Vanguard Restaurant; earns $100 per week
Education: 10th grade
Criminal record: Eight juvenile arrests, runaway, possession of marijuana, illegal possession of firearms, and four burglaries, convicted of firearms charge and two burglaries; spent two years in juvenile facility.
Comment: Arrested after being identified as assailant in a street holdup. Alleged leader of a street gang. Police consider dangerous. No indication of drug usage.

Case 5
Name: Walter Lollar   Age: 34
Charge: Possession of stolen mail and forgery
Residence: 5361 Texas Street, lives with common-law wife and two children by a prior marriage.
Employment: Works 30-hours per week at a service station, earns minimum wage
Education: Quit school after eighth grade; no vocational skills
Criminal record: Nine arrests — mostly drunk and disorderly and vagrancy. Two convictions: (1) driving while intoxicated (fined and lost license); (2) forgery (completed two years' probation).
Comment: Arrested attempting to cash a stolen social security check. Probation officer indicates defendant has a drinking problem.

What's your opinion of the bail system? Should it be easier or harder to get out of jail prior to trial? Discuss your reasons.

After an arrest, the accused may be fingerprinted, photographed, and required to participate in a lineup.

(10 percent of the total) to the bonding company. If a person released on a bail fails to return, the court will keep the money.

The Eighth Amendment to the U.S. Constitution states "excessive bail may not be required." However, a poor person unable to raise any money could be detained in jail before trial and without conviction. Many people consider this unfair, and in recent years, courts have started programs to release defendants without requiring any money.

To be eligible for release on **personal recognizance,** or personal bond, the defendant must promise to return and must be considered a good risk to show up for trial. In determining the likelihood of the defendant's return, judges consider factors such as the nature and circumstances of the offense, the accused's family and community ties, financial resources, employment background, and prior criminal record.

In addition to personal recognizance programs, courts may set a variety of nonmonetary conditions designed to ensure the return of the defendant. These conditions include third-party custody, requiring the defendant to maintain or get a job, to reside at a certain address, or to report his or her whereabouts on a regular basis.

Despite the advantages of these programs, statistics indicate that a large number of defendants commit crimes while out on bail. As a result, some people argue that it should be harder, not easier, to get out on bond. They say that courts should be able to consider danger to the community when setting bail. On the other hand, supporters of pretrial release say that it prevents punishment prior to conviction and gives defendants the freedom to help prepare their case.

Preliminary Hearing

A **preliminary hearing** is a screening device. It is used to determine if there is enough evidence to require the defendant to stand trial. At a preliminary hearing the prosecutor is required to establish the commission of a crime and the probable guilt of the defendant.

In most states, the defendant has the right to be represented by an attorney, to cross-examine prosecution witnesses, and to call witnesses in his or her favor. If the judge finds no probable cause, the defendant will be released. However, dismissal of a case at the preliminary hearing does not always mean the case is over. This is because the prosecution may still submit the case to a grand jury.

A preliminary hearing.

Grand Jury

A grand jury is a group of between 16 and 23 persons charged with determining whether there is sufficient cause to believe that a person has committed a crime and should be made to stand trial. The Fifth Amendment to the U.S. Constitution requires that before anyone can be tried for a serious crime in federal court, there must be a grand jury indictment.

To secure an indictment, a prosecutor will present evidence designed to establish that a crime has been committed and that there is probable cause to believe the defendant committed it. Neither the defendant nor his or her attorney has a right to appear before a grand jury. Also, the prosecutor is not required to present all the evidence or call all the witnesses as long as the grand jury is satisfied with the merits of proceeding to trial.

Grand jury indictments are required only in federal court. However, many states also use a grand jury indictment process. Other states bring defendants to trial following a preliminary hearing or based on a criminal **information.** This is a formal accusation detailing the nature and circumstances of the charge — filed with the court by the prosecutor.

Felony Arraignment and Pleas

After an indictment is issued, the defendant will be required to appear in court and enter a plea. If the defendant pleads guilty, the judge will set a date for sentencing. If the defendant pleads not guilty, the judge will set a date for trial and ask the defendant if he or she wants a jury trial or a trial before a judge alone.

Nolo contendere is a plea by the defendant that does not admit guilt but also does not contest the charges. It is equivalent to pleading guilty. The only advantage of this plea is that it cannot be used as evidence in a later civil trial for damages based on the same set of facts.

Pretrial Motions

An important preliminary proceeding is the pretrial **motion.** A motion is a formal request for a court to make a ruling or take some other action. Prior to trial, a defendant may file motions seeking to have the case dismissed or to obtain some advantage or assistance in preparing the case. Common pretrial motions include *motion for discovery of evidence,* which is a request by the defendant to examine, before trial, certain evidence in the possession of the prosecutor; *motion for a continuance,* which seeks more time to prepare the case; and *motion for change of venue,* which is a

Pretrial motions are an important part of the criminal justice process.

request to change the location of the trial to avoid community hostility, for the convenience of witnesses, or for other reasons. Perhaps the most important and controversial pretrial motion is the motion to suppress evidence.

The Exclusionary Rule

The Fourth Amendment protects citizens against "unreasonable searches and seizures" by the government. But it doesn't say what happens if the police violate the amendment. To put teeth into the amendment, the U.S. Supreme Court adopted the **exclusionary rule.** This rule holds that any evidence illegally seized by law enforcement officials cannot be used in court against the accused. It also applies to evidence obtained from illegal questioning of the accused.

The rule is used by criminal defense lawyers who file a **motion to suppress evidence.** This motion asks the court to exclude any evidence that was illegally obtained. If the judge agrees that the evidence was obtained in violation of the accused's constitutional rights, it will be suppressed. This does not mean the evidence is returned to the defendant. For example, if the police illegally seize contraband, such as marijuana, it cannot be used at trial, but it does not have to be given back to the defendant.

The exclusionary rule has been used in federal courts since 1914. However, the rule was not extended to state courts until the 1961 case of *Mapp* v. *Ohio*. This famous case made the exclusionary

Under the "exclusionary rule" evidence obtained in an illegal search and seizure cannot be used against a defendant at trial.

rule binding on the states. Over the years since the *Mapp* decision, the courts have modified and reevaluated the exclusionary rule, but the basic rule remains.

The exclusionary rule does not prevent the arrest or trial of a suspect. However, in some cases, it does mean that guilty people may go free. This is because when an important piece of evidence is excluded from the trial, the case is often dismissed or the defendant is acquitted.

The exclusionary rule is very controversial. Many people claim that it is a legal loophole that allows dangerous criminals to go free. Others say that rule is necessary to safeguard our rights and to prevent police misconduct. The two major arguments in support of the rule are *judicial integrity* and *deterrence*. Judicial integrity is the idea that courts should not be parties to law-breaking by the police. Deterrence means that police will be less likely to violate a citizen's rights if they know illegally seized evidence will be thrown out of court.

Critics of the rule claim it doesn't work. They say it doesn't deter because the police simply don't understand the complexities of the Fourth Amendment. Moreover, critics claim the rule doesn't work because it doesn't punish the police but rather, rewards the criminal.

As a practical matter, police are sometimes more concerned with arrests than with convictions. They frequently make arrests to seize contraband, gather information, or disrupt criminal activity. Even when they are seeking a conviction, they sometimes make mistakes.

In 1985, criticism of the rule led to the adoption of a so-called "good faith exception." In the case of *United States* v. *Leon*, the Supreme Court held that the "exclusionary rule should not apply to bar evidence obtained by police acting in reasonable reliance on a search warrant, issued by a detached and neutral magistrate, that is later found to be invalid."

PROBLEM 30

a. What is the exclusionary rule? How does it work?

b. Why do you think the Supreme Court adopted the exclusionary rule? What are some agruments in favor of the rule? Against the rule? Do you favor or oppose the rule? Explain your answer.

c. What is meant by the good faith exception to the exclusionary rule? What are some arguments in favor of the rule? Should it be extended to warrantless searches?

THE CASE OF A PURSE SEARCH

Ms. Chen, a high school teacher, found two students holding lit cigarettes. Since smoking violated school rules, Chen took the girls to the principal's office. When the principal asked the girls whether they had been smoking, one student, T.L.O., denied it and claimed that she did not smoke.

The principal then asked for her purse, which she handed to him. When he opened it, he saw cigarettes and a pack of rolling papers. T.L.O. denied that these belonged to her. However, on the basis of experience, the principal knew that rolling papers often indicated marijuana. When he looked farther into the purse, the principal found marijuana, drug paraphernalia, $40 in $1 bills, and written documentation of T.L.O.'s sale of marijuana to other students.

PROBLEM 31

a. Should the exclusionary rule apply to searches by school officials of students in high school? Why or why not?

b. How much evidence should a school official have before searching a student's purse or locker? Should probable cause be required? Reasonable suspicion?

c. Do you believe that the principal had the right to open T.L.O.'s purse? Could the marijuana and drug paraphernalia be used against her in court?

d. Should high school students have more rights, fewer rights, or the same rights as adults in the community? Explain your answer.

Plea Bargaining

Contrary to popular belief, most criminal cases never go to trial. Rather, most defendants who are convicted plead guilty before trial. In minor cases, such as traffic violations, the procedure for pleading guilty is simple. The defendant signs a form waiving the right to appear and mails the court a check for the amount of the fine. In major cases, guilty pleas result from a process of negotiation between the accused, the defense attorney, and the prosecutor. This process is known as **plea bargaining**. It involves granting certain concessions to the defendant in exchange for a plea of guilty. Typically, the prosecution will allow the defendant to plead guilty to a less serious charge or recommend a lighter sentence on the original charge.

YOU BE THE JUDGE

In each of the following situations, decide whether the police conduct was reasonable or unreasonable. Then decide whether the evidence obtained could be used at the trial of the accused. Be prepared to explain your answers.

a. Police officers see two masked men flee from a jewelry store in an unidentified dark-colored van. The officers approach the store, find the owner shot dead, his store ransacked. There are no witnesses. Several hours later, in a neighboring town, other police alerted to the crime see two men in a dark-colored van. They stop the van and question the occupants. Their answers are unhelpful. With only their intuition to rely upon, the police search the van and find the stolen merchandise, the murder weapon, and the masks. Arrested, confronted with the evidence, and told their rights, the suspects confess to robbery and murder.

b. The police see Ringo, a long-haired musician hanging out in a park. Because they don't like his looks, they decide to stop and search him. The search reveals nothing illegal.

c. Acting on a tip, police go to the home of Rossi, a suspected narcotics pusher. Finding the front door open, they go upstairs, where they find Rossi in bed with his wife. When Rossi sees the police, he grabs two pills from the bedside table and puts them into his mouth. The police try to prevent Rossi from swallowing the pills. When this fails, they handcuff him and rush him to the hospital, where police recover two morphine tablets. Rossi is charged with possession of narcotics.

d. Schmerber, who is accused of drunken driving, is taken to a hospital after an accident. At the hospital the police ask him to submit to a blood alcohol test. When he refuses, the police have a blood sample forcibly taken.

e. Jail guards routinely conduct body cavity searches of pretrial detainees to deter visitors from smuggling drugs or other con-

Plea bargaining allows the government to avoid the time and expense of a public trial. The defendant, on the other hand, often receives a lighter sentence than if the case had resulted in a conviction at trial. When accepting a guilty plea, the judge must decide if the plea was made freely, voluntarily, and with knowledge of all the facts. Thus, once a defendant pleads guilty, withdrawing the guilty plea is very hard.

Plea bargaining is controversial. Critics charge that plea bargaining allows dangerous criminals to get off with light sentences. Others, more concerned with the plight of the defendant, argue that the government should be forced to prove guilt beyond a reasonable doubt at trial. They say that the system is unfair to the accused, particularly if the prosecution has a weak case.

traband to inmates. A rectal search of defendant Odom reveals a quantity of illegal pills.

f. Amtrak officials in San Diego observe two persons loading a footlocker onto a train bound for Boston. They become suspicious when they notice the trunk is unusually heavy for its size and is leaking talcum powder, a substance often used to mask the odors of marijuana and hashish. The railroad officials notify federal agents, who meet the train in Boston two days later. The agents and a police dog that is trained to detect marijuana watch as the footlocker is unloaded. When the dog signals the presence of marijuana, the agents emerge and arrest the owners of the footlocker.

g. Williams is suspected of kidnapping and murdering a 10-year-old girl. Soon after the girl's disappearance, witnesses see Williams carrying a large bundle with two feet sticking out of it. Williams is later arrested and advised of his Miranda rights. He then talks with an attorney, who advises him to keep quiet. He tells the police that he will not discuss the case until he sees his attorney. Later, during a ride to a jail in another city, one of the officers, knowing the girl's body had not been found, remarks, "We could stop and locate the body because this little girl's parents are entitled to give her a Christian burial." After apparently thinking this over, Williams says, "Turn around, I'll show you where the body is."

h. The police receive a tip from an informant of unproven reliability that Sanchez and others are selling narcotics out of a house in Burbank. Police investigate and observe many people with prior narcotics arrests coming and going from the house. They see other people carrying small packages. Based on this evidence, police apply for and receive a search warrant from a magistrate to search the houses and automobiles owned by the defendant. Illegal drugs are found in the search, but a court later finds that the search warrant was improperly issued by the magistrate (i.e., there had not been sufficient evidence to issue it).

PROBLEM 32

a. Should plea bargaining be allowed? Do you think plea bargaining offers greater advantages to the prosecutor or to the defendant? Explain your answer.

b. Marty, who is 22 years old, is arrested and charged with burglarizing a warehouse. He has a criminal record, including a previous conviction for shoplifting and two arrests for auto theft. The prosecution has evidence placing him at the scene of the crime. The defense attorney tells him the prosecution will reduce the charge to petty larceny in exchange for a guilty plea. If you were Marty, would you plead guilty to the lesser charge? Why or why not?

c. Suppose Marty pleads guilty after being promised probation by the prosecutor, but instead he receives a long prison term. Is there anything he can do about this?

d. Do you think anyone accused of a crime would plead guilty if he or she were really innocent? Explain your answer.

THE TRIAL

In all criminal prosecutions, the accused shall enjoy the right to a speedy and public trial, by an impartial jury of the State and district wherein the crime shall have been committed, which district shall have been previously ascertained by law, and to be informed of the nature and cause of the accusation; to be confronted with the witnesses against him; to have compulsory process for obtaining witnesses in his favor, and to have the assistance of counsel for his defense.

— Sixth Amendment to the U.S. Constitution

Due process of law means little to the average citizen unless and until he or she is arrested and charged with a crime. This is because many of the basic rights set out in the U.S. Constitution apply to people accused of crime. Accused people are entitled to have a jury trial, in public and without undue delay, to be informed of their rights and of the charges against them, to confront and cross-examine witnesses, to refuse to testify against themselves, and to be represented by an attorney. These rights are the essence of due process of law. Taken together, they make up the overall right to a fair trial.

Right to Trial by Jury

The right to a jury trial is guaranteed by the Sixth Amendment to the U.S. Constitution. It is applicable in both federal and state courts. However, a jury is not required in every case. In fact, juries are not used very much. Most criminal cases are resolved by guilty pleas before ever reaching trial. Jury trials are not required for certain minor offenses — generally, those punishable by less than six months in prison. Defendants can *waive* (give up) their right to a jury trial; in some states, waivers may occur in the majority of cases.

Jury panels are selected from voter registration or tax lists and are supposed to be generally representative of the community. In federal courts, juries consist of 12 persons who must reach a unanimous verdict before finding a person guilty. State courts are not required to use 12 jurors, nor are the jurors required to reach a unanimous verdict. However, the U.S. Supreme Court has held that juries in state courts must have at least 6 jurors.

PROBLEM 33

a. Why is the right to a jury trial guaranteed by the Bill of Rights? Why would someone choose not to have a jury trial?

b. Do you think jury verdicts should be unanimous? Why or why not?

Public defenders represent people who cannot afford to hire a lawyer.

Right to a Speedy and Public Trial

The Sixth Amendment to the U.S. Constitution provides a right to a speedy trial in all criminal cases. The Constitution does not define *speedy*, and courts have had trouble deciding what this term means. To remedy this problem the federal government and some states have set specific time limits within which a case must be brought to trial.

If a person does not receive a speedy trial, the case may be dismissed. However, defendants often waive the speedy trial requirement. They do this because of the unavailability or illness of an important witness, or because they need more time to prepare their cases. Before dismissing a case, courts will consider the cause and reasons for the delay and whether the defendant was free or in jail during the pretrial period.

PROBLEM 34

a. Why is the right to a speedy trial important? How soon after arrest should a person be brought to trial? What are some reasons for and against bringing a defendant to trial in a short time after arrest?

b. Do you think that televising criminal trials is a good idea? Why or why not?

Right to Confront Witnesses

The Sixth Amendment provides people accused of a crime with the right to confront (face-to-face) the witnesses against them and to ask them questions by way of cross-examination. Although a defendant has the right to be present in the courtroom during all stages of the trial, the U.S. Supreme Court has said that this right may be restricted if the defendant becomes disorderly or disruptive. In such instances, judges have the power to remove the defendant from the courtroom, to cite him or her for **contempt of court,** or in extreme circumstances, to have the defendant bound and gagged.

Freedom from Self-incrimination

Freedom from self-incrimination means that you cannot be forced to testify against yourself in a criminal trial. This right comes from the Fifth Amendment and can be exercised in all criminal cases. In addition, the prosecutor is forbidden to make any statement drawing the jury's attention to the defendant's failure to testify.

Although a defendant has a right not to testify, this right can be waived. Moreover, a defendant who takes the witness stand in his or her own criminal trial must answer all questions.

Related to the right against self-incrimination is the concept of **immunity.** Immunity laws force a witness to answer all questions — even those that are incriminating. In exchange for the testimony, the witness is granted freedom from prosecution. Prosecutors often use these laws to force people to testify against co-defendants or others involved in the crime.

PROBLEM 35

a. If you were a defense attorney, what would be the advantages and disadvantages of allowing a criminal defendant to testify at trial?

b. If you were a member of the jury in a criminal trial, what would you think if the defendant failed to testify? Would you be affected by the judge's instruction not to draw any conclusion from the defendant's failure to testify?

c. If a defendant is forced to stand in a lineup, give a handwriting sample, or take an alcohol breath test, does this violate the privilege against self-incrimination?

Right to an Attorney

The Sixth Amendment provides that "in all criminal prosecutions, the accused shall enjoy the right to have the assistance of counsel for his defense." At one time this meant that, except in capital cases, a defendant had the right to an attorney only if he or she could afford one. However, in 1938 the Supreme Court required the federal courts to appoint attorneys for indigent defendants in all federal felony cases. Twenty-five years later, in the case of *Gideon* v. *Wainright,* the Supreme Court extended the right to counsel to *all* felony defendants, whether in state or in federal court. In 1972 the Supreme Court further extended this ruling by requiring that no imprisonment may occur, even in misdemeanor cases, unless the accused is represented by an attorney.

As a result of these decisions, criminal defendants who cannot afford an attorney are appointed one free of charge by the government. These attorneys may be either public defenders or private attorneys.

PROBLEM 36

a. Do you think court-appointed attorneys are as good as those who are privately paid? Why or why not?

b. Assume a defendant wants to handle his or her own defense. Would this be allowed? Do you think this is a good idea?

c. Assume a lawyer knows that his or her client is guilty. Is it right for the lawyer to try to convince the jury that the person is innocent? Why or why not?

SENTENCING

The final phase of the criminal justice process begins with the sentence. Once found guilty, the defendant will be sentenced by the judge, or in some states, by the jury. The sentence is perhaps the most critical decision in the criminal justice system. This is because it can determine a defendant's fate for years or, in some cases, for life.

Most criminal statutes set out a basic sentence structure, but judges generally have considerable freedom with respect to actual sentence, including the type, length, and conditions of the sentence. Depending upon the state, judges may choose from one or a combination of the following options:

■ *Suspended Sentence.* A sentence is given, but the convicted person is not required to serve it and is released with no conditions attached.

■ *Probation.* The defendant is released to the supervision of a probation officer after agreeing to follow certain conditions, such as getting a job, avoiding drugs, or not traveling outside of the area.

■ *Fine.* The defendant must pay an amount of money set by the court.

■ *Restitution.* The defendant is required to pay back or make up for whatever loss or injury was incurred by the victim of the crime.

■ *Work Release.* The defendant is allowed to work in the community but is required to return to prison at night or on weekends.

■ *Imprisonment.* The defendant is sentenced to a term in prison. Some states require that a *definite* sentence be given, in which case the judge would specify the exact number of years to be served (e.g., 2 years). Some states provide for an *indeterminate* term, in which case the sentence is not stated in a specific number of years but as a minimum and maximum term (e.g., not less than 3 years nor more than 10 years).

Many factors go into the sentencing decision. These include the judge's theory of corrections and what he or she thinks is in the best interest of society and of the individual. In addition, most states authorize a **presentence report.** This report is prepared by the probation department. It contains a description of the offense and the circumstances surrounding it. The report also sets out the defendant's past criminal record, data on the defendant's social, medical, educational, and employment background, and a recommendation as to sentence. After studying the report and listening to recommendations from the defense attorney and the prosecutor, the judge will impose sentence.

Purposes of Sentence

Over the years, the criminal sentence has served a number of different purposes, including **retribution, deterrence, rehabilitation,** and **incapacitation.**

At one time, the primary reason for punishing a criminal was retribution. This was the idea of "an eye for an eye and a tooth for a tooth." Criminals were punished as a kind of revenge for their wrongdoing.

Another reason for sentencing criminals is deterrence. Many people believe that punishment will discourage the offender from committing another crime in the future. In addition, the punishment will serve as an example to deter other people from committing crimes.

A third goal of sentencing is rehabilitation. Rehabilitation means helping convicts change their behavior so that they can lead useful and productive lives after release. Rehabilitation is based on the idea that criminals can be helped to overcome the social, educational, or psychological problems that caused them to commit a crime and that they can be helped to become responsible members of society.

WHERE YOU LIVE

Does your community have any prisons, jails, or halfway houses? Who is kept there? What are living conditions like in these institutions? What rights do the inmates have?

A sentencing hearing.

People convicted of a crime may be sent to a correctional institution. Where are offenders from your community sent?

A fourth reason for sentencing is incapacitation. This means that society will be protected by physically separating the criminal from the community. While locked up in prison the offender will not pose a threat to the safety of the community.

Today there is no single purpose behind the criminal sentence, and many people disagree over how to handle people convicted of a crime. When sentencing a criminal, the court may have one or more of these purposes in mind.

PROBLEM 37

a. Refer to the bail hearing on page 86. Assume that all five defendants in this hearing were tried and found guilty. Consider the information provided and impose a sentence in each case.

b. Be prepared to explain your decision and discuss those factors that you considered most important in each case. Which of the purposes of punishment would you hope to achieve in each sentence?

c. Should all people convicted of the same crime receive the same sentence, or should the judge look at each case and determine each sentence on an individual basis? Explain your answer.

CORRECTIONS

When a person is convicted of a crime, state and federal governments have the right to punish the offender. The system of corrections includes the entire range of treatment and punishment options available to the government. These include community corrections, halfway houses, jails, reformatories, and prisons.

Life Behind Bars

Today, almost half a million people are locked up in American prisons. Another 200,000 people fill local jails on any given day. All across America, prisons and jails are packed to overflowing.

The major reason for the booming prison population is a get-tough attitude toward crime. Legislatures and courts are acting to ensure that more criminals are sentenced to longer terms. In recent years, most states have passed **mandatory sentencing** laws. At the same time, many states have doubled or tripled the length of minimum prison sentences. The crackdown on drunk driving, and tougher bail and parole laws are other reasons for overcrowding.

The growing prison population has created many problems. Overcrowding sparks fights and riots. Drug use, sexual assault, and violence are all common occurrences. Life behind bars is often dangerous and unpleasant. Many prisoners live in tiny cells in spartan conditions.

An inmate's life is controlled by many rules. Inmates are told when to get up and when to go to sleep. Mail is screened. Access to radio, television, and books is controlled. Visitors are limited, and inmates are subject to constant surveillance and searches. Some inmates work at prison jobs, which pay almost nothing; others spend all day locked in their cells.

Until the 1960s, courts had a hands-off policy toward prisons. Inmates had few, if any, rights. Prison officials could make almost any rules they wanted. As a result, harsh treatment, solitary confinement, and beatings were all fairly common.

Today, courts have established the concept of prisoner rights. The U.S. Supreme Court has said that people who enter prison must give up many of their rights. However, the Court has set out certain rights that inmates have, even after entering prison. These include the right to be free from cruel and unusual punishment, the right to freedom of religion, the right to due process, the right to medical treatment if ill, and the right of access to law libraries and the courts.

Many state prisons and local jails are now under court order to alleviate overcrowding and improve conditions. Courts and prison officials are constantly being asked to balance the rights of prisoners against the need to maintain security and order in prison.

PROBLEM 38

a. Should prisoners have rights? If so, what rights should they have? Make a list of these rights.

b. If you were a prison warden, what rules would you make to control the prisoners? Make a list of these rules.

c. What, if anything, should be done to reduce prison overcrowding? Should we build more and bigger prisons, or should we be more selective about who is locked up?

PRISONS AND JAILS: WHAT'S THE DIFFERENCE?

■ Prisons are operated by federal or state governments. They are used to incarcerate people convicted of more serious crimes, usually felonies for which the sentence is more than one year.

■ The nearly 700 U.S. prisons range in size from small, well-designed facilities to huge maximum security penitentiaries sprawling over thousands of acres.

■ Some U.S. prisons are so big that they resemble small cities. For example, Louisiana's State Prison at Angola and Michigan's State Penitentiary at Jackson each contain over 4,000 inmates and thousands of employees.

■ Jails, on the other hand, are operated by cities and counties. They are used to detain people awaiting trial and to temporarily hold mental patients, drug addicts, alcoholics, juvenile offenders, and felons awaiting transfer to other facilities. Jails also hold people convicted of minor crimes for which the sentence is a year or less.

■ The 3,400 U.S. jails vary in size from big-city facilities holding over 1,000 inmates a day to small rural jails consisting of an office and a few cells.

■ Another difference between prisons and jails is the length of stay. The average stay in jails is only 11 days. In prison, the average time served is almost 2 years.

CAPITAL PUNISHMENT

Capital punishment, also known as the **death penalty,** has a long history in America. The first person executed for murder was hung in 1630. In colonial years, the death penalty was imposed for a number of different crimes. Gradually, however, capital punishment was restricted to the most serious crimes — usually murder or rape.

For many years, people have argued about capital punishment. Public protest against the death penalty gradually reduced the number of executions from a peak of 199 in 1935 to only one in 1967. For the next ten years, executions were halted while the courts studied the legality of capital punishment.

In the 1972 case of *Furman* v. *Georgia*, the Supreme Court held that the death penalty as then applied was unconstitutional. States rewrote their capital punishment laws, and in 1976, the Court ruled the new laws were constitutional if certain factors were considered in sentencing. Executions soon resumed, and to-day over 1,400 inmates are on death row.

Thirty-eight states now have death penalty statutes. Most of these laws call for two trials, one to decide guilt or innocence and another to set the sentence. They spell out guidelines for deter-mining whether death or life imprisonment is appropriate. Judges and juries are required to consider both *aggravating* and *mitigating* circumstances. These include such things as the nature of the crime and the background and prior record of the accused.

The controversy over capital punishment involves legal, po-litical, and moral issues. Is the death penalty constitutional? Is it a moral punishment for murder? Does it deter crime? Is it applied fairly?

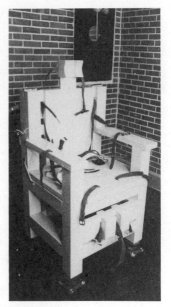

What is your state's law regarding capital punishment?

Opponents of capital punishment answer no to all these ques-tions. They say anyone who values life cannot approve the death penalty. They argue that "thou shalt not kill" means no one should be executed. They say the death penalty does not deter murder. To support this idea, they cite statistics showing that murder rates are the same in states with the death penalty as those without it. Opponents also argue that the death penalty is applied in an unfair manner, that members of minority groups are more likely to be executed, and that it violates the Eighth Amendment's ban against "cruel and unusual punishment."

Advocates of the death penalty say that killers get what they deserve. They argue that the threat of death does deter crime. They concede that studies on deterrence are inconclusive, but they say that people fear nothing more than death. Advocates say the public wants the death penalty. They also point to opinion polls showing that most Americans favor capital punishment. They argue that execution protects society and saves the government money. Fin-ally, they say the death penalty is fairly applied and that the Supreme Court has upheld this view.

PROBLEM 39

a. Do you favor or oppose use of the death penalty? Explain your answer. If you favor it, to what crimes should it apply?

b. If you oppose the death penalty, what do you think is the strongest argument in favor if it? If you favor the death penalty, what do you think is the strongest argument against it?

JUVENILE JUSTICE

In the United States, juveniles involved with the law are treated differently from adults. However, this has not always been the case. In earlier times, children were thrown into jails with adults. Long prison terms and corporal punishment were common. Some children were even sentenced to death for their crimes.

Reformers concerned over the harsh treatment of children urged the establishment of a separate court system for juveniles. The idea behind juvenile court was that children in trouble with the law should be helped rather than punished. Central to the concept of juvenile court was the principle of **parens patriae.** This meant that instead of lawyers fighting to decide guilt or innocence, the court would act as parent or guardian interested in protecting and helping the child. Hearings would be closed to the public. Proceedings would be informal. If convicted, children would be separated from adult criminals.

In 1899, Cook County, Illinois, set up the country's first juvenile court. Today, every state has a separate court system for juveniles. These courts generally handle two different groups of juveniles: the delinquent offender and the status offender. A **delinquent** child is one who has committed an act that is a crime under federal, state, or local law. **Status offenders,** on the other hand, are youths who are considered unruly or beyond the control of their legal guardians. Status offenses are not crimes. They are illegal acts which can only be committed by juveniles. Status offenses include: running away from home, skipping school, refusing to obey parents, or engaging in immoral behavior. In different states status offenders are called PINS, CHINS, or MINS — *pe*rsons, *chi*ldren, or *mi*nors *in ne*ed of *su*pervision.

JUVENILE LAW TERMS

The vocabulary used in the juvenile justice system is different from that used in the adult criminal justice system. The following is a comparison of the major terms used in the adult and juvenile systems:

Adult	*Juvenile*
Crime	Delinquent act
Arrest	Contact or take into custody
File charges	Petition
Not guilty plea	Denial
Guilty plea	Admission
Trial	Hearing
Verdict of guilty	Found to be involved
Sentence	Disposition or placement

PROBLEM 40

a. Explain the concept of parens patriae. Do you agree with this idea?

b. Should juveniles and adults accused of the same crime be treated the same or differently? Should they have the same rights? The same punishment? Explain your answer.

WHERE YOU LIVE

In your state, what is the maximum age jurisdiction of juvenile court?

Can juveniles be transferred to adult court in your state? If so, at what age and under what circumstances?

Who Is a Juvenile?

Before the establishment of juvenile courts, children under the age of seven were never held responsible for criminal acts. The law considered them incapable of forming the necessary criminal intent. Children between the ages of 7 and 14 were generally thought to be incapable of committing a criminal act; but this belief could be disproved by showing that the youth knew that the act was a crime or would cause harm to another and committed it anyway. Children over the age of 14 could be charged with a crime and handled in the same manner as an adult.

Today, all states set age limits that determine whether a person accused of a crime is treated as an adult or as a juvenile. In most states, young people are considered juveniles until age 18. However, some states set the limit at 16 or 17.

In most states, a juvenile charged with a serious crime, such as robbery or murder, can be transferred to criminal court and tried as an adult. States that allow transfers require a hearing to consider the age and record of the juvenile, the type of crime, and the likelihood that the youth can be helped by the juvenile court. As a result of a get-tough attitude involving juvenile crime, many states have revised their juvenile codes to make it easier to transfer youthful offenders to adult court.

PROBLEM 41

In each of the following situations, decide whether the person should be tried as a juvenile or transferred to criminal court and tried as an adult. Explain the reasons for your decisions.

a. Eric, age 15, is accused of robbing an 86-year-old woman at gunpoint. Eric, who has a long juvenile record including acts of burglary, brags about the robbery.

b. Marcia, age 17, is accused of killing a pedestrian while driving a stolen car. She has never been in trouble before, is remorseful about the killing, and claims that she planned to return the car after a short joyride.

Juvenile Court Today

The juvenile court system was founded with high goals. In theory, the system was supposed to help and rehabilitate young offenders. It was designed to act as a guardian looking out for the best interests of children. In practice, juvenile court often failed to rehabilitate. It also denied young people the protection and rights guaranteed to adults. In many cases, juveniles were processed through a system with few safeguards and little hope of treatment. In 1966, the U.S. Supreme Court began to change the theory and operation of the juvenile justice system. To help you understand the juvenile court process, refer to Figure 11.

THE CASE OF GERALD GAULT

Gerald Gault, age 15, was taken into custody and accused of making an obscene phone call to a neighbor. At the time Gerald was taken into custody, his parents were at work, and the police did not notify them of what had happened to their son. Gerald was placed in a detention center. When his parents finally learned that he was in custody, they were told that there would be a hearing on the next day, but they were not told the nature of the complaint against him.

Mrs. Cook, the woman who had complained about the phone call, did not show up at the hearing. Instead, a police officer testified to what he had been told by Mrs. Cook. Gerald blamed the call on a friend and denied making the obscene remarks. No lawyers were present, and no record was made of what was said at the hearing.

Since juries were not allowed in juvenile court, the hearing was held before a judge, who found by a preponderance of the evidence that Gerald was delinquent and ordered him sent to a state reform school until age 21. An adult found guilty of the same crime could be sent to county jail for no longer than 60 days.

PROBLEM 42

a. Make a list of anything that happened to Gerald Gault that you consider unfair. Explain your reasoning for each item on the list.

b. How would you change any of the things you thought were unfair?

In deciding the *Gault* case, the U.S. Supreme Court held that juveniles were entitled to many of the same rights as adults. Specifically, the Court ruled that juveniles charged with a delinquent

Today, juveniles are given many of the same rights as adults.

act were entitled to be notified of the charges against them, to be represented by an attorney, to confront and cross-examine witnesses, and to remain silent.

PROBLEM 43

a. What rights that adults have were not granted in the *Gault* decision?

b. Do you agree with the *Gault* decision? Why or why not? Should adults and minors have the same legal rights? Why or why not?

c. Do you think Gerald Gault's hearing would have turned out differently if he had been given the rights the Supreme Court later ruled he was entitled to?

The *Gault* decision gave young people accused of a crime many of the same rights as adults, but it also left many unanswered questions. In the case of *In re Winship* (1970), the Supreme Court decided that juveniles charged with a criminal act must be found "delinquent by proof beyond a reasonable doubt." This is the same standard required in adult court. However, in *McKeiver* v. *Pennsylvania* (1971), the Supreme Court decided that jury trials were not required in juvenile cases. In reaching this decision, the Supreme Court restated the protective philosophy of juvenile court and expressed concern that jury trials could hurt juveniles by destroying the privacy of juvenile hearings. Thus, although juveniles now receive many of the rights available to adults, the Supreme Court has made it clear that not all of the procedures used in an adult court apply in a juvenile proceeding.

Status Offenders   When a juvenile court is confronted with a status offender, special problems arise. Youths who fall into this category are charged with the status of being "beyond control" or "habitually disobedient," or with truancy from school or other acts that would not be crimes if committed by an adult.

Status offenders are usually emotionally troubled youths who need help. Many status offenders are runaways or young people with drinking and drug problems. It is estimated that over 500,000 minors run away from home each year. Over 80 percent of these are between the ages of 15 and 17. Although most runaways return home of their own accord, others are picked up by the police and referred to the juvenile court.

In recent years, a number of programs have been set up to help runaway youths. These include counseling centers, shelter homes, and a nationwide toll-free phone number that runaways can call for assistance (see Appendix B).

As a general rule, a single act of unruly behavior is not enough to support a finding that a youth is in need of supervision. Rather, most states require a showing that the youth is habitually disobedient or has repeatedly run away, skipped school, or been out of control.

Because of problems at home, parents sometimes ask the court to file a PINS petition against their own child. Youths charged with status offenses are entitled to have an attorney, and they may defend their conduct by showing that it was justified or that it was the parent who was unreasonable and at fault. In such cases, the PINS petition might be withdrawn and replaced by a neglect petition against the parents.

PROBLEM 44

a. Who are PINS, CHINS, and MINS? Explain how such people differ from delinquents.

b. Do you think courts should interfere in disputes between parents and children? If not, why not? If so, why and under what circumstances?

c. Should attendance at school be mandatory? Why or why not? What should be done about students who are chronically absent from school?

Procedures in Juvenile Court

Suppose a young person is accused of a delinquent act. What happens to this person from the time he or she is taken into custody until release from the juvenile justice system? The exact procedures vary from state to state, but the general process that follows is similar throughout the country.

Taking into Custody   On the whole, young people may be taken into custody for all the same reasons the police might arrest an adult. In addition, juveniles can be taken into custody for status offenses. These are acts that would not be considered criminal if committed by an adult. These offenses include running away from home, truancy, promiscuity, disobeying one's parents, or other actions suggesting the need for court supervision.

After taking a juvenile into custody, the police have broad authority to release or detain the juvenile. If the offense is minor, the police may give the juvenile a warning, release the youth to his or her parents, or refer the case to a social service agency. If the offense is serious or if the youth has a prior record, the police may detain the youth and refer him or her to juvenile court.

Intake is the informal process by which court officials or social workers decide if a complaint against a youth should be referred to juvenile court. This decision is usually made after interviewing the youth and considering the seriousness of the offense, the past record of the accused, the youth's family situation, and other factors.

The estimate is that as many as one-half of all complaints received by juvenile courts are disposed of during the intake process. Although some of these cases result in outright dismissal, other cases are referred to social service agencies or otherwise diverted from the juvenile justice system.

Initial Hearing   Youths who are taken into custody and formally referred to juvenile court are entitled to an initial hearing on the validity of their arrest and detention. At this initial hearing, the state must generally prove two things: that an offense was committed and that there is reasonable cause to believe that the youth committed it. If the state wants to further detain the youth it must prove that the juvenile is a danger to himself or to others, or is likely to run away if released. If the youth does not have an attorney, the court will usually assign one at this time and set a date for a hearing on the facts.

Adjudicatory Hearing   Instead of a trial, a juvenile charged with a delinquent act is given a hearing. Generally known as an adjudicatory hearing, the purpose is the same as an adult trial: to determine the facts of the case. Unlike an adult trial, a juvenile hearing

WHERE YOU LIVE

Where are juvenile offenders placed in your state and community? What is the maximum length of time a juvenile can be committed to a juvenile institution? What happens to status offenders in your community?

FIGURE 11   Typical Juvenile Court Process

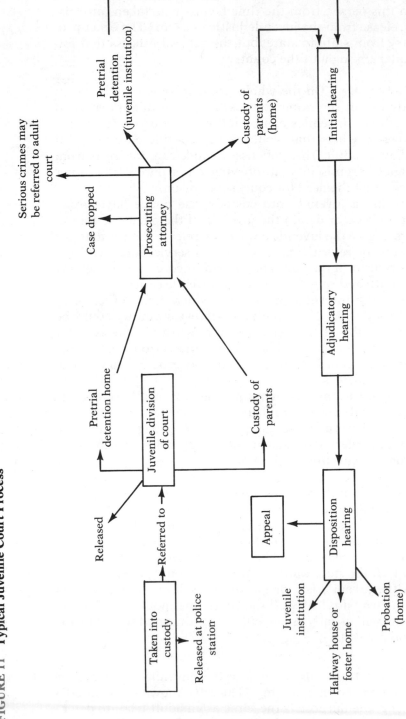

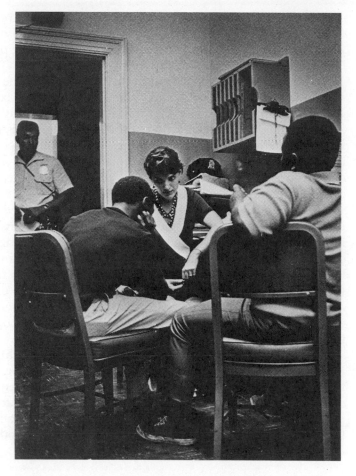

After juveniles are taken into custody, a decision is made to either release the youths to their parents or guardians or detain them pending trial.

is generally closed to the public, and the names of the accused and the details of the offense are withheld from the press.

At the adjudicatory hearing, the juvenile is entitled to be represented by an attorney. The attorney can offer evidence, cross-examine witnesses, and force the prosecution to prove its case beyond a reasonable doubt. If the judge finds the juvenile non-delinquent (not guilty), he or she is free to go. If the judge decides that the facts, as set out in the petition, are true, the court will enter a finding of delinquent. This is similar to a conviction.

Dispositional Hearing   The dispositional hearing is perhaps the most important stage in the system for juveniles who are found delinquent. At this hearing, the judge decides what sentence, or **disposition,** the juvenile offender should receive. The judge's sentence is usually based on the presentence report prepared by the probation department. This report is the result of an investigation of the juvenile's social, psychological, family, and school background.

**WHERE
YOU
LIVE**

What are the provisions
for the appeal of a juv-
enile case in your state?
Does your state allow
records to be sealed or
destroyed? Who is al-
lowed to inspect juven-
ile records?

In theory, courts try to provide individualized treatment for
each youth. In practice, the alternatives are usually probation,
placement in a group home or community treatment program, or
commitment to a state institution for juveniles.

Probation is the most common disposition. The judge can
impose a number of conditions on the juvenile. For example, the
juvenile might be ordered to attend school regularly, to hold a
steady job, to obtain counseling at a treatment center, to be home
by 8:00 p.m. at night, or to stay away from certain people. Juveniles on probation will probably have to meet with a probation
officer on a regular basis. Violation of the conditions set by the
court can result in revocation of the probation.

For serious offenses, the juvenile can be committed to a juvenile institution. Most courts have the power to place a youth for an
indeterminate length of time. This means that no matter what the
offense, the youth can be locked up for the maximum period allowed by state law. This generally varies from one to three years.
In some cases, it lasts until the youth reaches the **age of majority.**
Although most youths never serve the maximum sentence, the
exact time of release is usually up to the agency that operates the
institution.

What happens to status offenders presents special problems.
Should they be taken out of the home? Should they be committed
to institutions? Should they be mixed with delinquents or adult
offenders? In response to these concerns, many states have removed status offenders from large institutions and placed them in
foster homes, halfway houses, or other community facilities.

PROBLEM 45

a. Do you think juvenile offenders should be treated and rehabilitated, or punished? Explain your answer.

b. Do you think there should be a set penalty for each juvenile
offense, or should the judge have the discretion to set a different
sentence for each offender?

Post Disposition   Most states give young people the right to appeal decisions of a juvenile court. However, because the U.S. Supreme Court has never ruled on this issue, the provisions for appeal vary greatly from state to state.

Once released from an institution, a juvenile may be placed on
aftercare. This is the equivalent of parole in the adult system.
Aftercare usually involves supervision by a parole officer, who
counsels the juvenile on education, jobs, vocational training, or
other services.

Unlike an adult criminal a juvenile delinquent does not lose any of his or her civil rights. Upon reaching adulthood, the juvenile can still register to vote. In addition, all states make juvenile court records confidential and limit public access to them. Despite this confidentiality, a juvenile record can still cause problems. Only certain states have juvenile records permanently sealed or destroyed, and even though juvenile court records are confidential, a number of people and agencies may gain access to them.

HEARING ON A PINS PETITION

Assume that a parent goes to the county prosecutor and asks that a PINS petition be filed against his 15-year-old son. The petition asks the court to take the son out of the home and place him in a county institution because he is beyond control and needs the state's supervision. An attorney is appointed and defends the youth, saying that his father is guilty of neglect.

The PINS statute reads: A child may be declared a person in need of supervision (PINS) for continually refusing to obey the lawful orders of his or her parents, being beyond the control of the parents, running away from home on a repeated basis, or being a habitual truant from school.

The neglect statute reads: A child may be declared neglected if the child's parents fail to provide necessary support or education required by law, abandon or abuse the child, or fail to provide the supervision and care necessary for the child's well being.

Statement of Mr. Jones (father): I give up. There is nothing more I can do with my son. He won't do anything I say. He stays out all night with his friends, and he constantly gets into trouble. He has been arrested at least three times — once for possession of drugs and twice for burglary. Two times he was released, but he got six months' probation for the second burglary when he was 14. He has run away twice. He is failing in school. His mother died three years ago, and things haven't been the same since. I need him at home to help take care of his two sisters. They are 10 and 12 years old. I may sometimes go out for a drink after work and miss dinner, but I'm not an alcoholic. Now he refuses to be home at dinner time, and I know he's out using drugs and committing crimes.

Statement of Billy Jones (age 15): Sure, I've gotten into some trouble, but there is never any food in our house, and my father won't give me any money to go out to eat. I had to get money somehow. Dad is almost never home at dinner time. He comes home drunk almost every night of the week and gives me a bad time. Sometimes he hits me across the face when he has been drinking. We are always arguing, and he often yells at me. He's acted weird since mom died, and I can't take it. So, I run away or stay out all night.

Roleplay Mr. Jones and his attorney (the county prosecutor), Billy Jones and his attorney, and the judge, following these steps:

1. The judge should announce the case and ask the county attorney to call his or her witness. The father should be questioned by the county attorney as to his reasons for wanting the PINS petition.

2. The father should be cross-examined by Billy's attorney (the judge may interrupt with questions at any time).

3. Billy should be called to the stand and questioned by his attorney.

4. Billy should then be cross-examined by the county prosecutor.

5. At this point, the judge may ask additional questions of anyone involved and should ask the attorneys to make summations if they desire.

6. Finally, the judge should decide whether Billy is a PINS or whether he is neglected. Depending upon what the judge decides, an order may be issued to remove him from the home, either temporarily or permanently, and place him in a juvenile institution, group home, or foster home; leave him in the home; have a social worker or court psychiatrist provide some follow-up treatment; or place other conditions on the father or the son that the judge believes are appropriate.

Until the 1960's, prison officials usually determined the rights and treatment of prisoners.

three
CONSUMER
LAW

Have you ever bought a meal in a restaurant or a pair of sneakers at a sporting goods store? Have you ever ridden a bus to work or had your car repaired at a service station? If you did any of these things, you were a consumer. A **consumer** is a person who buys goods and services from another. Since everyone buys goods and uses services, everyone is a consumer.

When sellers agree to provide, and consumers agree to pay for, goods or services, the parties have entered into a legal agreement. The agreement is called a **contract.** Every time you buy a meal in restaurant, you promise to pay for it, and the restaurant promises to give you a meal that is fit to eat. If the seller and the consumer have a dispute they can't settle themselves, the law will help determine how the dispute is decided.

For many years, consumer law was symbolized by the legal expression **caveat emptor.** This means "let the buyer beware." In other words, consumers had to look out for unfair and misleading sales practices before buying or else be prepared to suffer the consequences. Once consumers bought something, they were stuck with the purchase, even if they got less than they bargained for, such as poor-quality goods or products that were unsafe or defective.

Today the law is more balanced. Consumers now have a right to be correctly informed of important information, such as quality, price, and credit terms. Sellers must avoid sales and advertising practices that mislead, deceive, or are otherwise unfair to consumers; and sellers may only market products that will not harm consumers in normal use. This increased concern for consumers is based on the fact that sellers are better informed about the products or services being offered and are usually in control of the sales transaction.

Even though the law has changed, the best protection is still a careful purchase. Many consumers do not realize that learning about products or services and knowing their rights as consumers are the best ways to avoid a problem. You should also recognize that if you receive poor quality merchandise or fall victim to a deceptive practice, all is not lost. You can often solve the problem yourself. And when you can't the law may provide a remedy. This chapter will help you become a better consumer — able to recognize, avoid, and, where necessary, resolve consumer problems.

PROBLEM 1

Make a list of ten goods or services that you have purchased in the last week.

a. For each item, explain how you decided to purchase that particular good or service. What information did you consider before buying each item?

b. Have you ever had a problem with a product or service you bought? What was the problem? What did you do?

PROBLEM 2

Read each of the following statements. Decide whether you strongly agree (SA), agree (A), are undecided (U), disagree (D), or strongly disagree (SD) with each statement. There are no right or wrong answers.

a. Minors (persons under 18) should not be allowed to make contracts.

b. Contracts should always be in writing.

c. Consumers should not purchase items, except a house or car, unless they can pay the full price at the time of the purchase.

d. Merchants who trick consumers into making purchases should be sent to jail.

FIGURE 12   Where Consumers' Dollars Go

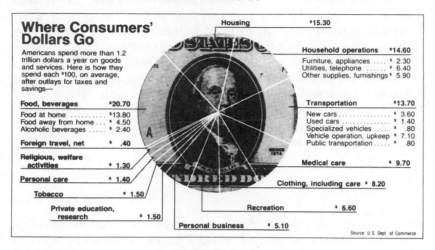

Reprinted from *U.S. News & World Report*, May 1, 1978.

e. Most consumers are not affected by television advertising.

f. A car dealer who provides financing should be able to take back the car if the consumer misses a payment.

g. The government should forbid the sale of any product harmful to consumers.

HOW LAWS PROTECT THE CONSUMER

The federal, state, and local governments all have laws that protect the consumer. As you go through this section, and whenever you think about consumer protection problems, ask yourself: What are my rights under federal law? Under state law? Under local law?

Federal Law

Congress has passed many consumer protection laws. These laws protect consumers in three ways. First, they prohibit unfair or misleading trade practices, such as false advertising, unfair pricing, or mislabeling. The *Federal Food, Drug, and Cosmetic Act*, for example, requires that certain important information be listed on most food and drugs offered for sale.

Second, federal laws set standards for the quality, safety, and reliability of many goods and services. Failure to comply with these standards can result in legal action against the seller. For example, the *Consumer Product Safety Act* allows the government to ban, seize, or prevent the sale of harmful products.

Third, the federal government has many agencies that enforce consumer laws and help consumers. For example, the Federal Trade Commission (FTC) has the power to prohibit unfair or deceptive trade practices (such as false advertising) and can take legal action to stop such practices.

State Law

States also have consumer protection laws. These laws often copy the *Federal Trade Commission Act* and make unfair and deceptive trade practices a violation of state law. State laws allow consumers to bring complaints into state court and before state agencies. They also enable agencies, such as the state attorney general or the state Office of Consumer Affairs, to halt illegal practices.

Like federal consumer protection laws, state laws give the government power to stop unfair and deceptive practices and provide consumers with a variety of remedies. For example, some laws make consumer fraud a crime and subject the offender to fine or imprisonment. Other remedies include **cease and desist orders,** by which an agency can require a business to stop a forbidden practice; **consent orders,** which are voluntary agreements to end a practice that is claimed to be illegal; and **restitution,** which is an order to refund or repay any money illegally obtained. In some cases, consumers can join together to bring **class actions,** which allow one or more persons to bring suit on behalf of a larger group.

Local Law

Cities and counties also have consumer protection laws. Most of these laws have been passed quite recently, and they range from requiring the inspection of restaurants for health hazards to declaring certain trade practices illegal.

HOW YOU CAN PROTECT YOUR RIGHTS AS A CONSUMER

Consumers can have a wide variety of problems. The following section will help you avoid some of these problems and will explain how to deal with difficulties that may arise.

PROBLEM 3

Responding to a radio ad, Harriet purchased a 10-speed bicycle from Ron's Speed Shop. She paid $200 in cash for the bicycle but was told that she'd have to wait a week for the bicycle because it was presently out of stock. The bicycle arrived a week later, but when Harriet unpacked it she found a 3-speed bicycle instead of the one she had ordered.

a. Is there anything Harriet could have done differently at or before the time of purchase?

b. What steps should Harriet take after discovering this error?

c. If this happened in your community and the seller refused to exchange bicycles, where could Harriet go for help?

What to Do Before Buying

Generally, making large purchases on impulse is not wise. When shopping for products or services, you should learn as much as possible about them before buying. Careful consumers always

Wise consumers compare prices on different brands and check food for freshness.

comparison shop before making an important purchase. They purchase the item only after considering other products that could also meet their needs. They shop at stores that offer the best prices, service, and selection.

PROBLEM 4

Select either a good or service that you would like to buy (e.g., sports equipment, clothes, vacation). After you have selected the item, answer the following questions.

a. Is the item you have chosen something you need or something you want? What is the difference between a need and a want?

b. List all the places you could buy the good or service. What factors are important to you in deciding where to buy the item?

c. Are there different brands or models for the same item (e.g., different model cars)? If so, what factors do you consider important in deciding which brand to purchase?

d. How can you learn more about products and services and the firms that provide them?

Become Informed About the Product or Service   When you go shopping, information is your most important resource. Informed consumers need information on the product or service, the seller or manufacturer, and the terms or conditions of the sale. You should naturally consider price when shopping for products or services, but you need other information as well. Before you buy a product, you need to know how to use it safely, how long it will last, how to take care of it, where to take it if it needs service or repair, how much it will cost, and whether it has a warranty.

Before you buy a service, you need to know who will perform it and what their qualifications are. You should also find out if there are any guarantees and what happens if you are not satisfied. Finally, you should find out when the service will be started and completed.

To help you find the information you'll need, many reliable publications discuss the price, quality, and reliability of everything from food to furniture. *Consumer Reports* and *Consumer Bulletin* can be found on newsstands and in most public libraries. You can often get information on a particular product by contacting the dealer or manufacturer. In addition, federal, state, and local governments provide information on many goods and services. Perhaps most important, you should ask friends or neighbors about their experiences with particular products or services.

Check Out the Seller   Whether you buy wholesale or retail, from another person or from a huge store, it is always wise to check out

Informed consumers read
publications such as these.

the seller's reputation for honesty and reliability. Find out the
seller's return policy. If you return defective merchandise, will you
get a cash refund, a credit toward future purchases, or a replacement at no extra cost? What is the seller's attitude toward service
and repair? Will you get prompt, courteous service, or will you get
the runaround?

To learn about sellers, ask your friends and other consumers
who have dealt with the particular business. In addition, many
groups can provide information and assistance. These include consumer groups and business organizations, such as the local Chamber of Commerce or Better Business Bureau.

Better Business Bureaus (BBB) are nonprofit organizations
sponsored by local and national businesses. BBBs can be found in
more than 150 cities. Most of them keep records of consumer complaints registered against a business as well as some indication of
how a business has resolved complaints.

Be Sure You Understand the Terms of the Sale   Most purchases
require no special knowledge, but understanding the terms and
conditions of the sales transaction can prevent problems and save
money. Consumers need to know the *total* purchase price. Are there
any hidden costs or conditions? Is delivery free, or is there a
charge? If you charge the item or buy on time, what is the **interest**
rate and how much will you pay? Is there a guarantee? If so, what

Impulse buying can cost you money. Before buying an expensive product such as a camera, you should shop around.

does it cover and how long will it last? Finally, ask yourself if the price is reasonable and whether this is the best time to buy.

After gathering information, shop around. Watch for genuine sales and specials. Prices often vary from day to day and from store to store. Comparison shopping saves money and helps you make the best possible purchase.

What to Do After Buying

Sometimes even careful shoppers have problems. When this happens, it is important to remain calm and be persistent. If you keep the following suggestions in mind, you can usually solve your problem. If you can't, there may be an agency or organization that can help you.

First, you should always try to contact the seller. Reputable businesspeople are interested in a customer's future business, and most problems and misunderstandings can be cleared up with a face-to-face discussion or a telephone call.

Provide the seller with all the necessary information — identify the item (including model or serial number), give the date and location of purchase, describe when and how the problem arose, and explain what you want done. Be sure to bring along your sales receipt, warranty, or other pertinent information. Be polite but firm. If the seller refuses to help or gives you the runaround, send a written complaint to the owner or store manager. Mention that you will take other measures if you do not receive satisfaction within a reasonable amount of time. Be sure to date the letter and keep a copy for your records.

If the seller still refuses to help you, consider contacting the product's manufacturer. If you don't know the name of the manufacturer, ask your librarian for the *Thomas Registry*, a volume listing thousands of products and their manufacturers. If the seller is part of a chain store, consider writing to the corporate headquarters of the store. If you don't know the address of the manufacturer or the corporate headquarters, go to your local library and look it up in *Standard and Poor's Register of Corporations*. Many companies have consumer affairs departments, but you may get faster action by writing directly to the company president. State the facts clearly and send photocopies of any important documents (e.g., canceled checks, past letter to the seller). Describe the problem. Explain what you've tried to do about it and what you want the company to do. Consider sending copies of your letter to local and state consumer protection organizations and to your local Better Business Bureau.

If you are still dissatisfied, it may be time to seek outside help. Many agencies and organizations may be able to help you. These groups are discussed in the next section. Above all, don't give up if you feel you have a valid complaint.

GOVERNMENT CONSUMER PUBLICATIONS

The federal government has hundreds of consumer publications, many of them free. Subjects include Automobiles, Budget, Children, Clothing, Consumer Education, Food, Health, Housing, Insurance, Landscaping, Recreation, and Senior Citizens.

A free list of publications is available in both English and Spanish. Write to: Consumer Information, Pueblo, CO 81009.

**ADVICE ON
COMPLAINING**

■ Get together all the
key facts. Save all im-
portant documents
(e.g., warranties, bills,
canceled checks, repair
estimates).
■ Give the seller a
chance to correct the
problem.
■ If this doesn't work,
contact the manu-
facturer of the product
or the store's head-
quarters (if it's a
chain).
■ If you still aren't
satisfied, take your
complaint to a con-
sumer protection
agency, a media action
line, or a small claims
court. You may also
wish to contact an at-
torney at this point.

PROBLEM 5

Terry and Martha Tubman saw a newspaper ad for major brand
color TV sets on sale at Tally's Radio & TV Shop. They rushed
down to Tally's, where they bought a 21-inch model for $435.
Several weeks later the TV completely lost its picture. A TV service mechanic who came to their home told them the picture tube
had blown and that it would cost $200 to repair. The next morning,
Terry and Martha returned to the store and asked to speak to Mr.
Foxx, the salesperson who had sold them the TV.

a. Roleplay the meeting between the Tubmans and Mr. Foxx.
What should the Tubmans say, and what should Mr. Foxx say?

b. If Foxx refuses to help, what should the Tubmans do then? If
they decide to write a letter of complaint, to whom should it be
sent? Make a checklist of information needed in the letter. Write a
letter for the Tubmans.

c. What should the Tubmans do if they get no response to their
letter?

Consumer Protection Agencies and Organizations

You can solve most disputes on your own, but there may be occasions when you will need the help of one or several of the various
agencies and organizations that have been set up to aid consumers.

Consumer Groups   Many private organizations help consumers.
National organizations, such as the Consumer Federation of America and the Consumers Union, educate consumers and lobby for
passage of consumer protection legislation. Other state and local
consumer groups give advice, investigate complaints, contact
sellers, try to arrange settlements, and make legal referrals. To
find these organizations, contact a local university, your state attorney general's office, or a member of your city council. You
should also check the phone book under both "Consumer" and
"Public Interest Organizations."

Business and Trade Associations   One of the best known con-
sumer-help organizations is the Better Business Bureau (BBB). In
many places, the BBB investigates consumer complaints, contacts
the company involved, and tries to arrange a settlement. Reasonable complaints can often be settled with the BBB's help, but the
BBB can act only as a negotiator and cannot force a business to
settle.

In communities that do not have a BBB, you can contact the local Chamber of Commerce. If your problem involves an appliance, and both the dealer and the manufacturer have been unhelpful, consider contacting the Major Appliance Consumer Action Panel (MACAP) (address listed in Appendix B), which can help with complaints.

Media   More than 100 local newspapers and about 50 radio and television stations have special "action line" or "consumer affairs" services which help consumers. Even when a consumer complaint service does not exist, the media are often interested in publicizing legitimate stories of consumer problems. Publicity is a powerful weapon, and many consumers find that problems can be settled simply by contacting, or even threatening to contact, the media. To use these services, check with your local newspaper and radio and television stations.

Professional Associations and Unions   Many business and professional people belong to associations that act on behalf of the

WHERE YOU LIVE

Does your community have a consumer mediation program? Does it have a Better Business Bureau? A media "action line"? If so, what do each of these programs do?

entire profession or occupation. While such an association may have no legal enforcement powers over its members, a consumer complaint may result in pressure or dismissal of the offending member. For example, if you have a complaint against an attorney, you could contact the American Bar Association or the bar association for your state.

State and Local Government All states and many local governments have consumer protection agencies. These agencies deal with everything from public utility regulation to making sure you get a fair deal when having your car repaired. These departments are often located within the state attorney general's office, the Consumer Affairs Bureau, Consumer Protection Agency, Public Advocate's Office, or Public Utilities Commission.

In addition, states and cities have boards or agencies that set minimum standards for health and safety. For example, local public health inspectors routinely inspect restaurants to ensure that they are clean and free of health hazards.

Finally, there are over 1,500 state boards that license or register more than 550 professions and occupations. Commonly regulated occupations include accountants, architects, attorneys, barbers, bill collectors, doctors, electricians, engineers, funeral directors, nurses, plumbers, and real estate agents. Professional and occupational licensing was started by state legislatures to protect the public's health, safety, and welfare. State boards also have the power to revoke (take away) licenses for violations of established standards.

PROBLEM 6

Choose a service that you or your family has used. (e.g., medical care, legal aid, auto repair, etc.)

a. Is there a union, professional association, licensing board, or other agency that could assist you if you had a problem with this service?

b. What steps must a consumer take to register a complaint with this agency or association?

c. What power does this agency have?

Federal Government It is usually best to try to solve your problem on a local level, but for certain problems, the federal government may provide the only remedy. Even if a federal agency can't help, it can often suggest a way to solve your problem. Some of the major federal consumer protection agencies follow. The address for each of these agencies appears in Appendix B.

The Office of Consumer Affairs (OCA) conducts consumer education and is concerned with all kinds of consumer problems. If you don't know where to turn, or if you just want advice, the OCA will refer you to the state or federal agency that may be able to help you.

The Federal Trade Commission (FTC) is the federal government's main consumer protection agency. The FTC acts to prevent unfair or deceptive trade practices, such as false or misleading advertising, unfair pricing, false or mislabeled goods, and problems with bills, credit, or warranties. The FTC has regional offices throughout the country and has the power to order a business to stop an unlawful activity.

The Food and Drug Administration (FDA) regulates the safety of food, drugs, cosmetics, and medical devices. It conducts tests to assure the safety of these items and can order unsafe products off the market.

The Consumer Product Safety Commission (CPSC) makes and enforces safety standards for most consumer products, with the exception of food, drugs, automobiles, airplanes, boats, and firearms. It may ban or seize unsafe products and require that warnings be placed on hazardous substances and products.

The U.S. Postal Service (USPS) can investigate mail order companies and seek criminal prosecutions for mail fraud. If you receive unordered goods through the mail, or if you suspect mail fraud of any kind, the USPS may be able to help.

The Occupational Safety and Health Administration (OSHA) regulates health in the workplace. If your complaint concerns

dangerous conditions or hazardous substances on the job, OSHA can investigate and seek a solution.

The Department of Transportation (DOT) sets standards for the regulation of air and railroad travel. If you have a complaint against an airline or Amtrak for overcharging, mistreating, or illegally "bumping" you or for losing or mishandling your baggage, the DOT's Consumer Affairs Office may provide a remedy.

The Interstate Commerce Commission (ICC) regulates rates and services of interstate bus, railroad, truck, and moving companies.

The National Transportation Safety Board (NTSB) sets standards for vehicle safety and handles complaints related to auto dealer fraud or tampering with odometer (auto mileage) readings.

PROBLEM 7

How would you handle each of the following problems? If you think an agency or organization could help you, indicate which one and explain your answer.

a. You plan to fly from St. Louis to Chicago for your brother's graduation. You purchase a ticket in advance, but when you arrive at the airport, you are told that the flight is overbooked and you will have to wait for the next plane. Four hours later you arrive in Chicago, but you miss the graduation and think the airline should compensate you.

b. You become ill after eating a can of sardines purchased from a local supermarket. You know several friends who have also gotten ill from eating this particular brand of sardines. You protest to the supermarket, but they do nothing.

c. You apply for a charge account at a local department store. You are over 21 and have a good job but are turned down anyway. You receive no reason for the rejection and wonder what you can do.

d. You see an ad stating, "You'll have a glamorous career as a disc jockey after only 20 home lessons." You pay $100 and complete the correspondence course, but radio stations tell you your training is useless. None will hire you.

e. Your three-year-old sister is badly injured when one of her toys shatters and cuts her. You think the toy is too dangerous; your family wants compensation for her injuries.

f. You buy a new set of radial tires. Three weeks later, one of them blows out. You run off the road, causing minor damage to your car. The dealer offers to replace the tire, but you are not satisfied.

g. You buy some furniture on a time payment plan. When you get your first bill, you discover the total cost of the payments is over

$1,000, while the price of the furniture was only $700. You call the store and they tell you that the interest amounts to 20 percent a year. You wouldn't have bought the furniture if you had known it would cost so much.

Taking Your Case to Court

If you can't settle your complaint and a consumer agency has been unhelpful, you may wish to take your case to court. Anyone can go to court. Minors can sue through their parents or guardians. In some places, free or low-cost legal services may be available to consumers who cannot afford an attorney.

Civil Court   If the dispute involves a large amount of money, the case will be brought in your local civil trial court. Taking a case to court can be costly and time-consuming, but a consumer can ask for a number of different **remedies.**

First, you can sue for **damages.** Damages is money that a court orders paid to a person who has suffered a loss or an injury. For example, if you are injured because of a defective power drill, you can ask for money for a new drill, medical expenses, time lost from your job, and other related costs.

A second remedy is **rescission and restitution.** This means you could ask the court to cancel the contract (rescission) and order the person you are suing to give back any money you have already paid (restitution). This releases you from any further performance under the contract, but you would have to return any benefit already received under the contract. Assume, for example, that you sign a contract to purchase a set of pots and pans and that a pan melts the first time it is exposed to a direct flame during cooking. In such a case, you might seek rescission and restitution. You would get your money back and would have no further obligations under the contract. The seller would get back all the pots and pans.

The third civil remedy is **specific performance.** This means you ask the court to order the seller to carry out the specific terms of the agreement. For example, if you ordered goods that were never delivered, the court could order the company to deliver the goods. However, you would still have to pay for them.

A suit for damages or specific performance is designed to place you in approximately the position you would have been in if the contract had been successfully completed. A suit for rescission and restitution is designed to return both the buyer and the seller to the position each was in before the contract began.

Criminal Court   In some cases, the seller's action may be a crime as well as a violation of civil law. These acts can be prosecuted as criminal fraud. Criminal fraud occurs when a salesperson knowingly misstates or misrepresents some important fact, with the intent to defraud you resulting in harm.

For example, assume you contract with a builder to construct a deck on your home. You pay the builder several thousand dollars to purchase the necessary materials. However, the builder never intends to build the deck. He simply uses the scheme to take your money. In such a case, you're the victim of a crime. You should contact the police or your local prosecutor. Cases like this can be prosecuted by the government in criminal court. State laws not only provide a fine or jail term (or both) for a convicted defendant

MOCK TRIAL: JAMES PHILLIPS v. THE RADIO SHOP

FACTS
In this case, James Phillips purchased an inexpensive radio from the Radio Shop and later attempted to exchange it because it did not work. The date of the sale was November 14; the return was made 10 days later. The sales slip has the following language typed at the bottom: "This product is fully guaranteed for five days from the date of the purchase. If defective, return it in the original box for credit toward another purchase."

The store refuses to make the exchange, and James brings this action in small claims court.

EVIDENCE
James has (1) the sales slip for $25 dollars paid to the Radio Shop and (2) the broken radio. He claims to have thrown away the box the radio originally came in.

WITNESSES
For the Plaintiff
1. James Phillips
2. Ruby Phillips, James's sister

For the Defendant
1. Al Jackson, the salesman
2. Hattie Babcock, store manager

COURT
The judge should provide an opportunity for James to make his case and should give the representatives of the store a chance to tell the court why the money should not be returned. Both sides should call their witnesses.

At the end, the judge should decide the case and provide the reasons for the decision.

WITNESS STATEMENT: James Phillips
"I went into the Radio Shop to buy a transistor radio. I looked at a few different radios, but the salesman talked me into buying the Super Electro Model X-15. I paid the $25 price, and he gave me the

but may also require that the defendant pay back the defrauded consumers.

PROBLEM 8

Each of the following consumers has a problem. If the consumer has to go to court in each matter, what is the best remedy? Why? Could any of these situations result in a criminal prosecution? Why?

radio in a cardboard box. When I got home to listen to the radio, I found that it didn't work. I went back to the store to get my money back, but the salesman wouldn't return it. He said I should have brought it back right away. I explained to him that my mother had been sick and I'd been busy. Here's the broken radio and the receipt as proof. I want my money back!"

WITNESS STATEMENT: Ruby Phillips
"All I know is that when James got home the other day, he was all excited and wanted to show me something. He called me into the kitchen to show me his new radio. I said, 'Let's hear how it works.' He turned it on and nothing came out but static. He moved the dials around but couldn't get it to play. Was he ever mad! I told him that he ought to take it back to the store and demand his money back."

WITNESS STATEMENT: Al Jackson
"I sold the kid the radio, but as far as I know it worked OK. All the table models worked well enough, so why shouldn't the one boxed and straight from the factory? I'll bet what really happened is that he dropped the radio on his way home. Or maybe he broke it during the 10 days he had it. That's not my fault, is it?"

WITNESS STATEMENT: Hattie Babcock
"As Jackson said, all the other X-15s have worked fine. We've never had a single complaint about them. We have a store policy not to make refunds unless the merchandise is returned within five days in the box we sold it in. Also, the guarantee on the radio says that the radio must be returned in the original box. That's the reason Jackson didn't give the kid his money back. Otherwise, we'd have been more than happy to give him credit toward a new purchase. After all, pleasing our customers is very important to us. Personally, I agree with Jackson. The kid probably didn't bring back the box because it was all messed up after he dropped it."

**WHERE
YOU
LIVE**

Is there a small claims
court in your com-
munity? If so, where is
it located? What is the
filing fee? What is the
largest amount of
money that can be
awarded? Are lawyers
permitted in this court?

a. Jeanine takes a floor length dress, originally belonging to her mother, to the dry cleaners. When she picks it up, she finds several holes in it. The store claims the holes were there when the garment was brought in. Jeanine is certain that they are the result of the cleaning.

b. The Gonzales family hires the Weedout Chemical Company to spray their lawn twice a month during May, June, July and August. Weedout sends a monthly bill. By June 10, Weedout has not yet sprayed, although it sent a bill in May, which the Gonzales family paid. Weedout is behind schedule with its spraying because there is a great demand for its product, a successful new formula not yet available from other local companies.

c. Sergio, a college student, has a summer job selling books door to door. He is paid a commission on every book sold. To make extra money, he uses phony order forms. The top page is a receipt for the sale of one book. The copy beneath, which has its signature line in exactly the same place as the top copy, includes an agreement to purchase another book every month for two additional months.

In June, Mr. and Mrs. Joiner pay $12 for a book. The next month, Sergio returns with another $12 book and asks for payment. The Joiners say they never agreed to buy the second book. Sergio shows them the receipt with their signature. The Joiners had not kept their copy of the receipt. Reluctantly, they pay for the second book. Later they discover that several neighbors are in the same situation.

Small Claims Court   In the early twentieth century, court reformers recognized that the typical civil court was too slow, expensive, and complicated for many minor cases. These reformers proposed a "People's Court". It was designed to give citizens their day in court for small claims.

Every state has a **small claims court,** where you can sue for small amounts of money. The maximum award varies from $200 to $5,000, depending on the state. Filing a suit in small claims court is very inexpensive. Attorneys are not required (in some states they are not allowed), and there are few time-consuming delays. Filing a suit in small claims court involves three steps.

First, contact the court clerk to determine if the court can handle your claim. If so, you'll be required to fill out some forms and pay a small filing fee (from $2 to $15). To fill out the forms, known as a complaint or statement of claim, you'll be asked for the name and address of the party you are suing, the reason for your complaint, and the amount you are asking for.

Second, prepare for your case in advance. In most states, the court will notify the defendant of the date and place of the hearing. In the meantime, you should gather all the evidence necessary to present your case. This includes receipts, letters, canceled checks, sales slips, and estimates of repair. If a defective product is involved, be sure to bring it along, if possible. Contact all witnesses to be sure they come to court. Uncooperative witnesses can be **subpoenaed.** This means they can be ordered to appear in court. If you have time, visit court before your hearing so you'll know what to expect. Also, practice presenting your case to a friend beforehand.

Third, be on time for court on the date scheduled for the hearing. If for any reason you can't make it, call the court clerk to

How can a small claims court help consumers?

FIGURE 13   **Complaint Form for Small Claims Court**

SUPERIOR COURT OF THE DISTRICT OF COLUMBIA
CIVIL DIVISION
SMALL CLAIMS AND CONCILIATION BRANCH
613 G STREET, N.W.   THIRD FLOOR
WASHINGTON, D. C.   20001   Telephone 727-1760

_____
                                 Plaintiff   (1) _____

_____   vs.   (2) _____

_____   (3) _____
  Address   Zip Code   Defendant

No. SC _____

STATEMENT OF CLAIM

DISTRICT OF COLUMBIA, *ss:*

_____ being first duly sworn on oath says the foregoing is a just and true statement of the amount owing by the defendant to plaintiff, exclusive of all set-offs and just grounds of defense.

_____   _____
      Attorney for Plaintiff   Plaintiff (or agent)

_____
  Address   Zip Code

Subscribed and sworn to before me this _____ day of _____, 19___

_____
Deputy Clerk (or notary public)

NOTICE

To:
(1) _____   (2) _____
                 Defendant   Defendant

                                     CHECK ADDRESS
_____☐ TO BE USED FOR   _____☐
  Home Address   Zip Code   MAILING   Home Address

_____☐   _____☐
  Business Address   Zip Code   Business Address

You are hereby notified that _____

_____ has made a claim and is requesting judgment against you in the sum of _____ dollars ($_____).

as shown by the foregoing statement. The court will hold a hearing upon this claim on _____ at 9:00 a. m. in the Small Claims and Conciliation Branch located at 613 G Street, N. W., third floor.

Chief Deputy Clerk
Small Claims and Conciliation Branch

BRING THIS NOTICE WITH YOU AT ALL TIMES   [86401]

ask for a postponement. Once your hearing begins, tell your story. Do this by presenting your facts, witnesses, and any evidence you may have. Don't get emotional. Be prepared for questions from the judge. After both sides have presented their stories, the judge will make a decision.

PROBLEM 9

a. Using the complaint form in Figure 13 (or a copy of the form used in your local small claims court), fill out the form with a complaint that you, a friend, or a family member may have had. Write a short description of the events giving rise to your claim.

b. What would you do if you were notified that you were being sued in small claims court for failing to pay a bill? What would happen if you ignored the notice or did not show up in court?

c. Do you think small claims courts should follow normal court rules? Should lawyers be allowed? Why or why not?

DECEPTIVE SALES PRACTICES

Most sellers are honest, but some are not. A few use deceptive or unfair sales techniques. As a result, consumers should be able to recognize and avoid deceptive sales practices.

Federal law gives you three days after the sale to cancel any purchase made from a door-to-door salesperson.

THE CASE OF THE HOME FREEZER/FOOD PLAN

For Mr. and Mrs. Richardson, feeding a family of four was a struggle, so they were especially interested when they saw an ad for a family food plan. The ad declared:

> Veribest Family Foods beats inflation and saves you money. Top-quality meats, vegetables, and other foods delivered to your home for three years with no increase in price. Start the Veribest plan now and receive a freezer free of charge. Call today.

The Richardsons had doubts, but they called anyway. Sam Jones, a Veribest salesman, came to their home the same evening. Jones explained that for only $40 a week over the next three years, Veribest would supply enough top-quality food to feed their entire family. Since the food would be delivered once a month, the Richardsons would need a freezer, and Jones would "throw this in" for only $100 down and $25 a month for the next three years.

The Richardsons said they thought the freezer was free, but Jones replied that it would last a lifetime and was really like a gift, since the Richardsons would save so much on food. To make the offer even better, Jones said that for every person the Richardsons referred as a possible customer, he would deduct $30 from the price of the freezer.

The Richardsons still weren't sure, but Jones wouldn't take no for an answer. They soon signed the contract. The next day, the Richardsons saw an identical freezer selling at a local store for only $390, but they had already signed the contract and figured they were stuck.

When the food started coming, it was of poor quality and in such small amounts that it ran out by the middle of the month. After several months the freezer no longer kept food frozen, and the Richardsons decided they had had enough. Mrs. Richardson called Veribest to tell them about the food and broken freezer. She also demanded the $150 they expected for giving Jones the names of five friends as possible customers. She was told that they could not cancel the plan and that there would be a small service charge to repair the freezer. Also, for the Richardsons to get the $150 reduction, the referrals actually had to buy the plan. None, had, so the Richardsons weren't entitled to anything.

PROBLEM 10

a. Did any unfair or deceptive practices take place in the Richardsons' story? If so, explain why they were unfair or deceptive.
b. Did the Richardsons make any mistakes? What could they have done to prevent the problems from occurring?
c. What can the Richardsons do now? Can any state or federal agencies help them? If so, which ones?

Door-to-Door Sales

Most door-to-door salespeople are honest. They offer products and services consumers may need and want. Some, however, use high-pressure tactics and smooth talk to get you to buy things that you otherwise wouldn't buy. Once in the door, this type of salesperson won't take no for an answer and will do almost anything to make the sale.

Mr. and Mrs. Richardson had the misfortune to meet a high-pressure salesperson. They signed the contract, but after Mr. Jones left they began to have doubts. What could they have done? *They could have canceled the contract.* A Federal Trade Commission rule gives consumers a three-day "cooling off" period after they have signed a contract for over $25 with a door-to-door salesperson. During this period, the Richardsons could have notified Veribest in writing that they wished to cancel the contract. The FTC rule also requires door-to-door salespeople to tell their customers about the right to cancel and put it in writing. If the seller does not do this, the consumer may be able to cancel the contract.

PROBLEM 11

Have you ever bought anything from a door-to-door salesperson? If so, what was it? Were you happy with the product? Did you have any problems after the sale?

Referral Sales and Phony Contests

Jones tricked the Richardsons with a referral sales technique. He did this by misleading them into thinking that they would save money by referring him to other customers. Jones used this technique to help make the sale and also to get the names of new victims. In many states, referral sales are unlawful, and the consumer is entitled to cancel the contract and demand a refund.

Advertising and the Consumer

Advertising has an enormous impact on consumer behavior. Advertisements are designed both to inform and to influence. They try to create a desire for the products advertised. Every day, American consumers are bombarded by countless ads telling them what to eat, how to dress, where to travel, when to shop, and how to look and feel better.

THE CASE OF THE FREE DINING ROOM TABLE

Ron Harris received a call telling him that he had won a contest at the Finkel Furniture Store. The caller announced that Mr. Harris had won a "free" dining room table. All he had to do was buy the chairs to go with it at their regular price of $160 per set. After investigation, it was discovered that the entire dining room set (table and chairs) was regularly sold for only $160. Has the store done anything wrong?

Ron Harris has been the victim of a phony contest. It is illegal to use the word *free* and then require the consumer to do something to get the free item. Mr. Harris can get his money back if he was lured into buying the chairs as a result of the phony contest.

PROBLEM 12

Assume that Ron Harris was suspicious about the contest and decided not to purchase the chairs.

a. Should Harris report the call even though he was not a victim of this practice? Why?

b. Would you report a deceptive consumer practice you knew about even if you were not harmed by it? Why?

PROBLEM 13

a. Have you ever bought anything after seeing or hearing an ad? What did you buy? How did the ad affect your decision to buy the item?

b. Give an example of an ad you consider effective. Give an example of an ad you consider ineffective or misleading. What type of ads are most effective? Least effective?

Advertising can, of course, be beneficial. For example, merchants use advertising to tell potential customers about their products. Ads can also help consumers by telling them about new goods and services and by providing other useful information. The primary purpose of ads, however, is to sell products. Although ads can be helpful, they can also mislead, deceive, and confuse.

Ads sometimes mislead consumers by vague claims or, in a few cases, outright lies. Other ads try to create a desire for products that consumers don't really need or want. Many ads appeal to emotion rather than providing the kind of factual information needed to make a wise buying decision.

The federal and state governments have laws that prohibit false or deceptive advertising. Despite these laws, deception takes many forms and these laws are difficult to enforce.

When the public is widely exposed to a misleading ad, the FTC can order the seller to stop the false advertising. They can also order **corrective advertising.** This means that the advertiser must admit the deception in all future ads for a specified period of time. For example, a well-known mouthwash company advertised that its product cured sore throats and colds. When an investigation proved this claim false, the FTC ordered that all new ads admit that the previous claims were untrue.

As a general rule, false or misleading ads are illegal; however, one type of ad is an exception to this rule. Ads based on the seller's opinion, personal taste, or on an obvious exaggeration, are called **puffing.** While perhaps not literally true, ads that puff are not illegal. For example, a used car dealer that advertises the "World's Best Used Cars" is engaged in puffing. This is because a reasonable person should know better than to rely on the truthfulness of such a statement.

The difference between illegal advertising and puffing is small, so consumers should be on guard. If the statement tends to mislead about an important fact concerning the product, it is illegal; but if an ad is merely an opinion, it is puffing and legal.

PROBLEM 14

Based on ads you have seen or heard, give two examples of puffing. Then decide whether the italicized language from the following ads, if untrue, is false advertising or puffing. Explain your answer.

a. "... *handsewn* crepe sole shoes."

b. "You'll love Gerry's *famous* hamburgers."

c. "... *jump higher, run longer* with Sportsman Joggers."

d. "Lose 3 to 10 pounds in *a week or less* with Body Toner."

THE CASE OF THE PHONY SALE

The ad read, "Giant Sale. Top-Quality Stereos formerly $220 — now only $175." In fact, the stereos had never cost $220 and could be bought for $175 even when not on sale. Is this ad legal?

Ads that make false claims are clearly illegal. The FTC could order this stereo ad discontinued because it is untrue.

Until the law began to regulate advertising, advertisements often made grandiose claims.

For many consumers, the biggest problem is not false advertising. Rather, it is legal advertising that influences them to buy things they really don't want, need, or know much about. Many ads try to sell products by appealing to your emotions. For example, some ads *associate* products with popular ideas or symbols, such as family, motherhood, wealth, or sex appeal. These ads try to convince you that purchasing these products will associate you with the same ideas or symbols.

The *bandwagon approach* is a technique that promotes the idea that everybody's using the product, so you should too. Related to this is *celebrity appeal*. This technique involves having famous athletes or movie stars advertise the product. These people bring glamour and style to ads, but this does not necessarily mean the products are of high quality.

Still other ads try to convince consumers by resorting to the *claims of authorities*, such as doctors, or by citing test results or studies that appear scientific. A common television technique is based on the notion that *seeing is believing*. These ads often show everyday people successfully using certain household products.

Some ads simply try to make you laugh or feel good. The advertiser hopes you'll think of their product whenever you want to feel good. Some advertisers don't care what information you have about their product as long as their brand is the only one you consider. The people who make these ads know that many shoppers select nationally advertised brands even though local or store brands may cost less and be of equal quality. Whatever technique advertisers use, you should learn to separate the product from the characters and images in the ad.

PROBLEM 15

Read and analyze the following ads. What is the technique or appeal used in each ad? What important information is missing from each ad? To whom is this ad trying to appeal: children, adults, women, men, or some other group?

a. "Don't wait until your house burns down. Buy Homeowners Insurance now."

b. "Nine out of ten doctors recommend 'Super Strength' Pain Reliever."

c. "If you want to get that special man in your life, use AvecMoi Perfume."

d. "Going out of business! Bargains galore! Everything at the Pants Palace is priced to sell, sell, sell."

e. "Be the first in your neighborhood to drive the new Super-Sport Sedan."

Have you ever bought anything because of advertising? Were you pleased or disappointed with your purchase? Where are some places that ads can be found?

f. "Your mother used Stuart's Baby Powder; shouldn't you too?"

g. "For the time of your life drink Brewmeister Beer."

h. "You've come a long way, baby. Why not smoke a woman's cigarette?"

i. "Try Crunch King cereal, and you'll get a free surprise in every box."

PROBLEM 16

a. Bring in three ads from a newspaper or magazine. Analyze each ad: What is the purpose of the ad? Who is the ad aimed at? How much information is given about the product or service? What advertising technique does the ad use? How effective is it?

b. Select a product and create an advertising slogan for it. Did you use an advertising technique or appeal. If so, which one?

Bait and Switch

THE CASE OF THE APPLIANCE SWITCH

Ms. Moss saw an ad in the paper that read, "Beautiful Microwave Oven. Only $200 at A-1 Appliances." She then went to A-1's store and encountered Sam Shifty, who said to her, "You don't want that oven. It doesn't have the latest features. But look over here at our other ovens."

Ms. Moss is about to fall victim to the sales technique known as **bait and switch.** This technique involves an offer to sell a product on what sounds like very good terms — an almost-too-good-to-be-true deal. The seller does not really want to sell the product or "bait" being offered. It is simply used to get the buyer into the store. Once the consumer is in the store, the product turns out to be much less appealing then expected, enabling the seller to "switch" the consumer to a more expensive item.

Bait and switch is the offering of one product to get consumers into the store in order to switch them to a higher-priced item. Salespeople who use bait and switch "talk down" the advertised product and then refer the consumer to another higher-priced item. As encouragement, salespeople may be given a higher commission if they sell the higher-priced item. On some occasions, the product advertised as bait may not even be in stock.

Bait and switch gives sellers a strong advantage over unwary consumers. Already in the store and anticipating purchase but disappointed in the quality of the bait, the consumer is a captive audience unlikely to bother with comparison shopping. The Federal Trade Commission has rules against bait and switch and will take appropriate action when it receives complaints from consumers. Many state and local agencies also handle these complaints. If local law prohibits bait and switch, a consumer may be able to cancel the contract with a seller.

PROBLEM 17

Mr. and Mrs. Rose are looking for a new washing machine. They see an ad that says, "Come to Dyco Discount for the best deal in town on an inexpensive washer." The salesperson in the appliance department has been instructed to try selling a washer-dryer combination to every customer seeking a washer. If the combination can't be sold, the salesperson is to try selling a more expensive washing machine before showing the cheaper models.

a. Roleplay this encounter.

b. Have you ever encountered a situation like this? If so, how did you handle it? What are the advantages and disadvantages of aggressive selling? For the customer? For the store?

> **ADVICE FOR SHOP-PING BY MAIL**
>
> ■ Carefully read the product description.
> ■ Be certain the order form is filled out correctly and that all required information is provided.
> ■ Pay by check or money order. Never send cash.
> ■ Keep a copy of the order blank, the seller's name and address, and the date you sent in the order.
> ■ Note the promised delivery time.
> ■ Carefully inspect all mail-order packages upon receipt to be sure that nothing is missing or broken.

Mail-Order Sales

> ### THE CASE OF THE ELECTRIC KNIFE
>
> One day, Barry received a package in the mail containing an electric knife from the Super-Knife Corporation. A letter was enclosed that said he was getting the knife for a free 10-day trial. Barry used it once and then forgot about it. Three weeks later, a bill came for $39.95. Must Barry pay?
>
> Barry does not have to pay for the knife, nor does he have to return it. Under federal law, all unordered merchandise received by mail may be kept as a gift. Sending unordered merchandise is unlawful, and such activity should be reported to the U.S. Postal Service or the Federal Trade Commission. It is lawful to send free samples and to ask for charitable contributions, but the receiver of the goods cannot be forced to pay.

Millions of consumers shop by mail. Mail-order shopping is convenient. Items may cost less, and shoppers may not be able to find what they need in their local stores. However, mail-order shopping can also cause problems. Mail-order packages can arrive late, broken, or not at all. According to federal law, you have a right to

ADVICE ON REPAIRS

■ Become generally familiar with how cars and major appliances operate.

■ Get estimates from several repair shops. Beware of free estimates.

■ Demand and keep an itemized written estimate.

■ Insist that any repairs not listed on the estimate be made only after getting your approval.

■ Request that replaced parts be saved and returned to you.

know when you can expect merchandise to be shipped. Sellers must follow the promises in their ads (e.g., "will be rushed to you within a week"). If no shipping date is stated the merchandise must be shipped within 30 days. If the seller does not ship within 30 days, you have the right to cancel the order. The Federal Trade Commission monitors compliance with this rule.

Consumers should watch out for ads sent through the mail offering "free" items in exchange for subscriptions or memberships. Free items almost always require a commitment to purchase other items in the future (e.g., "four free books now if you purchase four more during the next year at the member's price"). Book and record clubs often mail catalogs to members on a monthly basis. The clubs preselect an item that will be sent to you unless you take some action (usually within 10 days) to make another selection or to reject all selections. These plans are legal, but they can be inconvenient and possibly expensive if you are not careful.

PROBLEM 18

Shannon receives 3 unordered records in the mail. An enclosed letter states that she can have the records for two dollars if she joins a record club and promises to buy 10 more records within a year.

a. Is this mailing legal?

b. Does Shannon have to pay the two dollars? If she doesn't pay the two dollars, does she have to return the records?

c. If she does send in the two dollars, is she obligated to buy the other records?

d. Have you ever bought anything through the mail? If so, what was it? Were you pleased with your purchase?

Repairs and Estimates

THE CASE OF THE COSTLY ESTIMATE

Nichole takes her car to Scott's Repair Shop. The mechanic tells her the car needs a tune-up and estimates the cost at $30. Nichole tells the mechanic to go ahead with the tune-up, but when she returns to pick up the car, the bill amounts to $85. Did Nichole do something wrong? What can happen if she refuses to pay?

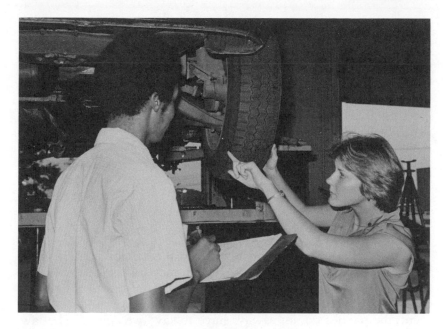

Consumers should check out repair shops for service, reliability, and honesty.

Nichole is the victim of an "open-ended estimate." Service mechanics often estimate the cost of the repair but then have you sign a repair agreement, which provides (usually in small print) that you authorize all repairs deemed necessary. You should always get a written estimate and insist that any repairs not listed on the repair agreement be made only after getting your specific approval.

Some places have laws that require repair shops to give written estimates. Frequently, these laws limit the percentage difference between the estimate and the final bill.

You should also watch out for "free estimates." Sometimes the estimate is free only if you agree to have the particular shop make the repairs.

A final protection when having repairs made on your car or appliance is to ask the repair shop to save and return all used and replaced parts. This identifies you as a careful consumer. Also, if you suspect fraud, you will have the old parts as evidence to make it easier to prove your case.

Being careful ahead of time is particularly important because if you refuse to pay for repairs after they have been made, the repair shop or garage can place a **lien** on the repaired item. This means that the repair shop can keep your car or appliance until you pay the bill.

CONTRACTS

A **contract** is an agreement between two or more persons to exchange something of value. In a contract, each person is legally

**WHERE
YOU
LIVE**

Is there a repair and estimate law in your community? If so, how does it work?

bound to do what is promised. For example, in the Case of the Home Freezer/Food Plan, a contract was signed in which Veribest promised to deliver the freezer and monthly supplies of food, and the Richardsons promised to make their payments. The Richardsons entered into a formal contract, but you also make a contract when you buy a hamburger or a movie ticket. If one party to the contract does not carry out the promise, the other party can go to court for help. To protect yourself as a consumer, it is important to understand how contracts are formed and how contracts affect your rights.

Elements of a Contract

A legally binding contract must have certain elements. There must be an **offer** by one party and an **acceptance** by the other. In addition, the two parties must agree exactly to the terms of the contract. This is called **mutual agreement.** To have mutual agreement, the parties do not always have to say "we agree." The law infers agreement from certain actions, such as signing a contract or beginning to carry out the terms of the bargain.

In every valid contract, there must also be an exchange of **consideration.** This means something of value is given for something else of value. For example, when you buy an item at a store, your consideration is the money you pay, and the merchant's consideration is the item you are buying.

People entering into a contract must be legally competent to make contracts. This means they cannot be mentally ill or intoxi-

A consumer should always read a contract before signing it.

cated. Also, agreements to do something illegal or against public policy are not enforceable in court.

If Kevin says to Sally, "I will sell you my motorcycle for $150," this is an offer. If Sally says, "OK," or if she pays the $150 to Kevin, or if she signs an agreement to pay $150, there is an acceptance. They have agreed to the exact terms. The motorcycle being exchanged for the money is the consideration. Both parties are competent, and the agreement is not illegal or against public policy. Therefore, a contract has been made.

You should not be too quick to enter into a contract. Be sure you understand and agree with all the terms before you accept; otherwise it may be too late to back out of the deal.

PROBLEM 19

For each of the following situations, decide whether a contract has been made. Be prepared to give your reasons.

a. An auctioneer says, "What am I bid for this antique sofa?" Someone in the crowd says, "$300."

b. Adam says to Basil, "I'm going to sell my car for $500." Basil replies, "All right, here is the money. I'll take it."

c. The citizens of a small town collect $1,000 and offer it as a reward for catching a suspected criminal. The sheriff captures the suspect and seeks the reward.

d. Sara's father promises to pay her $1,000 when she turns 18. On her eighteenth birthday, she seeks the money.

e. Standing at one end of a long bridge, Shelly says to Lynn, "I'll give you five dollars if you walk across the bridge." Lynn says nothing but starts walking across the bridge.

f. Liz offers Sharon $100 to steal four hubcaps for her sports car. Sharon steals the hubcaps, brings them to Liz, and asks for the money.

Minors and Contracts

THE CASE OF THE REQUIRED COSIGNER

Keith, 16, a drummer in a popular rock band, goes to a local music store to purchase a new set of drums. The drums cost $750. He offers to put down $150 and make monthly payments on the remaining amount. Because Kevin is only 16, the manager of the store refuses to sell him the drums. Is this fair? Is this legal?

A minor is a person under the age of legal majority (18 in most states). Minors may make contracts. However, as a general rule they cannot be forced to carry out their promises and may cancel or refuse to honor their contracts. Minors who cancel contracts usually must return any goods or consideration still in their possession. This rule is designed to protect minors from being taken advantage of because of their age and lack of experience. However, because of this rule, minors have a tough time getting credit. Many stores require minors to have a parent or other adult **cosign** any major contract. The adult cosigner is responsible for making payments if the minor backs out of the deal.

Minors may, however, be held to contracts that involve necessities, such as food, clothing, shelter, or medical aid. Minors can be required to pay for the reasonable value of such goods and services.

In most states, a minor who continues making payments on a contract after reaching the age of majority is considered to have **ratified** the contract. Once the contract has been ratified, it can no longer be canceled.

Written and Oral Contracts

Most contracts may be either written or oral (spoken). However, certain kinds of contracts must be in writing to be enforceable. These include contracts for the sale of land or real estate, the sale of goods priced at $500 or more, agreements to pay another person's debt, and agreements that cannot be performed within a year from the date of the agreement.

The law favors written contracts. For your protection, it is always better to have a written contract. Otherwise, it can be difficult to prove that a party promised to do something. If there is a written contract, a court will not even listen to evidence of promises made before the signing of the contract except when the written contract is unclear or one party was tricked into entering the contract.

THE CASE OF THE BROKEN PROMISE

Ruth orally agreed to sell her car to Mike for $2,000. A few days later, she got an offer of $2,300 from Paul. Thereafter, she refused to sell her car to Mike. Can Mike hold her to the agreement? Should he be able to?

Because the car sold for more than $500, a court would not force Ruth to sell her car to Mike unless they had a written contract.

Illegal Contracts

> **THE CASE OF THE DEAL TO STEAL**
>
> Gilbert makes a written agreement to pay Lionel $200 if he will steal a valuable painting. Lionel steals the painting, but Gilbert refuses to pay him. Can Lionel take Gilbert to court to force him to pay?
>
> No court would enforce this contract! It is an agreement to commit a crime and is therefore void.

Some contracts are unenforceable in court. This is because they are illegal or against the interests of society. Also, courts sometimes find that a contract is so unfair, harsh, and oppressive that it should not be enforced. Such a contract is considered to be **unconscionable.** However, courts will usually require more than just a very high price before refusing to enforce a contract.

PROBLEM 20

In each of the following situations, decide whether the contract could be enforced. Explain your answer in each case.

a. Mrs. Williams buys a stereo from a store where she has made many credit purchases in the past. Every time she buys a new item, the store has her sign a contract which says that until she pays the full price on everything, the store still owns each item. The store knows that she is unemployed and receiving public assistance. She misses two payments on the stereo. Can the store take back all the merchandise?

b. Roe, a candidate for governor, promises to appoint Doe, also a candidate, to a high government office if he will withdraw from the race. Doe withdraws. Roe wins. Can Doe force Roe to make the appointment?

c. Paolo rents a bike from Rainbow Rental Company. Before he can take the bike he has to sign a form that says, "Rainbow will not be responsible for damage or injury caused by any accident involving this bike." As a result of careless maintenance, the brakes fail on Paolo's bike and he is injured. Can Rainbow use the contract to defend against a lawsuit by Paolo?

WARRANTIES

A **warranty** is a promise or guarantee made by a seller concerning the quality or performance of goods offered for sale. A warranty is

A contract is a promise or agreement that creates legal obligations that can be enforced in court.

also a statement of what the seller will do to remedy the problem if the item doesn't perform as promised. There are two types of warranties: express and implied. Warranties give consumers very important rights. You should always be aware of the warranties that exist when you make a purchase.

Express Warranties

An **express warranty** is a statement — written, oral, or by demonstration — concerning the quality or performance of goods offered for sale. For example, if a salesperson tells you "This TV will not need any repairs for five years," this is an express warranty. Similarly, an express warranty would be created if you purchased a vacuum cleaner from an appliance store after seeing a demonstration of the vacuum picking up small particles from a deep shag rug. Since oral warranties and warranties by demonstration are difficult to prove, it is always best to get a written warranty.

Express warranties are created by statements of fact, but not everything a seller says is a warranty. If the seller's statement is merely an opinion or an obvious exaggeration, it is considered puffing or sales talk and cannot be relied on. For example, a used car lot advertising "Fantastic Used Cars" is engaged in puffing. No warranty is created, and no customer should rely on such a statement.

What happens if your TV blows a tube or your watch won't tell time? The first thing to do is check the warranty. One TV may be guaranteed for 90 days, while another may be covered for a full year. All warranties provide a remedy when things go wrong. You may be able to return the item for a refund, exchange it for another, or have it repaired.

Sellers do not have to give written warranties. However, if they do, the *Magnuson-Moss Warranty Act* requires that written warranties (1) disclose all the essential terms and conditions in a single document, (2) be in simple and easy-to-read language and (3) be made available to the consumer before sale. Written warranties must also tell you exactly what is included and what is not included. For example, if the product breaks and needs repair, the warranty must explain which repairs are covered and who will make them. The Warranty Act does not apply to products that cost $15 or less.

Under the act, warranties are labeled either "full" or "limited." A full warranty means:

■ a defective product will be fixed or replaced free, including removal and reinstallation, if necessary;

■ the consumer will not have to do anything unreasonable to get the warranty service (such as shipping a piano to a factory);

■ the product will be fixed within a reasonable time after the consumer complains;

■ if the product can't be fixed after a reasonable number of attempts, the consumer can get a refund or a replacement (this is called the Lemon Law);

■ the warranty applies to anyone who owns the product during the warranty period (not just the first purchaser).

Any protection less than this is called a limited warranty. Part of a product could have a full warranty, and part could be limited. Read all of the warranty carefully.

PROBLEM 21

Read and evaluate the one-year limited warranty provided and answer the following questions.

a. Who is making the warranty? Who will make any repairs — dealer, service center, manufacturer, or independent repairer?

b. How long is the warranty in effect? Does the buyer have to do anything to make the warranty effective?

c. What is covered — the entire product or only certain parts? What is promised — repair, replacement, labor, postage? Are there any limitations or exclusions? Is this a full or limited warranty? Why?

Implied Warranties

An **implied warranty** is an unwritten promise, created by law, that a product will do what it is supposed to do. In other words, the law requires products to meet certain minimum standards of quality and performance, even if no express promise is made. Implied warranties apply only to products sold by dealers. Implied warranties do not apply to goods sold by casual sellers. For example, if a friend sells you her bike, no implied warranties are involved. The three types of implied warranties are (1) warranty of merchantability, (2) warranty of fitness for a particular purpose, and (3) warranty of title.

A **warranty of merchantability** is an unwritten promise that the item sold is of at least average quality for that type of item. For

ONE-YEAR LIMITED WARRANTY

Electro Toasters fully guarantees this entire product for one year from purchase date to owner against defects in material or workmanship.

Defective product may be brought to purchase place, authorized service center, or Service Department, Electro Toasters, Inc., 3rd & Maple Streets, Arlington, PA, freight prepaid, for free repair or replacement at our option.

Warranty does not include: cost of inconvenience, damage due to product failure, transportation damages, misuse, abuse, accident, or commercial use.

For information, write Consumer Claims Manager at above Arlington address. Send name, address, zip, store or service center involved, model, serial number, purchase date, problem.

This warranty gives specific legal rights. You may have other rights which vary from state to state.

This warranty becomes effective upon purchase. Mailing the enclosed registration card is one way of proving purchase date but is not required for warranty coverage.

A sample warranty.

WARRANTY AND CONSUMER INFORMATION AVAILABLE

What is the purpose of a warranty?

ADVICE ON WARRANTIES

■ Not all warranties are the same. It's worth checking warranties when comparison shopping.
■ When you look at a warranty, consider the duration (how long does it last?); the scope (what parts or problems are covered or excluded?); and the remedy (what do you get under the warranty? what must you do to get the remedy?)
■ Check out your own state's law. Sometimes it gives you rights that are not in the warranty.

example, a radio must play, a saw must cut, and a freezer must keep food frozen. This warranty is always implied unless the seller expressly disclaims it. Be especially wary of goods marked "as is" or "final sale".

A **warranty of fitness for a particular purpose** exists when a consumer tells a seller before buying an item that it is needed for a specific purpose or will be used in a certain way. A salesperson who sells an item with this knowledge makes an implied promise that the item will meet the stated purpose. For example, if you tell a salesperson you want a waterproof watch and the salesperson recommends a watch, which you then buy, an implied warranty of fitness has been created. If you then go swimming and water leaks into the watch, the warranty is breached.

A **warranty of title** means that the seller promises that he or she owns the item being offered for sale. Sellers must own the goods and be able to transfer title or ownership to the buyer. If a person knows an item is stolen but still sells it, the warranty of title has been broken.

If any of the implied warranties or promises are broken, you usually have the right to return the goods, cancel the contract, and demand a refund or replacement. In most cases, however, you'll only be entitled to have the item repaired.

PROBLEM 22

Is there a warranty created in any of the following situations? If so, what type of warranty? Has the warranty been broken?

a. John sells Terri his used car. On the way home, the car completely breaks down. The cost of fixing the car is greater than the sale price.

b. Deitra buys a dress after telling the salesclerk that she plans to wash it in a washing machine. The clerk replied, "That's fine. This material is no trouble at all to clean." The dress shrinks after being washed in a washing machine.

c. A salesperson tells Sharon, "This is the finest camera on the market. It will last for years." Eight months later, the lens breaks.

d. Mike steals a diamond ring from a jewelry store and sells it to Marie after telling her his mother had given it to him.

e. Sandy orders a baseball bat from a catalog. The catalog read, "31-inch baseball bat, $7.95," and included a picture of a wooden bat. Two weeks later, Sandy receives an aluminum bat in the mail.

f. Ned buys a new sofa from a furniture store. One of the legs falls off two weeks after delivery.

Disclaimers

THE CASE OF THE GUITAR THAT QUIT

Sherry buys a new guitar for $100. Her sales receipt has a clause that reads, "This writing is the exclusive statement of the terms of the agreement between the parties. Seller makes no warranties either express or implied with respect to this product." The third time Sherry plays the guitar, one of the strings pops. Can she return the guitar?

A **disclaimer** is an attempt to limit the seller's responsibilities should anything go wrong with a product. The clause quoted in the Case of the Guitar That Quit is a disclaimer. It is an attempt by the store to avoid responsibility if anything goes wrong with the guitar. The quoted clause makes it clear that an express warranty is not being offered. But does the clause disclaim the implied warranty?

The implied warranty of merchantability can usually be disclaimed by using such expressions as "with all faults" or "as is." Unless these or other easily understood words are used, the seller must actually use the word "merchantability" to disclaim the implied warranty of merchantability. In addition, to be effective, the disclaimer must be written so as to be easily seen by the consumer. Because the language in the sales receipt for the guitar did not contain "as is," "with all faults," or the word "merchantability," it is probably *not* effective as a disclaimer. The implied warranty of merchantability protects Sherry if she returns the guitar.

Consumers should also know that under the *Magnuson-Moss Warranty Act*, sellers offering a written warranty may not disclaim or modify any implied warranty during the effective period of the written warranty.

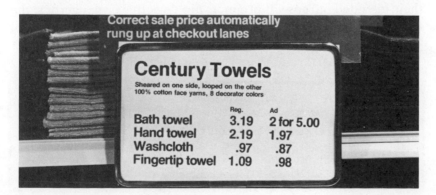

What warranty, if any, is the seller making here?

FIGURE 14 Hazardous Products

The Consumer Product Safety Commission has rated the following common items as the most hazardous around the home. This index is based on the seriousness and frequency of accidents, with greater weight for those involving young children.

Hazard Index
1. Bicycles and equipment   40.6
2. Stairs, ramps, and landings   23.5
3. Footballs and football gear   13.7
4. Baseballs and equipment   12.9
5. Playground equipment   12.5
6. Power lawn mowers   12.0
7. Skates, skateboards, scooters   11.1
8. Swimming pools and equipment   11.1
9. Nonglass tables   11.0
10. Beds and bunk beds   9.7
11. Chairs, sofas, and sofa beds   8.3
12. Basketballs and equipment   7.8
13. Floors and flooring materials   7.4
14. Nails, carpet tacks, thumbtacks   7.2
15. Architectural glass   6.3

Sellers sometimes use disclaimers to limit the consumer's remedy. For example, a contract may read, "It is expressly understood and agreed that the buyer's only remedy shall be repair or replacement of defective parts. The seller is not liable in damages for injury to persons or property." Courts generally enforce these clauses. However, courts sometimes find it unfair to limit a consumer's remedy for personal injuries arising out of a purchase. Therefore, a consumer who buys a television set and signs a contract containing the previous clause could sue for medical expenses, despite the contract, if the television exploded and caused personal harm.

You should remember that if you fully examine the goods (or had this opportunity) before making a purchase, the implied warranty will not apply to those defects you should have discovered during the inspection. Therefore, *carefully inspect for defects any goods you buy*. Be especially careful with used cars. It is wise to have a mechanic you trust examine the car before you purchase it.

Be sure to carefully read all instructions that come with a product. If you fail to use the product properly, or if you use it for an improper purpose, you may invalidate the warranty.

UNSAFE OR DANGEROUS PRODUCTS

Occasionally, a product is not only poor-quality but also defective. In these instances, the product may actually harm or even kill the person using it. The area of law that deals with the problem of injury to consumers is known as product liability law.

Each year, millions of Americans are injured as a result of home accidents involving consumer products. In addition, thousands of people are killed driving cars, trucks, or motorcycles. Thousands more die in accidents involving falls, burns, firearms, poisons, and recreational activities.

Consumers have a right to safety. But how safe do you have a right to be, and who is responsible if you are injured in your home or on the highway? Sellers are expected to make products safe for their intended purpose. If products are defective or dangerous, the maker may be liable for the resulting harm. This liability is based on warranty, negligence, or strict liability.

THE CASE OF THE EXPLODING BOTTLE

John's mother doesn't have anything to serve her guests, so she asks John to run to the store and get a bottle of soda. As John is on his way home, the bottle suddenly explodes, injuring his eye and cutting his hands. Who, if anyone, is responsible for the injury to John?

In the Case of the Exploding Bottle, the bottle was not of ordinary quality. Thus, there is probably a breach of the warranty of merchantability. The results of the breach, however, are far more serious than usual. Another way to look at the case is in terms of **negligence.** Negligence law deals with a person's lack of care toward another to whom a duty is owed, resulting in harm. Here it is possible that the soda company, the bottle manufacturer, the store, or all three, failed to exercise sufficient care in designing, manufacturing, or handling the bottle that injured John.

It is often hard to prove negligence. As a result, the trend in products liability law is to hold the manufacturer and others in the chain of supply (e.g., distributor, retailer) strictly liable if someone is injured because of a defective product. Using **strict liability,** the consumer must prove the purchase, defect, and injury but need not pinpoint who was at fault in causing the defect.

Does your state have a "helmet law" for motorcycles? What are some other examples of laws affecting consumer safety?

Some manufacturers are required to put warnings on potentially dangerous products, such as drugs, cigarettes, power tools, machinery, and cleaning fluids. If you ignore these warnings, you may not be able to recover damages if you are injured by the product. Also, there may be no liability if you use a product for an unintended purpose or use it in a careless manner.

The U.S. Consumer Product Safety Commission handles complaints and deals with the safety of most consumer products and

The *Federal Hazardous Substance Labeling Act* requires warning labels on any potentially dangerous household product.

Many consumers use credit cards.

product-related injuries. The commission has the power to force dangerous products off the market and will advise consumers on the safety of products.

PROBLEM 23

a. Make a list of five items that are or can be dangerous to use.

b. For each item, decide whether the government should ban it, regulate it (e.g., provide warnings), or take no action at all.

c. Explain why you treated each item as you did. Consider in your explanation both the danger and the benefits of each item.

CREDIT

Credit means buying goods or services now in exchange for a promise to pay in the future. It also means borrowing money now in exchange for a promise to repay it in the future. People who loan money or provide credit are called **creditors.** People who borrow money or buy on credit are called **debtors.** Creditors usually charge debtors additional money over the amount borrowed for the privilege of being given the credit. This additional money owed to the creditor is called **interest.**

Types of Credit

The two general types of credit are unsecured and secured. **Unsecured credit** simply means using credit (buying goods or bor-

FIGURE 15   Credit Card Application

Applicant's Information
Please read special instructions*

BANK USE ONLY

FIRST NAME | MIDDLE NAME | LAST NAME

STREET ADDRESS | CITY | STATE | ZIP

SOCIAL SECURITY NUMBER | HOME PHONE NUMBER | APPLICANT'S AGE | NO OF DEPENDENTS

PRESENT ADDRESS YRS ___ MOS ___ | HOME W/RELATIVES ___ BUYING ___ RENTING ___ OWN ___ | IF BUYING/OWN VALUE ___

TO WHOM DO YOU PAY RENT/MORTGAGE | ADDRESS | BALANCE | MONTHLY PAYMENT

FORMER ADDRESS | CITY | STATE | ZIP | FORMER ADDRESS YRS ___ MOS ___

NAME OF NEAREST RELATIVE (not living with you) | ADDRESS | RELATIONSHIP

EMPLOYER | POSITION | HOW LONG YRS ___ MOS ___

BUSINESS ADDRESS | CITY | STATE | ZIP | BUSINESS PHONE NUMBER

PREVIOUS EMPLOYER | POSITION | ADDRESS | HOW LONG YRS ___ MOS ___

GROSS MONTHLY INCOME | AMOUNT AND SOURCE OF ADDITIONAL INCOME (See special instructions)* | IF OBLIGATED TO PAY ALIMONY/CHILD SUPPORT LIST MONTHLY AMOUNT

IF ALIMONY/CHILD SUPPORT | NAME AND ADDRESS OF PAYER

BANK AND BRANCH | CHECKING ACCT NO | SAVINGS ACCT NO | LOAN ACCT NO

BANK AND BRANCH | CHECKING ACCT NO | SAVINGS ACCT NO | LOAN ACCT NO

AUTO MAKE | YEAR | FINANCED BY/ADDRESS | PRESENT BALANCE | MO PAYMENT

CREDITORS | ADDRESS | ACCT NO

TOTAL OF ALL DEBTS AND MONTHLY PAYMENTS (See special instructions)*

CL ___ NO CDS ___

SOURCE ___

DR ___ BANK AND BRANCH

FULL SIGNATURE

rowing money) based only on a promise to repay in the future. Credit cards and store charge accounts are examples of unsecured credit. **Secured credit** means consumers must put up some kind of property as protection in the event the debt is not repaid. For example, a person who buys a house must give the lender a security interest (called a mortgage) in the house until the debt is repaid. If the home buyer fails to pay off the mortgage the lender can sell the house and use the proceeds of this sale to pay off the debt.

Credit Cards and Charge Accounts   Today, many stores and companies issue credit cards and allow their customers to maintain charge accounts. Consumers can use credit cards to buy gasoline, take a vacation, go out to dinner, buy furniture, clothing, and hundreds of other things.

Credit cards are engraved with the holder's name and identification number. They entitle you to buy goods or services on credit. Some companies provide these cards free; some charge a yearly fee, typically between $25 and $50. Consumers are given a credit limit and can make purchases up to that limit.

Companies issuing credit cards send out monthly statements that show you how much is owed. Most credit card companies allow you to pay bills over time, making minimum monthly payments. If you pay the entire bill on or before the due date, there is no extra charge. However, if you pay only part of the amount owed, there is usually a finance or interest charge on the unpaid monthly balance. Interest charges vary from 12 to 24 percent a year.

Various companies use slightly different methods of computing interest. However, you can estimate the interest charge by multiplying the balance owed by .015 (i.e., if the interest is 1.5 percent per month). For example, if the balance owed is $500.00, the monthly interest charge will be about $7.50 ($500.00 × .015). The total amount owed for the month will be approximately $507.50 ($500.00 + $7.50 interest).

If your credit card is lost or stolen, you should report it immediately to the credit card company. For protection, any person with credit cards should keep a list of the following information:

THE CASE OF THE LOST CREDIT CARDS

Sally lost her wallet containing a MasterCard and a Sears credit card. By the time Sally realized her wallet was missing, someone had charged $800 on the MasterCard and $100 on the Sears account. Does Sally have to pay these bills?

(1) the name of the company issuing the card; (2) the account number on each card; and (3) the number to call if the card is lost or stolen.

If your credit card is lost or stolen, you are not responsible for any unauthorized charges made after you notify the issuer that the card is missing. The law limits your liability for charges made before notification to $50 per card. In the Case of the Lost Credit Cards, Sally would probably be liable for $50 on each card. If she had notified Sears and MasterCard before any charges were made, she would have owed nothing.

Billing errors can be a real headache. It takes time and energy to sort them out, and they can cost you money if you don't discover them. To avoid billing problems, check *all* sales slips carefully, save receipts and canceled checks, and go over each bill or monthly statement carefully.

If you still encounter a problem, The *Fair Credit Billing Act* provides you with a measure of protection. If you have a complaint about your bill, this law requires creditors to acknowledge and respond to your written complaint within 90 days. You may withhold payment of the disputed amount pending the investigation; however, undisputed amounts must be paid as normally required. Until your complaint is settled, the law forbids the creditor from reporting the matter to a credit bureau.

To receive the protection of the *Fair Credit Billing Act*, your communication to the creditor must meet certain requirements. You must complain in writing. Phone calls do not protect your rights under this act. Your notice must be received at the creditor's address within 60 days after the statement was first sent to you. In the notice you must include your name and your account number. Finally, you must explain why you believe there is a billing error and state the amount of the error.

If the bill is correct, you may have to pay a finance charge on the unpaid amount in dispute. However, a creditor who does not follow the requirements of this law may not collect the first $50 of the disputed amount, even if the bill turns out to be accurate. A consumer can sue such a creditor for damages and can also recover attorney's fees.

THE CASE OF THE CHARGE ACCOUNT BILLING ERROR

You pay the bill on your monthly department store charge account. The next month, you are again charged for the amount already paid. You call the store to straighten out the mistake, but the next month you receive the same bill plus a letter threatening to close your account. What can you do? Draft a letter to a local store explaining the problem and what you want done about it.

PROBLEM 24

Examine the billing statement reproduced in Figure 16 and answer the following questions.

a. Who is the creditor?

b. Who is the debtor?

c. What is the new balance? How did the creditor arrive at the new balance?

d. How much credit is available? How did the creditor determine the credit available?

e. Assume the debtor had a store receipt from the camera shop for $77.67. Draft a letter to the creditor about this billing error.

FIGURE 16   Billing Statement

PAYMENTS SHOULD BE ADDRESSED TO:
UNITED VIRGINIA BANK CARD CENTER
7818 PARHAM RD . P. O BOX 27182
RICHMOND. VIRGINIA 23270

UNITED VIRGINIA BANK CARD
STATEMENT

ACCOUNT NUMBER	STATEMENT CLOSING DATE
4366-040-878-010	03/12/86

CREDIT LIMIT	CREDIT AVAILABLE
1,000	810.50

CUSTOMER REPRESENTATIVE TELEPHONE NUMBER
(804) 270-8414

INQUIRIES SHOULD BE ADDRESSED TO:
UNITED VIRGINIA BANK CARD CENTER
7818 PARHAM RD. P. O. BOX 27172
RICHMOND. VIRGINIA 23261

JOHN Q. CONSUMER
1000 MAIN STREET
ANYWHERE, USA

POSTING DATE	REFERENCE NUMBER	TRANSACTION DATE	TRANSACTION DESCRIPTION			AMOUNT
07 18	*76145324	07 07	DODGE STATE PARK	FT WAYNE	IN	30 03
07 25	*81983773	07 03	ECONOMY HOTEL, INC.	ASHVILLE	NC	19 71
08 02	21407856	08 02	PAYMENT - THANK YOU			100 00-
08 08	21575724	07 27	THRIFTY MOTEL	SOUTH HILL	VA	14 51
08 09	22161982	08 05	SNAP SHOT CAMERA	WASHINGTON	DC	87 67

VISA.   VISA.

TYPE OF CREDIT	PREVIOUS BALANCE	CREDITS	PAYMENTS	NEW TRANSACTIONS	PERIODIC RATES	CORRESPONDING ANNUAL PERCENTAGE RATES	BALANCE ON WHICH COMPUTED	FINANCE CHARGE	NEW BALANCE
ADVANCES	00	00	00	00	1.00%	12.0%	00	00	00
OTHER EXTENSIONS OF CREDIT	136 08	00	100 00	151 92	1.50%	18.0%	100 36	1 50	18950
TOTALS	136 08	00	100 00	151 92	ANNUAL PERCENTAGE RATE 18.0 %		100 36	1 50	18950

171870
TO PAY IN INSTALMENTS
PAY THIS AMOUNT
BY THE PAYMENT
DUE DATE

PAST DUE	00
CURRENT DUE	10 00
MINIMUM PAYMENT DUE	10 00

DUE DATE
09/08/86

To avoid additional FINANCE CHARGE on other extensions of credit, pay this amount by the payment due date.

NOTICE: SEE REVERSE SIDE FOR IMPORTANT INFORMATION

Loans and Installment Sales Contracts The biggest difference between unsecured and secured credit transactions is the requirement that consumers post **collateral** in secured transactions. Collateral is property put up by the debtor that may be taken by the creditor if the loan is not repaid.

If Joan wants to buy a new car, she can go to a bank to borrow money. The bank loans her the money (if her credit is good) in exchange for her promise to repay it. The bank may also require collateral. For example, they may ask that she put up the car or other valuable property as security for the loan. This means that the bank can take the car if she **defaults** (misses payments) on her loan.

Who Should Use Credit?

To make an informed decision about a credit purchase you must first answer this question: Is it worth having a car, television, vacation, or other item before you have saved the entire purchase price, even though you'll pay more for the item in the long run?

Most American families answer yes to this question. In recent years, consumer debt has averaged approximately $1,000 for every man, woman and child in America! And this figure does not include money owed for home mortgages. Many American families are seldom out of debt.

Extensive use of credit is here to stay but consumers should know that credit purchases cost more than cash purchases. In addition, studies show that consumers who use credit spend more and buy more often. This is the reason many merchants offer "easy credit."

Consumers who buy on credit pay more, and they risk losing their products (and their payments) if they fail to make the required payments. As a general rule, consumers who spend more than 20 percent of their take-home salary to pay off debts (excluding mortgages) are using too much credit. Consumers who skip payments to cover living expenses or who take out new loans to cover old loans are also using too much credit.

PROBLEM 25

a. Make a list of products or services which you, your friends, or your family have bought on credit.

b. What are the advantages and disadvantages of using credit to pay for clothing to be worn at a formal party? Tuition for college or vocational school? A car to get you to work? A vacation?

c. Write out some rules that will help you decide when to use credit.

The Cost of Credit

You should shop for credit just as you shop for products and services. The cost of credit includes interest and other finance charges. Because there are different methods for calculating interest rates, always ask lenders for the **Annual Percentage Rate** (APR). This number is calculated the same way by all lenders, so you can use it to compare rates.

Interest Rates   Each state sets limits on the amount of interest that can be charged for various types of credit. Any amount charged above the legal limit is called **usury.** Lenders who charge interest rates above the legal maximum may be liable for both civil and criminal penalties.

THE CASE OF THE 50/50 CREDIT PLAN

Sally Saleswoman tells Linda, "This washing machine is a good buy—only $500. Now, if you don't have the cash, I can arrange easy credit for you. Only $50 down and $50 a month for 12 months, Just sign here." Linda signs and pays $50. How much interest will she pay if the contract calls for 12 monthly payments?

Linda will pay a total of $650 over 12 months ($50 down plus $600 in installment payments). Since the cash price of the washing machine was $500, she paid a $150 finance charge for the right to borrow $450 ($500 minus $50 down payment). According to the formula set up under federal law, the APR would be 49 percent!

Interest rate ceilings vary from state to state. Generally, however, loans from banks or finance companies carry interest rates of from 10 to 20 percent per year. Credit card companies and department stores usually charge 1.5 percent per month (18 percent a year). Installment contracts for consumer goods like new cars or furniture can vary by as much as 10 percent.

Other Finance Charges   Besides the interest paid on an installment sale, there are sometimes other charges added onto the basic price. These include:

■ *Credit property insurance*, which insures the purchased item against theft or damage.

TOLL-FREE NUMBERS FOR CREDIT CARD COMPANIES

Most major credit card companies have toll-free "800" telephone numbers which you can use to contact the company. Services offered by each company differ, but generally you can notify them of a stolen or lost credit card, make inquiries about your bill or your account, apply for a credit card, and register a change of address.

Bank credit card companies, such as BankAmericard and Master Charge, do not have toll-free numbers, since most business is handled by the issuing banks. However, if you need to contact the bank about any of the above problems, and you are out of the local calling area, try calling collect.

You can obtain toll-free numbers by calling 800/555-1212.

Banks loan money to consumers. Where else can a consumer borrow money?

■ *Credit life insurance,* which insures the life of the buyer and guarantees payment of the balance due if the buyer should die during the term of the contract. Note: you are *not required* to buy credit life insurance.

■ *Service charge,* which covers the seller's cost of bookkeeping, billing, etc.

■ *Penalty charge,* which covers the seller's inconvenience in case of late payments. May include court costs, repossession expenses, and attorney fees.

PROBLEM 26

Choose an item you would like to have but could purchase only by using credit.

a. Where could you shop for this credit?

b. What interest rates do the different sources of credit charge for this item? What is the APR for each creditor? What other finance charges are required?

Costly Credit Arrangements   Low-income consumers and persons heavily in debt may fall prey to **loan sharking.** This means lending money at high, often usurious (illegal) rates of interest. Loan sharks promise "easy" credit and appeal to people who have problems obtaining and keeping good credit standing.

Some creditors use **balloon payment** clauses in their agreements. In such agreements monthly payments are small, but the last payment is much larger. This may make it difficult for the consumer to make the final payment. Consumers should carefully consider any agreement with a balloon payment clause. Be sure you can save up enough for the large final payment.

Another clause to avoid in financing agreements is the **acceleration clause.** This clause permits the creditor to accelerate the loan, making all future payments due immediately in the event a consumer misses a single payment.

You should also beware of **bill consolidation.** This means combining all your debts into a single monthly payment. Lenders sometimes claim to wipe out all your bills with one easy monthly payment. However, the consolidation loan may require payments over a longer period of time and at a higher interest rate. In the long run you may pay more.

THE CASE OF THE HIDDEN CHARGES

Art buys some new furniture on the installment plan. When he receives an itemized bill, he discovers that he owes a total of $745, while the price of the furniture was only $553. He calls the store, and they tell him that he is paying 20 percent interest. He would never have bought the furniture if he'd known it would have cost this much. What mistakes did Art make? What can he do now?

Truth in Lending   To prevent credit abuses, Congress passed the *Truth in Lending Act.* This law requires creditors to give you certain basic information about the cost of buying on credit. The creditor must tell you — *in writing and before you sign a contract* — the finance charge and the Annual Percentage Rate (APR). The finance charge is the total amount you pay to use the credit including interest charges and any other fees. The APR is the percentage cost of credit on a yearly basis.

The law also requires that consumers be given a copy of the contract and be told the rules and charges for any late payments. Violators are subject to both civil and criminal penalties, and consumers who sue creditors under this act may recover damages, court costs, and attorney fees.

ADVICE ON USING CREDIT

■ Credit costs money. Don't buy things on credit you don't need or want. Resist high-pressure sales techniques.

■ Determine how much debt you can handle.

■ Comparison shop for credit. If you are suspicious, check to see if the lender is licensed and whether complaints have been filed.

■ Before making a credit purchase, read and understand the entire contract. Don't sign contracts with blank spaces.

■ If a contract has a large final payment, be sure you can afford it.

■ Once you've signed a credit agreement, keep a copy in a safe place. Keep receipts for each payment.

PROBLEM 27

Carefully read the retail installment contract reprinted in Figure 17.

a. What is the annual percentage rate in this contract?

b. Are there any balloon payments?

c. Must the consumer buy credit insurance?

d. What does the term "deferred payment price" mean?

e. Are there any blank spaces that should be filled in? If there are, what goes in the spaces?

f. If Jones misses a payment, can the store take back the refrigerator?

FIGURE 17 Retail Installment Contract

Seller's Name: *Lowell's Department Store*, *Pittsburgh, Pennsylvania* Contract # *32.83*

RETAIL INSTALLMENT CONTRACT AND SECURITY AGREEMENT

The undersigned (herein called Purchaser, whether one or more) purchases from *Lowell's Dept Store* (seller) and grants to *Lowell's Dept. Store* a security interest in, subject to the terms and conditions hereof, the following described property.

PURCHASER'S NAME *Mr. John Jones*
PURCHASER'S ADDRESS *74 Woods Place*
CITY *Pittsburgh* STATE *Pa* ZIP *15210*

1. CASH PRICE		$ *315.00*
2. LESS: CASH DOWN PAYMENT $ *50.00*		
3. TRADE-IN		
4. TOTAL DOWN PAYMENT		$ *50.00*
5. UNPAID BALANCE OF CASH PRICE		$ *265.00*
6. OTHER CHARGES: *Service Charge*		$ *8.00*
		$
7. AMOUNT FINANCED		$ *273.00*
8. FINANCE CHARGE		$ *49.14*
9. TOTAL OF PAYMENTS		$
10. DEFERRED PAYMENT PRICE (1+6+8)		$ *372.14*
11. ANNUAL PERCENTAGE RATE		*18*

QUANTITY DESCRIPTION AMOUNT

QUANTITY	DESCRIPTION	AMOUNT	
1	*Refrigerator*	*300*	*00*

Description of Trade-in:

Sales Tax	*15*	*00*
Total	*315*	*00*

Insurance Agreement

The purchaser of insurance coverage is voluntary and not required for credit. (Type of Ins.) insurance coverage is available at a cost of $ *10.00* for the terms of credit.

I desire insurance coverage

Signed_____ Date_____

I do not desire insurance coverage

Signed_____ Date_____

Purchaser hereby agrees to pay to *Lowell's Department Store* at their offices shown above the "TOTAL OF PAYMENTS" shown above in *12* monthly installments of $ *26.85* (final payment to be $ *26.85*) the first installment being payable *March 5*, 19 *79*, and all subsequent installments on the same day of each month until paid in full. The finance charge applies from (Date) *Feb. 5, 1979*

Signed_____

Notice to Buyer: You are entitled to a copy of the contract you sign. You have the right to pay in advance the unpaid balance of this contract and obtain a partial refund of the finance charge based on the "Actuarial Method."

Why should you shop for credit?

Obtaining Credit

Any store, bank, or credit card company that extends credit to consumers wants to know that the money will be repaid. Before making a loan, the creditor will want to know several things about the consumer:

■ Is the consumer a reliable person (e.g., does he or she move or change jobs frequently)?

■ Does the consumer have a steady income that is likely to continue into the future?

■ Is the consumer's income high enough to enable the consumer to pay for the items likely to be purchased?

■ Does the consumer have a good record in paying off other loans and previous bills?

Creditors are in business to make money; thus, it is understandable that they would ask questions such as these. However, creditors have sometimes unfairly denied credit for reasons such as the debtor's race, sex, or source of income (e.g., public assistance or alimony). Today a federal law, the *Equal Credit Opportunity Act*, protects consumers against credit discrimination based on sex, marital status, race, color, religion, national origin, old age, or source of income. The Federal Trade Commission handles credit discrimination complaints against finance companies, retail stores, oil companies, and travel and entertainment credit card companies. Bank regulatory agencies, such as the Federal Reserve Board and Comptroller of the Currency, handle complaints against banks and bank credit cards. If you think you have been discriminated against, you may complain to one of these agencies or sue the creditor in court.

Many states also have laws that forbid credit discrimination. Complaints should be directed to the state or local consumer affairs office or human rights commission.

PROBLEM 28

You are a loan officer at a local bank. Each of the following people is seeking a loan. Based on the information provided, evaluate each applicant and make a decision regarding each loan request. Discuss your reasons for granting or denying credit.

a. Alice Johnson is the mother of four children. Her only income consists of public assistance payments of $420 per month and $80 per month from the pension of her deceased husband. She wishes to buy a new stove and refrigerator totaling $700. She lives in a public housing development. Her rent and other expenses usually total about $375 a month.

b. Jerry Levitt is a carpenter seeking work wherever he can find it. Depending on the weather and other factors, he is subject to seasonal unemployment. He currently brings home about $650 per month and has car payments of $150 a month, stereo and TV payments of $105 a month, rent of $220 a month, and no money in the bank. He would like to borrow $2,500 to buy a motorcycle.

c. Sue Sullivan, 22, is in her second year of college. She has excellent grades and plans to attend medical school after graduation. Until recently, her parents paid her bills, but she is now on her own. She is seeking $2,000 for her college tuition and expenses. She has never borrowed money before, but she plans to repay all loans after finishing medical school.

PROBLEM 29

Susan and Sam Richards want to open a charge account at a local department store. Their application is reproduced in Figure 18.

a. If you were a credit officer, would you approve their application? Why or why not?

b. Is there information not on this form that would be helpful in making a decision? Is any of the information on the form unnecessary? Explain your answers.

What to Do If You Are Denied Credit

If you ever apply for credit, the creditor will evaluate your application according to certain standards. The creditor may investigate you personally or may pay a credit bureau to check your credit record. Many creditors do both. There are thousands of credit bureaus across the country. Financial and personal infor-

Federal laws apply when banks provide credit to consumers.

FIGURE 18   Charge Account Application

Applicant's Signature *Sam K Richards*	Identification *VA. Drivers License P831947*	Date *3-23-79*	
Co-Applicant's Signature *Susan Lynn Richards*	Identification *VA Drivers License C139246*	Date *3-23-79*	

Office Use Only

Account Previously Applied For?		Store Number	Date	Courtesy Card Amount	Approved By	Account Number
Applicant ☐ Yes ☒ No	Co-Applicant ☐ Yes ☒ No		Taken By No.	Courtesy Card Authorized By	Date	FLC CBC RI
Where	Where					
When	When					

Charge Card(s) To Be In The Name Of

1. First *SAM*   Initial *K.*   Last *RICHARDS*   Date of Birth Mo. Day Yr. *10 06 48*

Type of Account Requested ☒ Joint ☐ Individual	Number of Charge Cards Requested *2*	Co-Applicant's Name (If Joint Account Requested) 2. First *SUSAN* Initial *L.* Last *RICHARDS* Relationship To Individual Named In Box 1. *wife*

Present Residence (Mailing) Address-Street *089 South Maple Street*   Length of Time at This Address *3 years*

City, State *Alexandria, Virginia*   Zip *22314*   Area Code & Phone Number *(017) 342-8619*

Social Security Number *084-74-8574*   ☐ Own Home   ☐ Own Mobile Home   ☒ Rent   ☐ Room   ☐ Live With Parents   Monthly Mtge./Rent *$350*   No. of Dependents Including Self *2*   Other(s) Authorized To Use This Account — Relationship(s)

Applicant's Information		Co-Applicant's Information (If Joint Account Requested)	
Former Address - Street *012 West 14th Street*	How Long *3 yrs*	Former Address - Street *012 West 14th Street*	How Long *3 yrs*
City, State *Washington, D.C.* Zip *20036*		City, State, Zip *Washington, D.C. 20036* Social Security Number	
Employer's Name (Give Firm's Full Name) *Fix-It Plumbing Company*	How Long *3 yrs*	Employer's Name (Give Firm's Full Name) *West 12th St Elem. School*	How Long *2 years*
Employer's Address *389 "C" Street Wash.D.C.* Business Telephone *861-4819*		Employer's Address *1201 12th St. Wash.D.C.* Business Telephone *391-0842*	
Position *Plumber* Gross Salary (Monthly) *$1500.*		Position *Teacher's Aide* Gross Salary (Monthly) *$500.00*	

You Need Not Furnish Alimony, Child Support Or Separate Maintenance Income Information If You Do Not Want Us To Consider It In Evaluating Your **Application**.

Other Income – Source(s)	Amount (Monthly)	Other Income – Source(s)	Amount (Monthly)
Former Employer – Address *Garry Plumbing & Heating*	How Long *4 yrs*	Former Employer – Address *Franklin Elementary School*	How Long *2 years*
Position *Plumber* Gross Salary (Monthly) *$1000*		Position *Teacher's Aide* Gross Salary (Monthly) *$400*	
Bank – Branch *Security American Bank* ☒ Checking ☒ Savings ☐ Checking & Savings ☐ Loan		Bank – Branch *Security Amer. Bank* ☒ Checking ☒ Savings ☐ Checking & Savings ☐ Loan	
Nearest Relative Not At Your Present Address *Robert Richards* Relationship *brother*		Nearest Relative Not At Your Present Address *Sally M. Cook* Relationship *sister*	
Relative's Address *1001 Market Street Lanham, MD.*		Relative's Address *813 Apple Lane Vienna, Virginia*	

Credit Cards (Include Loan or Finance Companies)			Exact Name In Which Account Is Carried	For Office Use Only
Firm Name	Location	Account No.		Credit Bureau Report: In File Since _____ Last Checked _____
American Oil	*Richmond, VA.*	*M482-613*	*SAM K. RICHARDS*	
Hahns Dept Store	*Washington DC*	*014-892*	*Susan L. RICHARDS*	

mation about consumers is often stored in computers and may be passed among the various bureaus.

If a credit report indicates that you are a poor risk, the creditor will probably deny credit. Also, if you are trying to get credit for the first time and have no credit record at all, the creditor may deny credit. Sometimes creditors decide to deny credit based solely on information in the application, without taking the time to order a credit report.

The *Equal Credit Opportunity Act* says that creditors must tell consumers why they were turned down. The reasons given must be specific. For example, "applicant does not meet our standards" is not specific enough. On the other hand, "insufficient income" is a specific reason. It tells you how your circumstances must change to qualify for credit. If a credit report is involved, another federal law protects you from inaccurate credit bureau reporting. The *Fair Credit Reporting Act* requires creditors who deny credit based on information received from a credit bureau to tell you that fact. The creditor must also give you the name and address of the credit bureau that supplied the report.

Every consumer has the right to learn the nature of information in his or her credit file. Although credit bureaus are not required to show consumers copies of the actual file, they must disclose the nature and substance of the information it contains.

If you discover false, misleading, incomplete, irrelevant, or out-of-date information in your file, you can require the credit bureau to recheck its information and correct the errors. If the credit bureau does not cooperate in correcting your credit file, you may complain to the Federal Trade Commission or sue the bureau in court. If after reinvestigating the information the bureau still believes that it is correct, you have the right to have your version of the dispute inserted in the file.

How could a budget help this consumer?

DEFAULT AND COLLECTION PRACTICES

Consumers who use credit sometimes have difficulty making all their payments. Problems can arise because the consumer is over-extended or too deeply in debt. Problems can also arise because of unexpected unemployment, family illness, or a variety of other reasons. A consumer who is unable or unwilling to pay off a debt goes into **default.**

What a Consumer Can Do in Case of Default

If you have problems paying your bills, you should consider each of the following options.

1. Reassess your financial life-style to determine where the problem arose. If you are not already on a budget, you should consider starting one.

2. Notify each creditor of the problem and ask to have the term of debt extended (leading to smaller monthly payments) or to have the amount of the debt reduced or refinanced. Keep in mind that refinancing over a longer period usually results in increased finance charges.

3. Contact a consumer credit counseling service or a family service agency that offers free or low-cost financial counseling (see Appendix B for addresses).

4. Seek assistance from friends or relatives to reduce the debt to a manageable level.

**WHERE
YOU
LIVE**

What agencies and organizations in your community provide financial counseling services? Do they charge a fee for their services?

5. Consider debt reorganization under Chapter XIII of the Federal Bankruptcy Law. Under this plan, the wage earner, the creditors, and a court-appointed referee work out a plan to repay debts on an installment basis. The entire process is supervised by a federal court.

6. Declare voluntary **bankruptcy**. This option is usually the least desirable and should be considered only as a last resort. All assets (some states exempt your home and necessary clothing) are assembled and sold. The proceeds are distributed among the creditors.

Creditor Collection Practices

Creditors have many ways of collecting money from consumers who are unwilling or unable to pay their debts. It is understandable that creditors take action to recover money or property owed them. However, in the past, some bill collectors engaged in unsavory practices. As a result, some debtors suffered family problems, lost their jobs, and had their privacy invaded.

These practices prompted Congress to pass the *Fair Debt Collection Practices Act* in 1978. This act protects consumers from abusive and unfair collection practices by professional debt collectors. It does not apply to creditors collecting their own bills. Under the act, the debt collector's communications are limited to reasonable times and places. False or misleading statements as well as acts of harassment or abuse are strictly prohibited.

Calls and Letters   If phone calls or letters are unreasonable and become harassing, you should report the collection practice to the Federal Trade Commission or to your local consumer protection agency. Under federal law, you can send bill collectors a notice demanding that all collection contacts cease. You may still owe the money, but the collection contacts would have to stop. You should also consider contacting the phone company, which has the power to remove telephones from anyone using them for harassment.

Repossession   As mentioned earlier, consumers sometimes post collateral when they take out a loan or sign installment sales contracts. The creditor can usually **repossess,** or take back, the collateral if you default on the loan or obligation. Most states do not permit creditors to repossess if it involves violence or a breach of the peace.

The creditor can sell the collateral and then apply the proceeds of the sale to the amount you owe. Debtors are also charged for any costs incurred in the repossession and sale. After the sale, you are entitled to get back any amount received by the seller that is in excess of the amount owed (plus expenses). However, if the sale brings in less than the amount owed (plus expenses), the debtor must pay the difference. In some states, creditors who repossess give up the right to collect any amount remaining after the sale.

Court Action   As a last resort, creditors may sue debtors in court for the exact amount owed on the debt. At times, the trouble and expense of suing in court make creditors avoid this method. However, creditors often sue debtors in small claims court.

Just because you are sued does not mean the creditor is entitled to collect the disputed amount. Consumers often have legitimate defenses, such as the fact that the goods were defective. As a result, *if you ever receive a summons to go to court, don't ignore it.* Contact a lawyer immediately. If unable to afford one, you may call the local legal services or legal aid office, or ask the court to appoint a free attorney. However, unlike criminal trials, there is no constitutional right to an attorney in civil cases.

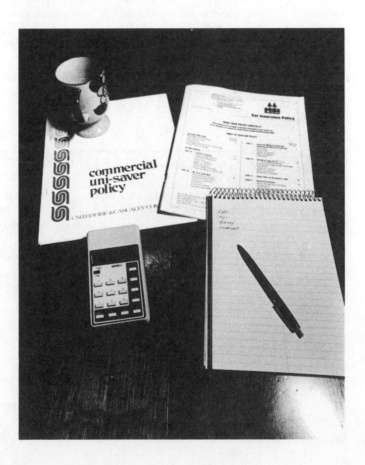

The main thing to avoid when being sued is a **default judgment.** This is a judgment entered for the plaintiff (creditor) and against the defendant (debtor). Most default judgments occur because the defendant simply fails to show up in court. Consumers who cannot appear in court on the date set in the summons should contact the court clerk in advance to arrange for a postponement of the trial.

Garnishment and Attachment   A creditor who wins a court judgment against a consumer may still have trouble collecting if the consumer does not pay voluntarily. It was once common practice to have people imprisoned for not paying debts; however, this is no longer allowed.

One solution creditors use is to get a court order that forces the debtor's employer to withhold part of the debtor's wages and pay it directly to the creditor. This is called **garnishment.** The federal *Wage Garnishment Act* limits the amount that can be garnished to 25 percent of your take-home pay (i.e., after taxes and social security deductions). If you are employed by the federal government or receive other federal money, such as welfare or unemployment compensation, you cannot have your income garnished (unless the money is used to meet court-ordered child support payments). The act also prohibits employers from firing employees who have their wages garnished for a single debt. State laws may further limit and sometimes completely prohibit garnishment.

Creditors can also get possession of debtors' money or property by **attachment.** This is a court order that forces a bank to pay

THE CASE OF THE MISSED PAYMENT

Orlando buys a used car from Top Value Cars for $1,200 and signs a contract calling for monthly payments for three years. After paying $800 he misses a payment because of large doctor bills. Leaving home one morning, he finds that the car is gone. Top Value had hired someone to repossess the car in the middle of the night.

PROBLEM 30

a. Assume that Top Value sold the car for $500 and incurred expenses of $200 in the repossession and sale. Will Orlando get money back, or will he still owe money to Top Value (even though he no longer has the car)? How much is owed and to whom?

b. Is the action taken by Top Value legal? Do you think the repossession laws are fair? What arguments could creditors make on behalf of these laws? What arguments could debtors make against them?

the creditor out of a consumer's bank account, or that allows the
court to seize the consumer's property and sell it to satisfy the
debt.

Garnishment and attachment are usually used by creditors
after a court judgment has been rendered. However, some states
permit creditors to use these remedies *before* suing consumers in
order to guarantee that funds will later be available. The U.S.
Supreme Court has ruled that a consumer's wages cannot normally be garnished, nor can his or her property be attached, without first giving the consumer notice and an opportunity to be
heard in court.

**WHERE
YOU
LIVE**

When buying a car in
your community, what
procedures must you
follow to register the
car and obtain license
plates?

CARS AND THE CONSUMER

One of the most important purchases you will ever make is an
automobile. Buying, owning, maintaining, and selling an automobile involves many legal issues. Earlier in this chapter, you
learned how the law affects car owners in cases of repair fraud and
repossession. Now you will apply some concepts you have already
studied (comparison shopping, contracts, warranties, and credit)
to automobiles. You will also look briefly at the sometimes confusing but important topic of insurance.

Buying a Car

When you shop for a new or used car, you should consider at least
five general characteristics: (1) safety, (2) price, (3) quality, (4)

Never purchase a used car
without checking to de-
termine if the car is in
good condition.

warranty, and (5) fuel economy. Many consumers fail to compare safety features when shopping for a car. Safety features are important because in an average year, one out of every three motorists has an automobile accident! Federal law requires car dealers to provide a pamphlet that details safety aspects of new cars. This pamphlet includes information on acceleration and passing ability, stopping distance, and tire load. In addition, you should always check visibility from the driver's seat (i.e., check for blind spots, windshield glare in strong sunlight, positioning of inside and outside mirrors); ability to reach all controls while sitting in the driver's seat with the seat belts fastened; and protection afforded by bumpers and safety belts.

THE CASE OF THE USED CAR PURCHASE

Having saved $500 from her summer job, Sharon responded to an ad for "like-new, one-owner used cars." A salesperson for A-1 Used Cars watched Sharon wander around the lot until she was attracted to a sharp-looking, late-model compact car. Sharon told the salesperson that this car looked just right for her. He replied, "You've made a good choice. This is an excellent car. It will give you many years of good service."

Although the sticker price was $1,550, the salesperson thought that he might be able to get her a $50 discount because she was "a nice young kid getting her first car." After conferring with the sales manager, he told her that she could have the car for $1,500 and that the dealer could arrange to finance the car and sell her all necessary insurance.

Sharon knew that she'd need a loan, and her parents had warned her that insurance was required by law. Her excitement increased as it appeared that all her problems could be solved in one stop.

The salesperson told her that A-1 would make any repairs to the engine, not caused by her misuse, for 30 days or 10,000 miles, whichever came first. Now she even felt confident about using all of her savings as a down payment. After all, what repair bills could she have with such a nice car accompanied by a terrific warranty?

PROBLEM 31

a. Make a list of things Sharon should have done or thought about before going to A-1.

b. Make a list of things she should have done at A-1 before agreeing to buy the car.

c. Did the seller make any promises to her? Did he say anything that could be considered puffing?

> **d.** What are the advantages and disadvantages of having the dealer provide Sharon with financing and insurance?
>
> **e.** Taking into account the lists you've made, roleplay Sharon's encounter with the salesperson.

When you shop for a car, remember that virtually no one pays the sticker price for a new or used car. Discounts are quite common. The size of the discount depends on the time of year, your negotiating ability, special sales, manufacturer's bonuses, rebates, and other factors.

PROBLEM 32

In addition to the purchase price, what other costs should you consider in deciding to purchase a car? Where is information available about each of these costs?

You should compare fuel economy, warranties, and the dealer's capability to make repairs the same way you compare

The U.S. Environmental Protection Agency publishes a booklet that lists average fuel economy for all passenger cars and trucks.

safety features and price. Many new cars have warranties covering most parts, except batteries and tires, against defects for 12,000 miles or 12 months, whichever comes first. Some manufacturers warrant the engine and drive train for a longer period. Other manufacturers offer a warranty as part of the purchase price but also make available an extended warranty (actually a service contract) for an additional price. Warranties vary, so be certain that you read and fully understand exactly what protections the warranty provides.

In some instances, used cars come with warranties. The Federal Trade Commission now requires used car dealers to place a large sticker — a "Buyer's Guide" — in the window of every vehicle offered for sale. The sticker must tell you whether the vehicle comes with an express warranty. If so, the sticker must tell you what the warranty includes. If the sticker says the car comes "as is," this means no warranty is provided. Finally, the sticker will advise you to get all promises in writing and to have the car inspected by a mechanic before you buy it.

Although car warranties are now easier to read and protections have been expanded, there are still time or mileage limits (or both) to the warranties. Also, a warranty may become ineffective if you fail to perform proper maintenance.

Always be sure the warranty and any additional promises are in writing. Keep these papers in a safe place.

Financing a Car

Most new car buyers and many used car buyers make their purchases on credit. Buyers may select the length of the repayment period, which may be as long as four years. The longer the repayment period, the lower the monthly payments will be (but a larger sum will have to be paid in interest). Figure 19 shows the total interest charges on a $4,000 loan, depending on the interest rate and the length of the repayment period. Interest rates are sometimes lower than 11 percent or higher than 12 percent.

FIGURE 19   Interest on a $4,000 Loan

	APR	LENGTH OF LOAN	MONTHLY PAYMENT	TOTAL FINANCE CHARGE
Creditor A	11%	3 years	$131	$ 716
Creditor B	11%	4 years	$103	$ 962
Creditor C	12%	3 years	$133	$ 783
Creditor D	12%	4 years	$105	$1,056

PROBLEM 33

Sam is buying a $5,000 car. He can make a down payment of $1,000 and needs to borrow the remaining $4,000. Assume that credit is available only from the four sources listed in Figure 19.

a. What is the total cost of the $5,000 car, using each of the loans?

b. If Sam decides to borrow, which credit arrangement would be least expensive? Which would be most desirable? Explain your answer.

Automobile financing is usually available from the following sources: car dealers, banks, credit unions, and finance companies. When comparing finance charges among lenders, make certain that the same down payment and repayment periods are used for each loan. In comparing terms, you'll mostly be concerned with the Annual Percentage Rate. However, you should also read all of the terms carefully so that you can answer such questions as:

1. Will there be a refund of finance charges if the loan is repaid ahead of schedule?

2. Will there be fair warning in the event of a repossession?

3. Is there a penalty for late payments? If so, how much?

4. Will all payments immediately become due if a payment is missed?

> **ADVICE ON BUYING AUTO INSURANCE**
>
> ■ Learn about the various types of insurance and comparison shop before making a decision.
> ■ Ask insurance agents several questions about the coverage (e.g., what is the company policy about raising rates if you have an accident?). Insist on clear answers.
> ■ Find out if there are any special discounts for people who've had driver's training or a good safety record. Young people are often required to pay higher insurance premiums.
> ■ Check to see which company charges less if young people are insured under the parents' policy and not issued a separate policy.

Insuring a Car

Auto **insurance** protects you against possible losses you can't afford. Insurance cannot prevent losses, but it can provide some compensation. Insurance can pay for the cost of repairing your car, medical bills, lost wages, and pain and suffering of those injured in an accident.

When you buy insurance, you can choose from various coverage combinations. Coverage depends on the kind of protection you want and how much you can afford to pay. Common coverages include liability, medical, collision, comprehensive, uninsured motorist, and no-fault.

Liability insurance pays for injuries to other people and property if you are responsible for the accident. Liability coverage pays for damages up to, but no more than, the limits of the policy. If injuries and property damages are greater than the policy limits, the person at fault will have to pay the difference. Policies gen-

Does your state require insurance coverage on all registered cars? If so, how much insurance must be carried? How much is insurance likely to cost a 17-year-old youth in your area?

erally have three limits: (1) on bodily injury per person, (2) on bodily injury per accident, and (3) on property damage per accident. For example, a "10/20/5" policy would pay up to $10,000 per person for personal injury, $20,000 per accident for personal injury, and $5,000 per accident for property damage. Accidents sometimes result in lawsuits where injured people are awarded damages of $100,000 or more. Therefore, careful consideration should be given to how much insurance a person carries. Also, the insurance company usually promises to defend any lawsuit resulting from an accident.

THE CASE OF THE NONSTOP CAR

Pulling left into the outside lane to pass a slow-moving truck, Larry saw the traffic light ahead turn yellow. "If I step on it, I'll make this light," he thought. Just then, an oncoming car made a left-hand turn in front of him. Larry hit the brakes. Nothing happened. Two seconds later, pinned against the steering wheel, he saw the other driver, Charles, stagger out of the car, bleeding and holding his shoulder in pain.

The kind of insurance policies each driver had, or didn't have, will determine the insurance benefits, if any, they will receive.

PROBLEM 34

Who should be responsible for paying for the medical bills and car repairs resulting from this accident? In most cases, who pays for repairs resulting from auto accidents?

Medical coverage pays for your own medical expenses resulting from accidents involving your car or the car you're driving. It also pays the medical expenses of any passengers in your car, no matter who is at fault. The amount of medical benefits, and the kind of medical costs (e.g., hospital bills, office visits), are limited in the policy. For example, medical coverage may be limited to $1,000 per person injured.

Collision coverage pays for accident damage to your own car. This is true, even if the collision was your fault. Collision coverage usually pays an amount up to the actual value of the car (not its replacement by a new car). You can lower the cost of collision insurance by including a *deductible*. This is an amount that you pay toward repairs before the insurance pays anything. For example, $100 deductible means that if there are $250 in damages, the insurance company will pay $150 and you will pay $100. The greater the deductible, the less costly the insurance.

Comprehensive coverage protects you against damage or loss to your car from causes other than collision. For example, damages due to vandalism, fire, or theft are covered under the comprehensive section of your policy. Read your policy carefully to determine whether valuables in your car, such as a tape deck, are covered in case of theft. Insurance policies sometimes include, usually at an extra charge, coverage for towing costs or car rental costs. These coverages are subject to certain limits and conditions, so read your policy carefully.

Uninsured motorist coverage protects you from drivers who don't have insurance. It does this by paying for the personal injuries or damage they cause. Be sure to find out how much your policy pays for personal injuries caused by an uninsured motorist, and, in the event you don't have collision coverage, whether it pays for damages to your car. Uninsured motorist coverage is usually an inexpensive and worthwhile addition to your policy.

No-fault insurance pays you up to a certain amount for injuries you receive in an accident, regardless of fault. With liability insurance, your company pays the other driver only if you were at fault. No-fault laws allow settlement of these claims without the delay and expense of determining fault in a court case. No-fault benefits are limited (e.g., $5,000 or $10,000) and are usually only for personal injuries. When injuries are greater than the no-fault limits, the injured person can still sue the other party. Some states now require no-fault insurance.

PROBLEM 35

Read the Case of the Nonstop Car. Assume that the accident happened in a state without no-fault insurance and that both Larry and Charles had full insurance coverage. Also assume that Larry was at fault.

a. Whose insurance company pays for Charles's hospital and car repair bills?

b. Whose insurance company pays for Larry's hospital and car repair?

c. What do you think would happen if the damages to Charles were greater than the limits of Larry's policy (i.e., Charles has personal injury damage of $200,000, and Larry's policy limit is $100,000)?

PROBLEM 36

Assume that the insurance policy you have on your new car includes collision insurance with a $250 deductible. Answer the following questions.

a. Skidding off an icy road into a guard rail, you dent your bumper. The repair cost is $200. Who has to pay for this damage?

b. Your fender is smashed, and the repair cost is $1,000. Who has to pay in this situation?

c. After you have had your car for six years, its market value is only $600. If the state doesn't require collision insurance, should you continue to take it out? Why?

What to Do in Case of an Accident

If you are involved in an accident, there are certain important things to do and not to do. Many of these tasks are based on common sense, but accidents can be emotionally upsetting and physically dangerous, so it is best to think about how to handle these problems ahead of time.

First, check to see if there are any injuries. Then, call the police and set up a system of routing the traffic around the automobiles. All drivers involved in the accident should exchange names, addresses, and phone numbers; driver's license numbers and registration numbers; make, model, and year of each car; name, address, and phone number of insurance agents; and names and phone numbers of any witnesses (or at least their license plate numbers so you can locate them later if needed).

Do not tell people the extent of your insurance; *do not* confess guilt; *do not* say your insurance company will take care of everything; *do not* sign any paper that says you were not injured, because some auto accident injuries are not noticeable for several days.

What should you do if you're involved in an auto accident?

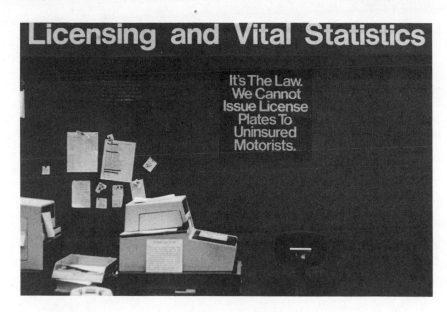

Licensing and Vital Statistics

It's The Law. We Cannot Issue License Plates To Uninsured Motorists.

Many states require that licensed drivers carry auto insurance.

Record the names and badge numbers of any police officers responding to the accident. The police may make notes as to the circumstances surrounding the accident, but you should also keep a record of this information. Write down all important information as soon as possible after the accident. Do it while your memory is still fresh, but don't give this to anyone except your insurance agent or attorney.

After an accident, contact your insurance company as soon as possible. Keep a copy of your insurance agent's name and phone number in your glove compartment. After speaking with your agent, you should also send a registered letter, including your policy number, fully describing the accident to your insurance company. Failure to notify your company within a certain limited period of time may allow the company to deny all financial responsibility.

Let your insurance agent handle calls and letters from other parties involved. If the accident involves personal injury or death, it may be wise to have a lawyer handle all calls and letters.

PROBLEM 37

On a winter's evening after dinner, your car is hit in the right rear fender. The accident occurred as you proceeded through an intersection on a yellow light. No one seems to be injured. In speaking with the driver of the other car, you notice that his eyes are bloodshot.

a. Make a list of all the information about this accident that you would need in order to write a thorough report.

b. Roleplay a meeting between the two drivers at the scene of the accident.

c. Making reasonable assumptions about information you need but that has not been given, draft a letter to your insurance company about your accident.

four
FAMILY
LAW

The family is the basic unit of our society. It is the most intimate and important of all social groups. Most people consider family life a private matter, and in many ways it is. If you argue with your brother or decide to have 10 children, the law won't interfere. All the same, the law is very much a part of family life.

Every time a birth, a death, a marriage, or a divorce takes place, the law is involved. Every state has laws affecting the family. For example, state laws set requirements that must be met before anyone can be married. Likewise, every state has laws that outline the basic rights and duties of family members. Other laws govern areas such as adoption, alimony, child care, custody, divorce, and family support.

When it comes to identifying a family, most of us would say we know one when we see one. We are surrounded by families wherever we go, and most of us live in family settings. However, because families come in all shapes and sizes, defining the term *family* is sometimes difficult.

Legally, the word *family* is used to describe many relationships: parents and children; people related by blood, marriage, or adoption; a group of people living together in a single group, sharing living space and housekeeping. Because the word *family* does not have a precise meaning, most laws include a definition of the term when they use it. For example, zoning laws that set aside certain areas for single-family homes define family one way. Laws involving insurance, social security, or inheritance define family in other ways.

PROBLEM 1

Examine the photos at the beginning of this chapter. For each photo, answer the following questions:

a. Is this a family? Why or why not?

b. Is this a common living arrangement?

c. What are the characteristics of a family? How would you define the term *family*?

d. How does the law affect each living arrangement?

THE CHANGING AMERICAN FAMILY

The American family has changed dramatically during the past 80 years. One way in which the family has changed is its size. The family has gotten smaller. In 1900, the average family size was 5.7 persons. By 1985, the average family had shrunk to 2.8 persons. Today, couples are having fewer children or, in some cases, no children at all.

Another reason families have changed is because women's roles have changed. During the early part of this century, most women did not work outside of the home. Today, however, over 60 percent of all married women hold jobs outside of the home. Now, most families are two-income families.

Single-parent families are yet another area of change. During the last decade, the number of one-parent families has doubled. There are two reasons for this. First, the number of divorces is at an all-time high. Second, there are a lot more unwed parents.

Americans have always been people on the move. Today's families are perhaps more mobile than ever. New jobs, new homes, and new life-styles can all result in moves from one community to another. Families are often spread across the country.

There are many different styles of family living. It is clear that families are changing. These changes have caused problems and conflicts that often involve the law. Nevertheless, the family is the bedrock of our society and it will no doubt continue to adapt and prosper.

FIGURE 20   Changes in American Families, 1970–1980

In One Decade—
10 Ways Families Have Changed

	1970	Latest		Percent Change
Marriages performed	2,159,000	2,317,000	Up	7.3%
Divorces granted	708,000	1,170,000	Up	65.3%
Married couples	44,728,000	47,662,000	Up	6.6%
Unmarried couples	523,000	1,346,000	Up	157.4%
Persons living alone	10,851,000	17,202,000	Up	58.5%
Married couples with children	25,541,000	24,625,000	Down	3.6%
Children living with two parents	58,926,000	48,295,000	Down	18.0%
Children living with one parent	8,230,000	11,528,000	Up	40.1%
Average size of household	3.3	2.8	Down	15.2%
Families with both husband and wife working	20,327,000	24,253,000	Up	19.3%

Reprinted from *"U.S. News & World Report"* copyright, 1980, U.S News and World Report, Inc.

PROBLEM 2

a. Discuss how the family has changed over the past 50 years. Discuss how your family has changed. Has it gotten bigger or smaller? Has it moved around more or less?

b. How many children did your grandparents have? How many children do your parents have? How many children would you like to have?

c. Where did your grandparents live? Where do your parents live? How often did they move during their lives?

d. Did both your grandparents hold jobs outside of the home? Do both your parents hold jobs outside of the home?

e. What do you think families will be like in the future?

PROBLEM 3

The law reflects the idea that marriage and the family are essential to the strength of society. As a result, the law affects families and family life. Before studying family law, here is a survey that asks for your ideas about law and the family. Read each statement, then decide whether you strongly agree (SA), agree (A), disagree (D), strongly disagree (SD), or are undecided (U) with each of the statements. Discuss your answers.

a. Getting married should be made harder for a couple.

b. Wives and husbands should have an equal say about all decisions in their marriage.

c. Adopted children have a right to know who their natural parents are.

d. Mothers with small children should not work outside the home.

e. All children should be required to go to school until age 18.

f. Parents should be able to discipline their children in any way they see fit.

g. Getting divorced should be made harder.

h. Spouse abuse should be a crime.

i. Grown children should be required to support their parents when they become elderly or disabled.

j. When a women gets married, she should keep her own name.

k. Husbands and wives should own everything equally regardless of who earns it or pays for it.

l. If parents get divorced, their children are better off living part-time with each parent.

MARRIAGE

Marriage is a personal, social, religious, economic, and legal relationship. Over 90 percent of all Americans will be married at some time during their lives. Marriage is the first step toward forming a new family. The family is the basic unit of our society. As a result, the law is very much involved in family life. This section examines the legal aspects of marriage. You will learn the steps that one must follow to get married, the requirements for a legal marriage, and the difference between formal and common-law marriage.

PROBLEM 4

a. Marriage involves many considerations. How important is each of the following to a successful marriage? Happiness, children, money, sexual relations, religion, common interests, romance, relationships with in-laws, faithfulness, age differences. Rank these considerations in order of importance. Are there any other factors that are important to a successful marriage?

b. Make a list of all the questions you would ask yourself before deciding to get married. Do any of these questions involve the law?

c. If you were getting married within the next six months, what social, religious, and legal arrangements would you have to make?

In legal terms, marriage is a **contract** between two persons who agree to live together as husband and wife. Marriage creates legal rights and duties for each partner. However, marriage is different from other contracts in several important ways. The marriage contract involves three parties: the husband, the wife, and the state. For this reason, anyone who wants to get married must meet certain legal requirements.

In the United States, marriage laws are set by the individual states. The legal rules vary from state to state. However, all states agree on the following requirements:

■ **Age.** A couple must be old enough to get married. Usually, females must be 16 and males 18. Some states allow younger couples to get married if their parents consent. Some states also allow marriage below the minimum age if the female is pregnant.

■ **Relationship.** Every state forbids marriage between close relatives. A person cannot marry his or her parent, child, grandparent, grandchild, brother, sister, uncle, aunt, niece, or nephew. Many states also prohibit marriages between first cousins. Marrying or having sexual relations with a close relative is a crime known as **incest.**

■ **Two people.** Marriage is between two persons only. Marrying someone who is already married is illegal. Having more than one husband or wife is a crime known as **bigamy.**

■ **Man and woman.** Marriage is a relationship between a man and a woman. Marriages between two persons of the same sex are illegal.

■ **Consent.** Both persons must agree to the marriage. No one can be forced to marry someone against his or her will. For example, no one can be forced to marry someone at gunpoint.

As a general rule, if a marriage is legal in one state, it will be recognized as legal in all other states. However, if a couple goes through a wedding ceremony without meeting the requirements for a legal marriage, the marriage may be annulled. **Annulment** is a court order that the marriage never existed. It is different from a **divorce**, which is a court order that ends a valid marriage. In other words, a divorce means that a man and woman are no longer husband and wife. An annulment means that a man and a woman were never husband and wife.

The grounds for annulment vary from state to state, but common reasons for an annulment include the following:

■ **Age.** The couple was too young to get married.

■ **Bigamy.** One spouse was already married.

■ **Fraud.** One spouse lied to the other about an important matter, such as the desire to have children.

■ **Lack of consent.** One spouse was forced to marry against his or her will, was too drunk to understand that a wedding was taking place, or was insane.

PROBLEM 5

Read Figure 21, a marriage license application. Then answer the following questions:

a. Can William and Myra be legally married in Colorado? Why or why not?

b. Why do you think states make rules about marriage?

c. Explain the difference between an annulment and a divorce.

d. How old do you think someone should be before getting married? Do you think that allowing females to marry at an earlier age than males is fair? Why or why not?

Getting Married

To get legally married, a couple will have to follow certain steps. These steps usually include a blood test, a marriage license, a waiting period, and a wedding ceremony.

Blood Test   Most states require a couple to have a blood test for venereal disease (VD) before getting married. A few states also require a physical examination. These tests make the couple aware of any medical problems that may affect their marriage.

Marriage License   All states require a marriage license. To apply for a marriage license, the couple will be asked to provide certain information, such as proof of age and a copy of their blood test results. They will then have to swear to the truth of the information and pay a small fee.

Waiting Period   After applying for a marriage license, there is often a short waiting period before the couple can pick it up. In some states, there is another waiting period between getting the license and the marriage ceremony. These waiting periods help ensure that people are serious about marriage. For example, the waiting period could prevent someone from getting married as a joke or while they were intoxicated.

Wedding Ceremony   A wedding ceremony is required for a valid marriage. This can be either a religious or a civil ceremony. Weddings may be conducted by public officials such as judges or jus-

FIGURE 21   Marriage License Application

APPLICATION FOR A MARRIAGE LICENSE

TO THE CLERK OF THE CIRCUIT COURT:

I hereby make application for Marriage License, to be issued in accordance with the Laws of this state, under penalties of perjury, the following statement, to wit:

Male's Name   Female's Name
William Halder   Myra Gambrell

Age 16   Age 15

Date of Birth 9/17/64   Date of Birth 5/8/65

Birthplace   Colorado   Birthplace   Louisiana
                State   State

Residence   Residence
6220 Clay Street   311 Mountain View Drive

Denver, Colorado   Boulder, Colorado

Marital Status: Marital Status
Single _____✓_____   Single _____✓_____

Widowed _____   Widowed _____

Divorced _____   Divorced _____

(If previously married list exact date of death and place or exact date of divorce decree and where granted for all previous marriages)

Relationship, if any ___NONE_____

Signature of person consenting if male is a minor

_____
(Parent or Guardian)

Signature of person consenting if female is a minor

_____
(Parent or Guardian)

_____
(Applicant)

Sworn to and subscribed before me this ____ day of _____, A.D., 19__.

Check here if License is to be   _____
mailed:
To one of the contracting   Clerk of the Court or other
parties   Comparable Official
To Minister of the Gospel   County of _____

_____   State of _____
(Give name and mailing address)   (Give complete address and affix
                                        Court Seal)

**WHERE
YOU
LIVE**

Where does a person obtain a marriage license in your state? Is a physical exam or a blood test required? Is there a waiting period before you can get married? If so, how long is it?

tices of the peace. The law does not require any set form for the wedding ceremony. However, to be legally married, each person must state that he or she agrees to marry before an official and a witness. Once the wedding ceremony has been completed, the couple will receive a marriage certificate. See Figure 22 for an example.

Laws place many restrictions on marriage. Laws prescribe who can marry, what obligations are created by marriage, and how marriage can be ended. However, states cannot prohibit marriage between healthy adults without a good reason.

Customs and traditions also play a large role in marriage. For example, most marriages in the United States take place in a church or synagogue. In America, religious and cultural traditions are an important part of married life. However, these customs and traditions sometimes run afoul of the law. The following cases will help you understand why government regulates marriage and which regulations are appropriate.

FIGURE 22   **Sample Marriage Certificate**

VOID-SAMPLE ONLY

State of Alaska
Certificate of Marriage

I Hereby Certify That:

Samuel N. Trout
Bridegroom   and   _Dolly Varden_
Bride

of _Minto_   of _Nome_

Were United by Me in

Holy Matrimony

In Accordance with the Laws of the State of Alaska

on the _15th_ day of _January_ 19XX, at _Nome_, Alaska

Witnesses   Officiant

Signature _____   Signature _____
Signature _____   Official Title _MINISTER_

THE CASE OF REYNOLDS v. THE UNITED STATES

Today, the Mormon Church condemns polygamy and excommunicates members who espouse it. However, in 1878 George Reynolds, a Mormon living in the Utah territory, was arrested and charged with the crime of bigamy. At the time, the Mormon religion regarded plural marriages as a religious obligation. Mormons then believed that refusal to practice polygamy when circumstances permitted would lead to "damnation in the life to come." Reynolds argued that the antibigamy law violated his constitutional right to freedom of religion. After his conviction, he appealed his case to the U.S. Supreme Court. How would you decide this case? Why?

In the *Reynolds* case, the Supreme Court upheld the antibigamy law. It ruled that religious *belief* cannot justify an *illegal act*. Reynolds could believe anything he wanted, but he could not put into practice a belief that society condemned. The Court reasoned that no one would assume, for example, that human sacrifices could be justified as a religious practice.

THE CASE OF LOVING v. VIRGINIA

In 1958, Harvey Loving, a white man, and Diana Jeter, a black woman, decided to get married. Both legal residents of Virginia, they traveled to Washington, D.C., to get around a Virginia law forbidding marriage between people of different races. After their marriage, they returned to Virginia, where they were arrested and charged with violating the ban on interracial marriages. The Lovings pleaded guilty and were sentenced to one year in jail. The judge, however, suspended the sentence on the condition that the Lovings leave Virginia and not return for 25 years. The Lovings moved to Washington, D.C., but appealed their case to the U.S. Supreme Court. They asked that the law against interracial marriages be declared unconstitutional.

PROBLEM 6

a. What happened in the *Loving* case? Why was the couple arrested?

b. What arguments do you think the state made in favor of the law? What arguments do you think the Lovings made against the law?

c. How would you decide this case? Explain your answer.

d. Some marriage regulations are appropriate, and others are not. Should the state regulate marriage based on age, mental capacity, health, religion, race, or other factors? Explain your answer.

Before getting married, the couple must fulfill the legal requirements set by the state.

Common-Law Marriage

> ### THE CASE OF THE COMMON-LAW MARRIAGE
>
> Kim Johnson and Arthur Little move in together and live as husband and wife. They never obtain a marriage license or have a formal marriage ceremony, but Kim signs her name as Mrs. Kim Little. Are Kim and Arthur legally married? If they split up, can either of them legally marry someone else without first getting a divorce?

Common-law marriage is a marriage without a blood test, a license, or a wedding ceremony. It is created when two people agree to be married, hold themselves out to the public as husband and wife, and live together as if married. Only the District of Columbia and 13 states — Alabama, Colorado, Georgia, Idaho, Iowa, Kansas, Montana, Ohio, Oklahoma, Pennsylvania, Rhode Island, South Carolina, and Texas — allow common-law marriage.

Some states require a couple to live together for a certain number of years before "the knot" is legally tied. In other states, people could be married in a matter of days if they actually agree to be married (now, not sometime in the future), live together, and hold themselves out as husband and wife. If a couple decides to split up after entering into a common-law marriage, they must get a divorce before either may remarry. Someone who remarries without first getting a divorce can be charged with the crime of **bigamy.**

States that do not allow common-law marriages will still recognize such a marriage if it took place in one of the states listed above. Also, the children of a common-law marriage are **legitimate** and have the same rights and duties as other children.

PROBLEM 7

Rick Rockstar and his girlfriend, Blondie, live together in the mountains of Montana. They talk about having a wedding but never get around to it. Anyway they are in love and think it is just as simple to tell people that they are married. They buy a house, open a joint bank account, and are known everywhere as Mr. and Mrs. Rockstar. The situation is fine for a while, but eventually Rick gets bored and leaves. He soon finds a new girlfriend, Pinkie. Being from a traditional background, Pinkie insists that they get married right away.

a. What are the requirements of a common-law marriage?

b. Do Rick and Blondie have a valid common-law marriage? Why or why not?

c. If Rick and Blondie had lived together in Utah instead of Montana, would they have a valid common-law marriage?

d. Can Rick marry Pinkie? Why or why not?

WHERE YOU LIVE

Does your state allow common-law marriage? If so, how long must a couple live together to make the common-law marriage valid?

HUSBANDS AND WIVES

In the traditional marriage the husband was the provider, and the wife was the homemaker. As a result, the husband was considered the head of the household. He had a duty to support his wife and children. In return for this support, he was entitled to his wife's household services and companionship. The law reflected this traditional view by giving husbands the legal right to make decisions such as where the family would live, how money would be spent, and other important matters.

Over the last 20 years, the traditional marriage has been challenged by economic and social changes in our society. Today, the role of the husband as the sole breadwinner and the wife as the sole homemaker has changed. Married women now play a large role in the ranks of the employed, and responsibilities are divided more equitably within the family. The law is also changing to reflect the idea that marriage is a partnership between equals.

Financial Responsibilities

The law now requires husbands and wives to support one another in accordance with their respective needs and abilities. Many states require both spouses to pay for necessary family items purchased by either of them. However, some states retain the traditional rule that the husband has a legal duty to provide his wife with food, clothing, shelter, medical care, and other **necessities.** If the husband fails to provide such essentials, the wife can purchase the necessary items and make her husband pay for them. At the same time, the wife has no legal duty to pay her husband's bills.

In addition to the basic necessities, some courts require the husband to maintain the family in accordance with his economic position. In general, however, a woman can not obligate her husband to pay for luxury items bought without his knowledge.

The law regarding ownership of marital property has also changed. At one time, the law considered a husband and wife as one person. This meant the wife had no property rights. Any money or property a woman owned before marriage or acquired during marriage became the property of her husband. In 1887, the *Married Women's Property Act* changed the law. This act gave married women the right to own and control their own property.

Today, any property owned by either spouse before the marriage remains the property of that person throughout the marriage. In most states, any property acquired during the marriage belongs to the person who acquired it. Under this **separate property** system, whoever earns it, pays for it, is given it, or has title to it is considered to own it. Husbands and wives may make gifts to

THE CASE OF THE UNPAID BILLS

Bryan and Kelly have been married for five years. Both work, and each earns about $12,000 per year. They have problems paying their bills and often fight over money. Kelly goes shopping and charges groceries, clothes for the children, and a stereo costing over $400. Bryan gets angry and tells Kelly that he is not paying for anything.

PROBLEM 8

a. Is Bryan responsible for the debts of his wife?

b. Suppose Bryan were out of work and charged the previously mentioned items without telling his wife. Would she have to pay?

c. Do you agree or disagree with the following statement? "Husbands should be required to support their wives, but wives should not have to support their husbands." Explain your answer.

each other or place property, such as bank accounts, real estate, or automobiles, in both names. When they do this, the property is considered to be **joint property** of both spouses.

Eight states — Arizona, California, Idaho, Louisiana, Nevada, New Mexico, Texas, and Washington — have a **community property** system derived from French and Spanish law. Under this system, all property acquired during the marriage belongs equally to the husband and wife. If the marriage breaks up, either by death or divorce, each spouse is entitled to one-half of all the property acquired during the marriage.

Contrast the community property system with the separate property system by considering the case of a married woman who does not work outside the home. In a community property state, the wife owns half of the combined wealth of the couple, including the income of her husband. In a separate property state, the wife owns only that property which she herself acquires or which is acquired in the name of both the husband and the wife.

PROBLEM 9

a. Lloyd and Gloria were married four months ago. Before they were married, Gloria inherited a piece of land from her grandfather. Now that they are married, to whom does the land belong?

b. Frances and Leon are married and have two children. Frances is an architect making $30,000 a year. Leon is an artist who earns very little. Frances uses some of her income to buy a vaction home. If Frances and Leon split up, who owns the vacation home in a community property state? In a separate property state?

c. Which is fairer: a separate property or a community property system? Why?

Decisions in a Marriage

Married life involves many decisions and responsibilities. Couples need to cooperate, share, and work out the details of married life. How will housework be divided? Who will take care of the money? Will the couple have children? If they do, how will they be raised?

Today, most couples view marriage as a partnership. However, in the past, the husband was considered the head of the household. The law gave the husband the right to make most of the decisions. For example, the husband could decide where the couple would live and how his wife spent her time. When a woman married, everything she owned became her husband's property. A woman could not buy property or borrow money without her husband's permission. In return, the husband was expected to support and protect his wife and children.

Marriage is viewed differently today. More than half of all married women now hold jobs outside of the home. Women can do anything they want with their money and property. There is a greater sharing of household chores and child care. Despite these changes, however, married life still involves many decisions:

■ Will a woman take her husband's name or keep her own?

■ Will the couple have children, and if so, how many?

■ Which last name will the children use: the husband's, the wife's, or a combination of both names?

■ How will the children be raised?

■ Where will the couple live?

■ Will one spouse be willing to move if the other is offered a job in another city?

■ How will the housework be divided?

■ How will the money be handled? Will the husband and the wife pool their incomes or keep them separate?

■ How will the couple settle differences over religion or life-style?

THE CASE OF THE NAME CHANGE

Rose Palermo and Walter Dunn are getting married. A successful businesswoman, Rose would like to keep her maiden name, but someone tells her that this is against the law. What does the law require?

In most matters, husbands and wives are free to make their own decisions and work out their own problems. Except in rare cases, the law does not interfere in everyday family life. You should, however, know a few legal rules.

Name Change   Women have traditionally used their husbands' names as a matter of social custom. However, a woman is not legally required to do so. Legally, a woman can keep her maiden name, take her husband's name in combination with her own (e.g., Smith-Larkin) or make the traditional choice: use her husband's name.

Support   In most states, the husband still has the legal duty to support his wife and children. However, the law is changing to make the duty of support more equal. Today, many states require the husband and wife to pay for necessary family items bought by either of them. For more information about support, see page 204.

Privileged Communications   The law considers certain relationships private and confidential. For example, attorney-client, doctor-patient, and husband-wife relationships are considered privileged. This means that neither person can be forced to disclose information received as part of the relationship. At common law, a husband cannot be forced to testify against her husband. In 1980, the Supreme Court decided that one spouse could *voluntarily* testify against another in federal criminal prosecutions. One spouse can also testify against the other under other circumstances, for example, if a husband abuses his wife or children.

Spouse Abuse   Beating or assaulting one's spouse is illegal. Spouse abuse does occur, but beating anyone including one's husband or wife is a crime. For more information about spouse abuse, see page 208.

Inheritance   If a husband or wife dies, the other spouse is automatically entitled to a share of the deceased's estate. This amount varies from one-third to one-half depending on state law. One spouse may will to the other more than the statutory share, but not less. Even if a spouse is left out of a will, state law requires the survivor to receive a portion of the estate.

PROBLEM 10

Consider each of the following statements and decide whether you agree or disagree with it. In each case, discuss your answer.

a. Wives should take care of the house and children, and husbands should provide the family income.

How are the roles of women and men changing in our society?

b. When a woman gets married, she should keep her own name and not change it to that of her husband.

c. Married women should work only if they have no young children.

d. The husband should have the sole right to choose where the family will live.

e. Husbands and wives should own everything equally, regardless of who earns it or pays for it.

PROBLEM 11

a. What are some important decisions that families have to make?

b. Kevin Dunn is in an auto accident with a delivery truck. At the hospital, he tells his wife, Rita, that the accident was all his fault. Later, in a lawsuit for damages resulting from the accident, the delivery company subpoenas Rita to testify about Kevin's statements at the hospital. Does Rita have to testify against her husband?

c. Howard argued with his wife, Jean, for years. In a fit of anger, he rewrites his will, leaving his entire fortune to charity. If Howard dies, will Jean be left with nothing? Explain your answer.

Spouse Abuse

Spouse abuse is a serious problem. It occurs when one spouse beats or physically assaults the other. Women sometimes assault their husbands, but most cases involve men abusing their wives. Spouse abuse takes place in all kinds of families. It occurs among all ethnic, racial, and economic groups. In the past, spouse abuse victims were often afraid to talk about the problem. Today, however, family violence is getting lots of attention.

How should spouse abuse be handled? Some people believe that family life is a private matter and that legal interference can make things worse. They say that abused women are unlikely to testify when it comes time for trial. They also argue that arrests are a waste of time because most women don't want their husbands sent to jail. They just don't want to be beaten.

On the other hand, critics say that women are often too embarrassed or afraid to call the police. They claim some police don't take spouse abuse seriously. They say that police often won't make an arrest or even take the victim out of the home to a safe place. Critics also charge that courts are too lenient on those accused of spouse abuse.

To help abused spouses, many changes have been proposed. These include training police to be sensitive to the problems of abused women, setting up shelters for abused women and their children, and requiring criminal prosecution of abusers.

Today, spouse abuse cases are handled differently from area to area. Many states try to keep abuse cases out of court. Others have set up special programs to help battered women. One new method for dealing with spouse abuse is family mediation. Family mediators work with couples to help them solve their disagreements. However, an abused spouse can always take the following steps:

■ **Move out.** An abused woman can move out of her house. The law does not require her to stay in a home where she is being beaten. However, she should tell someone (a friend or relative) why she is leaving. This will prevent the husband from charging her with abandonment.

■ **Seek counseling.** Most places have counseling programs for people with marriage problems. Many larger cities also have special programs for battered women. These programs may have shelters where a woman and her children can live temporarily. To find a counseling program or shelter in your community, look under Social Services in the Yellow Pages of your phone book.

■ **Obtain a protective order.** Getting a court order forbidding the abusing spouse from harming his or her mate is sometimes possible. Courts may order the abuser to (1) stop the abuse, (2) leave his or her spouse alone, (3) move out of the house, (4) get counseling, or (5) do something else. Violating a court order is considered **contempt of court.** A person in contempt of court can be jailed or fined.

■ **Call the police.** Assaulting one's spouse is a crime. Police called in to stop a family fight can arrest the abuser. Sometimes police simply break things up and urge the couple to "kiss and make up." Many women have complained about this approach. As a result, some police departments give their officers special training in this

210 Street Law

WHERE YOU LIVE

What programs are available in your community to help abused women? Are there facilities where abused women can go if they decide to leave home?

area. Even if the police don't make an arrest, a police report can help back up a later legal action such as divorce or protective order. Moreover, a woman can still file charges and testify against a husband accused of injuring her.

■ **Get a divorce.** An abused spouse can seek a divorce or legal separation. If the couple is legally separated, the abusing spouse has no right to enter his wife's home. To obtain information about divorce, contact a legal aid office, family court, bar association, or women's organization.

A CASE OF SPOUSE ABUSE

Late one night, you hear screams and the sounds of crashing furniture coming from the apartment next door. You look out in the hall and see your neighbor, Mrs. Darwin, being slapped and punched by her husband. Before she can get away, Mr. Darwin pulls her back in and slams the door. You hear breaking glass and more screams. You know that Mr. Darwin has a drinking problem. You also know that this isn't the first time he has beaten his wife.

PROBLEM 12

a. If you were the neighbor in the case above, what would you do? Would you call the police? If you would, what would you tell them? If you wouldn't call the police, explain why not.
b. Suppose you are a police officer and you receive a call that a man is beating his wife. When you and your partner arrive at the Darwins, you find that Mrs. Darwin is cut, bruised, and obviously beaten up. Roleplay the encounter between the Darwins and the police.
c. As the police, decide what you should do in this situation. Would you question the couple? Would you arrest the husband? Would you take the wife out of the house?
d. As the husband, decide how you would react to the police in this situation. As the wife, decide how you would react. Would you press charges against your husband? Would you stay in the home? Would you do something else?
e. Suppose you are a judge confronted with the Darwin case. Would you send Mr. Darwin to jail? Would you take some other action?
f. Besides calling the police, what are some things Mrs. Darwin could do about her problem?

PROBLEM 13

In most states, a husband may not be criminally prosecuted for raping his own wife.

a. What do you think are the reasons behind this law? Should the law be changed or kept as it is?

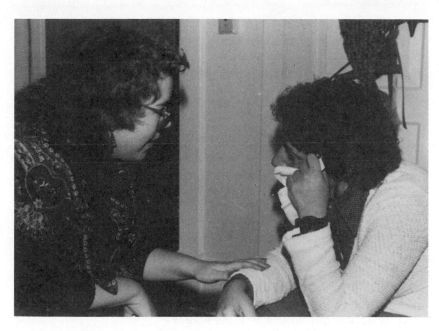

Spouse abuse often goes unreported.

b. Assume you are a prosecutor in one of the states where a husband can be prosecuted for raping his wife. A woman tells you that
she and her husband have been having violent arguments for
years. She says that during one of these arguments, her husband
forced her to have sexual intercourse. Assuming that a rape conviction carries a possible penalty of 20 years in prison, would you
file a rape charge against the husband? Explain. Is there anything
else you could do?

LEGAL RIGHTS OF SINGLE PEOPLE

Single people are adults who have never been married or who are
divorced or widowed. Today, the legal rights of single people is an
important topic because of the growing number of unmarried
couples. Many of these couples eventually get married. Others do
not. In any case, understanding how the law affects single people is
important.

In the past, unwed couples had few rights. In most states, if a
man and women lived together, shared household duties and expenses, and then split up, both could go their separate ways without legal obligation. On the other hand, if the couple had been
married, numerous laws would have set out their legal rights and
duties concerning divorce, alimony, child support, and other
issues.

However, the situation is changing. Unmarried adults may
think that their love lives are their own affair, but they should

beware. Legal problems can arise when single people live together. Today, unmarried couples do have certain legal rights and responsibilities.

Palimony

Until recently, courts would not enforce agreements between unwed couples as to support or property ownership. Courts refused because they said that contracts could not be based on an immoral relationship. However, since the California Supreme Court's 1976 decision in *Marvin* v. *Marvin*, many state courts have upheld support agreements between unwed couples.

Palimony is the name given to support payments made by one ex-lover to another after an unwed couple splits up. In the past when an unwed couple split up, any property went to the person who had legal title to it. In relationships in which the man was the wage earner and the woman the homemaker, this meant that the man got the property. This was because the wage earner "owned" the property acquired through his wages.

THE CASE OF MARVIN v. MARVIN

Movie actor Lee Marvin met singer Michelle Triola while filming a movie in 1964. Later, Michelle moved in with Lee. They never married, but they lived together for almost seven years. Michelle changed her name to Marvin and became Lee's lover, homemaker, and companion. After splitting up in 1970, Michelle sued Lee, asking for support payments and half of Lee's property and money. Michelle claimed that Lee had promised to support her for life. She also said they had an unwritten agreement to share all property acquired by either of them. Lee denied making these promises. He also said that even if he had made such a promise, it was unenforceable because of the immoral character of their relationship.

PROBLEM 14

a. Who are Lee Marvin and Michelle Triola? Why did Michelle sue Lee Marvin?
b. Should Michelle be awarded support payments and be given half of Lee's property even though they never married? Why or why not?
c. What effect will enforcing support agreements between unmarried couples have on marriage? What effect will it have on relationships between unmarried couples?

The California Supreme Court held that unmarried adults who voluntarily live together can make contracts regarding their earnings and property rights. It also held that if Michelle could prove an express agreement or if an agreement could be implied from their conduct, then a court could award her support payments and part of the property.

At the trial following the Supreme Court's ruling, Michelle could not prove that she and Lee had a contract to share property and earnings. However, what is important about *Marvin* v. *Marvin* is not the actual result of the case but the legal principle established. It held for the first time that unwed couples could acquire property rights similar to those of married couples. Although state court decisions are binding only on lower courts within that state, other state courts followed the California example. Today, many (but not all) state courts recognize the contract and property rights of unmarried couples.

Paternity

> ### THE CASE OF THE UNWED FATHER
>
> Martha, age 17, becomes pregnant. She claims that Michael, age 20, is the father, but Michael denies it and refuses to marry her or support the child. Does the law require Michael to marry Martha or to provide support for the child?

No one can ever be forced to marry someone against his or her will. If this happens, the marriage is invalid and can be annulled. However, an unwed couple can always decide to get married, and an unwed father can be required to support his child.

When an unmarried woman becomes pregnant, both the father and the mother have a duty to support the child. If a man denies being the father, the mother may bring a **paternity** action against the father to force him to pay support.

The purpose of a paternity suit is to establish that a particular man is the father of the child. In some states, blood tests may be used to prove that the man is *not* the child's father. For example, suppose both the mother and alleged father have blood type A and the child has blood type B. In this case, the man cannot be the father. A child cannot have type B blood unless either the father or the mother has the same type.

A paternity suit is usually started by the mother of the child. If the mother is a **minor** (under the age of legal adulthood), some states allow the lawsuit to be started by her parents. In either case, an unwed father can be forced to pay pregnancy expenses and child support until the child becomes an adult.

FIGURE 23 Singles Living Together in the U.S.A.* Unmarried Persons Living with Someone of the Opposite Sex

Year	
1970	523,000
1980	1,508,000

*U.S. Census Bureau Reports

Why do you think the number of unmarried persons of different sexes living together changed between 1970 and 1980?

PROBLEM 15

a. What is palimony?

b. What is paternity?

c. Bob, age 28, and Cory, age 23, have been dating for two years. Cory discovers she is pregnant. Who is responsible for supporting the child? If Bob denies that he is the father, can Cory force him to provide child support? Explain.

PARENTS AND CHILDREN

The relationship between parents and children is very special. Being a parent involves many rewards. It also involves many responsibilities. The law can't guarantee a happy family, nor can it make someone a good parent. But the law requires parents to care for, support, and control their children. When parents are unable or unwilling to fulfill their responsibilities, the law gets involved. This section explores the legal rights and responsibilities of parents and children. It discusses how the law affects family planning, child rearing, and adoption.

PROBLEM 16

a. What do you think are some of the rewards of being a parent?

b. What do you think are the responsibilities of being a parent?

Family Planning

Most married couples have children. Parenthood ranks as one topic on which most Americans can favorably agree. Today, however, many couples have fewer children and in some cases, no children at all. Influenced by the availability of **contraceptives,** the high cost of living, concerns about overpopulation, and changing attitudes toward marriage, careers, and childbearing, the national birth rate has moved slowly but steadily downward. The number of children per family has fallen from 3.5 at the end of World War II to a low of 1.4 in 1984.

Family planning allows couples to determine whether and when to have children. Some couples oppose certain methods of family planning for religious or other reasons, but most agree that some sort of planning is desirable. Among the best sources of family planning information are the family doctor, neighborhood health center, public health department, or family planning clinic.

In past years, abortion was considered a crime, and infor-

FIGURE 24   The U.S. Birth Rate Drops

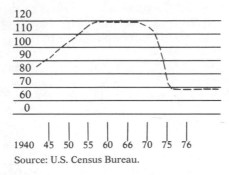

Births per 1,000 women 15-44 years old

Source: U.S. Census Bureau.

Why do you think the U.S. birthrate has gone down? Do you think family planning is a good idea? Why or why not?

mation about birth control and contraceptive devices was restricted. In 1965, the U.S. Supreme Court struck down a state law that prohibited the use of contraceptives by married couples. Later, the Supreme Court declared that a law prohibiting the sale of birth control devices to unmarried people was also unconstitutional because it violated the right to privacy. Today, states allow the sale of birth control devices to any adult, whether married or single. However, some states restrict the sale of contraceptives to minors.

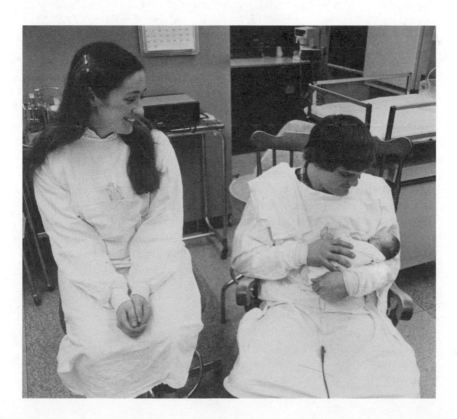

THE CASES CHALLENGING ABORTION LAW

Before 1973, Texas and Georgia had laws making **abortion** a crime except when performed to save the life or health of the mother. Citizens in these states filed suits asking that the laws be declared in violation of the U.S. Constitution. The plaintiffs argued that a woman has a constitutional right to control her body. Texas defended by saying that the law was necessary to safeguard the life of unborn children and to preserve and protect the health of pregnant women. If you were a justice on the Supreme Court, how would you decide this case and why?

In the cases of *Roe* v. *Wade* and *Doe* v. *Bolton,* the U.S. Supreme Court decided that women, married or single, have a legal right to an abortion. Basing its decision on the constitutional right to privacy, the Court defined the right to abortion in three stages:

1. First trimester (first 12 weeks of pregnancy) — a woman can have an abortion upon demand without interference by the state.
2. Second trimester (thirteenth week until viability, somewhere between the twenty-fourth and twenty-eighth week) — the state can establish regulations to make abortions safe but cannot prohibit them.
3. Third trimester (the child may be capable of living outside of the woman's body) — the state can regulate or forbid all abortions except to save the life of the mother.

Abortions are now legal in every state. However, the 1973 Supreme Court decision did not end the debate over abortions, nor did it settle all the issues: Does a woman need her husband's consent to have an abortion? Can a minor have an abortion without her parents' permission? Can the government be required to use Medicaid funds to pay for abortions? Is abortion moral?

In 1976 the Supreme Court reached a decision on the first two issues. It ruled that a law requiring a woman to get her husband's written consent for an abortion during the first trimester of her pregnancy was unconstitutional. It also ruled that a law giving parents an absolute veto right over abortions sought by their minor children was unconstitutional. The Court said both laws violated the right to privacy. However, in 1981 the Court upheld a Utah law that requires physicians to notify the parents of a minor before performing an abortion.

On the third issue, the Supreme Court upheld three state laws that prohibited states from having to pay for elective abortions. The Court reasoned that the right to have an abortion does not mean that states must use Medicaid funds to pay for abortions or that hospitals are required to provide free abortions for women who can't pay for them.

Since 1973, controversy over the Supreme Court decision on abortion has continued. Opponents of abortion have proposed measures at the local, state, and federal level designed to restrict the availability of abortion. On the other hand, people who believe that abortion is a woman's decision have worked equally hard to make abortions freely available.

Public opinions about abortion are strongly divided.

PROBLEM 17

a. Whose rights are involved in the abortion controversy? What are the legal, moral, and social arguments for and against abortion? What do you think of these arguments?

b. If you support legalized abortion, under what circumstances, if any, would you find abortion least acceptable? If you oppose legalized abortion, under what circumstances, if any, would you find abortion most acceptable?

c. Do you agree with the Supreme Court decision that a woman does not need her husband's consent to have an abortion? Explain your answer.

d. If given a choice, would you support or oppose a constitutional amendment designed to prevent or regulate the availability of abortions? Why?

Responsibilities between Parents and Children

Parents have certain legal responsibilities to their children. One basic responsibility of parents is to support their minor children. This means that parents must provide the basic necessities of life, including food, clothing, shelter, education, and medical care.

All parents, both rich and poor, are expected to support their children. However, the amount of support varies depending on what the family can afford. For example, a poor family would not be expected to buy expensive clothes or serve fancy meals.

In most states, financial support is the father's legal responsibility. This is true even if the parents are unmarried or divorced. In other states, new laws make the father and mother equally responsible for child support. This does not mean each parent pays

the same amount of money. It means that each parent provides according to his or her ability.

Parents have other legal responsibilities. They must provide for their children's education, medical care, and social and moral development. Parents also have a duty to control and supervise their children.

Education   All children have a right to a free public school education through the twelfth grade. The state may set standards for an adequate education, but parents have a right to send children to the school of their choice — public, private, or parochial. School attendance is generally required for all children ages 7–16, although state laws vary. A child who misses school is considered a **truant.** Parents who fail to send their children to school may be fined or arrested.

Medical Care   Parents have a duty to protect and supervise their children's health. This means that they must provide proper medical and dental care. Children must usually have their parents' permission to obtain medical treatment. For example, suppose a 14-year-old wants braces on her teeth. Without her parents' permission, a dentist could not put on the braces. Although parents have a right to supervise medical care, they can be charged with neglect if they ignore their children's health. Also, in life-threatening emergencies, a court may give permission for doctors to treat a child without parental consent.

Discipline   Parents have a right and a duty to supervise their children. Likewise, children have a legal duty to obey their parents and follow reasonable rules. Parents are entitled to ask children to do chores around the house and yard. Parents may also decide where their children live, what school they attend, what religion they practice, and other aspects of a child's life.

As long as parents don't abuse or neglect their children, the law gives them the authority to make their own decisions about their children's welfare. However, parents' authority is not absolute. Children do not have to obey parents who order them to do something dangerous or illegal. Parents who mistreat their children can be charged with child abuse. Moreover, parents cannot allow their children to run wild or do anything they want. If they do, the parents can be charged with **contributing to the delinquency of a minor.** For example, a father who encourages his son to use drugs could be convicted of this crime.

Children who *continually* disobey their parents or run away from home may be charged as status offenders. **Status offenses** are not crimes. They are illegal acts that can be committed only by children. Status offenses include running away from home, skipping school, refusing to obey parents, or engaging in immoral or dangerous behavior. Status offenders may be placed under court supervision. When this happens, the child is known as a PINS,

CHINS, or MINS — a person, child, or minor in need of supervision. Courts may order counseling, special schooling, or in serious cases may place the child in a juvenile facility or a foster home.
(For more information about status offenders, refer to Chapter 2.)

THE CASE OF POLOVCHAK v. POLOVCHAK

For years, Anna and Michael Polovchak had dreamed about leaving
Russia and immigrating to America. But like many immigrants, the
Polovchaks had trouble adjusting to life in a new country. After
living in Chicago for several years, the Polovchaks decided to return
to the Soviet Union.

The Polovchaks' 12-year-old son, Walter, was not pleased about the
decision to return to Russia. Walter had developed a taste for ice
cream and bicycles. He loved America and wanted to stay. When his
parents insisted he return to Russia, Walter ran away from home.
He sought refuge in a foster home while his parents went to court to
get him back.

The Polovchaks argued that the U.S. Constitution gave parents the
right to control the destiny of their minor children without government interference. They said that the government had no right to
prevent them from taking Walter back to Russia. "If we were going
back to England, I don't think anyone would interfere," they said.

Walter's attorney said that the child's decision to seek political
asylum was paramount. He said that Walter had a right to make his
own political judgments. He also argued that if Walter returned to
Russia, he would be branded a defector and would suffer grave
consequences.

PROBLEM 18

a. Why did the Polovchaks want to return to Russia? Why did their
son, Walter, want to stay in America?
b. Should the Polovchaks be allowed to take Walter with them?
Why or why not? What if Walter were an infant?
c. Which is more important: the Polovchaks' right to control their
own family or Walter's right to live in a free country?
d. Do you think the Polovchaks have the legal right to take Walter
with them? Why or why not? How do you think the court decided
this case?

Earnings and Employment   In most families, children who work
keep and spend their own money. Nevertheless, parents have the
the legal right to take the earnings of their minor children. Children may keep only the wages that their parents want them to
keep. However, parents have no right to use other money that

belongs to their children. For example, if a child receives an inheritance or recovers damages in a lawsuit, the child has the right to have this money set aside in a bank account until he or she becomes an adult.

Responsibility for Injuries   At one time, parents were not responsible for injuries caused by their children, whether accidental or intentional, unless a parent was somehow to blame. For example, if a parent gave a child a gun to play with, the parent could be liable for any injuries caused by the child.

Today, all states have laws that make parents responsible for harm caused by their children, up to a certain dollar limit. This amount varies from $200 to $5,000 depending on state law. A special rule known as the **family car doctrine** makes parents responsible for damages caused by any driver in the family. This means that if a child causes an accident while driving his parents' car, the parents may have to pay for the damage.

Emancipation   Parents are not required to support an adult child. Parents' legal responsibility ends when their children become emancipated. **Emancipation** means that children are set free from the legal control and custody of their parents. It also means that parents are no longer required to support their children. Emancipation takes place when the child reaches adulthood — age 18 in most states. It can also occur if a child gets married, joins the armed forces, or becomes self-supporting.

THE CASE OF THE RICH SON

Ira, 42, owns a successful business. His mother, 65, will retire from her job at the end of the year. Her meager savings and social security payments will not be enough for her to continue paying rent where she lives. She can move to a publicly supported home for the elderly but would prefer to stay in her own apartment. Does Ira have a legal obligation to support his mother? Should the law require adult children to support their parents when they are in need?

A long tradition of law and social custom has called upon adult children to support their parents when in need. Some states have **family responsibility laws.** These laws require children to care for elderly parents. Other states have abolished these laws, and almost all states limit the support obligation to what a relative can fairly afford.

PROBLEM 19

Consider the following situations. In each case, decide whether the parents have the legal authority to make the decision involved.

What rights do you think the children have in each situation? What arguments can you make in support of the parents? In support of the children?

a. Mr. McBride disapproved of the lifestyle of his 18-year-old son, Larry. When Larry, who attends college, moves out of the dorm into a commune, Mr. McBride cuts off his support, including tuition.

b. Monica, age 17, has a birthmark on her cheek. On the advice of a friend, she decides to have plastic surgery to remove the birthmark. Her parents absolutely forbid it.

c. Murray, a high school senior, does not want to move to a new city with his parents. He wants to finish high school with his friends. His parents insist that he live with them.

d. Mr. and Mrs. Parham think that their 16-year-old daughter is mentally ill and needs psychiatric treatment. The daughter objects, but her parents decide to commit her to a mental institution.

Child Abuse and Neglect

The legal system tries to stay out of most disputes within families. However, all states have laws that protect children against parental neglect and abuse. The legal definition of **child abuse** includes physical abuse, abandonment, and failure to provide adequate support or care. Despite the legal definition, determining exactly what is child abuse is sometimes difficult.

PROBLEM 20

Consider each of the following situations. Then decide whether the action of the parent or parents should be considered child neglect or abuse. Explain your answer.

a. An unmarried parent goes to work and leaves her two children, ages seven and three, at home unattended.

b. A parent beats his 12-year-old son until he is black and blue.

c. A father tells his 14-year-old daughter that she can stay out all night or do anything else she wants as long as she doesn't bother him.

d. A mother spanks her four-year-old son until he cries.

e. A married couple refuses to allow their teenage son to date or go anywhere without them.

> **WHERE YOU LIVE**
>
> Does your state have a neglect or child abuse law? Who is required to report evidence of child abuse in your state?

Parents have a right and a duty to discipline their children. However, they may be prosecuted for using excessive force, and children who are injured or mistreated can be taken from the parents. An estimated one million child abuse cases occur each year in the United States. One of the problems with neglect and child abuse is that many cases are not reported. Understandably, most people are reluctant to interfere in the family affairs of others. To help solve this problem, most states require doctors, nurses, teachers, social workers, and in some cases the general public to report suspected child abuse cases.

After a child abuse case is reported, several questions arise. How should the police handle such a case? What should courts do? Should the child be returned home or removed from the parents' care? Should parents found guilty of child abuse be fined, imprisoned, or provided with counseling?

PROBLEM 21

Assume that you see the father of the family next door beating his 10-year-old son. The boy is screaming in obvious pain.

a. What, if anything, would you do?

b. Roleplay a visit by the police to this family's home. What should the police say and do?

c. If the father is taken to court for continually beating and injuring his son, what should the court do? Do you think child abuse should be a crime? What should happen to abusive parents?

d. Some say that children learn to be violent when they are victims of violence. Do you agree?

How are suspected cases of child abuse handled in your community?

FOSTER CARE AND ADOPTION

Children who are neglected or abused may be removed from the family home, placed in a foster home, or made available for adoption. Sometimes parents may simply decide to give up their children for adoption.

Foster parents are people who take care of minors who are not their natural children. Foster parents are usually not the legal guardians. Full legal guardianship and custody rights are still held by the natural parents or by a government agency. Foster parents are usually paid for child care, and children can be removed from foster homes at any time with the agency's permission. Though foster parents have few legal rights regarding foster children, they often form close attachments and sometimes apply to adopt the child.

Adoption is the legal process by which an adult or adults become the legal parents of another person. Though adults usually adopt children, most states permit adults to adopt another adult.

Few legal restrictions are placed on who can adopt another. Therefore, people — regardless of marital status, race, religion, or age — are eligible to adopt anyone else. In practice, however, adoption agencies and courts try to make the child's new family as much like that of the natural parents as possible. This means adoption agencies are sometimes reluctant to place children with parents of a different race or religion.

Most adoptions are set up through public or private adoption agencies. People wishing to adopt apply to these agencies and are investigated as to whether they will be suitable parents. Public agencies usually charge little or no fee for this service. Private agencies may charge much more. Because there is a shortage of children available for adoption, some people adopt children living in foreign countries. Other people turn to **black market adoptions**, in which go-betweens arrange for women to have their babies and turn them over to adopting parents without going through an adoption agency. This practice is illegal in most states.

People who wish to adopt must contact an adoption agency. They must then apply to a court to have the adoption legally

Adopted children have all the legal rights and responsibilities of natural children.

approved. An attorney is often necessary to take the legal steps to make the adoption final. An adoption agency will submit its report on the parents and will seek written consent from the natural parents. In most states, consent is required, but in some cases, even if the natural parents refuse consent or cannot be found, courts may still grant adoptions that they decide are in the best interest of the child. A child who has reached a certain age (often 12 or 14) must also consent to the adoption.

In most states, when the court approves an adoption, a temporary order is issued. This means the agency or natural parents remain the legal guardian for a specified waiting period, such as

---

THE CASE OF SCARPETTA v. SPENCE-CHAPIN ADOPTION SERVICE

Olga Scarpetta, 32, comes from a wealthy California family. During an affair with a married man, she becomes pregnant. Rather than embarrass her family, Olga goes to New York to have the baby. The child, born May 18, is turned over to the Spence-Chapin Adoption Service four days later. On June 1, Olga signs a document giving the agency full authority to find new parents for the child.

The agency has no trouble finding interested couples. They place the child with the DeMartino family on June 18. Mr. DeMartino, a doctor, and his wife have already adopted a four-year-old boy from the same agency and everything worked out very well.

Within two months following the baby's birth, Olga changes her mind and asks for the return of her baby. The agency refuses to help her and will not tell her who has the child. After several weeks of arguing with the agency, Olga goes to court. She tells the judge that she was physically and emotionally upset following childbirth. She is sure that she now wants to keep the child. Her family in California has learned the truth and also wants Olga to get the baby back.

PROBLEM 22

Read the following opinions and decide which one you agree with. Be prepared to give reasons for your choice. Note that the adoption agency is the defendant in this case because the DeMartinos had not yet received final legal custody of the child. The court must decide whether to return the child to the natural parent or leave the child with the adoptive parents.

Opinion 1
There are a number of reasons why this court believes it is in the best interest of the child to leave her with her adoptive parents, the DeMartinos.

First, Olga waited six weeks after putting the child up for adoption before requesting the child's return. During this period, the DeMar-

six months or a year. After this, a new birth certificate is issued. It shows the adopting parents as the parents of the child. The adopted child and the adoptive parents then assume the same rights and responsibilities as natural born children and their parents.

A controversy regarding adoption is whether adopted children have a right to know who their natural parents are. Traditionally, adoption records have been sealed, and adopted children were not allowed to find out the names or whereabouts of their natural parents. However, adoptive children are often interested in learning about and meeting their natural parents. Some adoptees even

tinos formed a strong attachment to the child and made many sacrifices because they had every reason to believe the child would be their own.

Secondly, the background of the DeMartinos is greatly superior to that of Olga. Olga is thirty-two, unmarried, and, from the evidence before us, appears emotionally unstable. As for the adoptive parents, the agency selected them because they had already adopted a four-year-old boy and proved themselves well able to provide for the child's moral and physical well-being. They can give the attention of two parents to the child. To take the baby away at this point would cause a great deal of suffering to them.

Finally, the mother freely gave up the child and the agency acted in a proper manner in obtaining her consent.

Opinion 2
There is a presumption in the law that unless proven unfit the natural mother is best suited to provide adequate support and care for the child. This court believes Olga Scarpetta is such a natural parent.

First, Olga was under a great deal of pressure when she placed the child for adoption. She had just gone through an unwanted pregnancy, labor and delivery. She was very worried about the reaction of her highly religious family. I believe this decision could not have been freely given under the circumstances.

Second, she now clearly wants the child and is very able to provide for the child's welfare. Her wealthy family also supports her in this decision and will help her out if she needs financial assistance.

Finally, there is no evidence that Olga will be an unfit parent, and even though the DeMartinos may be good or even better parents, this does not mean they should be given rights ahead of the natural mother.

ADOPTION RECORDS HEARING

Assume that your state proposes the following law: "All adopted persons over the age of 21 shall have the right to obtain a copy of their original birth certificate and shall be given the name and last known address of their natural parents." At a hearing on the proposed law, two people testify.

Mrs. Margaret Jones says, "When I was 16, I became pregnant. The father, a soldier at a nearby army base, was transferred and I never saw him again. My parents could not afford to support another child in our family, and I didn't want to leave high school. I was also embarrassed, so I went to visit my aunt in another town. I had the baby, and then placed him for adoption. I returned to my home town and finished school. I am now happily married and the mother of two children, ages 11 and 14. My husband does not know about my earlier affair or the child I gave up. The adoption agency promised that they would never tell anyone my name. I do not wish to see the child I put up for adoption, and I believe it best that we live our own separate lives."

Michael Franklin says, "I am 19 years old, and only last year my adoptive parents told me that I was adopted at birth. I love my adopted parents very much, but I feel a strong need to find out who my natural parents are and to meet them. I want to know where I came from and a little more about why I am the way I am. Everyone needs to belong somewhere. It's inhuman not to let me know who my real parents are."

PROBLEM 23

a. If you were a member of the legislature and heard these two witnesses' testimonies, how would you vote on the adoption records law? Explain your answer. Would the law be better if it allowed adopted children to look at records only when the natural parents were first asked and gave their consent?

b. Would fewer people place children for adoption if they knew the children would later find out their names? Would opening adoption records result in more abortions or more black market adoptions?

c. What problems do you think may arise if the proposed law is passed? Can you rewrite the law to improve it?

d. Do you think Michael's adopted parents should have told him sooner that he was adopted? If they know, should they tell him who his natural mother is and why he was placed for adoption?

spend a great amount of time, seeking information on their family history. Today, a few states allow them to look at adoption records. However, some states have laws that provide adopted children,

What is your state's law regarding whether adopted children can find out who their natural parents are?

reaching the age of majority, with the right to obtain the names of their natural parents. Some people oppose these laws. They believe that the natural parents have a right to privacy and a right not to see children they put up for adoption unless they desire to do so.

FAMILY PROBLEMS

Though many couples are happily married, some problems occur in all marriages. Minor disagreements are usually settled by the couple working together. Major differences may require the couple to seek the help of a marriage counselor, psychologist, social worker, or minister. Although most problems can be solved, marriages do break down. The hard reality of everyday life can wear away a couple's love and compatibility. At such times, a husband and wife may consider ending their marriage.

This section discusses resources available to help people with family problems. It also deals with the procedures that can be used to end a valid marriage, namely separation and divorce. It discusses some of the issues that arise when a marriage breaks up. These include child custody, support, alimony, and property division.

Marriage Problems

A couple should never rush into a divorce. Divorce is a serious step that will affect them and their children for the rest of their lives. A couple should not seek a divorce in the heat of anger or without at least trying to work out their problems.

If a husband and wife cannot settle their differences together, they may wish to consult a **marriage counselor.** Marriage counseling can help them explore the reasons for their problems and ideally work out a solution. To locate a qualified marriage counselor, couples can contact the American Association for Marriage and Family Therapy (see Appendix B). They can also ask friends or members of the clergy.

Many people who consider divorce see it as a way to end forever a relationship that has become unbearable. Yet, this is not always the case. It is almost never true if children are involved. Children can tie a couple together for many years after divorce. Divorce may change the relationship between spouses, but it won't necessarily end it.

Anyone thinking about divorce or separation should also know that splitting up can be very costly. Some of the major considerations are legal fees, alimony, and child support payments. The couple will also have to divide all their property, such as their house, car, furniture, life insurance, cash, bank accounts, and everything else they own.

A national survey found that the most common problems in a marriage were conflicts with in-laws or relatives, job and career pressures, cheating, conflicts about children, sexual problems, a breakdown in communication, excitement or fun gone out of marriage, alcohol or drug abuse, money problems, and loss of shared goals or interests.

PROBLEM 24

a. What do you think are the five most common marital problems that lead to separation or divorce?

b. Before someone marries, can that person anticipate marital problems and decide whether they are likely to occur? Explain.

c. If problems occur, what can a couple do to try to work them out?

d. What are some costs involved in getting a divorce?

Separation

A lasting relationship is the goal of most married couples. The marriage ceremony usually includes the words "in sickness and in health, till death do us part." However, in America, over one million couples are divorced each year. Today, over 30 percent of all marriages end in divorce.

If a married couple decides that their marriage has broken down, they can legally consider any of the following:

■ An **informal separation.** The couple may decide to live apart.

This separation may be for a short cooling-off period, or it may be permanent. In either case, the couple is still legally married and may get back together at any time.

■ **A legal separation.** A legal separation is much like an informal separation except that the terms of the separation are put into a written separation agreement. This written agreement is approved by a court.

■ **A divorce.** A divorce is a court order that legally ends a valid marriage. Once a divorce is final, the couple may legally remarry.

WHERE YOU LIVE

What marriage or family counseling agencies exist in your community? Are these privately or publicly operated? How much do they charge?

For religious reasons, some couples won't consider divorce. Other times, a husband and wife need time alone to consider the future. In these situations, a separation rather than a divorce may be the best idea.

If a married couple separates, they still have legal and financial responsibilities between themselves and to their children. They remain husband and wife, and neither may remarry. For these reasons, it is a good idea to have a formal separation agreement. This is a written document that sets out the continuing rights and duties of each spouse. It also states the couple's understanding on alimony, child custody, support, division of property, and so forth.

Once a separation agreement is signed by both the husband and wife, it becomes a legal contract, which can be enforced in court. For example, if a husband refuses to pay promised support money or won't leave home as agreed, the wife can take him into court.

A separation agreement can say anything the couple wants it to. However, once signed, it cannot be changed unless a court changes it or both spouses agree to a change. If the husband and wife later seek a divorce, the terms of the separation agreement are usually made part of the divorce **decree.**

It is not absolutely necessary to have an attorney draw up a separation agreement or represent a couple in a divorce. Many cities have **pro se** (or do-it-yourself) divorce classes and groups for people who want to handle their own divorces. To learn more about this, check with the local court, law school, or legal aid office. However, do-it-yourself divorce should be considered only if the couple has no children, agrees on the divorce and other matters, and has little property or money to divide.

If the split involves children, large sums of money or property, or any disagreement, then each spouse should have an attorney or should consult a family mediation service. Even if a couple decides not to get a divorce, it is wise to consult a lawyer to learn their legal rights and obtain other information. A couple should consider getting help in the following situations: if one spouse is violent toward the other or toward the children, if one spouse declares that he or she wants a divorce, if one spouse leaves the other, if one spouse does not support the children, and if one spouse consults a lawyer about a possible divorce.

Until recently, most divorcing couples hired a lawyer and prepared for battle. Now, however, an alternative is available. Today, couples can use the services of a new kind of professional: the family mediator.

A family mediator works directly with a couple, guiding them through a series of negotiations designed to achieve an agreement both can live with. The agreement is then reviewed by lawyers before being filed in court. The mediator can help divorcing couples work out their own settlements without the time, expense, or acrimony of the traditional adversary process.

Some people say that lawyers are always necessary in a divorce. They believe that one spouse may take advantage of the other without an attorney. Others believe that mediation is better because it helps couples work out a mutually acceptable agreement. Most experts agree that a mediated settlement should be reviewed by a lawyer for each person before it is finalized. For a list of organizations involved in family mediation, see Appendix B.

PROBLEM 25

Bill and Rachel married when they were both 21. One year later, they had a baby. After two years of marriage, they are constantly fighting and are generally miserable. They are unsure about a divorce, but both think it might be better to live apart for awhile. Bill works as an auto mechanic and brings home $1,000 a month. Rachel used to work as a teller in a local bank, making $800 a month, but has not worked since having a child. They rent an apartment for $300 a month, and they own the following property: $500 in a savings account, a car worth $1,500, and furniture and appliances.

a. Do Bill and Rachel have any choices besides divorce? Explain.

b. Do Bill and Rachel need a lawyer to help them? How could a mediator help them? Who else could help them?

c. List the things that Bill and Rachel must decide before agreeing to a separation. Then roleplay a meeting between the two of them in which they try to work out a separation agreement.

d. Explain the difference between an informal separation, a legal separation, and a divorce.

Divorce

At one time, most states allowed divorce only if one spouse could show that the other spouse had done something wrong or was at fault. Typical "faults" or grounds for divorce include the following:

- Adultery — sexual intercourse between a married person and someone other than his or her spouse

- Desertion — leaving one's spouse with no intention of returning

- Mental cruelty — behavior that make normal married life impossible

- Physical cruelty — acts of violence or physical abuse against one's spouse

- Insanity — mental illness

Proving that one spouse was at fault was often hard. Divorce was also embarrassing. Many couples went to a foreign country or to another state to get a divorce.

In recent years, the laws have changed. Most states now permit **no-fault divorce.** To obtain a no-fault divorce, a spouse does not have to prove the other spouse did something wrong. Instead, the husband or wife has to show only that there are irreconcilable differences. This means that the marriage has completely broken down. Many states also allow divorces when a couple can show that they voluntarily lived apart for a certain period of time, usually one year or more. Despite the easier divorce laws in most places, a few states still require one of the fault grounds to be proven before a divorce will be granted.

PROBLEM 26

a. Why do you think the divorce rate has doubled over the last 15 years?

b. Do you think states should make it harder or easier to get a divorce? Why?

c. Some courts require couples to see a marriage counselor before granting a divorce. Do you think this is a good idea?

d. Explain the difference between a fault divorce and a no-fault divorce.

Steps in a Divorce

The legal procedure for obtaining a divorce varies from state to state. However, the following basic steps are the same throughout the country:

1. File a complaint. The person seeking the divorce (known as the **plaintiff**) files a **complaint.** The complaint, also called a **petition,** asks that a divorce be granted based on some ground such as adultery, desertion, or voluntary separation. The complaint may

WHERE YOU LIVE: What are the grounds for divorce in your state? Does your state allow no-fault divorce or divorce by consent? How long does it take to obtain a divorce in your state?

also ask for alimony, child support, custody of the children, or division of property.

2. Serve the defendant. The person seeking the divorce must give his or her spouse formal legal notice of the divorce action. This is done by serving the **defendant** with a copy of the complaint and a summons. A **summons** is a legal document that tells the defendant that a court case has been started.

3. File an answer. Once the defendant has received legal notice of the divorce action, he or she must file an **answer.** An answer either admits or denies the facts and demands in the complaint. If the defendant objects to the complaint, this is known as a **contested divorce.** The issue will then be settled in court. If the defendant does not file an answer or admits the facts in the complaint, the divorce may then go forward **uncontested.**

4. Pretrial actions. Before going to trial, the husband and wife may try to reach an agreement. This may be negotiated by the couple themselves, through their lawyers, or with the help of a mediator. Also, the court may refer the couple for counseling to see if the marriage can be saved. If child custody or alimony are issues, the court may order an investigation of the parents or call for a list of each spouse's earnings and assets.

5. A court hearing. In all cases, a court hearing will take place. If the divorce is **uncontested** or the couple has reached an agreement on all issues the hearing will be short. If the divorce is **contested,** or if there is a disagreement on other issues, there will be a trial. At this time, each spouse may **testify** about the divorce. The court will then decide whether to grant a divorce. The court will also decide issues such as alimony, child support, property division, and custody of the children.

6. The divorce is granted. Once the divorce is granted, there is sometimes a short waiting period before it becomes final. During this time, a spouse can **appeal.** Neither spouse may remarry. However, once the divorce is final, either party is free to remarry.

Over one million couples are divorced each year. Why do you think there are so many divorces?

Until recent years, divorced fathers rarely received custody of their children.

Child Custody

For better or worse, divorce is a fact of American life. If a couple splits up, one important question is: With whom will the children live? In legal terms, the question is: Who will have **custody** of the children? The importance of the custody issue is illustrated by the fact that in 1985, over nine million minor children in the United States were living with divorced or separated parents.

Custody decisions are important because the parent with custody can decide most aspects of the child's life, such as where the child will live and go to school. Custody may be temporary, or it may be permanently awarded to one parent. Once custody is awarded, it is rarely changed. However, courts can change custody if circumstances change. For example, if the custodial parent became addicted to drugs, the court might order a change of custody. The noncustodial parent is usually given visitation rights. This means that he or she can visit the child on certain days and times of the year. This parent is also usually required to contribute money for the child's support.

Sometimes courts award custody to both parents. This is known as **joint custody.** In this situation, the children can legally live with both parents. This basically means the child lives part-time with the father and part-time with the mother. For example, some children switch homes every week. Others switch every month. Both parents have full responsibility for supervision of the child, and both have an equal say in important issues such as schooling and religion.

Today, joint custody is becoming more common. However, courts have not favored it. This is because of the belief that parents who cannot cooperate enough to stay married often do not work well together after a divorce.

PROBLEM 27

What are the advantages and disadvantages of each of the custody arrangements? Which custody arrangement do you think children would prefer?

If parents cannot agree on custody, the decision is made by the court. For many years, the law presumed that young children were better off with their mothers. This presumption was called the *tender years doctrine*. Today, all states have changed their laws to treat men and women equally in custody disputes.

In determining custody, courts now ask: What is in the best interest of the child? This is often difficult to determine. Courts look at factors such as the youth's actions in the home, school, and community. Courts also consider the emotional and economic stability of the parents, and the religion of each parent. Many courts listen to the children's desires, especially if they are over a certain age (e.g., 12). To help with this decision, judges often order a social service agency to do a study of the parents and children. The results of this study are then used as the basis for a custody recommendation.

Increased mobility and high divorce rates have created a new legal term: *grandparents' rights*. Today, 47 states have laws permitting grandparents to sue for the privilege of visiting their grandchildren after the parents are divorced or separated.

PROBLEM 28

a. Should a child's wishes be considered in determining custody? Does it make a difference if the youth is 4 years old? 12? 16?

b. Should children have their own attorneys in custody cases? Why or why not?

c. Should courts make decisions regarding child custody? If not, who might be better able to make such decisions?

d. Do you think that joint custody is a good idea? Why or why not?

Most divorced parents try not to fight over their children. However, custody disputes provide courts with some of their toughest cases. The worst kind of custody dispute is a case of **child snatching.** This occurs when a noncustodial parent physically abducts his or her child and moves to another state. Many people blame child snatching on the failure of courts to honor other states' custody decrees. They also point to a legal loophole which

BILL OF RIGHTS FOR CHILDREN IN DIVORCE ACTIONS*

    I. The right to be treated as an interested person and not as a pawn or possession of the parents

   II. The right to grow up in that home environment which will best guarantee an opportunity for the child to grow to mature and responsible citizenship

  III. The right to the day-by-day love, care, discipline, and protection of the parent having custody of the child

  IV. The right to know the parent they don't live with and to have the benefit of that parent's love and guidance through adequate visitation

   V. The right to a positive relationship with both parents, with neither parent being permitted to degrade or downgrade the other in the mind of the child

  VI. The right to have moral and ethical values developed and to have limits set for behavior so that the child may develop self-discipline and self-control

 VII. The right to the most adequate level of economic support that can be provided by the best efforts of both parents

VIII. The right to the same opportunities for education that the child would have had if the family unit had not been broken

  IX. The right to a regular review of living arrangements and child support orders as the circumstances of the parents and the benefit of the child may require

   X. The right to recognition that children involved in a divorce are always disadvantaged parties and that the law must take steps to protect their welfare, including a social investigation and the appointment of an attorney to protect their interests

*Adapted and printed with permission from "A Bill of Rights," developed by the Family Court of Milwaukee County, Wisconsin.

Do you think that any changes should be made in this bill of rights for children? Explain any you propose. Do you think that the protections in this document should be the law in your state? Why or why not?

---

exempts parents from prosecution under federal kidnapping laws. To remedy the first problem, Congress passed the *Parental Kidnapping Prevention Act of 1980*. This law provides resources to help parents locate missing children. It also prevents parents who abduct their children from getting new custody orders in a different state.

Alimony, Property Division, and Child Support

Since the development of no-fault divorce, most divorce disputes now center on two issues: children and economics. The major economic issues are alimony, child support, and property division.

Most of these issues are negotiated between the parties, who then make a brief courtroom appearance to finalize the breakup.

Alimony is money paid to support an ex-wife or ex-husband after a divorce. It covers household and personal expenses, work-related costs, educational expenses, and recreation. Alimony is usually paid by men to support their ex-wives. However, men can and sometimes do receive alimony. In 1980, the U.S. Supreme Court ruled that state laws that restrict alimony to women are unconstitutional.

Alimony is based on need. As a result, alimony awards vary in each case. When awarding alimony, courts consider the couple's standard of living, the financial status of both husband and wife, and the wage-earning capacity of each spouse.

Dividing the property owned by the couple is another important issue. Property division means deciding who gets the house, the car, the furniture, the bank account, the life insurance, and so on. In all states, property owned by one spouse prior to the marriage belongs to the same person after divorce. In community property states, all the property acquired during the marriage is divided in half. In other states, property is divided based on what the court considers equitable, or fair. Alimony and property division are separate concepts. Property includes all physical possessions that have been acquired by the family up to the time of the divorce. Alimony consists of future payments of support money after the end of the marriage.

THE CASE OF THE MEDICAL SCHOOL DEGREE

When Mark and Janet Sullivan sought a divorce to end their 11-year marriage, the case seemed simple. The couple had little property to divide and with California's no-fault divorce law, seemingly little to argue about. However, at the time of the divorce, Ms. Sullivan argued that she deserved part of her ex-husband's income as a physician because she had helped him earn his medical degree.

Ms. Sullivan claimed that she was entitled to a share of Mark's total projected lifetime income as a doctor. Mark countered that Janet might be entitled to reimbursement for part of the *cost* of his education but not for the *value* of his degree. To understand the difference, imagine that a couple buys a stock for $100 when they first married and the stock is worth $1,000 when they divorce. Should the court give the ex-wife $50 or $500?

PROBLEM 29

a. What happened in this case? What is Ms. Sullivan asking for?
b. What is fair reimbursement: the cost of Mark's education or the value in terms of his increased earnings? Explain your answer.
c. Explain the difference between alimony and property division.

If a divorcing couple has children, they will also need an agreement on child support. Both parents have a legal duty to support their children after a divorce. All states require divorced fathers to support a child not in their custody. Some states impose the same obligation on noncustodial mothers. The level of support is based on the parents' ability to pay and the amount necessary to cover the child's needs. Child support is usually paid until the child becomes an adult or is emancipated.

Problems sometimes arise when one spouse fails to provide the agreed-upon financial support. If this happens, the other spouse may go to court and seek an order requiring payment. Many states provide free legal aid to needy spouses trying to collect such payments. In addition, the federal government has a nationwide locator service that helps find spouses who are behind in their support payments.

PROBLEM 30

In each of the following situations, the couples are divorcing. Should either spouse pay alimony or child support? If so, which one should pay? How much should be paid and for how long?

a. Miguel, a successful plumbing contractor, earns $50,000 per year. His wife, Carmen, stays home and takes care of their four children. When they divorce, the two older children — a junior in high school and a freshman in college — wish to stay with Miguel; the two younger children prefer to stay with Carmen.

b. Angela, a social worker for the city, divorces her husband, Leroy, an occasionally employed writer. He had been staying home, taking care of their two-year-old son. Angela's yearly salary was $23,000; Leroy earned $3,000 in the past 12 months.

GOVERNMENT SUPPORT FOR NEEDY FAMILIES AND OTHERS

Since the economic depression of the 1930s, the government has operated social programs to provide for needy families. This section discusses issues such as: Who benefits from these programs, how much individuals receive, and how government aid programs operate.

The U.S. government estimates that there are 35 million poor people in America. The government defines poor people as those who make less than a certain annual income. (In 1985, it was less than $10,610 per year for a nonfarm family of four.) In the mid-1980s, federal, state, and local governments spent close to $300 billion a year on social service programs. However, at least half of this money goes to the nonpoor through social insurance programs, such as social security, Medicare, and unemployment compensation. These programs provide benefits to people who are retired, disabled, or otherwise in need of assistance.

Programs designed to aid the poor include *Aid to Families with Dependent Children*, food stamps, Medicaid, and public housing. How much a person receives under these programs depends on individual state laws. The federal government pays a minimum amount to the states and asks them to increase this with state funds. The state contributions vary. As a result, an unemployed person or someone receiving welfare in one state may receive two or three times as much as a similarly situated person in another state.

PROBLEM 31

a. What do you think are the causes of poverty in America? Can government programs help solve these problems? If so, how?

b. Should people receiving money under social programs receive the same amount no matter what state they live in? Why or why not?

Social Insurance Programs

Some government aid programs protect all Americans regardless of income. Most of these programs act like insurance policies whereby people receive benefits based on the amount of money they paid to the government when they were working.

Social Security When you apply for a job, the employer will ask for your social security number. Although this may seem unimportant now, your social security number will be a valuable asset when you retire. Social security works like an insurance policy. When you work, a percentage of your wages are deducted by your employer, who pays an equal amount to the federal government. Once you reach retirement age, you are entitled to benefits based on the amount paid into your account.

Almost all Americans — men, women, and children — have social security protection either as workers or as dependents of workers. The following section summarizes some of the major provisions of the social security law. For additional information, contact the nearest office of the U.S. Social Security Administration.

■ *Retirement benefits.* Workers age 62 or older may retire and receive a monthly social security check. A worker's spouse and children may also be eligible. The amount a person receives is a percentage of earnings In 1985, it ranged from $361.00 a month to $903.60 for those who had retired.

■ *Disability benefits.*   Workers who are blind, injured, or too ill to work can receive monthly checks if the disability is expected to last at least 12 months or result in death. Spouses and children are also eligible.

■ *Survivor's benefits.*   When workers die, their families become eligible for payments. This is like a government life insurance policy.

   To illustrate how social security works, consider the case of Mary Smith, age 28, a single parent with two children. She works in a bakery for five years. Then, Mary becomes very ill and stops working. After a required waiting period, social security will pay Mary and her children a monthly check until she is able to return to work. If Mary dies, social security will continue to pay each of her children until they reach age 18, or 22 if they are full-time students.

Medicare   Medicare is a federal health insurance program for people age 65 or older. It also aids people of any age with permanent kidney failure, and certain disabled people. Medicare has two parts: hospital insurance and medical insurance. Hospital insurance helps pay for major hospital expenses and certain follow-up care. Medical insurance helps pay for physician fees and other medical expenses. Local Social Security Administration offices take applications for Medicare, assist people in filing claims, and provide information about the program.

Unemployment Compensation   Each state has an unemployment compensation system to help workers who lose their jobs. To

WHERE YOU LIVE

Where in your community does a person apply for Medicare benefits? For social security benefits? What is the procedure for applying?

ADVICE ON HOW TO OBTAIN UNEMPLOYMENT COMPENSATION

■ Contact the state employment office in your area.

■ Visit the office and apply for compensation.

■ Be interviewed by a case worker, who will decide whether you are eligible.

■ Your former employer will be sent a letter asking why you are no longer employed.

■ If you are awarded benefits, you must report on a regular basis to pick up your check and report on your efforts to find new employment.

■ If you are denied benefits or if they are reduced for some reason, you may request a written explanation. If you are not satisfied, you may file an appeal, and a hearing will be held to rule on your eligibility.

**WHERE
YOU
LIVE**

What are the maximum and minimun monthly benefit levels that a person in your state can receive for un- employment com- pensation? Where does a person apply for this compensation?

receive benefits, you must work for a certain period of time, prove you lost your job through no fault of your own, and be willing to take a similar job if one becomes available. In most states, you are not entitled to benefits if you quit or if you are fired for misconduct.

To apply for unemployment compensation, you must contact the state employment office. Benefits vary from state to state. The number of weeks you may receive benefits also varies, although most states limit benefits to a maximum of 26 weeks.

Programs to Aid the Poor

Government welfare programs are designed to maintain a mini- mum standard of well-being for everyone. This is done by pro- viding the poor with benefits to bring their standard of living up to a minimum level. Various welfare programs exist at the federal, state, and local levels. All of these programs help people who qualify for aid on the basis of need. The programs discussed next provide benefits to needy people in the form of cash, medical care, and housing.

Supplemental Security Income   The federal Supplemental Secur- ity Income program (SSI) provides money for needy aged, blind, and disabled people. This federal program provides monthly ben- efits at a standard rate all over the country. States may add their own benefits to those of the federal government. To receive SSI benefits, a person must be age 65 or older, be legally blind, or have a major disability that prevents employment for a year or more. Applications for SSI are handled by local social security offices.

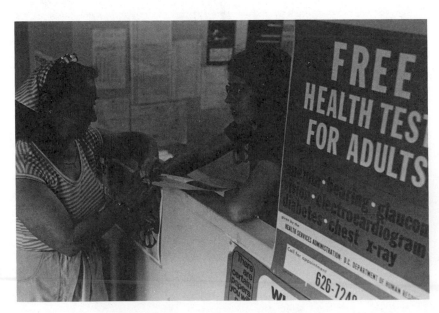

Medicare is a program to help the aged and disabled with hospital and medical costs.

Aid to Families with Dependent Children (AFDC)   AFDC is a joint federal-state program that provides aid to needy families with dependent children. The program provides cash for the support of a needy dependent child and the relative with whom the child is living.

A child is considered dependent if one parent has died, has left home, or is physically or mentally unable to fulfill parental duties. The child must be under age 18, or under 21 and attending school regularly. Every state sets a minimum income level to be eligible for benefits. Eligibility requirements vary from state to state. In most cases, AFDC goes to single-parent families, such as a mother with small children.

To receive AFDC benefits, the recipient can be required to get a job. However, there are some exceptions. For example, the recipient is not required to work if the dependent child is under six or if the recipient is old or ill. Applications for AFDC are made at local offices of state welfare agencies.

Welfare programs are sometimes controversial. Critics say that welfare discourages people from working, because welfare payments are reduced based on income received from employment. Others argue that it breaks up the family, because many states will not pay AFDC if the father is living in the home. Still others contend that the cost of the program is too high. Although nearly everyone agrees that the present system needs improvement, welfare reform has been slow in coming, and programs differ from state to state.

Some communities make direct payments of money, called general assistance, to poor people who are not covered by other programs or who receive inadequate assistance. Approximately 27 states provide such money, but it is often limited to short-term emergencies.

PROBLEM 32

Discuss whether you approve of the following aspects of AFDC. Explain your answer.

a. Fathers may not live in the home with the mother and children to receive payments.

b. Families are usually given money under this program without working

c. The amount one receives varies substantially from state to state

d. It is possible for parents to receive AFDC payments during the entire time they have a child under the age of 18

PROBLEM 33

Some people propose abolishing the welfare system and replacing it with a program that would guarantee all Americans a certain minimum income. Do you agree or disagree with this proposal? Explain your answer.

Medicaid   Medicaid is a government program that provides private medical care to poor people. It covers most common medical services, including hospital and outpatient care, nursing home services, hearing aids, eyeglasses, drugs, dental care, physician fees, medical supplies, and transportation to and from hospitals or doctors offices.

Anyone receiving welfare (AFDC) is automatically eligible for Medicaid. In addition, persons over 65 or those who are blind or totally disabled are eligible for Medicaid if they are U.S. citizens or

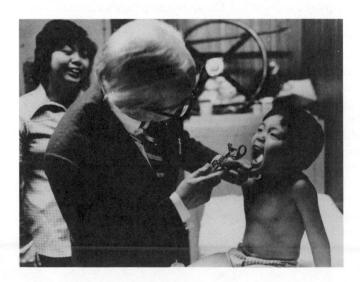

What public health facilities exist in your area?

legal aliens, live in the state where they apply, and have a low income. Application for Medicaid can be made at local welfare offices.

Food Stamps   People who have incomes below a certain level may be eligible to receive food stamps. Food stamps are coupons of various denominations that can be exchanged like money for food at authorized stores. Food stamps can be denied to illegal aliens and to people who refuse to seek employment. The program is funded chiefly by federal money through the U.S. Department of Agriculture. It is administered under uniform national standards, so eligibility requirements and amounts a household can receive are the same in all states.

Housing Assistance and Employment Training   Federal, state, and local governments have programs designed to provide poor people with housing assistance. These programs include government-operated housing projects, direct payments of rent money, low-interest loans and insurance to help people buy homes.

In addition, there are programs to train people in skills necessary to obtain a job. Some programs also provide full-time, part-time, or summer jobs. Interested people should check with their state personnel, labor, or employment agency. The U.S. Department of Labor may also be able to provide information on government programs in your area (See Appendix B).

> **WHERE YOU LIVE**
>
> What government job programs exist in your community? Are there any government-operated housing projects in your area?

PROBLEM 34

The people in the following situations call a local government office and ask if they can receive aid. To what program or agency should each be referred?

a. Gerald retires at age 70 after 50 years as an employee of Banks & Company. He needs money for living and medical expenses.

b. Monique is about to have a baby. She had to quit her job, and the father has run off. She needs money for living and medical expenses now and after the baby is born.

c. Gertrude is laid off from work. Several weeks later, her husband (who had a good job) is killed in a construction accident. She needs money for living expenses for herself and their one child.

d. William and Mildred have four children and can't afford to pay their bills for food, housing, clothes, and medical expenses.

e. John, age 17, drops out of high school. He has little money and is having trouble finding a job.

f. James, age 65, is in very poor health but can't afford a nursing home.

DEATH AND THE LAW

When a loved one dies, families are overcome with grief and sadness. Death strikes a deep emotional blow. It is also a major expense. Funerals in the United States are expensive. Making funeral arrangements is never easy, yet many decisions must be made: Should the deceased be buried or cremated? What kind of service should be held? What will the funeral cost? How will it be paid for?

Being totally unprepared for the death of a loved one can be emotionally upsetting. It can also be costly. To ease the burden of death on their families, some people plan ahead for their own funerals. Planning ahead makes sense, like buying insurance, making a will, or choosing a cemetery plot.

This section outlines the choices available to people faced with the death of a loved one. It discusses the considerations involved in planning a funeral, burial, or cremation. It also discusses social security and veterans' death denefits and the legal requirements relating to funerals and other aspects of dying.

Funerals

When someone dies, his or her family should know what choices they have. The first decision is the type of service. Services after death are a way of paying respect to the **deceased** and his or her family. Services after death are also a way of bringing people together to comfort one another.

Funeral services are the most common choice. At a funeral service, the body is present in a casket. Funeral services are usually held in a church, synagogue, or funeral home. **Memorial services** are a second choice. A memorial service is usually held after the deceased has been buried. As a result, it can be held at any suitable time or place. The focus of this type of service is on the life of the deceased.

The second major decision involves the body of the deceased. Does the family prefer burial, cremation, or bequeathal?

The most common choice is **burial.** People can be buried underground in a grave or above ground in a **mausoleum.** A burial can be, but doesn't have to be, very costly. Often a person's body is embalmed before burial. **Embalming** is not legally required in most circumstances. However, embalming does allow the body to be displayed. It is usually required if the person died of an infectious disease, the body is to be shipped across state lines, or the body is to be preserved for a long period before burial.

The second choice is **cremation.** About 10 percent of all deaths in this country result in cremation. Cremation reduces the body to ashes, which may then be scattered, stored in a simple urn, or buried. Cremation is not permitted by certain religions. Also, caskets are not legally required for cremation. As a result, cremation usually costs less than burial.

The final choice is **bequeathal.** This means that the body is donated to a medical school for use in research. Bequeathal is also an inexpensive alternative because the medical school pays for all arrangements. In some cases, people choose to donate parts of their bodies — such as their eyes, liver, or heart — to a medical school. In these cases, the body is returned to the family for burial as soon as the organ is removed.

To donate an organ for medical research, you need a written agreement with a medical school. The ideal donor is someone less than 60 years old with no infectious or incurable diseases. For example, cancer patients cannot be donors. Organ donors carry a Uniform Donor card. This card can usually be obtained by filling out a form at your state's Department of Motor Vehicles.

Funeral Expenses   Some families want an expensive funeral and can pay for it. In 1985 the average funeral cost over $2,000. Many funerals cost much more. Being a careful consumer isn't the first thing on your mind when a loved one dies. Therefore, knowing how much a funeral costs ahead of time makes sense. Funeral costs include embalming, caskets, burial plot, grave markers or monuments, use of a funeral home, transportation of the deceased, and so on. Costs can vary a lot. For example, one can buy a plain pine box or an expensive casket.

Most people qualify for death benefits, which help pay funeral costs. For example, social security will pay cash death benefits. This money is payable to the surviving spouse of anyone who is covered by social security.

Veterans may receive an additional amount, plus a U.S. flag and a grave marker from the Veterans Administration. Moreover, some veterans and their families are entitled to free burial in a national cemetery. To obtain more information about government death benefits, contact the nearest offices of the Social Security Administration and the Veterans Administration.

Some trade unions, fraternal organizations, and employers also provide death benefits. Likewise, insurance policies and pension plans may also help. For more details, contact your employee benefits office, insurance broker, or union representative.

PROBLEM 35

a. Have you ever attended a funeral or memorial service?. Would you know what to do if there were a sudden death in your family? What are some things that must be considered when a loved one dies?

b. Angela Antonio dies in an auto accident. Her family wants to have a funeral right away and does not want an open casket. Does the law require the body of the deceased to be embalmed? Explain your answer.

c. What is the difference between a funeral and a memorial service?

d. What are the major costs involved in a funeral?

e. Every religion and nationality follows its own traditions concerning the ceremony, the type of burial or cremation, and the period of mourning. Explain the type of funeral or service suggested by your own religion.

Dying and the Law

The law does not define the exact moment when death occurs. Determining whether someone is dead and the exact cause of death is a medical, not a legal, decision. Courts generally accept

THE CASE OF KAREN QUINLAN

One night, for no apparent reason, Karen Quinlan, age 22, stopped breathing for two 15-minute periods. She was admitted to a local hospital, where doctors did everything they could to help her. She went into a coma, and could not breathe without a mechanical respirator. Her doctors said that she was in a "vegetative state" and had no chance of recovery.

Karen remained in this condition for over three months. Her parents gradually gave up hope. Finally, they asked the doctor and the hospital to stop using the respirator and all other extraordinary measures to keep Karen alive. Her parents agreed that it would be wrong to stop Karen's breathing, but believed it would not be wrong to turn off a machine that did the breathing for her. Karen's doctor refused to turn off the respirator. He said that doing this would violate his professional oath. The parents then asked a court to order the hospital and doctor to comply with the family's decision.

PROBLEM 36

a. What happened to Karen Quinlan? Why did her parents ask the hospital to end treatment? Why did the doctor refuse?

b. What legal and ethical values are at stake in this case?

c. What would you have done if you were Karen's parents? If you were the doctor?

d. How should the court decide this case?

the opinion of qualified doctors. However, new scientific advances
have created many legal and ethical dilemmas.

The New Jersey Supreme Court ruled that the right to privacy
was more important than the hospital's opinion that the respirator
should not be removed. The court said that if a medical ethics
committee agreed that the prospect of recovery was remote, then
the hospital could not interfere with the private decision of Karen's family. The respirator was then removed, and Karen continued to live in a coma for several years.

Right to Die   Controversy over the *Quinlan* case raised an important issue: Does a person have a legal right to die? The New Jersey
decision gave residents the right to decide whether life support
systems can be disconnected from someone who will never regain
consciousness. How this decision would apply to other situations
was not clear.

Several states now have right-to-die statutes. These laws give
patients the power to tell doctors to cut off life support systems
when death is near. These laws are designed to give people the
right to die with dignity and without undue suffering and pain.
However, most states place limits on these laws. For example, in
one case, a court would not allow an auto accident victim who was
eight months pregnant to refuse a blood transfusion. The court
ruled that this would be unfair to the unborn child.

PROBLEM 37

In each of the following situations, decide whether the court
should order treatment or not order treatment. Explain your
decision.

a. A woman whose religion forbids blood transfusions is in an automobile accident. She needs a blood transfusion to live, but she refuses to have one.

b. A nine-year-old whose religion forbids blood transfusions is in a coma. He will die if he doesn't have a blood transfusion, but his mother refuses to allow one.

c. A mentally alert 73-year-old man, suffering from a painful and incurable form of cancer, wishes to stop treatment and leave the hospital.

d. A 26-year-old professional athlete is permanently paralyzed from the neck down as a result of a motorcycle accident. Doctors say that he may not be able to live without a respirator but the athlete asks that the respirator be turned off.

e. A child is born with brain damage and physical problems that require an operation if she is to live. The father refuses to consent to surgery.

Living Wills   Concern about the dying process and the consequences of terminal injury or illness has led to the development of a new legal document known as a **living will.** This is a document that terminally ill people use to try to determine the course of their own treatment. These documents say that if a person is ever in a situation in which there is no reasonable hope of recovery from injury or illness, then extraordinary efforts to keep the person alive should be stopped. These documents are legally binding in some states but not in others. However, a court might give consideration to such a document when deciding cases like that of Karen Quinlan.

PROBLEM 38

Read the living will on page 251. Then decide whether you would ever consider signing such a document. What are the ethical and legal reasons for and against living wills?

Missing Persons   The law considers a missing person to be alive unless there is a reason to believe the person is dead. For example, if a missing person was last seen boarding an airplane that crashes in the ocean, this would be reason to believe the person is dead. When there is no evidence that a missing person is dead, the law will presume death after seven years. This seven-year rule has been shortened in some states.

Most states will not assume that a missing person is dead if there is good reason for the person not to return. For example, a person who commits a crime and then disappears is not presumed

A LIVING WILL*

To my family, my physician, my lawyer, my clergyman and to any medical facility in whose care I happen to be. To any individual who may become responsible for my health, welfare and affairs.

Death is as much a reality as birth, growth, maturity and old-age — it is the one certainty of life. If the time comes when I, ... can no longer take part in decisions for my own future, let this statement stand as an expression of my wishes, while I am still of sound mind.

If a situation ever arises in which there is no reasonable hope of my recovery from physical or mental illness, I request that I be allowed to die and not be kept alive by artificial means or "heroic measures." I, therefore, ask that medication be mercifully given to me to end suffering even though this may hasten the moment of death.

This will is made after careful thought. I hope you who care for me will feel morally bound to follow my directions. I recognize that this appears to place a heavy responsibility upon you, but it is with the intention of relieving you of such responsibility and of placing it upon myself in accordance with my strong convictions, that this will is made.

                                          Signed_____
Date_____
Witness_____
Witness_____
_____

*Adapted from Model Living Will distributed by Concern for Dying Council.

dead. Also, most states will not presume death unless a serious search is made for the missing person.

Death Certificates   Every state requires the issuance of a **death certificate.** This is a document that lists the name of the deceased and the cause and date of death. Death certificates are official records of death. However, they cannot be used as legal proof that someone caused the death.

Wills and Inheritance

A **will** is a document that tells how a person wants his or her property distributed after death. Everyone who has money or property should consider making a will. A will ensures that anything you own goes to whom you wish in the amount you choose.

Why should someone make a will?

If you die without a will you die **intestate.** This means that any property or money you own will be distributed according to state law. This could result in a property distribution different from what you would want.

Intestacy laws differ greatly from state to state. As a general rule, if the person who dies is married and has children, part of the property will go to the surviving spouse (usually one-third or one-half) and part to the children. If the person who dies is widowed but has children, the children will usually receive all the property. If an unmarried person dies, any property will go to the parents, brothers and sisters, or other relatives, depending on the state. If a person dies without a will and without any living relations, all the property can go to the state. Dying without a will can sometimes cause real hardship for the survivors.

In most states, a person cannot legally make a will until reaching the age of majority. Usually, wills must be in writing. However, in some states, oral wills are permitted if made during a person's final sickness before death. Approximately half the states allow wills to be in a person's own handwriting, but a typewritten will is best. Many states require the will to be witnessed by at least two, and sometimes three, witnesses.

Most states require a husband or wife to provide for the other in the will. If they do not, the law usually gives the living spouse a *share* — usually one-third or one-half of the property. If a married woman dies and leaves all her property to a brother, her husband can still claim and receive a share of her property. The law also requires parents to provide for minor children in a will. However, once children reach the age of majority, there is no requirement to include them.

Many rules and technical details are involved in writing a will. As a result, most people should consult an attorney. A good lawyer can usually draft a simple will and advise on tax-saving ways to divide a person's estate.

The following is an example of a simple will. *It should not be copied under any circumstances. It may be incorrect for your circumstances or invalid under your state law.*

Last Will and Testament of Martha Yates Schwartz

I, Martha Yates Schwartz of 621 Marshall St., Jamestown, Virginia, being of sound mind, do declare this to be my last will and testament and hereby **revoke** all prior wills I have made.

1. I direct my **executor,** named below, to pay my debts, taxes, and funeral expenses as soon after my death as possible.

2. I give and bequeath to my oldest friend, Jennifer Schmidt, my red sapphire ring, which is kept in the bureau in my bedroom.

3. All the rest, residue, and remainder of my estate, real and personal, of which I am now or may hereafter be possessed or to which I may be entitled, I give to my husband, Mark Schwartz, if he survives me. If he does not survive me, I give the rest to my children, Peter and Ellen.

4. I appoint my husband, Mark Schwartz, to be the executor of my last will and testament to serve without **bond** or **undertaking.** In the event he does not survive me or fails to serve for any reason, I appoint my brother, Ken Yates, to serve as executor without bond or undertaking.

5. If my husband dies before me or at the same time, I nominate our good friends, Jacob and Wilma Stern, to be the guardians of our children. If they are unable or unwilling to serve, I nominate my brother, Ken Yates, and his wife, Elizabeth, to be the children's guardians.

In witness hereof I have hereunto set my hand this ___ day of
_____, 19_____

_____

Martha Yates Schwartz

The foregoing instrument was signed, published, and declared by said Martha Yates Schwartz as her last will and testament in our presence, and we, at her request and in her presence and in the presence of each other, have hereunto fixed our signatures as witnesses thereto.

Date	Name	Address
_____	_____	_____
_____	_____	_____
_____	_____	_____

WHERE YOU LIVE

How old does a person have to be to write a will in your state? How many witnesses are required?

PROBLEM 39

Refer to Martha Schwartz's will and answer the following questions:

a. Who will get Martha's property if she dies the day after she makes the will?

b. Who will take care of her children if she and her husband die in an accident?

c. Most states require two witnesses. Why do you think there are three spaces for witnesses here?

d. Are wills really necessary? Couldn't Martha accomplish her wishes by just telling her husband what to do if she dies? Explain.

Wills may be simple, or they may be very detailed. A detailed will may contain instructions on what happens to every item the person owns, exactly what happens at the funeral, and many other things. People with young children often include a clause naming someone a guardian for their children. The courts are not required to follow this direction, but they usually do unless there is a strong reason not to or the named guardian is unwilling to take the children.

Wills can usually be revoked by ripping them up. Wills can also be changed by adding a **codicil** or an amendment to the original will. However, any significant change should usually be accomplished by destroying the old will and writing a new one.

When someone dies, the executor or executrix named in the will becomes very important. If there is no will, this person is named by the court and is called an **administrator.** The executor or administrator usually arranges the funeral and the burial or cremation; locates the will and delivers it to the register of wills, who will **probate** it (verify and read it); takes charge of the deceased's property; keeps records; pays income, estate, and inheritance taxes; and, with court approval, gives out the property to the persons named in the will, called **heirs.**

The executor will often hire a lawyer to assist with the prior responsibilities. The attorney may charge an hourly fee or a fixed percentage of the value of the property left by the deceased (e.g., 6 percent). Some executors, depending on their own knowledge and the rules in the local probate court, may be able to probate a will without an attorney. The executor is also eligible for a fee. This is usually a fixed percentage of the value of the property and must be approved by the probate court.

PROBLEM 40

a. If you died today, what would happen to what you own?

b. At what stage in your life would you consider drawing up a will?

c. If you were named as executor in a will, could you perform the duties listed in the text? Would you need to have a lawyer to carry out the duties? Would you want to pay the lawyer a percentage of the value of all the property or an hourly fee? Explain.

five
HOUSING
LAW

Whether you live in a farmhouse or a high rise, a mobile home or a suburban split-level, a condominium or a walk-up flat, you and your family use and pay for housing. Many Americans own their own homes. Many others rent houses or apartments owned by someone else. Whether you own or rent, you need to be aware of some of the practical issues and problems involving housing.

In this chapter, you will find information on the advantages and disadvantages of renting and buying, where and how to find a place to live, and how to calculate the amount you can afford for housing. You will also learn what to do if you are discriminated against in buying or renting a home, what to look for in an apartment, and what to look out for in a lease.

PROBLEM 1

Assume you and your family are moving to a new home.

a. Make a list of all the features you would like in a home (house or apartment, size, type, location, price, convenience, etc.).

257

b. Look in the classified section of your local newspaper to see what you find that meets your description. Could you and your family afford to live there?

c. Are there more listings for some locations than others? Does the cost of houses and apartments vary, depending on where they are located? Why? What advantages and disadvantages are claimed for the various neighborhoods and housing types? In choosing a place to live, what do you think is the most important consideration? Why?

CHOOSING A PLACE TO LIVE

Choosing where to live is an important decision. Every year, over 40 million Americans move into a new house or apartment. This change of residence often involves a move into a new neighborhood, a different city, or another part of the country. Before looking for a place to live, you should ask yourself three questions: Where do I want to live? What can I afford? Do I want to rent or buy?

Location

A key factor in finding a place to live is location. In considering location, you should decide whether you prefer a city, suburban, or rural setting. If you have to travel to work or school every day, you should consider the cost of commuting, including how long it will take and whether public transportation is available. If you have children, you should consider the quality and availability of schools and child care facilities. You should also consider community services and neighborhood character. Find out if stores and shopping areas are conveniently located, and if police, fire, and sanitation services are reliable. Try to determine whether the neighbors seem friendly. Before deciding on a location, walk and drive around the neighborhood or community you're considering. Talk with people who live there, and give careful thought to whether you really want to live in the area.

PROBLEM 2

a. Would you rather live in a city, suburb, small town, or rural area? Why?

b. What are some advantages and disadvantages of each location?

Cost

People can't always live where they want. The choice of housing is often limited by what is available. Even more often, our choice of

What are some advantages and disadvantages of living in the city?

housing is limited by price. You may find a house or apartment in the area you like, but the price is too high. How much you can afford to pay is often the key factor in determining where you live.

A person who rents a house or apartment is known as a **tenant.** Tenants have to pay a set amount of money every month to the **landlord.** Depending on the agreement with your landlord, you may also have to pay utilities (electricity, gas, water, etc.). Remember that utility costs can be expensive, so consider them along with the rent. *Before renting or buying, find out what the average monthly utilities were for the past year.* It is usually best to ask to see copies of recent bills.

If you buy a home, you will probably be required to make a cash **down payment** before you can move in. The amount can vary from no down payment, under certain government loan programs, to as much as 20 or 30 percent of the house's price. The remainder of the cost of the house, called a **mortgage** loan, must be paid by the buyer over time. For example, if you buy a house for $60,000, you might be required to make a down payment of 25 percent, or $15,000. The remaining $45,000 would be your mortgage. This amount would be repaid in monthly payments over a number of years (e.g., 30 years). Buyers are also responsible for paying other costs relating to the property.

The traditional rule for either renting or buying is that you should not pay more than 25 percent of your monthly take-home income for housing. Using this formula, your rent or mortgage payment should be no more than $250 per month if you take home $1,000 a month. In recent years, the high cost of housing has forced many home buyers to spend more than 25 percent of their income for housing. This is not necessarily bad, especially if you buy a house that is a good investment. However, people who are forced to spend a large portion of their income on housing will naturally have less money for other things. In some cases, people spend so much on housing that they are not able to pay their other bills.

When deciding whether to rent or buy, what things should you consider?

PROBLEM 3

Mr. and Mrs. Furlong look at an apartment for $275 per month. The cost of the rent does not include utilities. They have a monthly income of $1,500. Consider the information provided on the chart "Record of Housing Expenses 1985," and then answer the following questions.

a. Using the 25 percent formula, how much can the Furlongs afford to pay each month for housing?

b. What was the average cost per month for utilities?

Record of Housing Expenses 1985			
MONTH	HEATING BILL	WATER BILL	ELECTRIC BILL
January	$ 80.00	$ 12.00	$ 21.05
February	83.40	13.00	22.60
March	64.60	12.46	21.55
April	50.02	12.52	18.00
May	36.78	13.80	18.43
June	-0-	18.00	23.90
July	-0-	19.67	25.40
August	-0-	22.40	26.92
September	34.60	19.01	20.23
October	50.90	14.06	19.27
November	69.41	12.36	20.34
December	78.50	12.38	21.70
	$548.21	$181.66	$259.39

c. Will the Furlongs be able to afford the apartment if the utilities stay the same? If they go up?

d. How can the Furlongs try to keep down the cost of utilities?

Renting Versus Buying

Should you buy or rent? Whatever you decide, each choice has advantages and disadvantages. Cost is a key consideration. If you're thinking of buying, you will need a certain amount of cash for a down payment. This prevents many people from buying. Mortgages usually run for 20 or 30 years, and the homebuyer is required to keep up monthly payments for the entire time. In addition, homeowners must pay for utilities, taxes, maintenance, repairs, insurance, and home improvements. Another disadvantage of buying is that the mortgage lender can take the house and sell it if you fail to make the mortgage payments.

Home ownership can be expensive, particularly in the beginning, but buying also has many advantages. First, the monthly mortgage payment is a form of forced savings, which can usually be recovered when the house is sold. This means that each month, part of your mortgage payment pays off part of the total loan. Second, buying a house is a good way to fight inflation. This is because housing prices usually rise while the monthly mortgage payment remains the same. Third, there are tax advantages to owning a home. The interest on a mortgage (usually a sizable part of your payments in early years) and the amount of any property taxes can be deducted from your federal income tax each year. Fourth, owning a house is usually a good investment. In most places, housing values have increased faster than the rate of inflation. Finally, many people buy houses for the "pride of ownership.'' Homeowners can generally change or improve the house or yard in any way they see fit, and the fact of ownership often builds pride in and concern for the community.

Like buying, renting also has it pros and cons. Renters have fewer responsibilities. They can call the landlord to make major repairs and don't have to worry about property taxes or home-owner's insurance. Renting gives people more freedom to move on short notice, and if renters lose their source of income, their commitment to pay lasts only as long as the **lease.**

In the short run renting probably costs less, although over a period of years renters have little but receipts or canceled checks to show for their payments. Moreover, the monthly rent can go up periodically, while monthly mortgage payments usually remain the same. Renters may have more flexibility if they decide to move, but they generally also have more rules and less privacy than homeowners. Deciding whether to buy or rent is a difficult decision. During a lifetime, many people do both.

PROBLEM 4

Fred and Jill, both 23 years old, decide to get married. They both have jobs paying about $12,000 a year. Each takes home $800 a month ($1,600 total). Between them they have about $5,000 in savings. They are trying to decide if they should rent or buy. They visit a real estate agent, who takes them to see a small two-bedroom house. The agent says the owner is willing to rent or sell

It is illegal to discriminate in the sale, rental, or financing of housing.

it to them. If they rent, the owner wants $375 a month rent, plus utilities, which average $50 a month. The owner will give them a one-year lease and make the major repairs. If they buy, the price of the house is $40,000 and a cash down payment of $5,000 would be required. They would also need a mortgage loan of $35,000 from a local bank. This would require monthly loan payments of $400 a month, plus $1,000 a year in real estate taxes, $300 a year in insurance, and $1,200 in closing costs.

a. List all the reasons why Fred and Jill should buy the house.

b. List all the reasons why they should rent the house.

c. Roleplay a discussion between them in which they decide whether to rent or buy.

Discrimination in Housing

THE CASE OF THE UNWANTED TENANT

Since the death of her husband, Mrs. Amy Weaver has run a small five-unit apartment house. She lives in one unit and makes a meager income by renting out the other four. She doesn't really dislike members of minority groups but knows that several of her regular tenants have threatened to move out if she rents to such people. Anyway, she feels she has the right to do whatever she wants in her own building.

Nuy Van Tran, a refugee from Vietnam, is looking for an apartment to rent. When a friend at work tells him about a vacancy at Mrs. Weaver's, he calls and makes an appointment to inspect the apartment. When Mr. Van Tran arrives for the appointment, Mrs. Weaver takes one look at him and tells him the apartment has been rented. "After all," she says to herself, "it's my property, and no one has the right to tell me whom I must allow to live here."

PROBLEM 5

a. What happened in this case? Why did Mrs. Weaver refuse to rent the apartment to Mr. Van Tran?
b. Do you think what Mrs. Weaver did was legal or illegal? Why?
c. Should the law allow landlords to rent to whomever they want?
d. Which do you think is more important: the right to control one's own property or the right to live where one chooses?
e. Is there anything Mr. Van Tran can do? Explain.

Choice of housing is sometimes limited by discrimination. For various reasons, some landlords, real estate agents, mortgage

**WHERE
YOU
LIVE**

What laws prohibit
housing discrimination
in your state or com-
munity? What state or
local agencies enforce
these laws and inves-
tigate complaints?

lenders, and owners prefer to sell or rent to certain types of people
over others.

Usually, a major consideration of those who sell or rent is
whether the money owed them will be paid in full and on time. To
help ensure this, they usually want to know several things about
potential tenants or buyers, including:

■ Does the person have a steady income that is likely to continue
into the future?

■ Is the income high enough to enable the person to pay for the
housing?

■ Does the person have a good record in paying off previous bills
or loans?

■ Will the person take good care of the property?

The *Federal Fair Housing Act of 1968* forbids discrimination
because of a person's race, color, sex, national origin, or religion.
This law covers the rental, sale, or financing of privately owned
houses and apartments with four or more units. An executive order
also prohibits discrimination in federally owned, operated, or assisted housing, including public housing.

Many states and cities also have antidiscrimination laws.
These laws sometimes provide more protection than the federal
law by forbidding discrimination against unmarried people, families with children, homosexuals, handicapped people, and others.

Discrimination can take many forms. It exists when owners
say their homes are sold when they're really not, or when real
estate agents practice **steering.** This means directing buyers or
renters to particular areas because of their race or other reasons.

Another type of housing discrimination is **redlining.** This is a practice whereby banks and others refuse to make loans to homebuyers
in certain areas or neighborhoods. Redlining violates federal law
and the laws of many states.

Not all discrimination is illegal. For example, landlords and
sellers may refuse to rent or sell to people who have poor credit
ratings.

Proving discrimination is not always easy, and there are some
valid reasons for turning down would-be tenants or homebuyers.
Nevertheless, if you think you've been unfairly discriminated
against, you may file a complaint with the U.S. Department of
Housing and Urban Development's (HUD) Fair Housing Office (see
Appendix B for the address). HUD has the power to investigate the
complaint and can attempt to solve the problem.

You may also be able to file a complaint with a local or state
antidiscrimination agency or take the case to court. U.S. district

courts have the power to order an end to the discrimination and can award money to the person discriminated against.

THE CASE OF NO KIDS ALLOWED

Bonnie and Ron Pomerantz owned a home in an adults-only housing development in Tamarac, Florida. They were attracted to the area by the quiet life of a child-free environment. "We liked the way the area was kept up . . . and we didn't plan to have kids," says Ron. Then Bonnie got pregnant and later gave birth to a baby girl, Erika.

When Bonnie became pregnant, the Homeowners Association asked the Pomerantz couple to move. They refused. After Erika's birth, the association sued them in state court. The Homeowners Association says that children increase maintenance and security costs, and that they destroy the peace and quiet of adults-only complexes. The association also says the Pomerantz couple breached the homeowner's contract they signed when buying the house. This deed restricted the housing development to adults.

The Pomerantz couple responded by saying that the Homeowners Association is discriminating against children. They contend that this discrimination is wrong and that the deed restriction is illegal. They also say they have the right to live where they want, and no one should be forced to choose between keeping their home or keeping their child. Finally, they say that children are no noisier than many adults or pets.

PROBLEM 6

a. What happened in the case? Why is the Pomerantz family being asked to move?

b. What arguments can you make for the Homeowners Association? For the Pomerantz family? What social values are involved in this case?

c. Do you think the Pomerantz family should be forced to move? If so, why? If not, why not?

d. Should certain housing be restricted to singles, senior citizens, or other groups? Explain your answer.

PROBLEM 7

Consider each of the following situations and decide whether you think the action of the landlord, homeowner, lender, or sales agent was legal or illegal under the *Federal Fair Housing Act*. If the action is legal under the act, do you think the law should be changed to prohibit the discrimination?

a. A real estate company has a policy of taking whites to white neighborhoods and blacks to black neighborhoods.

b. A woman seeking a two-bedroom apartment is turned down by the landlord, who thinks the apartment is too small for her and her three children.

c. A landlord turns down a man who collects unemployment benefits because the landlord is worried he won't be able to pay the rent.

d. A homeowner refuses to sell to a Hispanic couple because he thinks the neighbors won't approve.

e. A woman is rejected for a mortgage by a bank officer who believes her divorce makes her a financial risk.

f. A zoning change to allow a group home for the retarded is blocked by a neighborhood association.

g. A young lawyer is rejected as a tenant because the landlord is afraid he'll complain too much and stir up the other tenants.

h. A young musician is rejected by a landlord who thinks he looks like a hippie and might make too much noise.

i. A credit union official discourages an elderly man from buying a house because the official thinks the man won't live long enough to pay off the mortgage.

EQUAL HOUSING OPPORTUNITY

We Do Business in Accordance With the Federal Fair Housing Law

(Title VIII of the Civil Rights Act of 1968, as Amended by the Housing and Community Development Act of 1974)

IT IS ILLEGAL TO DISCRIMINATE AGAINST ANY PERSON BECAUSE OF RACE, COLOR, RELIGION, SEX, OR NATIONAL ORIGIN

- In the sale or rental of housing or residential lots
- In advertising the sale or rental of housing
- In the financing of housing
- In the provision of real estate brokerage services

Blockbusting is also illegal

An aggrieved person may file a complaint of a housing discrimination act with the:

U.S. DEPARTMENT OF HOUSING AND URBAN DEVELOPMENT
Assistant Secretary for Fair Housing and Equal Opportunity
Washington, D.C. 20410

RENTING A HOME

Many people rent their homes. A renter pays the owner a certain amount of money in return for the right to live there for a period of time. The person who receives rent money is called the **landlord,** and the person who pays rent money is called the **tenant.**

The landlord-tenant relationship is created by a type of contract called a lease or rental agreement. A lease sets out the amount of rent that must be paid and the length of time the apartment may be rented. It also states the rights and duties of both landlord and tenant.

Before you rent an apartment or a house, at least two things should be done to protect your interests. First, completely inspect the dwelling to ensure that it meets your needs. Second, because most leases are written to the advantage of the landlord, carefully read the lease. If you don't understand or can't read the lease, get help from someone else before signing.

PROBLEM 8

Assume that you are looking for a new apartment. You are married and have a two-year-old child and a small dog.

a. Make a checklist of all the things you would look for in an apartment.

b. What questions would you ask the landlord?

c. If you inspect an apartment, what things should you look for? Look out for?

The House or Apartment

Once you've decided to rent, your first job is to find a suitable house or apartment. Sometimes landlords put For Rent signs on their property. More often, you'll have to look in the classified section of the local newspaper or on community bulletin boards. Many landlords use real estate agents or brokers to rent property for them. These agents can make promises on behalf of the owner and are paid a fee for finding tenants and managing the owner's property.

Before you look at an apartment, it is wise to make a list of your needs and wants. Ask yourself questions such as: Where do I want to live? How much rent can I afford? What facilities and services do I need? How much living and storage space do I require? What other costs such as utilities or maintenance may be involved?

Once you've found an apartment, you can avoid problems by giving it a thorough inspection *before* signing the lease. You should

If you were looking for a rental house or apartment, how would you find one?

do this to determine the apartment's condition and to see that it meets your needs. Talking with other tenants is also a good idea. Ask them about their experience with the building and the landlord. Most important, never rent an apartment you haven't seen, even if you're shown a model apartment and told yours will be just like it.

ADVICE ON WHAT TO INSPECT BEFORE RENTING

- What is the condition of the building?
- Are hallways, lobbies, and common areas clean and well lighted?
- Does the building have laundry facilities?
- Is there enough parking space?
- Are there any signs of insects or rodents?
- How is routine and emergency maintenance handled?
- Is storage and closet space adequate?
- Is the apartment soundproof?
- Are the plumbing, heating, and electrical fixtures in working order?
- Are kitchen appliances clean and in good condition?
- Is there any evidence of water stains or peeling paint on walls and ceilings?
- Does the building provide protection against burglars or uninvited guests?
- Is it likely to be too cold in winter or too hot in summer?
- Is the apartment furnished or unfurnished?
- Do windows and doors open easily?
- Are there any broken windows or screens?
- Are fire extinguishers and safety exits available?
- Is the apartment big enough?

The Lease

Once you've inspected a rental house or apartment, you'll probably be asked to fill out a **lease application.** This is a form that the landlord uses to determine whether you qualify for the rental. You will be asked for information such as your name, age, address, place of employment, source of income, and a list of previous residences. You will also be asked for credit references. Landlords use this information to determine your ability to pay the rent. If the landlord approves your lease application, you will then have to sign a lease.

A lease is a legal agreement or contract in which both the landlord and the tenant agree to certain things. A lease usually includes the date you may move in, the amount of the rent, the dates on which the rent is to be paid, and the length or term of the lease. It also includes the amount of any **security deposit**, the

Tenants should always inspect the apartment before signing a lease.

conditions under which the rent may be raised, and rules governing repairs, maintenance, and other conditions in the apartment.

Depending upon your particular situation, one type of lease may be better than another. For example, if you are planning to rent for only a short period, or if your job requires you to move on short notice, you might prefer a **month-to-month lease.** This type of lease usually enables you to leave after 30 days' notice. However, it has the disadvantage of allowing the landlord to raise the rent or evict you with just 30 days' notice.

Another type of lease allows a tenant to move in with the understanding that the lease is for an indefinite period. This arrangement is called a **tenancy at will.** It allows the tenant to leave or be told to leave at any time.

A lease for a fixed period of time — such as six months or a year — is called a **tenancy for years.** This type of lease generally prevents the landlord from raising the rent or evicting the tenant during the period of the lease. If you are planning to rent for a long period of time, this may be the best type of lease for you.

Written leases are generally difficult to read and understand. To protect yourself, be sure to read all clauses in the lease carefully before signing it. Never sign a lease unless all blank spaces are filled in or crossed out. If you're unsure of anything in the lease, consult with a tenant organization, legal aid office, or private attorney. Also make sure any promises made by the landlord are written into the lease. For example, if the landlord promises to paint the apartment before you move in, get the promise in writing.

THE SUMMER RENTAL CASE

A college student goes to a resort town to work for the summer and rents an apartment for three months. After a month, she moves to a cheaper apartment down the street. The landlord demands rent for the two remaining months, but the young woman claims she doesn't owe any money because the lease was not in writing.

PROBLEM 9

a. Is the student obligated to pay the additional two months' rent? Would it make a difference if the landlord rented the apartment immediately after she moved out?

b. What should the woman have done when she found the cheaper apartment?

c. Roleplay a phone call between the woman and the landlord after she finds the cheaper apartment and wishes to get the landlord's permission to move.

Leases for less than one year do not have to be written to be legal. Because the lease in the Summer Rental Case was for only three months, the landlord is right. The oral agreement is binding, and the tenant still owes rent for two more months. To avoid problems, you are *always* better off getting a written lease, signed and dated by both you and the landlord. Leases that are for more than one year must always be in writing.

In most places, you'll probably be asked to sign a standard form lease. These leases are written to the landlord's advantage. Some even contain illegal clauses that are unenforceable in court. The lease reprinted in the text contains many provisions found in standard form leases. A few of the clauses contained in this lease are illegal in some states. However, before examining the lease, remember that landlord-tenant law differs from state to state. You should always inform yourself about the landlord-tenant laws in your own state.

PROBLEM 10

a. What are the key provisions of the lease on pages 272–273? Who is the landlord? Who pays for utilities? Is the tenant allowed to have a pet?

b. As a tenant, would you object to any of the provisions in this lease?

RANDALL REAL ESTATE CO.
PROPERTY MANAGEMENT — INVESTMENT
PROPERTY — SALES — INSURANCE

THIS AGREEMENT, Made and executed this _____ day of _____ A.D., 19____, by and between RANDALL REAL ESTATE COMPANY, hereinafter called the Landlord, and _____

_____ , hereinafter called the Tenant.

WITNESSETH, That Landlord does hereby let unto Tenant the premises known as Apartment No. 301, at 12 Marshall Street in Johnstown, for the term commencing on the ____ day of _____, 19____, and fully ending at midnight on the day of ____, 19____, at and for the total rental of _____ Dollars, the first installment payable on the execution of this agreement and the remaining installments payable in advance on the ____ day of each ensuing month, to and at the office of RANDALL REAL ESTATE COMPANY, 1000 Columbia Road, in Johnstown.

On the ____ day of _____, 19____, a sum of _____shall become due and payable. This sum shall cover the period up to the day of _____, 19____; thereafter, a sum of _____ shall be due and payable on the _____day of each month.

AND TENANT, does hereby agree as follows:

1. Tenant will pay the rent at the time specified.

2. Tenant will pay all utility bills as they become due.

3. Tenant will use the premises for a dwelling and for no other purpose.

4. Tenant will not use said premises for any unlawful purpose, nor in any noisy or rowdy manner, or other way offensive to any other occupant of the building.

5. Tenant will not transfer or sublet the premises without the written consent of the Landlord.

6. Landlord shall have access to the premises at any time for the purpose of inspection, to make repairs the Landlord considers necessary, or to show the apartment to tenant applicants.

7. Tenant will give Landlord prompt notice of any defects or breakage in the structure, equipment or fixtures of said premises.

8. Tenant will not make any alterations or additions to the structure, equipment, or fixtures of said premises without the written consent of the Landlord.

9. Tenant will pay a security deposit in the amount of $_____, which will be held by Landlord until

expiration of this lease and refunded on the condition that said premises is returned in good condition, normal wear and tear excepted.

10. Tenant will not keep any pets, live animals, or birds of any description in said premises.

11. Landlord shall be under no liability to Tenant for any discontinuance of heat, hot water, or elevator service, and shall not be liable for damage to property of Tenant caused by rodents, rain, snow, defective plumbing, or any other source.

12. Should Tenant continue in possession after the end of the term herein with permission of Landlord, it is agreed that the tenancy thus created can be terminated by either party giving to the other party not less than Thirty (30) Days' Written Notice.

13. Tenant shall be required to give the Landlord at least thirty (30) days notice, in writing, of his intention to vacate the premises at the expiration of this tenancy. If Tenant vacates the premises without first furnishing said notice, Tenant shall be liable to the Landlord for one month's rent.

14. Both Landlord and Tenant waive trial by jury in connection with any agreement contained in the rental agreement or any claim for damages arising out of the agreement or connected with this tenancy.

15. Landlord shall not be held liable for any injuries or damages to the Tenant or his guests, regardless of cause.

16. In the event of increases in real estate taxes, fuel charges, or sewer and water fees, Tenant agrees during the term of the lease to pay a proportionate share of such charges, fees, or increases.

17. Tenant confesses judgment and waives any and all rights to file a counterclaim, or a defense to any action filed by the Landlord against the Tenant and further agrees to pay attorney fees and all other costs incurred by the Landlord in an action against the Tenant.

18. Tenant agrees to observe all such rules and regulations which the Landlord or his agents will make concerning the apartment building.

IN TESTIMONY WHEREOF, Landlord and Tenant have signed this Agreement the day and year first hereinbefore written.

Signed in the presence of   _____

_____

_____

_____

_____

Landlord-Tenant Negotiations

In many places, housing is in big demand and short supply. In this kind of market, landlords generally have the upper hand and can often tell tenants to take it or leave it. Negotiating with a landlord can be difficult, but it is worth a try, particularly if you know your rights and know what you want in an apartment. If you do try negotiating with a landlord, it is best to be assertive, but tactful and polite. Landlords want to know you'll be a good tenant. But tenants expect something in return — namely, fair treatment and a clean, well-maintained place to live.

To strike a section from a lease, both the tenant and the landlord or rental agent should cross out the particular clause and put their initials next to the change. If anything is added to the lease, be sure the addition is written on all copies of the lease and signed by both the landlord and the tenant.

LEASE NEGOTIATION

Read the following information. Then two persons should roleplay the landlords (the Randalls). Two others should roleplay the tenants (the Monicos). Persons roleplaying the Monicos should inspect the apartment and ask the landlord all the questions a tenant should ask before deciding to rent the apartment. Persons roleplaying the Randalls should find out everything a landlord needs to know before renting to a tenant. The landlords should give a copy of the lease to the tenants. They should discuss it and reach a decision on whether to sign it.

Mr. and Mrs. Randall own an apartment building in the city of Johnstown. They have a nice two-bedroom apartment for rent. They require all their tenants to take a two-year lease, to pay a two-month security deposit, and to sign a lease (the same as the one printed in the text). They don't allow pets in the building. The rent is $400 per month plus utilities, which average about $50 a month. They are eager to rent the apartment right away because it has been empty for two weeks.

Mr. and Mrs. Monico have just moved to Johnstown, where they have new jobs. Mr. Monico's job may last only one year, and they may then move back to Williamsport, a city 100 miles away. They have a three-year-old son and a dog. Based on their salaries, they wish to pay only $350 a month in rent and utilities. They want a nice neighborhood and are a little worried about the crime in Johnstown. They want an apartment right away because they start work in three days. They see a notice advertising the Randalls' apartment. They don't know much about the neighborhood, but they decide to look at the apartment.

The apartment has two bedrooms, a living room, a dining area,

RIGHTS AND DUTIES OF LANDLORDS AND TENANTS

After a person signs a lease and moves into a rental home or apartment, both the landlord and the tenant take on certain rights and duties. Most rights and duties are set out in the lease. However, certain responsibilities exist without being stated in the lease. The following section discusses in detail several clauses from the lease reprinted in the text. This material is designed to help you read a lease and avoid problems.

Paying the Rent

Tenant will pay the rent at the time specified. (Clause 1)

A tenant's most important duty is paying the rent. Leases generally state the amount of rent to be paid and the date on which it

and one bathroom with a tub but no shower. It is on the second floor and has a small balcony overlooking a parking lot. The paint is peeling in the larger bedroom, and a small window is broken in the bathroom. The kitchen has a new refrigerator and sink, but the stove is old and worn and has a missing handle. The front door and the door to the balcony have locks that could easily be opened by an intruder.

After the roleplay, answer the following questions:

PROBLEM 11

a. Did the Monicos ask any questions about the neighborhood or building as a whole? Should they have?

b. What was decided regarding the amount of rent and other costs of the apartment? In reality, can tenants ever convince landlords to take less than they are asking?

c. In discussing the conditions in the apartment, did the tenants get the landlords to agree to any repairs?

d. Did the Monicos ask about such services as laundry, parking, and playgrounds? Should they have?

e. Are there any special rules in the lease that the Monicos didn't like? Did they ask the landlords to discuss these, and if so, what occurred? Could the Monicos have done a better job negotiating these rules?

f. Is it worthwhile for tenants to try to negotiate with landlords? Can tenants be hurt by doing this?

WHAT TO CONSIDER BEFORE RENTING

■ What kind of area do you wish to live in?

■ What are the costs, including rent, utilities, security deposit, maintenance fees, etc.?

■ What is the condition of the apartment or house? Will repairs be made by the landlord before you move in?

■ How long will the lease last and how can it be ended?

■ Will the landlord make or pay for repairs that occur after you move in?

■ What services (storage, trash removal, maintenance of yard, appliances) will the tenant receive?

■ Are there any special rules (no pets, no children, no parties)?

■ Do you understand all the clauses in the lease? Are any of them illegal or difficult for you to accept?

is due. Most leases require payment on the first day of each month. If you and the landlord agree to a date other than the first, be sure that it is written into the lease.

Historically, courts have required tenants to continue paying rent no matter what happened to the house or apartment. For example, if the apartment was damaged by fire, the tenant was still required to pay rent for the term of the lease. In recent years, courts and legislatures in most states have ruled that in situations in which the apartment is made unlivable by fire, landlord neglect, or other causes, the tenant cannot be forced to pay the rent. These situations are discussed more fully in the section on landlord-tenant problems. For now, keep in mind that tenants have a duty to pay the rent and that landlords generally have a right to **evict** tenants who don't pay the rent.

Raising the Rent

In the event of increases in real estate taxes, fuel charges, or sewer and water fees, Tenant agrees during the term of the lease to pay a proportionate share of such charges, fees, or increases. (Clause 16)

Generally, landlords cannot raise the rent during the term of a lease. When the term is over, the rent can normally be raised as much as the landlord wants. Some leases, however, include provisions (like Clause 16) that allow for automatic increases during the term of the lease. Many landlords include such clauses to cover

The rising cost of rental housing has caused many cities to enact rent control laws.

the rising cost of fuel and building maintenance. A lease with an escalation clause is obviously not favorable to a tenant.

Another factor that can affect whether the landlord may raise the rent is **rent control.** Many communities — especially large cities — have rent control laws, which put a limit on how much existing rents can be raised. Cities with rent control laws use various standards to control the rise in rents. Some places limit rent increases to a certain percentage each year. In other places, rent increases are tied to the cost of living, the cost of improvements in the building, or are allowed only when a new tenant moves in.

Rent control laws slow down the rising cost of housing. However, there are many arguments for and against rent control, and wherever it has been tried, it has been controversial.

> **WHERE YOU LIVE**
>
> Is rent control permitted in your state? If so, how does it operate and how successful has it been?

PROBLEM 12

Suppose your city council is considering rent control. Housing costs have been rising steadily, and a law is proposed limiting rent increases to 5 percent a year for all rental properties. Read the following statements. Decide which one you agree with and explain why.

Representative of a Tenant Group

There is a severe shortage of apartments and rental homes in the area. As a result, landlords have been able to charge just about any rent they want. During the last two years, rents have risen an average of 15 percent a year. The housing shortage and rent increases particularly hurt low- and middle-income tenants who are barely able to meet expenses and pay the rent. Only government control can stop the continued rapid rise in rents. Rent control should be passed by the legislature.

Representative of a Landlord Group

Rent control will mean more rundown housing, because area landlords won't be able to pay for repairs or improvements. Some landlords may be forced to sell or abandon their buildings because it will be uneconomical to operate them. In addition, if landlords can't expect reasonable profits, they won't build new apartment buildings. An even greater shortage of rental units will result.

Landlords raise rents only to meet the increased costs of heating fuel, electricity, taxes, and repairs. Also, landlords are in business to earn a profit and have a right to charge whatever they want. Besides, tenants can always move out and find another apartment if they think the rent is too high. Rent control would be a big mistake.

Quiet Enjoyment

THE CASE OF THE NOISY NEIGHBOR

Mike and Marcy O'Reilly sign a one-year lease, and they are pleased when they move into a beautiful old apartment building in their favorite part of town.

However, soon after moving, they discover that the building is incredibly noisy and disorderly. During the first week, their next-door neighbor throws several wild parties, keeping them up all night. They also discover that when their neighbor isn't having parties, he is receiving visitors at all hours of the day. These visits are almost always accompanied by loud music, shouting, and constant coming and going. The partying often carries out into the halls, and the O'Reillys are frequently hassled by the visitors.

The O'Reillys complain to the landlord on a dozen occasions, but the late-night parties and noisy visitors go on. Finally, the O'Reillys decide they have had enough and move out. The landlord then sues the O'Reillys, claiming they owe her for 11 months' rent. Will the O'Reillys have to pay?

One of a tenant's most important rights is the **right to quiet enjoyment.** This simply means that the tenant has a right to use and enjoy the property without being disturbed by the landlord or other tenants.

Tenants have a right to quiet enjoyment even if it is not stated in the lease, and landlords have a duty to ensure that other tenants don't unreasonably disturb the tenants in the building. If the O'Reillys (in the Case of the Noisy Neighbor) complained to the landlord and she did nothing about it, they were probably justified in moving out because of the failure to provide quiet enjoyment. As a practical matter, tenants should send a written complaint to the landlord if such conditions exist. It is also wise to keep a copy of the complaint. Unless the landlord knows of the problem, things are unlikely to improve.

Who is responsible for repair and upkeep in a rented apartment?

Upkeep and Repairs

Landlord shall be under no liability to Tenant for any discontinuance of heat, hot water, or elevator service, and shall not be liable for damage to property of Tenant caused by rodents, rain, snow, defective plumbing, or any other source. (Clause 11)

Traditionally, landlords did not have a duty to maintain the premises or make repairs to a rented house or apartment. In the few places where this is still true, tenants have to make all repairs that are needed to keep the property in its original condition.

Clause 11 from the sample lease states that the tenant must continue to pay the rent whether or not the landlord provides a dwelling fit to live in. In some states, this provision is unenforceable. Today, most states require the landlord to keep the house or apartment in a condition fit to live in. Many state courts have said that a **warranty of habitability** is implied in every lease. This means that the landlord promises to provide a place fit for human habitation. This promise is said to exist whether or not it is written into the lease. Thus, if major repairs are needed — the furnace breaks down, the roof leaks, or the apartment is overrun by insects or rodents — the landlord has a duty to correct the problems.

> **WHERE YOU LIVE**
>
> What is your state's law regarding repairs and the warranty of habitability?

PROBLEM 13

a. If you were a landlord, what repairs and maintenance would you expect the tenant to perform? Develop a list and explain it.

b. If you were a tenant, what repairs and maintenance would you expect the landlord to perform? Develop a list and explain it.

Besides the warranty of habitability, many communities have **housing codes.** These codes set minimum standards for repairs and living conditions within rental houses or apartments. Landlords are required to meet the standards of the housing code, and they may lose their license to rent if the standards are not maintained. Housing codes differ from area to area, but in most places tenants have the right to call in a government housing inspector to examine their apartment for code violations.

PROBLEM 14

Which of the housing code provisions reprinted on page 280 do you feel are most important? Are there any housing code requirements not listed that should be included?

While most places hold landlords responsible for major repairs, remember that the landlord's duty to make repairs differs from place to place and from lease to lease. It is always best to have the responsibility for repairs spelled out in the lease. Also, remember that tenants have a duty to notify the landlord when repairs are needed. If someone is injured as a result of an unsafe or defective condition, the landlord cannot be held liable unless he or she knew or should have known the condition existed.

WHERE
YOU
LIVE

Is there a housing code
in your community? If
so, what does it cover?
Who enforces it?

Use of the Property and Security Deposits

Tenant will use the premises for a dwelling and for no other purpose. (Clause 3)

Tenant will pay a security deposit in the amount of $_____ , which will be held by Landlord until expiration of this lease and refunded on the condition that said premises is returned in good condition, normal wear and tear excepted. (Clause 9)

SAMPLE HOUSING CODE

The following are examples of provisions included in a typical housing code.

Maintenance and Repair
■ Floors and walls shall be free of holes, cracks, splinters, or peeling paint.
■ Windows and doors shall be weatherproof, easily operable, free of broken glass, and equipped with workable locks.
■ Stairs and walkways shall be in good repair, clean, and free of safety hazards or loose railings.
■ Roof shall be free of leaks.

Cleanliness and Sanitation
■ Each unit shall be generally free of rodents and insects. Common areas shall be free of dirt, litter, trash, water, or other unsanitary matter.

Use and Occupancy
■ Each unit shall have a minimum of 120 square feet of livable floor space per occupant.
■ Each bedroom shall have a minimum of 50 square feet of floor space per occupant.
■ Each unit shall have a private bathroom.
■ Each common areas shall be accessible without going through another apartment.

Facilities and Utilities
■ Sinks, lavatories, and bathing facilities shall be in working order.
■ Every room shall have a minimum of two electrical outlets and no exposed wiring.
■ Water, electricity, gas, heating, and sewer services shall be in good operating condition.
■ Halls, stairways, and common areas shall be adequately lighted.
■ The building shall be free of fire hazards and secure from intruders or uninvited visitors.

Tenants pay for the right to use a landlord's property. As a general rule, tenants may use the property only for the purposes stated in the lease. For example, if you rented a house as a residence, you would not be allowed to use it as a restaurant or a dry cleaning business.

If you plan to operate any type of home business, you should get the landlord to agree to this in writing, or you run the risk of eviction. Likewise, committing a crime on the property may allow the landlord to end the lease and evict the tenant, regardless of what the lease says. Some leases contain language that specifies the names, ages, and number of people who will live on the premises. This can cause problems if there is a change in the family, for example, if a child is born or if a couple gets divorced.

Tenants have a right to use the rental property. But they also have a duty to take care of the property and return it to the landlord in the same general condition in which it was rented. Tenants are generally responsible for the upkeep of the property, including routine cleaning and minor repairs. Major repairs and upkeep of common areas, such as hallways, stairwells, and yards, are normally the responsibility of the landlord. However, the landlord and tenant can make different arrangements if they agree to do so.

Tenants are not responsible for damages that result from normal wear and tear or ordinary use of the property. For example, tenants are not liable for worn spots in the carpet caused by ordinary foot traffic. On the other hand, damages caused by a tenant's misuse or neglect are known as **waste.** The landlord can force the tenant to pay for such repairs. Moreover, tenants have a duty to let the landlord know when major repairs are needed and to take reasonable steps to prevent unnecessary waste or damage.

In most places, landlords have the right to ask for a **security deposit.** This deposit is an amount of money — usually one month's rent — that is kept by the landlord to ensure that the tenant takes care of the apartment and abides by the terms of the lease. If the tenant damages the landlord's property, the security deposit (or a part of it) may be kept to pay for the damage. Also, if the tenant does not pay all the rent, the landlord may be able to keep the security deposit to cover the portion of the rent still owed.

Some states put a limit on the amount of the security deposit. Some also require landlords to pay tenants interest on the money and return it within a specified time after the end of the lease. When a landlord requires a security deposit, the tenant should always get a receipt and should keep it until the deposit is returned. The tenant may also ask that the money be placed in an interest-paying bank account.

Whether damages result from normal wear and tear or from tenant neglect depends on all the facts. To protect yourself, make a list of all defects and damages that exist at the time you move in.

ADVICE ON SECURITY DEPOSITS

■ Before signing the lease, inspect the apartment and make a list of all defects or damages.
■ Give a copy of the list to the landlord and keep a copy for yourself.
■ Always get a receipt.
■ Ask to be paid interest on your money. In many places, you are entitled to this.
■ Before moving out, inspect the apartment and make a list of all damages.
■ Have a friend go through the apartment with you in case you later need a witness.
■ Clean the apartment. Repair any damage for which you are responsible, and remove trash so you won't be charged for cleaning.

**WHERE
YOU
LIVE**

What is the law in your
area regarding security
deposits? Is there a
limit on the amount
that can be required?
Does the landlord have
to pay interest on the
security deposit?

You should keep a copy of the list and give another copy to the
landlord.

When moving out, you should inspect the apartment again
and make a list of any damages. Sometimes an inspection with
both the landlord and the tenant present can help avoid any disagreements. Bringing a friend along as a witness can also be helpful in case you have a dispute with the landlord. If there are no
damages, the landlord should return your money. If part or all of
the money is withheld, you can demand a written statement item-
izing the cost of any repairs. If the landlord keeps the security
deposit and you disagree with the reasons for not returning it, you
have a right to sue for the money in small claims court.

Finally, tenants generally have no right to make any changes
in the structure or character of the property without the permission of the landlord. Even if the landlord agrees to changes or
improvements, the improvement becomes the property of the
landlord if it cannot be removed without serious damage to the
premises. For example, if you build new cabinets in the kitchen,
they become a **fixture** of the property and cannot be removed at
the end of the lease.

PROBLEM 15

In each of the following situations, the tenant is moving out and
the landlord wants to keep part of the tenant's security deposit.
Decide who should pay for the damages involved in each case.

a. The tenant moves without cleaning the apartment. The landlord is forced to remove trash, clean the walls and floors, wash the
windows, and clean out the oven and refrigerator.

b. The toilet overflows in an upstairs tenant's apartment. The
water leaks through the floor, ruining the ceiling and carpet in the
apartment below.

c. The tenant's pet stains the carpet. Suppose the lease allowed
pets.

d. The stove wears out. Suppose the tenant sells cookware and has
had numerous cooking parties in the apartment.

e. The walls are faded and need repainting.

f. The roof leaks and ruins the hardwood floors. Suppose the tenant never told the landlord about the leak.

g. The tenants panel the recreation room of their apartment, build
kitchen cabinets, and install drapes and two air conditioning
units. When they move, they remove all of their improvements and
keep them.

Housing codes help protect tenants from conditions such as these.

Responsibility for Injuries in the Building

Landlord shall not be held liable for any injuries or damages to the Tenant or his guests, regardless of cause. (Clause 15)

Many standard form leases contain clauses stating that the tenant cannot hold the landlord responsible for damages or personal injuries that result from the landlord's carelessness. For example, if a tenant were injured because of a broken guardrail that the landlord should have repaired, the lease may say that the tenant cannot sue the landlord.

This type of clause is known as a **waiver of tort liability.** Under this provision, you agree to **waive** (give up) the usual right to hold the landlord responsible for personal injuries. Most courts will not uphold such a clause. Therefore, if you or your guest are injured as a result of a landlord's carelessness, you can usually recover damages no matter what the lease says. However, you are always better off getting a lease without this type of clause because, if possible, you want to avoid going to court. Also, a few courts still enforce these clauses.

Landlord Access and Inspection

Landlord shall have access to the premises at any time for the purpose of inspection, to make repairs the Landlord considers necessary, or to show the apartment to tenant applicants. (Clause 6)

Most leases give landlords and their agents the right to enter the premises to make repairs, collect the rent, or enforce other provisions of the lease. This provision is called a **right of entry or access** clause. Taken literally, this provision would allow the landlord to enter your apartment at any time, day or night, without your permission.

However, the law in almost every state requires that visits by the landlord be at a reasonable time. Moreover, without your permission, landlords do not have the right to enter your apartment simply to snoop around or check on your housekeeping.

Rules and Regulations

Tenant agrees to observe all such rules and regulations which the Landlord or his agents will make concerning the apartment building. (Clause 18)

Some leases require tenants to obey all present and future rules that landlords make concerning the apartment. In many cases these rules are quite reasonable, but in other cases they aren't. Typical rules include: rules against having pets, rules against

---

THE CASE OF KLINE v. EMBASSY APARTMENTS

Seven years ago, when Sara Kline moved into her apartment, the management locked the building each night at 9:00 p.m. There was also a doorman and a 24-hour desk clerk who sat in the lobby. Her written lease, however, said nothing about the landlord providing security measures, and a few years later these services were discontinued. Since then, a number of tenants have been attacked in the building's common areas. One night about 10:00 p.m., Ms. Kline was mugged and seriously injured in a hallway. She sues the landlord for damages.

PROBLEM 16

Assume this case goes to trial. The following are two possible decisions of the court. Which one do you agree with and why?

Opinion 1

Landlords are not under a duty to provide police protection in their apartment buildings unless this is specifically promised in the lease. In this case, the lease said nothing about security or safety being provided by the landlord. To hold the landlord responsible now for what is not in the lease would be both unfair and very expensive.

The landlord's only duty is to make repairs and maintain common hallways and entrances. This means that if a tenant is injured as a result of a landlord's failure to repair such items as a broken step or handrail, the landlord can be held responsible. However, landlords

keeping bicycles or other items in the halls, and rules concerning visitors, cooking, storage, children, building security, and hanging pictures on the walls.

It is important to read all the rules and regulations before you move into a building. This is because you may lose your security deposit or be evicted for violating the apartment rules. If you are going to sign a lease that requires you to obey all rules — even those made in the future — it is best to have the lease state, "The tenant agrees to follow all reasonable rules and regulations."

PROBLEM 17

a. Suppose you own a three-bedroom house that you wish to rent. Make a list of all the rules and regulations you would want for your house.

b. Suppose you are a tenant seeking to rent the house in the previous example. Which rules would you consider reasonable and which unreasonable?

c. If tenants don't like some of the landlord's rules, what should they do?

> **WHERE YOU LIVE**
>
> Can tenants sue landlords for injuries or damage to property in your state? Will courts enforce a waiver of tort liability clause in the lease?

are not responsible for injuries caused by criminals or others over whom the landlord has no control.

If Ms. Kline was unhappy about the changes in services that occurred after she moved in or about the crime in the neighborhood, she was free to move to another apartment with better security. She had a month-to-month lease and could easily have moved out by giving the landlord 30 days' notice.

Opinion 2

Although courts have usually ruled that landlords are under no duty to provide security for tenants, this court believes that implied in every lease is a duty of the landlord to provide protective measures that are within the landlord's reasonable capacity.

Today's urban apartment building is different because there is no way the individual tenant can be protected in all the hallways. Common areas are under the landlord's control, and he has a duty to act reasonably in keeping them safe. In this case, the landlord knew that crimes had been committed in the building and still did nothing.

In addition, the tenant had come to expect a doorman, an employee at the desk in the lobby, and the front door of the building to be locked at 9:00 p.m. every night. Because these conditions existed when she moved in, the landlord had a duty to maintain the same degree of security all during her lease.

Sublease of a House or Apartment

Tenant will not transfer or sublet the premises without the written consent of Landlord. (Clause 5)

Clause 5 is a **sublease clause.** It requires you to obtain the landlord's permission before subleasing the apartment. A sublease takes place when the tenant allows someone else to live on the premises and pay all or part of the rent.

For example, suppose you sign a one-year lease on a small house. After six months, you find a larger house and want to move. If the landlord agrees, a sublease clause would allow you to rent the small house to someone else for the remainder of the lease. In a sublease situation, the original lease remains in effect, so if the new tenant fails to pay the rent, you are still responsible.

To avoid continued responsibility under the lease, a tenant can seek a **release.** If the landlord gives a release, this means the tenant is excused from all duties related to the apartment and the lease.

Landlords do not have to agree to tenants' requests to sublease. Therefore, you are better off with a lease that says, "The landlord agrees not to withhold consent unreasonably." This way, you would be able to sublease except when the landlord could give a good reason for refusing. Remember, even if your lease lets you sublet, you are still responsible for paying the rent to the landlord if the person to whom you sublet does not pay.

PROBLEM 18

a. Why do most leases require the tenant to get the landlord's permission before subleasing an apartment?

b. Assume the lease requires the tenant to get the landlord's permission before subletting. William, the tenant, leaves town and lets his friend Jose take over the lease, but Jose never pays the rent. Does William still owe the landlord the rent?

c. The Bridgewaters rent a four-bedroom house. When Mrs. Bridgewater loses her job, the Bridgewaters decide to take in a boarder to provide extra income. The boarder, a student from a nearby college, takes good care of his room, but the landlord objects and threatens to evict the Bridgewaters. Assume Clause 5 of the lease on page 272 is in effect. Do you think the landlord can evict the Bridgewaters for taking in a boarder? Explain your answer.

Tenants' Right to Defend Themselves in Court

Tenant confesses judgment and waives any and all rights to file a counterclaim, or a defense to any action filed by the Landlord against the Tenant and further agrees to pay attorney fees and all other costs incurred by the Landlord in an action against the Tenant. (Clause 17)

These students are renting an apartment for the summer. Do they need a lease?

WHERE YOU LIVE

Is there an agency in your area that handles tenant complaints? Does it enforce a housing code? If so, how effective is it?

A **confession of judgment** clause gives the landlord's attorney the power to go to court and admit liability of the tenant in any dispute with the landlord. In addition, the clause obligates tenants to pay the cost of any legal action against the landlord. For example, suppose a landlord wants to evict a tenant. The confession of judgment clause enables the landlord to start eviction procedures without even telling you about it. By signing such provision, you **agree in advance** to let the landlord decide without challenge if you have been at fault in any disagreement. This provision is illegal and unenforceable in some states. Even in states where the clause is illegal, it is frequently found in standard form leases.

LANDLORD-TENANT PROBLEMS

Landlords and tenants don't always live up to their responsibilities. Even after a thorough inspection of the apartment and a careful reading of the lease, problems may arise. When either the landlord or the tenant fails to fulfill the conditions of the lease, there is a violation or breach of the lease. Some breaches of a lease are minor and easily corrected. Other breaches of a lease are more serious and may result in an end to the lease, eviction, or other court action.

If the tenant is the cause of the problem, the landlord has certain remedies that can be used to solve the problem. These include evicting the tenant or bringing a suit to correct the problem. On the other hand, if the landlord is the cause of the problem, tenants also have certain things they can do.

What Tenants Can Do When Things Go Wrong

Some tenants think that once they move into an apartment, there is not much they can do if things go wrong. Although this was perhaps once the case, in most states this is no longer true; tenants now have many rights. When problems arise, tenants may take many actions:

■ Complain to the landlord

■ Complain to government agencies

■ Organize a tenants' group

■ Withhold rent

■ Sue the landlord

■ Move out

Complaints to the Landlord If you have a problem in your apartment, the first thing to do is to tell the landlord, the rental agent, or apartment house manager. Landlords have a duty to make repairs, but tenants have a duty to notify the landlord when such repairs are needed. Tenants can, of course, speak to the landlord about the problem, but it is often best to complain in writing. By keeping a copy of a written complaint, you'll have a reminder of your request and evidence that can be used in court, should that ever become necessary.

WHERE YOU LIVE

Are there any tenant organizations in your community? What do these organizations do? How effective have they been?

Complaints to Government Agencies Most local governments have agencies to handle tenant complaints and housing problems. Also, most communities have housing codes that set minimum standards for repairs, services, and living conditions in an apartment or rental house. Tenants may report unsafe or unsanitary conditions to the agency that enforces the housing code.

When you complain to the government agency that enforces the housing code, request a visit by a housing inspector. Find out when the inspector can come to your apartment. Then, be there for the inspection. Give the inspector a list of the defects in your apartment and point out all the problems. Get the name of the inspector and ask for a copy of the report. You may be surprised to find out that your apartment has violations you didn't even know about, such as faulty wiring, structural defects, or fire hazards.

The housing inspector's visit can be an important aid to the tenant. If the inspector finds code violations in the apartment, especially serious ones, the landlord may be ordered to correct the problem. Landlords who refuse to make ordered repairs can usually be fined or have their license to rent revoked. Sometimes the housing authorities may even make the repairs themselves and force the owner to pay for them. In extreme cases, the authorities can order the building vacated and have it demolished. In any event, a visit by the housing inspector puts the tenant in a strong position. It establishes a public record of the conditions in the apartment that can be used against the landlord in a court action.

Tenant Organizing Individual complaints to the landlord or the housing authorities can improve the position of a tenant. However, a complaint filed by a group of tenants may have even more force. If conditions in one tenant's apartment are bad, similar conditions may exist in apartments throughout the building. When this is the case, tenants may consider forming an organization or association. To form a tenant organization, it is helpful to contact an already established tenant association for advice and support. To find a local tenant group, check with the nearest legal aid office or contact the National Tenants Organization (address listed in Appendix B). Should the dispute with the landlord reach the stage where

In many places, tenants have organized to improve conditions in their buildings.

it becomes necessary to withhold rent or go to court, tenants who act together often achieve better results than those who act individually.

Rent Withholding   States that recognize the warranty of habitability also give tenants the right to withhold their rent if the landlord won't make repairs. This means not paying part or all of the rent until the landlord makes certain repairs or meets other tenant demands. Obviously, if several tenants in a building have similar problems and withhold rent as a group, this will have an economic effect on the landlord and is more likely to bring results.

Refusing to pay rent because of needed repairs is sometimes referred to as a rent strike. This is illegal in most states, so *tenants should always talk with a lawyer or legal services office before withholding rent.*

Another type of rent withholding may take place in states where the law allows tenants to make repairs themselves and then deduct the bill from the rent. Laws vary on when and how this can be done, but generally it may be done only if the landlord is given adequate notice of the repairs and has not made them. In most cases, tenants cannot withhold rent unless the repairs are of a serious nature, and most places restrict the amount that can be withheld.

Tenants who consider withholding rent should follow certain basic procedures. First, they should have a housing inspector inspect the building for code violations. Second, they should send the landlord a letter by registered mail announcing that they intend to withhold rent unless repairs are made by a certain date. Third, if repairs are not made by the date set, the rent money should be placed in a bank account known as an **escrow** account. In some states, establishing a bank account is required. In other states, the rent must be paid directly to the court.

If rent is being withheld, the landlord may decide to give in or may try to evict the tenant for not paying the rent. If the landlord tries to evict the tenant, the tenant can go to court and tell the judge about the needed repairs. The housing inspector's report, copies of letters to the landlord, and photographs of the apartment will all help to prove the tenant's case. Once again, remember that rent withholding is illegal in some states, so be sure to check your state law before taking this action.

> **WHERE YOU LIVE**
>
> Does the law in your community allow tenants to make repairs and deduct the amount from rent?

PROBLEM 19

The following law is proposed in your state: "Tenants may withhold rent whenever the landlord does not make repairs within two weeks of being notified that such repairs are needed."

a. Take a landlord's point of view and list all the arguments against the law.

b. Take a tenant's point of view and list all the arguments in favor of the law.

c. If you were a member of the state legislature, would you vote for or against this law? Why? Would you change the law in any way? If so, how?

Suing the Landlord In most places, if the landlord breaks the lease, the tenant may sue the landlord in court. In this kind of lawsuit, the tenant may ask the court to order that repairs be made or that part of rent previously paid to the landlord be returned to the tenant. If the tenants have made repairs themselves, it may also be possible to ask the court to order the landlord to pay them back. This kind of case may be costly in time and money. However, most places have small claims courts or landlord-tenant commissions which make the process easier and less expensive.

Moving Out A final remedy available to tenants is moving out. When a tenant ignores the lease and moves out, this is known as **abandonment.** If this happens, the landlord may sue for the remainder of the rent owed under the lease.

In extreme cases, however, tenants may legally break the lease and move without the landlord's permission. **Constructive eviction** occurs when the property is so run-down that it is unlivable, or when the landlord has denied the tenant's right to quiet enjoyment. Most states consider constructive eviction a valid reason for abandonment, but a few don't, so be sure to check your state law and talk with a lawyer before taking this action.

PROBLEM 20

Mr. and Mrs. Walker rented a one-bedroom apartment for $125 a month from Mr. Martinez. It was run-down, but they couldn't find anything else for the price. Two weeks after they moved in, the heat went out on a cold night, and the Walkers were forced to stay with relatives for several days. The Walkers also discovered that the roof leaked when it rained, the apartment was overrun by roaches, and the toilet continually overflowed.

a. If you were the Walkers, what would you do? Which of the possible tenant actions would provide the best solution for their problem? Why?

b. If you were the landlord, what would you do if the Walkers took each of the possible actions listed in this section?

c. Roleplay a telephone call from the Walkers to Mr. Martinez.

d. Assume the Walkers withheld one month's rent and the landlord brought the case to court. If you were the judge, what would you do?

What Landlords Can Do When Things Go Wrong

While tenants sometimes have problems with landlords there are also times when tenants don't live up to their responsibilities. If a tenant breaks apartment rules or fails to fulfill conditions in the lease, the landlord has a number of remedies. These include ending the lease, eviction, and court action.

Ending the Lease   Landlords and tenants sometimes come into conflict at the end of a lease. In most places, unless there is a clause that automatically continues the lease, or the landlord agrees to a new lease, the tenant must move out when the term of the lease is over. If a tenant refuses to move at the end of the lease, the landlord has three choices. First, the landlord can go to court and ask to have the tenant evicted. That is, the landlord can take legal action to have the tenant forced off the property. Second, the landlord can let the tenant stay in the apartment as a **holdover tenant.** In many states, if a tenant stays on after the lease is over, the landlord has the right to hold the tenant to a new lease identical to the one just ended. Third, a tenant who stays on beyond the end of the lease becomes a tenant at will in some states. This means that either the landlord or the tenant can end the lease with whatever notice the law requires — typically 30 days.

Tenants who are moving should always give the landlord adequate notice. Notice should be given in a letter and a copy should be kept. If there is a month-to-month lease, the landlord should be notified 30 days before the rent is next due. If the lease is for a fixed period, such as one year, the notice should be given at least 30 days before the end of the term.

A common problem arises when a tenant seeks to leave before the end of the lease. If this happens, it is always best to talk with the landlord and try to get a release. A landlord and tenant can always end a lease by mutual agreement, and in most cases this is what occurs.

**WHERE
YOU
LIVE**

What is the law in your state regarding retaliatory evictions?

PROBLEM 21

a. Walden signs a two-year lease for $200 a month. After six months, she decides to get married and now wants to get out of the lease. What choices does she have?

b. Larkin signs a one-year lease for an apartment near his college. After six months, he decides to move back to campus and just packs up and leaves. Is there anything the landlord can do?

Another option for the tenant is to sublet the apartment. While landlords may agree to let the tenants out of a lease or allow a sublease, they don't have to do this. If a tenant moves out or abandons an apartment without the landlord's permission, the landlord has the right to sue the tenant for damages in court. However, in most places the landlord is required to try to rent the apartment to another tenant. The landlord cannot let the apartment sit empty for 18 months and expect a court to award the full rent. If the landlord rents the apartment for the remainder of the lease, the original tenant will have to pay only for the period of time during which the apartment was vacant.

Eviction   Eviction is the legal process of having a tenant removed from the property. Many situations give a landlord the right to evict a tenant. The most common reason for eviction is a failure by the tenant to pay the rent. However, any serious breach of the lease can give the landlord cause for eviction.

When a tenant fails to pay the rent, the landlord may sue the tenant for the overdue rent or start legal action to have the tenant removed (or both). The landlord cannot physically throw the tenant out but must always file a case in court. A tenant who does not have the money to pay the rent or who intends to pay the rent late should always contact the landlord and explain the problem. Many landlords are willing to accept overdue rent or partial payments. Even if the landlord has started the eviction process, the tenant can usually stop the legal action by paying the amount owed plus any late fees or court costs.

Landlord-Tenant Court Process   Tenants may not be evicted unless the landlord files a case against them in court (See Figure 25). In some places, this occurs in the regular civil court system. In other places, evictions are handled by special housing courts or landlord-tenant commissions. Landlord-tenant courts often attempt to process cases quickly. In many places, cases are heard within a few days or weeks after they are filed.

Eviction procedures vary from state to state. However, the eviction process usually includes the following steps.

1. *Notice* — Before being evicted, the tenant must be given a written **notice** to quit (leave). This notice is a warning that unless the tenant corrects the problem (for example, removes a dog that violates a "no pet" rule), eviction action will be started. Leases often contain clauses through which tenants waive their right to written notice if they don't pay their rent.

2. *Complaint* — If the tenant does not meet the deadline for correcting the problem, the landlord may file a complaint in court, seeking an order to have the tenant removed from the apartment.

3. *Summons* — After the landlord files the complaint, an officer of the court will serve a summons informing the tenant of the eviction action and setting a date to appear in court. *A tenant should never ignore a summons. Many tenants have defenses to suits for eviction, but a failure to show up in court automatically results in a judgment in favor of the landlord.* In rare cases, a default judgment may be set aside if the tenant had a good reason for the failure to attend.

4. *Court Appearance* — Tenants should always go to court on the date set in the summons. When tenants appear in court, they are entitled to file an answer to the complaint. This is a written explanation of why the tenant should not be evicted. Another important reason for showing up is that the tenant may be able to reach a settlement with the landlord. For example, if the rent is overdue, the landlord might agree to a late payment.

5. *Trial* — If a tenant decides to defend against the eviction action, there will be a trial. Although most cases are decided by a judge, the U.S. Supreme Court has stated that tenants have a right to a jury trial. Possible defenses are that the tenant has paid the rent or

FIGURE 25   Landlord-Tenant Court Process

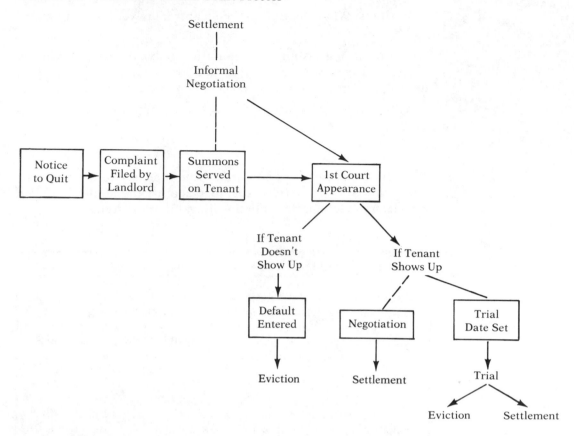

has not otherwise broken any provision in the lease. In most states, tenants may also defend by proving that the landlord has failed to make needed major repairs.

6. *Eviction* — If the case is decided in favor of the landlord, the court will issue an order telling the tenant to move out by a certain date. If the tenant does not move out voluntarily, the local sheriff can physically remove tenants and their belongings.

7. *Legal Help* — A tenant who receives a summons or notice to quit should seek legal help immediately. Tenants who cannot afford a private attorney should contact the nearest legal aid or legal services office. If this cannot be done ahead of time, a tenant who shows up in court may be able to have a lawyer appointed by the judge.

PROBLEM 22

Bill Williams has always paid his rent on time, but because of his wife's sudden illness and resulting medical bills, he is unable to pay this month's rent.

**WHERE
YOU
LIVE**

Is there a landlord-
tenant court in your
community? If so,
where is it located and
what procedures does it
follow? Is there a legal
aid or legal services
office in your area that
represents tenants?

a. What can Bill do? If the landlord files a suit for eviction, what can Bill do? What can Bill do if he wants a lawyer but can't afford one?

b. For what reasons might a tenant be unable or unwilling to pay the rent? If you were a judge in landlord-tenant court, which, if any, of these reasons would you consider valid excuses?

c. Do you think the typical eviction process is fair to both landlord and tenant?

Retaliatory Evictions   Landlords sometimes try to evict tenants who complain or otherwise organize against the landlord. Called **retaliatory eviction,** this action is illegal in most states.

THE CASE OF EDWARDS v. HABIB

Ms. Edwards rented a house from Mr. Habib on a month-to-month basis. Shortly after moving in, she called the city housing inspector and reported a number of unsanitary conditions. When an inspector came to investigate, he found more than 40 housing code violations. The landlord was ordered to correct them.

Instead of making the repairs, Mr. Habib notified Ms. Edwards that he was ending the lease and that she must move within 30 days. She went to court, claiming that she was being evicted as revenge for her report of the code violations. She said that the First Amendment to the U.S. Constitution gives citizens the right to petition the government and that Mr. Habib was interfering with this right.

Mr. Habib claimed his actions were legal. He said a month-to-month lease can be legally ended merely by giving the tenant a proper 30-day notice without stating any reasons for the action.

PROBLEM 23

a. What happened in this case? Why did Mr. Habib try to evict Ms. Edwards?

b. Do you think Mr. Habib's action is legal or illegal? Explain your answer.

c. What rights and interests are in conflict in this case?

d. Should landlords be able to evict tenants in cases such as this? List all the arguments in favor of Mr. Habib. In favor of Ms. Edwards.

e. If tenants have housing code violations or other problems in their apartment, what can they do?

For what reasons might a landlord evict a tenant?

BUYING A HOME

Many people never consider buying a home. They think homes are too expensive. Or they think home ownership involves too many responsibilities. But buying a home is easier than you may imagine. Each year millions of Americans buy homes. A few pay cash, but most use credit. They borrow money from banks, loan companies, and government programs. In addition, even renters should understand the financial, legal, and other important issues involved in owning a home. These issues affect their landlords, and, therefore, indirectly affect renters.

Things to Consider Before Buying

If you decide to buy a home, there are many things to consider. These include the type of area where you wish to live and whether you want to live in a house, an apartment, or some other type of dwelling. When considering purchase of a home, many people think only of single-family homes, but condominiums, cooperatives, and mobile homes are other alternatives.

A **condominium** is a form of ownership. Any type of building may be a condominium, but most condominiums are attached units in apartment buildings or townhouses. Each resident owns an individual apartment or townhouse. The rest of the property, including hallways, lobbies, elevators, grounds, and parking areas,

are owned jointly by all the residents. A person who buys a condominium makes monthly mortgage payments and also pays a
maintenance fee to take care of the jointly owned area.

Condominiums have many advantages. The condominium
owner has the economic advantages of ownership — tax benefits,
resale potential, and increase in value. However, like a renter, the
owner of a condominium is also free of responsibility for main-
tanence and upkeep of the grounds or common areas. In addition,
like apartment buildings, many newer condominiums offer extra
facilities such as swimming pools, health clubs, or recreation
areas.

Another form of ownership is the **cooperative.** Cooperative
ownership means the land and building are owned collectively.
Each resident buys shares in a business corporation and is given
the right to occupy an individual apartment. Residents of cooperatives don't own their apartment but own a share of the total
building. Owners are subject to rules set by the community as a
whole, and unlike condominium owners, residents of cooperatives
may not sell their units without the approval of the other
residents.

Cooperatives are common in big East Coast cities. In many
places, tenants get together, buy the building from the landlord,
and restore it. Because cooperatives and condominiums are new

forms of ownership, people considering this type of living space should be careful to get good legal and financial advice before buying. Nevertheless, these types of homes may be a good investment and generally cost less than traditional houses. The U.S. Department of Housing and Urban Development (HUD) estimates that over 10 million Amercians now live in condominiums or cooperatives.

Mobile homes are a low-cost alternative to traditional housing. They cost less than conventional homes, and most mobile homes come furnished, carpeted, and complete with all appliances. Despite what the name implies, most mobile homes aren't moved around. Rather, they are built in a factory and moved to a site where they usually remain.

Realtors can help both the buyer and the seller.

Like condominiums and cooperatives, mobile homes have become more popular as single-family homes have risen in price. However, there are certain drawbacks to mobile home ownership. First, mobile homes are financed more like cars than houses. Mobile home loans are typically for a shorter period than are home mortgages, and buyers are usually charged a higher rate of interest. Second, after buying a mobile home, the owner must find someplace to put it. This is sometimes a problem, because many cities restrict the areas where mobile homes may be located. Finally, because some mobile homes are poorly constructed, buyers should carefully check out the dealer's reputation for service and the warranty that accompanies their mobile home.

After deciding about the general area and type of housing desired, you should consider the size, quality and features you want in a home. Homebuyers should ask themselves the following questions: What features do you want in a home? A modern kitchen, a big yard, an extra bathroom, or a garage? Do you want a new home or an older home? If it needs repairs, can you fix it up yourself, or will you have to hire someone to do the work?

How much you can afford is an all-important consideration. Homebuyers should consult a banker, real estate agent, or attorney to determine their general price range. Finally, buyers must weigh all the costs associated with buying a home. You should consider the price of the house, but you should also consider the costs of taxes, insurance, maintenance, and travel to and from work.

PROBLEM 24

a. What are some of the factors that should be considered when planning to buy a home?

b. What are the advantages and disadvantages of condominiums, cooperatives, and mobile homes?

c. Read the real estate ads in your local newspaper. What do these ads say about costs and financing? What types of housing are available in your community?

Steps to Take in Buying

Real estate agents are representatives of sellers who allow the agents to offer their home. In return, the agents are paid a commission (usually a percentage of the total price, such as 6 percent) once the house is sold. Buyers should realize that agents wish to sell houses, and like salespeople in other consumer situations, they may sometimes exaggerate the facts to make a home sound better than it is. At the same time, agents can be very helpful to buyers.

Buying a house sometimes seems complicated. Real estate agents can help find homes that fit a buyer's special needs or explain about particular neighborhoods. Agents can also help arrange financing and explain local real estate procedures. To find a real estate agent you can trust, ask friends who have used agents whom they would recommend.

Shopping for a Home   As in any consumer purchase, your chances of obtaining a good buy will probably increase depending on the amount of time spent looking at different homes. Using more than one real estate agent may help, as well as checking out newspaper listings where real estate companies and other sellers advertise homes. Buying a home at a reduced price is sometimes possible if you purchase directly from a seller. This is because people who sell their own homes do not have to pay a commission to a real estate agent.

Before you buy a house, always determine its condition. Is it well constructed? Are repairs needed? Is any kind of warranty given? Is it worth the price asked? Once you find a home that you like, it is advisable to have the home inspected to determine if there are structural, electrical, plumbing, or other problems. Home inspectors can also determine how much the house is worth. This is done by conducting an **appraisal.** (This differs from the appraisal the bank or other organization does when considering giving the buyer a mortgage.)

Making an Offer   To make an offer on a home, a **sales contract** or purchase agreement must be written up and presented to the seller. (Note: sellers sometimes accept a lower price than the list price). The offer is sometimes called a **binder** and is usually accompanied by a deposit check, which may go to the seller if the buyer later backs out of the agreement. The sales contract should be reviewed by a lawyer or someone else experienced in buying homes. This is important, because all the major terms, including cost, financing arrangements, what comes with the house, and condition of the house, will be determined by this contract. Buyers should always make the offer contingent on financing. This means the sales agreement does not become legally binding until the buyer gets mortgage financing. It is also common to make the deal contingent upon a satisfactory home inspection or sale of other property owned by the buyer. When the seller agrees in writing to the buyer's offer it becomes a binding contract.

Obtaining a Loan   After the contract is signed, the buyer will have to apply to a bank, credit union, insurance company, or other source for approval of a mortgage loan. Comparison shopping is important, because mortgage interest rates vary from bank to bank. A small difference may result in thousands of dollars over the term of the mortgage. Figure 26 shows how different interest rates affect how much buyers pay each month. What can you conclude from this information about shopping for a mortgage loan?

WHERE YOU LIVE

What interest rate are homeowners in your area now able to obtain from mortgage lenders?

FIGURE 26   Comparing Mortgage Interest Rates

Cost of House	Down Payment %	Down Payment $	Loan Amount	Years	Monthly Payments at: 11%	13%	14.5%	15%
$60,000	10	$ 6,000	$54,000	30	524.15	597.78	661.50	683.10
	20	12,000	48,000	30	457.44	531.36	588.00	607.20
	25	15,000	45,000	30	428.85	498.15	551.25	569.25

Buyers will usually pay the same amount of money each month for the entire period of the loan. However, a new type of mortgage called a **flexible payment mortgage** permits buyers to pay less in early years, when the buyers' salaries are often lower, and more in future years, when the buyers may be making more money. There are also **adjustable rate mortgages.** With an adjustable rate mortgage, the payment changes as the interest rates in an area rise or fall over the years. This can help or hurt buyers, depending on whether future interest rates rise or fall.

Buyers should explore the possibility of a **mortgage assumption.** A mortgage is assumed when the seller and the mortgage holder (e.g., the bank) allow the buyer to take it over at the old interest rate. Also worth investigating is whether the seller will agree to take back or hold the mortgage for the buyer. In both situations, the buyer will not have to shop around for a mortgage. To obtain financing, all the considerations involving credit (discussed in Chapter 3) come into play, including the legal protections against discrimination because of race, color, religion, national origin, sex, marital status, and age (if old enough to enter into a contract).

Buyers trying to finance a home should consider whether they are eligible for a government-insured loan. The most common sources of government assistance are the Veterans Administration

WHERE
YOU
LIVE

What federal, state, or
local housing agencies
exist in your area? Do
they have mortgage
loan or housing re-
habilitation programs?
How do they operate?

(VA) and the Federal Housing Administration (FHA). Both agencies encourage banks and other lenders to make loans that otherwise might not be approved. The government does this by telling the lender that it will *insure* the mortgage loan. This means that if the buyer fails to pay, the government will.

VA loans are available only to veterans of the armed forces, their spouses, or dependents. They require little or no cash down payment and usually have a lower interest rate than conventional mortgages. FHA loans assist people who otherwise could not obtain a mortgage due to limited income or insufficient cash for a down payment. FHA loans require a small down payment, usually less than a conventional mortgage, and the interest rate may also be slightly less.

Another federal agency, the Farmers Home Administration, loans money directly to buyers in rural areas (having a population of 20,000 or less and being outside a city). This program may also require a smaller down payment and lower interest.

The federal government and some state and local governments promote the rehabilitation of older housing by loan programs to help pay for restoration. These programs are run by the U.S. Department of Housing and Urban Development and by state and local housing agencies. They provide low-interest loans to buyers interested in fixing up older houses. One program is called **homesteading.** This program sells older homes in run-down areas for low prices (one dollar in some places) to buyers who promise to live in and repair them.

One criticism of government housing programs is the amount of paperwork and the long waiting periods involved. Getting a loan approved by the government doesn't always take a long time, although banks and other private lenders generally process loan applications faster than government agencies.

Another problem with VA and FHA mortgages is that the seller is sometimes required to pay **points.** A point is equal to 1 percent of the total mortgage. This may reduce the seller's profit and result in some sellers refusing to sell to buyers who wish to get a VA or an FHA mortgage.

Title Searches and Insurance   Before a buyer can move into a new home, a **title search** must be conducted. This is a check of government land records to make sure the seller has the right to convey ownership or give good **title** to the property. Buyers generally pay a lawyer or a title company to conduct the title search.

Title searches are important, but land records don't always tell the whole story. At some time in the past, the home may have been sold or something else happened that gave another person some right to the property. As a result, mortgage lenders usually require buyers to obtain **title insurance** to protect against claims on the property. Buyers should also consider taking out owner's title insurance, which protects their own interest — not just the mortgage lender's.

If you buy a house, you'll also need homeowner's insurance. Homeowner's insurance protects you against fire, theft, storm damage, or other problems. Homeowner's insurance also protects the mortgage lender by requiring that the mortgage loan be paid out of the insurance settlement if there is a fire or other catastrophe.

Closing or Settlement   The **closing** is the final meeting between the buyer and the seller. At this meeting, the buyer officially becomes the new owner. Closings are ordinarily held 30 to 90 days after the signing of the sales contract but can be held whenever the buyer and seller agree. Any cash owed the seller is paid at the closing. **Closing costs** are also paid at this time. These costs include title search fees, attorney's fees, points, costs of recording deeds and mortgage notes, and insurance. The federal *Real Estate Settlement Procedures Act* (RESPA) requires the seller to give the buyer an estimate of these charges before closing. Buyers should always get an early estimate of their closing costs. This will give them a chance to shop around.

Recording Deeds and Mortgage   After the closing, the seller's attorney or agent will record the sale at the local courthouse. After this is done, a deed (or record of ownership) is mailed to the new owner.

PROBLEM 25

Examine the steps in buying a home and make a list of all activities for which you might need a lawyer. Do you think you could do any of these without a lawyer? Could someone else help you do any of them? If so, who?

Problems Associated with Home Buying

The most common problem new homeowners encounter is unexpected repairs. If the furnace breaks down, the roof leaks, or the plumbing system backs up, the financial benefits of home ownership can quickly disappear.

The law provides little protection to unwary buyers, so the best advice is to have the home inspected before signing a sales contract. Most communties have professional housing inspectors who will examine homes to see if they meet building and safety standards. If you buy an older house, you must be particularly careful. This is because the government usually does not provide any inspection either before or after a sale. In regard to mobile homes, the Department of Housing and Urban Development re-

quires that certain standards be met. Buyers should check to see if a state agency has inspected and approved the particular mobile home they are considering buying.

Today, builders will often give buyers a Homeowner's Warranty (HOW) on new houses. Some companies even inspect older homes and offer warranties for a fee. Buyers should be sure that any warranty or other promise regarding the home is in writing.

For many years, the law did not protect homebuyers. The general rule was "Let the buyer beware." The law has changed considerably over the past 20 years. Most states now protect "new homebuyers" through an implied warranty of habitability. This means that the law implies that new home builders promise that the house is well built and "fit to live in." In most states, if a buyer moves in and finds a major structural defect such as a leaky roof, the buyer can force the builder to correct it. This rule applies equally to houses that were not completed at the time of sale as well as to those that were finished.

Home warranties are also important if injuries occur as a result of a problem with the house. In one case, a baby was severely burned by hot water from a bathroom tap. The parents were awarded money damages because they were able to prove that the plumbing system had been installed without a mixing valve, which would have regulated the hot and cold water temperatures and prevented the accident.

PROBLEM 26

John and Martha buy a new home from a builder. Their sales contract doesn't provide them with a warranty or make any promises regarding repairs.

a. If the following things go wrong, should the builder or the homeowner pay for the damages?
- a refrigerator that comes with the house breaks after six months
- the toilet backs up after two months
- after a year a stair, made of poor-quality wood, cracks and Martha breaks her leg
- the electrical system can handle only two operating appliances at once
- whenever it rains, the basement floods
- pipes freeze in the winter and break

b. If the house Martha and John own is 20 years old, would any of your answers to the first question change?

c. What could Martha and John have done before they signed the sales contract to prevent any or all of the problems mentioned in the first part of this problem?

Rehabilitation of Older Housing

In recent years, the trend in many American cities and towns has been to restore and redevelop older homes and neighborhoods. Citizens have discovered that older buildings are an important part of a city's special identity and character. Moreover, home-buyers have been attracted by the lower prices and the convenience of inner-city living. This trend has resulted in the restoration of thousands of townhouses throughout the country.

Most people applaud rehabilitation because it preserves historic buildings and neighborhoods, brings in needed tax dollars, and reverses the flow of people moving out of the cities. On the other hand, revitalization can also bring problems. The major problem associated with restoration is the displacement of lower-income residents. As well-to-do citizens buy up urban properties, tenants and other lower-income residents are often forced to move out. In many urban areas, housing speculation is common. This means buying at a low price and then selling a short time later for a large profit. Likewise, the conversion of apartment buildings into condominiums can result in the eviction or displacement of many tenants.

**WHERE
YOU
LIVE**

How has the historic preservation movement affected your community? In what ways has it helped? Has it caused any problems?

Owning a home takes work as well as money.

WHERE YOU LIVE

What government housing assistance programs operate in your area? Are they working? What can be done to improve them?

Preserving healthy diverse neighborhoods, which offer housing for low- and middle-income people, is a major goal in many cities. City officials, neighborhood activists, and government agencies operate a number of programs to help displaced families and to give low-income residents a share in urban restoration. These programs include funds for subsidized housing, grants to help low-income residents buy their own homes, repair programs to help moderate-income homeowners keep pace with wealthier neighbors, and relocation assistance for families forced to move.

Housing for Low- and Moderate-Income Persons

People with low and moderate incomes often have difficulty finding decent affordable housing. Therefore, federal, state, and local governments have developed programs designed to provide opportunities for such families to rent apartments or buy houses at prices suitable to their incomes. These programs include:

■ building public housing where rent is charged in accordance with a person's ability to pay (the government pays whatever else it takes to support the project).

■ paying subsidies to landlords who rent to low- and moderate-income persons.

■ giving interest or tax discounts as encouragement to builders who construct housing for low- and moderate-income persons.

■ giving cash payments directly to poor persons so that they can afford to find and obtain standard housing on the private housing market.

To find out more about these programs, go to the local housing, social welfare, or human resources agency. Agency personnel should know where to apply. Also, free counseling and advice on housing is provided by local offices of the U.S. Department of Housing and Urban Development (HUD).

Government agencies have detailed rules — based primarily on family income — for determining who is eligible for government-sponsored housing. Even if you satisfy the eligibility standards, housing may not be immediately available. In such cases, applicants are placed on a waiting list. Some cities give preference to the elderly, minorities, persons displaced because of government projects, or families with small children. If a housing agency decides that you do not meet the income standards, you may be able to appeal. In this case, you should ask the agency for a personal interview or hearing to discuss your situation.

PROBLEM 27

a. What are the advantages and disadvantages of each type of government housing assistance program?

b. Assume that you are in charge of housing for poor people in your area and have a $3 million budget for the next year. Decide exactly how you would spend this money, and explain your decision. Who would be eligible for assistance, and where in your area would you build any housing projects?

six
INDIVIDUAL RIGHTS AND LIBERTIES

The United States Constitution is the framework of our government. It establishes the executive, legislative, and judicial branches. It is also the supreme law of the land, which all public officials are bound by oath to enforce. Moreover, the Constitution guarantees each American certain basic rights.

One remarkable feature of our Constitution is its endurance. It is the oldest written national constitution in use in the world. Another remarkable feature of the Constitution is its ability to adapt itself to changing conditions.

Our founding fathers knew that the Constitution might have to be changed. So they provided two methods of proposing **amendments:** by a two-thirds vote of both houses of Congress or by a national convention called by Congress at the request of the legislatures in two-thirds of the states. Once proposed, an amendment does not take effect unless it is ratified either by the legislatures in three-fourths of the states or by special ratifying conventions in three-fourths of the states.

The original Constitution, adopted in 1787, contained only a few provisions guaranteeing individual rights. However, citizens pressured their leaders to add a Bill of Rights. In response, the first 10 amendments were adopted by Congress in 1791 and then quickly ratified by the states.

These first 10 amendments contain most of our basic rights. The First Amendment protects the freedoms of religion, speech, press, assembly, and petition. The Second Amendment protects the right to bear arms. The Third Amendment protects against quartering of soldiers in private homes, and the Fourth Amendment protects against unreasonable searches and seizures.

The Fifth Amendment provides a right to due process of law and gives rights to accused people, including protection against self-incrimination and double jeopardy. The Sixth Amendment provides the rights to a lawyer, an impartial jury, and a speedy trial in criminal cases.

The Seventh Amendment provides for jury trials in civil cases. The Eighth Amendment bars cruel and unusual punishment and excessive bail or fines. The Ninth Amendment declares that the rights spelled out in the Constitution are not all the rights that people have. Finally, the Tenth Amendment reserves to the states and the people any powers not belonging to the federal government. (The full text of all 26 amendments can be found in Appendix A.)

The Bill of Rights was designed to protect Americans against the power of the *federal* government. Nothing in the Constitution specifically requires *state* governments to abide by the Bill of Rights. But in interpreting the Fourteenth Amendment, passed after the Civil War, the Supreme Court has extended most Bill of Rights protections to the states.

In addition to the Bill of Rights, later amendments provide other important rights. The Thirteenth Amendment forbids slavery and outlaws involuntary servitude, except as a punishment for crime. The Fourteenth Amendment requires equal protection of the laws for all citizens. It also provides that no state can deprive any citizen of "life, liberty, or property without due process of law."

Several amendments protect and broaden the right to vote. The Fifteenth Amendment forbids denying the right to vote based on race or color. The Nineteenth Amendment gives women the right to vote. The Twenty-fourth Amendment gives citizens of Washington D.C. the right to vote in presidental elections, and the Twenty-sixth Amendment gives all people 18 years of age or older the right to vote.

PROBLEM 1

a. Do we have any important rights not listed in the Bill of Rights? If so, what are they? Make a list.

b. Over the years, a number of new constitutional amendments have been suggested or proposed. Do you think we need any new amendments to the Constitution? If so, what amendments do you propose and why?

c. The following are some of our most basic and important rights. Based on your opinion, rank these rights in order from the most important to the least important. Explain your answer.

- right to privacy
- right to a jury trial
- right to freedom of religion
- right to travel freely
- right to freedom of speech
- right to be free from self-incrimination
- right to bear arms
- right to freedom of the press
- right to be free from cruel and unusual punishment
- right to legal counsel
- right to assemble peacefully
- right to vote

To understand constitutional law, you should keep three basic ideas in mind. First, the rights guaranteed in the Constitution are not, and cannot be, absolute. The totally free exercise of certain rights would, in some instances, restrict the rights of others. For example, suppose someone, as a joke, yells "Fire!" in a crowded theater. The right to free speech would not protect the person from arrest. In such cases, courts must balance one right or interest against another. In this case, a court would weigh the danger to the public against the individual's right to free speech. In this case, protecting the public is more important than protecting this individual's right to freedom of speech.

Second, the Constitution usually restricts "Congress" or "the States" from taking away basic rights. Although the Constitution protects citizens from certain actions by the government, its pro-

tection does not extend to situations that are purely private in nature. This means that actions by private citizens, businesses, or organizations are generally not covered by the Constitution. For example, the Fourth Amendment protects against unreasonable searches and seizures by the government. It does not protect against searches and seizures by private individuals. Therefore, if a neighbor comes into your house and seizes your television, this act does *not* violate the Constitution. It may, however, constitute the crime of larceny. As you will see later in this chapter, many private actions, though not unconstitutional, have been made unlawful by congressional action.

Third, remember that enforcing your rights can be time-consuming and expensive. Before trying to enforce a right, you should be aware of the time and money involved. You should then weigh these costs against the importance of the right. However, remember that you can do many things to protect your rights. So if you think you are right, don't give up.

This chapter focuses on freedom of speech and expression; freedom of the press; freedom of association; freedom of assembly and petition; freedom of religion; and the rights to privacy, due process, and equal protection. These are probably the most important rights we have, for without them all other rights would be meaningless.

FREEDOM OF SPEECH

Congress shall make no law . . . abridging the freedom of speech, or of the press; or the right of the people peaceably to assemble, and to petition the government for a redress of grievances.

—First Amendment

Freedom of speech guarantees the right to communicate information and ideas. It protects all forms of communication: speeches, books, art, newspapers, television, radio, and other media. The Constitution protects not only the person *making* the communication but also the person *receiving* it. Therefore, the First Amendment includes a right to hear, see, read, and in general to be exposed to different points of view.

Freedom of speech is not absolute and was not intended to be. However, expressing an opinion or point of view is usually protected under the First Amendment, even if most people disagree with the speaker's message. Remember that the First Amendment was designed to ensure a free marketplace of ideas — even unpopular ideas. Freedom of speech protects everyone, even people who criticize the government or express unconventional views.

The First Amendment enables citizens to express and obtain a diversity of opinions. It helps us to make political decisions and communicate these to our government. In short, the First Amendment is the heart of an open, democratic society.

Conflicts involving freedom of expression are among the most difficult ones that courts are asked to resolve. Free speech cases frequently involve a clash of fundamental values. For example, how should the law respond to a speaker who makes an unpopular statement, to which the listeners react violently? Do police stop the speaker or try to control the crowd? Courts must balance the need for peace and public order against the fundamental right to express one's point of view.

Political rallies are a form of free speech.

PROBLEM 2

a. A Supreme Court justice once wrote that the most important value of free expression is "not free thought for those who agree with us, but freedom for the thought we hate." What did the justice mean by this? Do you agree or disagree?

b. Can you think of any public statements or expressions of public opinion that made you angry? How did you feel about protecting the speaker's right to freedom of expression? What is the value of hearing opinons you dislike? What is the danger of suppressing unpopular thought?

The language of the First Amendment appears absolute (i.e., "Congress shall make *no* law"). However, freedom of speech is at times limited by government action. To understand these limits, you should be familiar with exceptions to the rule that protects all expression. These exceptions include obscenity, defamation, fighting words, and commercial speech.

Obscenity

The portrayal of sex in art, literature, and films is a troublesome topic in our society. The First Amendment guarantees freedom of expression. However, the government has the power to prohibit the distribution of obscene materials. In general terms, **obscenity** applies to anything that treats sex or nudity in an offensive or lewd manner or that exceeds recognized standards of decency.

As you might expect, courts have had difficulty developing a precise legal definition of obscenity. For example, in speaking about pornography, Justice Stewart once said that he couldn't define it, "but I know it when I see it." However, in 1957, the court ruled that obscenity is not protected by the Constitution. Later, in the 1979 case of *Miller* v. *California*, the Supreme Court set out a three-part guideline for determining whether a work is obscene. These guidelines are as follows:

1. Would the average person applying contemporary community standards find that the material, taken as a whole, appeals to prurient (i.e., purely sexual) interest?

2. Does the work depict or describe, in a patently offensive way, sexual conduct specifically outlawed by applicable state law?

3. Does the work taken as a whole lack serious literary, artistic, political, or scientific value?

Applying these standards, a medical textbook on anatomy is not obscene because it has scientific value. But a sex magazine

filled only with photos of nude women may be obscene depending on the standards of the local community.

Recently, state and local governments have developed new strategies for dealing with pornography. Some communities have tried to ban all pornographic works that degrade or depict sexual violence against women. Such works, they argue, are a form of sex discrimination that may lead to actual violence or abuse against women. Other communities regulate adult bookstores and movie theaters through their zoning laws. These laws restrict pornographic stores and theaters to special zones or ban them from certain neighborhoods. Finally, many communities have passed laws outlawing child pornography and greatly restricting minors' access to sexually oriented material. The Supreme Court has held that laws against child pornography are constitutional, even when the laws ban material that is not technically obscene.

PROBLEM 3

a. Should the government be allowed to censor books, movies, or magazines? If so, what kind and why?

b. Who should decide if a book or movie is obscene? What definition should be used?

c. Do you think pornographic books and movies encourage violence against women? Explain your answer.

Defamation

The First Amendment does not protect defamatory expression. **Defamation** is a false expression about a person that damages that person's reputation. When defamation is spoken, it is called **slander.** Written defamation is called **libel.** For example, assume a patient said that her doctor was careless and had caused the death of patients. If others heard this remark, the doctor could sue the patient for slander. If the patient had written the same thing in a letter, the suit would be for libel. However, if a damaging statement — written or spoken — is proved to be true, the plaintiff cannot win in court.

The Supreme Court has special rules that make it difficult for public officials or public figures to win a defamation suit. People who speak about public figures or officials have broader protection. This is because the Court has recognized the people's right to know about public affairs. A public figure can win a libel or slander suit *only* if the expression was false, damaging, and made with either malice or *reckless* (an almost intentional) disregard for the truth.

PROBLEM 4

In 1960 a civil rights group took out a full-page ad in the *New York Times* to solicit funds for a right-to-vote campaign in Montgomery, Alabama. The ad contained a list of complaints about the behavior of the Montgomery police force.

The Montgomery chief of police sued the newspaper and the sponsors of the ad. He said the complaints about his police force had harmed his reputation. At the trial, it turned out that some of the statements made about the police force were untrue.

a. If the police chief can prove harm to his reputation, should he be able to win his libel suit?

b. What effect might his winning the suit have on news coverage? What effect might his losing have on news coverage?

Commercial Speech

Another form of speech that is not fully protected by the constitution is **commercial speech.** All forms of advertising are considered commercial speech, as distinguished from individual speech. The Supreme Court has ruled that states may regulate and even ban commercial speech under certain circumstances. Specifically, they may prohibit deceptive or misleading advertisements. State and local governments may also place restrictions on the time, place, and manner of commerical speech. For example, cities can ban commercial billboards or restrict them to certain areas. However, cities cannot totally prohibit dissemination of commercial information. For example, states may not prevent abortion clinics from advertising in newspapers. Nor can professional associations totally prevent their members from advertising their services. For example, courts have outlawed rules that prevented lawyers from advertising and other rules that kept pharmacies from advertising prescription drug prices.

Under the commercial speech doctrine, government may regulate, even ban, commercial billboards.

Fighting Words

The First Amendment does not protect you if you use words that are so abusive or threatening as to amount to what the Court calls **fighting words.** These are words spoken face-to-face that are likely to cause a breach of the peace between the speaker and the listener. Fighting words are like a verbal slap in the face. Such expression is more like an assault than like information or an opinion, whose communication is safeguarded by the Constitution. For example, in 1942 a person was arrested for calling a city official a "goddamned racketeer" and a "damned Fascist." He was convicted because his words were considered "likely to cause an average addressee to fight."

Time, Manner, and Place Restrictions

Laws may regulate expression in one of two ways. Some laws regulate expression based on its content. These laws prescribe *what* a speaker is allowed to say. Other laws regulate the time, manner, and place of expression. These laws prescribe *when, how* and *where* speech is allowed.

As a general rule, government cannot regulate the content of expression (except in special situations such as obscenity, libel, or false advertising). But it may make reasonable regulations governing the time, manner, and place of speech. For example, towns may require permits to distribute handbills, use sound trucks, or stage protests in parks, streets, or other public property. Cities may regulate the time during which loudspeakers may be used, the places where political posters may be located, and the manner in which demonstrations may be conducted. However, government cannot favor some ideas over others. Nor can it prohibit groups with unpopular views from holding peaceful demonstrations.

PROBLEM 5

a. Why do you think courts generally approve of laws that regulate the time, manner, and place of expression but disapprove of laws that regulate the content of expression?

b. Which of the following laws regulate the content of expression, and which regulate the time, manner, and place of expression? Which, if any, violate the First Amendment?

■ A city ordinance prohibits the posting of signs on public property such as utility poles, traffic signs, and street lamps.

■ A regulation prohibits people from sleeping in federal parks, even though the sleeping is part of a demonstration.

■ A federal regulation prohibits public broadcasting radio stations from airing editorials.

■ A town ordinance prohibits commercial billboards anywhere within the town limits.

■ A city ordinance prohibits Communists, Neo-Nazis, and other groups espousing a different form of government from renting the city auditorium.

Vagueness and Overbreadth

Courts have ruled that laws governing free speech must be clear and specific. This is so that a reasonable person can understand what expression is prohibited. Laws also need to be clear so they can be enforced in a nondiscriminatory way. In addition, laws that regulate free speech must be narrowly drafted to prohibit only as much as is necessary to achieve the government's goals. Laws that unnecessarily prohibit too much expression are considered overbroad. Courts may strike down vague or overbroad statutes, even if the expression could have been prohibited under a clearer, more narrowly drafted law. Besides rules against **vagueness** and overbreadth, some actions that may not appear to be speech are sometimes given First Amendment protection. Foremost among these is symbolic speech.

Symbolic Speech

Expression may be symbolic as well as verbal. **Symbolic speech** is conduct that expresses an idea. Although speech is commonly thought of as verbal expression, we are all aware of nonverbal communication. Sit-ins, flag-waving, demonstrations, and the wearing of armbands or protest buttons are examples of symbolic speech. Symbolic speech is protected by the Constitution. However, there are limits. If the conduct involves illegal or violent action, it is not protected. For example, in 1968 the U.S. Supreme Court upheld a federal law that prohibited draft card burning. It upheld the law despite arguments that draft card burning is a form of symbolic speech.

PROBLEM 6

In the following cases, identify the speakers' interests in expressing their positions and the government's interest in regulating the expression. Then decide whether the action in each case should be protected by the First Amendment as symbolic speech.

a. Bill Spence taped peace symbols to an American flag. When he hung the flag upside down (a symbol of distress or danger) in the window of his apartment, he was arrested and convicted for violating a state law against improper use of the flag.

b. Raoul Ortega believes that discrimination against Hispanic-Americans is widespread. To protest discrimination, he throws a rock through a school window. Taped to the rock is the message "End Discrimination Now!"

Offensive Speakers and Hostile Audiences

THE FEINER CASE

In 1951 Irving Feiner made a speech on a street corner in a predominantly black neighborhood of Syracuse, New York. A racially mixed crowd of 75 to 80 persons gathered to hear the speech, forcing some pedestrians to walk in the street to pass by. In his speech, Feiner called the president a "bum," the American Legion a "Nazi Gestapo," and the mayor a "champagne-sipping bum." He said, "Negroes don't have equal rights; they should rise up and fight for them."

The speech produced angry muttering and pushing from some members of the crowd. One man told the two police officers observing the speech that if they did not "get the S.O.B. off the stand," he would do so himself. Police twice asked Feiner to stop the speech and then, when he refused, arrested him for disorderly conduct. The police claimed the arrest was necessary to prevent a fight.

PROBLEM 7

a. What happened in the Feiner Case? Why was Feiner arrested?
b. Do you think Feiner was legally arrested? Were his First Amendment rights denied? Why or why not?
c. Do you think people should ever be prohibited from voicing unpopular views? Explain your answer.

Cases like Feiner's pose a dilemma. Should the police arrest the unpopular speaker or try to control the hostile audience? Although the government has a duty to protect free speech, it must also protect the general welfare and prevent rioting. At different times, the Court has used different legal tests to untangle this thorny dilemma.

One of the oldest tests is the *clear and present danger test*. Using this test, a court looks at the circumstances under which the expression was made. It then decides whether, in that situation, there was a clear and present danger of a substantial violation of the law. For example, a speech that causes an audience to mutter and mill about in disagreement with a speaker does not present a clear and present danger. But a speech that begins to cause a riot does present such a danger.

Another test is called the *balancing test*. This means that courts balance the individual's interest in free expression against the interest the government seeks to protect by prohibiting the expression.

More recently, the Court has used the *incitement test*. This means that speech can be prohibited only when it is directed toward inciting or producing immediate lawlessness and is likely to produce such action. For example, a speaker who urges people to commit **treason** could be punished. However, merely supporting or teaching about a different system of government is protected under the First Amendment.

THE GREGORY CASE

During a period of racial turmoil in 1969, Dick Gregory and a group of civil rights advocates staged a peaceful and orderly march from city hall to the home of Chicago's mayor. The purpose of the march was to demand desegregation of Chicago's public schools. As the demonstrators marched through the mayor's neighborhood, several thousand bystanders cursed and threatened the marchers. The police, fearful that they could no longer contain the large crowd, asked the demonstrators to disperse. When the demonstrators refused, they were arrested for disorderly conduct.

PROBLEM 8

a. In what ways are the Feiner and Gregory cases similar? In what ways are they different?
b. As a police officer, how would you have handled each situation? Would you have arrested the demonstrators or the hecklers?
c. Assume that Feiner and Gregory are convicted for disorderly conduct. As a judge, how would you rule on their appeals?

FREEDOM OF THE PRESS

If it were left to me to decide whether we should have a government without a free press or a free press without a government, I would prefer the latter.

—Thomas Jefferson

The First Amendment guarantees freedom of the press. It protects us from government **censorship** of newspapers, magazines, books, radio, television, and film. Traditionally, courts have been strong defenders of press freedom. For example, in 1966 the Supreme Court said that "justice cannot survive behind walls of silence." It said this to emphasize our system's distrust of secret trials. In addition to providing information about news events, the press subjects all of our political and legal institutions to public scrutiny and criticism.

The Constitution's framers provided the press with broad freedom. This freedom was considered necessary to the establishment of a strong, independent press. An independent press can provide citizens with a variety of information and opinions on matters of public importance. However, freedom of the press sometimes collides with other rights, such as a defendant's right to fair trial or a citizen's right to privacy.

Among the difficult questions government and the press have confronted are: When can the government prevent the press from publishing information? When can the government keep the press

from obtaining information? When can the government force the press to disclose information? Is freedom of the press limited in places such as schools or prisons?

Prohibiting Publication

THE CASE OF THE GAG ORDER

In 1975, six people were brutally murdered in their home in a small Nebraska town. The murders and the later arrest of a suspect received widespread news coverage. At a pretrial hearing, which was open to the public, the prosecutor introduced a confession and other evidence against the accused. Both the judge and the lawyers believed that publication of the information would make it impossible for the suspect to have a fair trial before an unbiased jury. As a result, the trial judge issued a gag order, which prohibited the news media from reporting the confession and any other evidence against the accused. Members of the news media then sued to have the order declared unconstitutional.

PROBLEM 9

a. What happened in this case? Why did the judge issue a gag order?
b. Should judges be able to close criminal trials to the press? If so, when and why?
c. Which is more important: the right to a fair trial or the right to freedom of the press? Explain your answer.
d. As a practical matter, how could the court protect the rights of the accused without infringing on the rights of the press?

In the Gag Order Case, the judge was concerned about the defendant's Sixth Amendment right to a fair trial. The reporters were concerned about their First Amendment right to freedom of the press. This case presented a conflict between two important constitutional rights: free press versus fair trial.

In 1976, the U.S. Supreme Court decided that the gag order was unconstitutional. It held that the trial judge should have taken less drastic steps to lessen the effects of the pretrial publicity. The Court suggested postponing the trial until a later date; moving the trial to another county; questioning potential jurors to screen out those with fixed opinions; and carefully instructing the jury to decide the case based only on the evidence introduced at the trial.

If the gag order had been approved, it would have amounted to a **prior restraint** (censorship before publication) on the press.

Attempts to censor publications before they go to press are presumed unconstitutional by the courts. Prior restraint is only allowed if (1) publication would cause a certain, serious, and irreparable harm; (2) no lesser means would prevent the harm; and (3) the prior restraint would work.

Another example of a government attempt to impose censorship before publication took place in 1971 when a government employee gave top secret documents about the Vietnam War to several newspapers. The documents outlined America's past conduct of the war in Vietnam. The government sued to block publication of the so-called Pentagon Papers, but the Court refused to stop publication. It said that the documents, although perhaps embarrassing, would not cause "direct, immediate, and irreparable harm." On the other hand, if the documents had, for example, contained a secret plan of attack during a time of war, the Court might have blocked publication.

PROBLEM 10

A state law made it a crime to publish the name of any youth charged as a juvenile offender. A newspaper published an article containing the name of a juvenile charged with the murder of another youth. The newspaper learned the name of the arrested youth by listening to the police radio and by talking to several witnesses to the crime.

a. What is the state's interest in having and enforcing this law?

b. What is the newspaper's interest in publishing the juvenile's name?

c. How should the conflict be resolved?

Denying Access to Information

Another way in which the government tries to control the press is by denying the public access to certain information. Some argue that denying access to information does not violate the rights of the press. Others contend that freedom of the press implies a right to obtain information.

To protect the public's access to government information, Congress passed the *Freedom of Information Act* (FOIA) in 1966. This law requires federal agencies to release information in their files to the public. The law allows anyone to obtain government information and records unless the material falls into a special exception. Exceptions include information affecting national defense or foreign policy, personnel and medical files, trade secrets, investigatory records, and other confidential information.

The law guarantees citizens the right to learn about the business of government. Federal agencies must respond to requests for information within 10 days. Agencies that refuse to release unprivileged information can be sued in federal court.

A letter requesting information under the *Freedom of Information Act* (FOIA) should be sent to the head of the agency or to the agency's FOIA officer. For a sample letter requesting information

FIGURE 27   Sample FOIA Letter

Agency Head or FOIA Officer
Title
Name of Agency
Address of Agency
City, State, zip

Re: Freedom of Information Act Request.

Dear _____:

Under the provisions of the Freedom of Information Act, 5 U.S.C. 552, I am requesting access to (identify the records as clearly and specifically as possible).

If there are any fees for searching for, or copying, the records I have requested, please inform me before you fill the request. (Or: ... please supply the records without informing me if the fees do not exceed $_____.)

[Optional] I am requesting this information (state the reason for your request if you think it will assist you in obtaining the information.)

[Optional] As you know, the act permits you to reduce or waive fees when the release of the information is considered as "primarily benefiting the public." I believe that this request fits that category and I therefore ask that you waive any fees.

If all or any part of this request is denied, please cite the specific exemption(s) that you think justifies your refusal to release the information, and inform me of the appeal procedures available to me under the law.

I would appreciate your handling this request as quickly as possible, and I look forward to hearing from you within 10 days, as the law stipulates.

Sincerely,

Signature
Name
Address
City, State, zip

A sample letter requesting information under the *Freedom of Information Act.*

Source: House Committee on Government Operations, *A Citizen's Guide on How to Use the Freedom of Information Act and the Privacy Act Requesting Government Documents,* 95th Cong., 1st sess., 1977.

under the *Freedom of Information Act*, see Figure 27. The agency's address can be found in the *United States Government Manual* or in Appendix B. Write "Freedom of Information Request" on the bottom left-hand corner of the envelope.

Identify the records you want as accurately as possible. Although you are not required to specify a document by name, your request must reasonably describe the information sought. The more specific and limited the request, the greater the likelihood that it will be processed without delay. You are not required to demonstrate a need or even a reason for wanting to see the information. However, you are more likely to receive the documents if you explain why you want them.

PROBLEM 11

Rumors about the state prison had gone on for years. Ex-prisoners claimed that rape, suicide, murder, and mistreatment were all common occurrences. The warden denied the allegations but refused to provide any information about prison conditions. A newspaper asked permission to inspect the prison and interview the prisoners, but the warden denied the request. The newspaper then asked the state Department of Corrections for information about the prison. It asked for a list of inmates and for information about anyone who had died or been injured while in custody. The Department of Corrections refused to provide any information. The newspaper then did two things. It filed suit seeking admission to the prison and it filed a *Freedom of Information Act* request for information about the prison.

a. How would you decide the lawsuit against the prison?

b. What are the newspaper's rights under the *Freedom of Information Act?* How would you decide their request for information?

c. Draft a letter to the state Department of Corrections seeking information under the FOIA.

Requiring the Press to Disclose Information

The government and the press also argue over the extent to which the First Amendment protects a reporter's sources of information. Reporters contend that requiring them to reveal their sources makes it more difficult to gather and publish information. When this problem arises, the freedom of the press often conflicts with other important rights.

The Federal Communications Commission requires radio and television stations to present both sides of important public issues.

THE CASE OF THE SHIELD LAW

In 1976 the *New York Times* published a story suggesting that a doctor had murdered several patients. As a result, New Jersey authorities investigated the case and charged the doctor with murder. Defense attorneys asked the *New York Times* to turn over the names of everyone who had been interviewed during the investigation and any other information it had. The defense contended that they could not properly prepare their case without this information. The *New York Times* and the reporter who conducted the investigation refused to turn over any information. They argued that the First Amendment and a New Jersey law that protected a reporter's sources of information allowed them to withhold any unpublished material in their possession. Should the judge allow the reporter to withhold the information sought by the defense attorney? Why or why not?

FREEDOM OF ASSOCIATION AND FREEDOM OF ASSEMBLY

Two other rights protected by the First Amendment are freedom of association and freedom of assembly. Freedom of association means that people have the right to associate with one another and to join or form groups for political, social, economic, or religious purposes. Freedom of association does not appear directly in the Constitution; rather it grows out of other constitutional rights.

Freedom of assembly means that citizens have the right to gather together peacefully to petition government for some action or policy. Citizens exercise these rights in many ways. They write letters to government officials, they lobby in Congress or their state legislatures, and they march or demonstrate in the streets.

Like other rights, the freedom of assembly is not absolute. The government may make reasonable rules regarding the time, manner, or place of protests and demonstrations. However, although the government can restrict protests to certain areas or to certain times of day, it cannot prohibit all protests. Nor can government regulate a protest based on what people plan to say.

PROBLEM 12

The American Nazi party planned a demonstration in the town of Skokie, Illinois. Most of Skokie's residents are Jewish, and many were survivors of Nazi concentration camps during World War II. Many others had lost relatives in the gas chambers. Because of this, many residents strongly opposed the Nazis demonstrating in their town.

To prevent violence and property damage, the town passed a law that it hoped would keep the Nazis from demonstrating in Skokie. The law required anyone seeking a demonstration permit to obtain $300,000 in liability insurance. However, this requirement could be waived by the town. The law also banned distribution of material promoting racial or religious hatred and prohibited public demonstrations by people in military-style uniforms. The Nazis challenged the law as a violation of their First Amendment rights.

a. Why did Skokie's Jewish population feel so strongly about this demonstration?

b. Some claimed that the purpose of the demonstration was to incite Skokie's Jews and to inflict emotional harm rather than to communicate ideas. Do you agree or disagree? Should the motive of the speaker affect whether the speech is protected by the Constitution?

c. Does the government have an obligation to protect the rights of the Nazis and other unpopular groups, even if their philosophy would not permit free speech for others? Should Ku Klux Klan or Communist party rallies have this same protection?

d. How should this case be decided? In what ways, if any, should the town be able to regulate speech and assembly?

The Constitution protects the right to dissent, but the government may regulate the time, manner, and place of public demonstrations.

EXPRESSION IN SPECIAL PLACES

Schools, military bases, and prisons present special First Amendment problems. The rights of students, military personnel, or inmates often conflict with the rights of others or interfere with the need to preserve order. When this happens, courts must balance the competing interests in each case.

As a general rule, courts allow greater freedom of speech in public places such as parks and city streets. Somewhat less freedom of speech is allowed in publicly owned but special purpose facilities such as schools or prisons. In these places, you may speak freely only up to the point where the expression would interfere with the purposes of the facility. Finally, almost no freedom of speech is allowed on privately owned property.

THE TINKER CASE

Mary Beth Tinker and her brother John were opposed to the Vietnam War. They decided to wear black armbands to school as symbols of their objection to the war. When school administrators learned this, they adopted a policy that anyone wearing armbands would be asked to remove them. Students who refused would be suspended until they returned to school without the armbands. The Tinkers and three other students wore black armbands to school. Though some students argued the Vietnam issue in the halls, no violence occurred. The five protesting students were suspended from school until they came back without their armbands. Should wearing the armbands be considered a form of free speech protected by the Constitution?

In *Tinker v. Des Moines School District* (1969), the U.S. Supreme Court decided that the right to freedom of expression "does not end at the schoolhouse door." It held that wearing armbands was a form of "symbolic speech" protected by the First Amendment. However, the Court also held that the students' right to free speech could be restricted when the school could show that the students' conduct would "materially and substantially disrupt" the educational process. For example, a student could probably not insist on giving an antiwar speech during a biology class. This type of disruption did not occur in reaction to the Tinkers' armbands, nor could it reasonably have been predicted, so their suspensions were unconstitutional.

PROBLEM 13

For each of the following cases, give the arguments for and against permitting the expression. Then decide whether the expression is protected by the First Amendment. Explain your answers.

a. Candidates for national political office sought permission to enter Fort Dix military base to distribute literature and discuss issues with military personnel. Permission was denied because Fort Dix had a regulation against "demonstrations, sit-ins, picketing, protest marches, political speeches" and similar activities.

b. A prison warden confiscated personal writings from an inmate's cell. The warden claimed that the writings were "racist" and "inflammatory." The inmate was punished by sending him to solitary confinement for a month.

c. A group of college students marched to the county jail to protest the arrests of other students who had taken part in a civil rights demonstration. The sheriff warned them that they were trespassing and told them to leave immediately. Some left but others did not. Those who remained were arrested and charged with trespass.

d. Several hundred black students marched to the grounds of the state capitol to protest against segregation. A large crowd of police and onlookers gathered to watch. The protesters carried signs that read "Down with Discrimination" and sang freedom songs. After being warned to disperse, the protestors were arrested and charged with breach of the peace.

e. An urban high school has a long-standing rule against wearing *all* partisan buttons and badges. Whenever students wear buttons, school officials require their removal. A student wears a "white power" button to school. When the student refuses to remove it, she is suspended.

In recent years, many cases have raised questions about freedom of the press in schools. As you learned in the *Tinker* case, students carry their constititional rights with them into school. In some instances, however, freedom of the press may be more limited in school than in the community.

Courts have sometimes allowed school administrators to impose prior restraints on student publications. Courts have done this when administrators could reasonably predict that the publication would cause "a material and substantial disruption in the educational process." In addition, administrators can make reasonable rules for the time, manner, and place of distributing publications. However, courts examine these rules carefully to ensure that they are not unreasonably restrictive or that they do not represent an attempt to suppress unpopular expression.

PROBLEM 14

A student newspaper, funded in part by the county school board, lets the principal review articles before publication. The principal denied permission to print an article entitled "Sexually Active Students Fail to Use Contraceptives". The principal did this because the school board had banned teaching about birth control from the curriculum. The student editors believe that the First Amendment protects their right to publish this article.

a. Does the First Amendment apply to school publications? Should student publications be treated differently from the daily newspaper in your community? Why or why not?

b. In what ways can school officials regulate a school publication without interfering with First Amendment rights?

c. How would you decide the prior case? Give reasons for your decision.

YOU BE THE JUDGE

Sue Mills is a senior at a public high school. Sue has been active in the Women's Rights Caucus during her years at the school, which is coed and evenly balanced between males and females. Sue believes that sexism pervades the entire school system.

The following is a list of possible methods by which she could express her concern and dissatisfaction. Decide which of the activities would be protected as "speech" under our Constitution and which are not protected. Explain your answer.

a. Sue speaks on a corner near the school and calls for an end to sexism.

b. Sue hands out leaflets to the students as they enter the school. The leaflets, in an obscene and violent manner, accuse the school of sexism.

c. Sue enters the school library and asks for a book on sexism in America. When the librarian tells her that the library doesn't have such a book, Sue sits down and refuses to leave.

d. Sue pickets in front of the school with a sign saying "End Sexism."

e. Sue demands the right to speak about sexism to the student body at a school assembly.

f. Sue throws a rock through a school window. On it is written the message, "End Sexism."

g. During a physical education class, Sue begins speaking about sexism in athletics.

h. Sue uses a sound truck to express her views in front of the school.

i. Sue decides to express her displeasure by refusing to speak at any time during the school day.

j. Sue comes to school dressed like a five-year-old, declaring, "I will not dress like a woman until I am treated like one."

k. When a school club refuses to admit females, Sue puts a bomb under the building and blows it up.

l. Sue burns the American flag in front of the school, saying, "I will not respect this flag until the United States changes its sexist policies."

m. Sue buys space in the school newspaper to express her views.

n. Sue enters the school wearing a black armband to protest the school's sexist policies.

FREEDOM OF RELIGION

Congress shall make no law respecting an establishment of religion, or prohibiting the free exercise thereof . . .

—First Amendment

The first 16 words of the First Amendment deal with freedom of religion. The placement of these words at the beginning of the Bill of Rights reflects the deep concern the founding fathers had about the relationship between church and state, and about individuals' rights to practice their religion freely. Religious freedom is protected by two clauses in the Amendment: the establishment clause and the free excerise clause.

The **establishment clause** forbids the government from setting up a state religion. It also prohibits the government from preferring one religion over another or from passing laws that aid or promote religion. The **free exercise clause** protects individuals' right to worship or believe as they choose.

Taken together, the establishment and free exercise clauses require the government to be neutral toward religion. Government laws and practices must not endorse or disapprove of religion. However, it is important to recognize that America is a religious country and that Americans are religious people. Many of our national traditions have religious overtones. For example, our money includes the words "In God We Trust." The Pledge of Allegiance contains references to God. Christmas trees are set up at government buildings during the holidays. Although these traditions appear to violate separation of church and state, they have been upheld by the courts.

Establishment Clause

The establishment clause prohibits the government from enacting laws aiding one particular religion or all religions. It also forbids establishment of a government church. Thomas Jefferson once referred to the establishment clause as a "wall of separation between church and state." In America, there is a wall of separation, but it is not complete. Churches are indirectly aided by government in many ways. For example, churches do not have to pay real estate taxes, even though they receive government services such as police and fire protection. In addition, the Supreme Court has allowed states to provide **parochial school** students with certain benefits.

The Court uses a three-part test to decide whether a law is an unconstitutional violation of the wall of separation:

1. The law must have a secular (nonreligious) purpose.

2. The primary effect of the law must neither advance nor inhibit (hold back) religion.

3. The operation of the law must not foster excessive entanglement of government with religion.

Establishment clause cases are often controversial. This is particularly true when cases involve aid to parochial schools or prayer in public schools.

Over the years, the states have been permitted to provide many services to church schools. In addition, the Court has approved some forms of aid to parochial school students and their parents. For example, it has allowed states to provide bus transportation and loans of certain textbooks to parochial school students.

However, state and federal laws that provide financial aid directly to a religious institution or its instructors are less likely to be approved. For example, in 1985 the Court decided that Michigan could not pay parochial school teachers to teach after-school courses in parochial schools. Although the courses were non-religious, the Court outlawed the program because it provided direct aid to religious schools and had the effect of advancing religion.

Not all laws that provide financial aid to religious institutions are unconstitutional. The Court has upheld a federal law that funds construction of buildings and facilities at religious colleges, as long as the buildings are not used for religious purposes.

Perhaps the most controversial establishment clause issue is prayer in public schools. Is prayer in public schools allowable? What about Bible reading or silent meditation?

PROBLEM 15

A state board of education decided that a daily prayer should be recited by schoolchildren to help them develop the strength to defend the American way of life. The prayer the board developed read: "Almighty God, we acknowledge our dependence upon Thee and we beg Thy blessings upon us, our parents, our teachers and our country." Several children and their parents challenged the daily prayer as a violation of their freedom of religion.

a. Do you think that requiring children to say a daily prayer violates the First Amendment? Explain your answer.

b. What would you think if students could choose a different prayer depending on their religion or could choose not to pray?

c. Does reciting a daily prayer at school constitute an "establishment of religion"?

d. Should the First Amendment forbid all traces of religion in official public life — Christmas carols, the motto "In God We Trust," religious statements by the president?

Free Exercise Clause

The free exercise clause protects individuals' right to worship as they choose. However, when an individual's right to free exercise of religion conflicts with other important interests, the First Amendment claim has not always won. As a rule, religious *belief* is protected. *Actions* based on those beliefs may be restricted if the action violates an important government interest. For example, the Supreme Court ruled that members of a religion that allowed men to have more than one wife (a violation of the bigamy laws) could not practice this belief in the United States. This decision was based on the Court's opinion that preserving the traditional family is more important than permitting this particular religious practice.

THE AMISH CASE

Wisconsin had a law requiring all children to attend school until age 16. However, members of the Amish religion believe that children between the ages of 14 and 16 should devote that time to Bible study and training at home in farm work. The Amish believe that high school is "too worldly for their children." State officials prosecuted several Amish parents for not sending their children to school. The parents defended their actions as an exercise of their religion.

Wisconsin v. *Yoder* reached the U.S. Supreme Court in 1972. The Court weighed the rights of the Amish to practice their religion against the state's interest in requiring school attendance. The Court held that the Amish people's right to free exercise of religion was more important than the two years of required schooling. Among the factors the Court considered was the tendency for Amish children to become employed, law-abiding citizens after completing their religious education.

The Amish way of life is closely tied to their religious beliefs.

PROBLEM 16

The following cases involve government action and religion. For each case, determine whether the case involves the establishment clause, the free exercise clause, or both. Then decide whether the government's action violates the First Amendment.

a. A state government pays a chaplain to open each legislative session with a prayer.

b. A state law allows tax deductions for tuition expenses for the parents of students in public, private, and parochial schools.

c. A state law authorizes a one-minute period of silence in all public schools "for meditation or voluntary prayer."

d. A city erects a Christmas display which includes a Santa Claus, a Christmas tree, reindeer, and a nativity scene.

e. A state law requires that the Ten Commandments be posted in each public school classroom.

f. A state law makes it a crime to refuse to salute the American flag, even though Jehovah's Witnesses believe this is contrary to their religion.

g. A state university makes meeting space available for all student groups except religious groups.

The establishment and free exercise clauses are closely related and often come into conflict. Ensuring that a law does not establish a religion can interfere with free exercise of religion. For example, consider aid to parochial schools. Does the *failure* to aid parochial schools deprive some people of the free exercise of their religion? Similarly, laws that protect free exercise may appear to establish a religion. For example, Sunday closing laws protect Sunday as a day when individuals can attend church. But to people whose day of worship is not Sunday, these laws also appear to be an establishment of religion.

THE RIGHT TO PRIVACY

The makers of our Constitution . . . conferred, against the Government, the right to be let alone — the most comprehensive of rights and the right most valued by civilized men.

> *Olmstead* v. *United States*, (1928), dissenting opinion

Today, Justice Brandeis's words from the *Olmstead* case continue to have meaning in our daily lives. Although the words *right to privacy* or *right to be let alone* cannot be found anywhere in the federal Constitution, most citizens agree that **privacy** is a basic right and must be protected.

PROBLEM 17

a. What does privacy mean to you at home? At school? At work? On the phone? In other places?

b. How would you feel if someone listened in on your phone calls, opened your mail before your saw it, or inspected your locker without your permission?

c. In what other ways can privacy be invaded? How can the law protect the right to privacy?

Since the mid-1960s, the Supreme Court has recognized a constitutional right to privacy. This right is protected both where citizens seek to be let alone (as in search and seizure cases) and where citizens want to make certain kinds of important decisions (such as marriage and family planning) free of government interference.

The Court has said that the Constitution creates "zones of privacy." The zones are derived from the freedoms of speech and association (First Amendment), freedom from unreasonable search and seizure (Fourth Amendment), the right to remain silent (Fifth Amendment), the right to have one's home free of soldiers during peacetime (Third Amendment), and the unspecified rights kept by the people (Ninth Amendment).

The right to privacy sometimes conflicts with important government interests. For example, the government may need information about individuals to solve a crime or to determine eligibility for government programs. In such cases, the government can regulate certain acts or activities, even though an individual's interest in privacy is affected. Deciding whether a constitutional right to privacy exists involves a careful weighing of competing private and government interests.

PROBLEM 18

For each of the following situations, decide what rights or interests are in conflict and what arguments can be made for each side. Indicate whether you agree or disagree with the law or policy.

a. A public school requires students to obey a dress code and restricts the hair length of boys.

b. The government requires taxpayers to reveal the source of their income, even if it is from illegal activities.

c. A law forbids nude bathing anywhere at a community's beaches.

d. In a prison that has had several stabbings, inmates are strip-searched every day.

e. A state law requires motorcyclists to wear helmets.

f. The police place a small device in a phone, enabling them to record all numbers dialed on that phone.

The right to privacy protects citizens from unreasonable interference by state or federal governments. The right to privacy is also protected by laws passed by Congress or state legislatures. The *Fair Credit Reporting Act* (discussed in Chapter 3), for example, gives consumers a right to inspect their credit records and correct any inaccurate information. Do you know of any other laws that protect personal privacy?

Privacy in the Home

There is a saying that a person's home is his or her castle. Historically, the law has recognized that people may reasonably expect considerable privacy in their homes. However, in certain instances, such as when police carry out valid search warrants, the privacy of the home may be legally invaded.

THE CASE OF POSSESSING OBSCENE MATERIALS AT HOME

Georgia had a law prohibiting possession of obscene or pornographic films. A man was arrested in his own home for violating this law. He said (and the state prosecutor did not challenge him) that he had the films for his own use and not for sale.

In this case, the Supreme Court recognized a person's right to possess obscene materials in one's own home for private use. The Court indicated that individuals have the right to think, observe, and read whatever they please, especially in their own homes.

PROBLEM 19

a. Do you agree or disagree with the Court's opinion?
b. Would you decide the case differently if the man had showed the obscene films to people outside his home? Would your decision be different if people had to pay to see the films? Why?
c. Assume a person is arrested for possessing a small amount of illegal marijuana in her home. Could she successfully argue, based on the prior case, that the law violates her right to privacy? How are the cases the same? How are they different?

Privacy at School

WHERE YOU LIVE

How do schools in your community notify people of their privacy rights? What written procedures have been developed to implement this law?

Courts generally limit students' right to privacy in schools. For example, most courts uphold searches of students' desks and lockers. The courts reason that lockers belong to the school and that students cannot reasonably expect privacy on school property. Likewise, the Supreme Court has upheld searches of students' belongings without a warrant and without probable cause, as long as school officials have some reasonable suspicion of wrongdoing.

There is, however, a federal law that protects students' right to privacy. Known as the *Family Educational Rights and Privacy Act of 1974*, this law gives parents the right to inspect school records kept on their children. If parents find any inaccurate, misleading, or inappropriate information, they may insist on a written correction. The law also prohibits the release of school records without a parent's permission.

Students who reach age 18 or enroll in college have a right to see their own records. Requests to see school records must be honored within 45 days. Schools have a duty to inform parents and students of their rights under this law.

THE CASE OF THE TENTH GRADE DISCIPLINE PROBLEM

Michon, age 17, is getting ready to apply to college. Before filling out her college recommendation, the guidance counselor reviews her school records and finds this note from her 10th grade teacher: "Michon has a serious discipline problem. She can't control herself and will have problems succeeding in school because of this." Her counselor includes this remark on the college recommendation form.

PROBLEM 20

a. What, if anything, can Michon do about the comments in her recommendation form?
b. What are her rights under the *Family Educational Rights and Privacy Act?* What are her parents' rights?

Privacy on the Job

Privacy is an issue when one applies for or holds a job. How much personal information can an employer require from a job applicant or employee? What kind of information can an employer keep

Federal law prohibits information in school records from being given out without consent of students or their parents.

in an employee's records? Do future employers have a right to see these records? To what extent can an employer determine an employee's private habits such as dress, grooming, and personal behavior when on the job and during off-duty hours?

PROBLEM 21

A county police regulation requires male officers' hair "to not touch the ears or the collar except the closely cut hair on the back of the neck." The regulation also limits the length of sideburns and prohibits beards and goatees, although it allows neatly trimmed mustaches. Patrolman Johnson sues the police department because he believes the regulation violates his rights.

a. What rights and interests are in conflict in this case?

b. What arguments can be made for each side?

c. How would you decide this case? Give your reasons.

d. Should schools require certain dress and grooming standards for students and teachers? Should the military be able to do this for soldiers? Explain.

Except in cases of discrimination, the law does little to regulate the employment practices of *private* business. Some com-

WHERE YOU LIVE

Does your state or local government have any laws regarding the use of lie detectors? If so, what are they?

panies, however, have policies that allow open access to personnel records. A few states have passed laws to force business and state government employers to allow employees to see their records.

Today, many businesses use lie detectors in an effort to identify dishonest employees. Employers claim this helps prevent employee theft. Some employees believe that being forced to take a lie detector test is an unreasonable invasion of their privacy. They claim that lie detector tests are inaccurate and that innocent employees sometimes lose their jobs because of the tests. Some states have laws that limit the use of lie detectors.

A few government agencies, such as the CIA and the FBI require their employees to take lie detector tests. These agencies also restrict the off-duty activities of their employees. In 1982 Congress passed the *Intelligence Identities Protection Act*. This law makes it illegal for any government employee to reveal the identity of intelligence agents working on behalf of the U.S. government. All of those practices have been upheld on national security grounds.

PROBLEM 22

Ted takes a job with the federal government. On Monday he signs a contract agreeing not to disclose any information about his work without approval of his superiors. On Tuesday, Ted has lunch with a reporter for the *Washington Post*. The reporter, who is doing a story on U.S. intelligence operations, gets Ted to reveal the name of a U.S. undercover agent working in a foreign country. On Thursday, the U.S. government sues the *Washington Post* to prevent it from publishing its story on intelligence operations. On Friday, Ted is arrested.

a. Has Ted broken any laws? Has the reporter?

b. What rights or interests do Ted, the press, and the government have at stake in this case?

c. How would you decide the case against Ted? How would you decide the lawsuit against the *Washington Post?*

Information Gathering and Privacy

In recent years, computers have changed the way we live, work, and play. Computers enable public and private organizations to collect and store detailed information about individuals. Indi-

Data banks are kept by many agencies and organizations such as the Internal Revenue Service, state motor vehicle departments, retail credit companies, the FBI, Veterans Administration, state welfare departments, and the armed forces.

viduals are usually unaware that the information is being collected on them or being given to others.

The federal government's computers contain enormous amounts of information. Today, there are about 5,000 federal data banks. For example, the federal government requires banks to microfilm large checks passing through customer accounts. Most banks keep copies of *all* checks written or deposited by their customers. This information can be useful when authorities investigate white-collar crime, but it may be unfairly damaging if it falls into the hands of other investigators.

Courts have held that the right to privacy does not protect checks or deposit slips. However, limited protection is provided by a federal law that requires customers to receive notice whenever a federal agent seeks a copy of their financial records from a bank, savings and loan association, or credit card company. Individuals can then ask a federal court to decide whether the government's request should be honored. However, the law does not protect

THE CASE OF THE FINANCIAL DISCLOSURE LAW

In 1976 Florida voters passed a "Sunshine Law" requiring certain elected officials to make a complete, annual public disclosure of their financial interests. The required disclosure could be either a copy of the person's most recent federal income tax return or a sworn statement identifying each separate source and amount of income over $1,000.

Five state senators sued, arguing that the public's "right to know" was violating their "right to privacy." They also contended that the law placed an unfair burden on political candidates and would deter some people from running for office.

PROBLEM 23

a. Do you think it is important to have disclosure laws for public officials? If so, why?
b. In this case, which do you believe is more important: the public's right to know or the individual's right to privacy? Give reasons for your decision.

against requests from state and local governments, private investigators, or credit bureaus to see a person's financial records.

Although laws such as the *Freedom of Information Act* encourage the government to release information to the public, another law has tightened control over federal records. *The Privacy Act of 1974* prevents the government from releasing information about an individual without that person's written consent. It protects medical, financial, criminal, and employment records from unauthorized disclosure. The law also entitles individuals (with some exceptions) to see information about themselves and to correct any mistakes. If your rights are violated under this law, you may sue for damages in federal court.

THE CASE OF THE DAMAGING FILE

Marsha is a member of an organization that opposes the construction of nuclear power plants. She believes the FBI has been gathering information on her. She worries that if she applies for a government job, the FBI file may result in her not being hired. Can Marsha find out whether the FBI has a file on her?

DUE PROCESS

No person shall be . . . deprived of life, liberty, or property, without due process of law . . .

—Fifth Amendment

No State shall . . . deprive any person of life, liberty, or property, without due process of law . . .

—Fourteenth Amendment

The Constitution seeks to ensure justice by requiring the government to follow **due process** (fair procedures) when dealing with citizens. Due process procedures do not guarantee that the *result* of government action will always be to a citizen's liking. However, fair procedures do help prevent arbitrary, unreasonable decisions. Due process requirements vary depending on the situation. At a minimum, due process means that citizens must be given *notice* of what the government plans to do and have a *chance to comment* on the action.

Government takes many actions that may deprive people of life, liberty, or property. In each case, some form of due process is required. For example, a state might fire someone from a government job, revoke a prisoner's parole, or cut off someone's social

How does due process of law apply to school suspensions?

WHERE
YOU
LIVE

What due process procedures are followed by schools in your area before a student is suspended?

THE CASE OF GOSS v. LOPEZ

In 1971 widespread student unrest took place in the Columbus, Ohio, public schools. Students who either participated in or were present at demonstrations held on school grounds were suspended. Many suspensions were for a period of 10 days. Students were not given a hearing before suspension, although at a later date some students and their parents were given informal conferences with the school principal. Ohio law provides free education to all children between the ages of 6 and 21. A number of students, through their parents, sued the board of education, claiming their right to due process had been violated when they were suspended without a hearing.

In *Goss*, the Supreme Court decided that students who are suspended for 10 days or less are entitled to certain rights before their suspension. These rights include (1) oral or written notice of the charges; (2) an explanation (if students deny the charges) of the evidence against them; and (3) an opportunity for students to present their side of the story.

The Court stated that in an emergency, students could be sent home immediately and a hearing held at a later date. The Court did *not* give students a right to a lawyer, a right to cross-examine witnesses, a right to call witnesses, or a right to a hearing before an impartial person.

In *Goss*, the Court considered the due process interests of harm, cost, and risk. The Court ruled that reputations were harmed and educational opportunities were lost during the suspension; that an informal hearing would not be overly costly for the schools; and that while most disciplinary decisions were probably correct, an informal hearing would help reduce the risk of error.

security payments. Due process does not prohibit these actions, but it does ensure that certain procedures are followed before any action is taken.

You are probably familiar with some due process requirements from your knowledge of criminal law. Among the procedures that the government must use before sending someone to jail (thereby depriving the person of liberty) are notice of the charges, an opportunity to be heard at a trial, assistance of a lawyer, and the right to appeal.

If a person has a right to due process, the next issue is what process is due. Due process is a flexible concept. The procedures required in specific situations depend on several factors: (1) the seriousness of the harm that might be done to the citizen; (2) the cost to the government, in time and money, of carrying out the procedures; and (3) the risk of making an error without the procedures.

In addition to notice and an opportunity to be heard, due process may include a hearing before an impartial person, representation by an attorney, calling witnesses on one's behalf, cross-examination of witnesses, a written decision with reasons based on the evidence introduced, a transcript of the proceeding, and an opportunity to appeal the decision.

If you believe that the government has not followed fair procedures, you may want to consult an attorney. With the attorney's advice and assistance, you could file a complaint directly with the government agency. You may also be able to go to court and seek an order that the government follow due process in dealing with you.

Remember that when the Supreme Court decides a constitutional issue, it sets out the *minimum* protection required. No government can offer less. For example, a state could not decide to do away with the "notice" requirement in the *Goss* decision. However, government agencies can (and some do) offer greater due process protection than the Supreme Court requires.

PROBLEM 24

For each of the following situations, decide whether the citizen has any interest at stake. If there is an interest, is it in life, liberty, or property? If you think there is an interest, what procedures do you think the government should follow to protect the citizen's rights?

a. City welfare officials believe a person is no longer eligible for welfare. They end payments without a hearing.

b. A defendant, convicted of first degree murder, is sentenced to death. The state supreme court refuses to hear his appeal.

c. A student who is a discipline problem is paddled by the teacher. The student is not given a hearing before the paddling.

d. Federal officials plan to build a dam which will flood a privately owned farm. The farmer does not want to sell her land or move from her home. No hearing is held, but the farmer is offered the fair market value of her property.

e. A consumer misses two car payments in a row. The finance company takes the car back without any notice or a hearing.

f. A child has a series of bitter arguments with her parents. Her parents place her in a state hospital for the mentally ill. She does not receive a hearing.

DISCRIMINATION

We hold these Truths to be self-evident, that all Men are created equal, that they are endowed by their Creator with certain inalienable rights . . .

—Declaration of Independence

No state shall . . . deny to any person within its jurisdiction the equal protection of the laws.

—Fourteenth Amendment

The promise of equality set out in the Declaration of Independence and the Fourteenth Amendment, is one of our nation's most ambitious ideals. But what does equality mean? Does it mean equal result, equal treatment, equal opportunity, or something else? Citizens claiming they have been denied equality have flooded the courts and legislatures in recent years. However, the government has found the promise of equality difficult to explain and enforce.

Over time, ideas about equality have changed. For many years, the courts held that equal protection did not mean that all persons had to have access to the same facilities, such as schools, restaurants, railroad cars, or public restrooms. Instead, the law allowed separate facilities for white and blacks as long as the facilities were equal. This was known as the separate but equal doctrine. In the 1954 case of *Brown* v. *Board of Education*, the Supreme Court ruled that separate schools were "inherently unequal." It then ordered the public schools integrated "with all deliberate speed." In the years following the *Brown* case, other court decisions and laws required the desegregation of all other public facilities.

The *Brown* decision started a period of growing national awareness about discrimination. During the next 30 years, courts and legislatures confronted issues of discrimination based on race, **national origin, alienage,** sex, age, handicap, income, and **legitimacy.** Unquestionably, the civil rights movement improved the economic and social positions of millions of Americans. However, despite landmark Supreme Court decisions and numerous civil rights laws, equality remains an elusive goal rather than an accomplished fact. Today society faces the problem of overcoming past discrimination against minorites and women without causing reverse discrimination against others.

What Is Discrimination?

Many laws discriminate. They do this by classifying people into different groups. Discrimination is an unavoidable result of lawmaking. Not all types of discrimination are illegal. As long as classifications are reasonable, they do not violate the equal protection clause.

Everyone is familiar with laws that require a person to be a certain age to obtain a driver's license. These laws discriminate but are not unconstitutional. For example, in some states people over age 16 qualify for a license; those under 16 do not. This classification is considered reasonable. But what if the law required a person to be left-handed to get a license? Or what if whites but not blacks, or Polish-Americans but not Mexican-Americans, could get a license? Would these laws be constitutional? How do they differ from the age requirement?

PROBLEM 25

The following situations all involve some form of discrimination. Decide whether the discrimination is reasonable and should be permitted, or is unreasonable and should be prohibited. Explain your reasons.

a. An airline requires pilots to retire at age 50.

b. A business refuses to hire a man with good typing skills for a secretary's position.

c. The owner of a French restaurant wants to hire a head chef. She accepts applications only from chefs born in France.

d. People under age eighteen are not allowed into theaters showing X-rated movies.

e. Women sports reporters are excluded from men's locker rooms following major league baseball games.

f. A city's bus system is not designed for use by people in wheelchairs.

g. In selecting applicants for government jobs, preference is given to veterans.

h. Girls are not allowed to try out for positions on an all-boy baseball team.

i. A private club restricts its membership and does not allow whites to join.

j. Auto insurance rates are higher for young unmarried drivers.

The Fourteenth Amendment provides that no state shall deny to any person the equal protection of the law. To determine whether a law or government practice meets the equal protection standard courts use three different tests, depending upon the type of discrimination involved.

The Equal Employment Opportunity Commission works to end discrimination in hiring, promotion, firing, wages, and other conditions of employment.

The Rational Basis Test   The standard used to judge most laws and practices is called the rational basis test. Using this test, the law will be upheld if it is reasonable, that is, if a rational relationship exists between the classification and the purpose of the law. For example, not licensing drivers under age 16 discriminates against people under age 16. This classification is considered reasonable because a rational relationship exists between the classification (age) and the purpose of the law (prohibiting immature people from driving). On the contrary, issuing licenses to left-handers but not right-handers would violate equal protection. The classification has nothing to do with the law's purpose and is therefore unreasonable. When courts use the rational basis test, they give wide discretion to the government. In upholding a law judges sometimes say, "This law may not be wise, but it is not irrational or unreasonable. Therefore, it does not violate equal protection."

The Strict Scrutiny Test   Laws that discriminate based on race, national origin, or alienage are considered "inherently suspect." These laws are judged by a more exacting standard called strict scrutiny. This means that laws involving race, national origin, or alienage will be declared unconstitutional unless the government has a *compelling* interest requiring the classification. This strict standard is used to ensure that people are judged on their own merits, not as members of a group. Also, discrimination based on race, national origin, or alienage typically affects members of minority groups. Because they are a numerical minority, they are often unable to use the political process to help themselves.

In addition to showing a compelling interest for the law, the government must have no other less offensive way to achieve the purpose of the law. Issuing driver's licenses to whites but not to blacks, or to Polish-Americans but not to Mexican-Americans, would be judged under the strict scrutiny standard. Both of these classifications would fail to survive strict scrutiny. Although the state may have a compelling interest in highway safety, it is not advanced by a classification based on race or national origin.

Courts also use strict scrutiny to review laws that involve fundamental rights, such as freedom of religion or the right to travel. For example, if a state scheduled an election on a major religious holiday, forcing some people to choose between practicing their religion or voting, courts would use strict scrutiny to resolve the conflict. When this test is used, the person challenging the law or practice is often successful.

The Substantial Relationship Test   The Supreme Court has used a third test in sex discrimination cases. Laws involving classifications based on sex must "serve important governmental objectives and must be substantially related to achieving those objectives." In other words, there must be a *close* connection (not merely a *rational* one) between the classification and purpose of the law.

For example, a state law prohibited the sale of beer to males, but not to females, between the ages of 18 and 20. The law was based on the fact that more young males than females had been arrested for drunken driving. However, the law did not prohibit females from buying beer and giving it to males. The Supreme Court held the law unconstitutional because there was no close, substantial relationship between the classification and the law's purpose.

To some extent, the substantial relationship test allows the courts to second-guess the legislature. Although the exact meaning of this test is not yet clear, laws that discriminate based on sex will need to be more than reasonable to survive court review.

Equal protection cases are complicated. The courts first identify the type of discrimination involved and then analyze the problem using the appropriate legal test. As a general rule, laws and

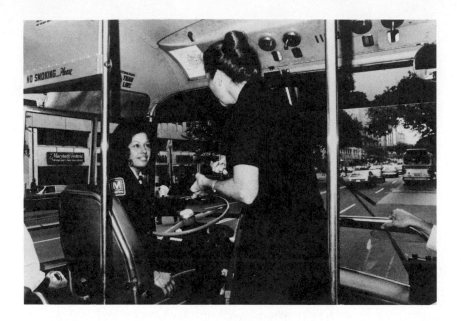

practices are likely to be challenged on equal protection grounds if they discriminate based on race, national origin, alienage, or sex, or if they affect a fundamental right. Although many other laws and practices discriminate, few can be successfully challenged under the Fourteenth Amendment.

The Fourteenth Amendment prohibits discrimination by state governments. The due process clause of the Fifth Amendment prohibits discrimination by the federal government. As a result, *private* acts of discrimination are not illegal unless they are forbidden by a specific local, state, or federal law. To deal with private discrimination Congress has passed a number of important civil rights laws.

Major Federal Civil Rights Laws

Equal Pay Act of 1963

■ Requires equal pay for equal work, regardless of sex.

■ Requires that equal work be determined by equal skill, effort, and responsibility under similar working conditions at the same place of employment.

■ Requires equal pay when equal work is involved even if different job titles are assigned.

(Enforced by the Wage and Hour Division of the U.S. Department of Labor or by private lawsuit)

Civil Rights Act of 1964 (amended in 1972)

■ Prohibits discrimination based on race, color, religion or national origin in public accommodations (e.g., hotels, restaurants, movie theaters, sports arenas). It does not apply to private clubs closed to the public.

■ Prohibits discrimination because of race, color, sex, religion, or national origin by businesses with more than 15 employees or by labor unions (this section is commonly referred to as Title VII).

■ Prohibits discrimination based on race, color, religion, sex, or national origin by state and local government and public educational institutions.

■ Prohibits discrimination based on race, color, national origin, or sex in any program or activity receiving federal financial assistance. It authorizes ending federal funding when this ban is violated.

■ Permits employment discrimination based on religion, sex, or national origin if it is a necessary qualification of the job.

(Enforced by the U.S. Equal Employment Opportunity Commission or by private lawsuit)

Voting Rights Act of 1965 (amended in 1970 and 1975)

■ Bans literacy and "good character" tests as requirements of voting.

■ Requires bilingual election materials for most voters who don't speak English.

■ Reduces residency requirements for voting in federal elections.

■ Establishes criminal penalties for harassing voters or interfering with voting rights.

(Enforced by the U.S. Civil Rights Commission)

Civil Rights Act of 1968

■ Prohibits discrimination based on race, color, religion, or national origin in the sale, rental, or financing of most housing.

(Enforced by the U.S. Department of Housing and Urban Development or by lawsuit in a federal court)

Age Discrimination in Employment Act of 1967 (amended in 1978)

■ Prohibits arbitrary age discrimination in employment by employers of 20 or more persons, employment agencies, labor organ-

izations with 25 or more members, and federal, state, and local governments.

■ Protects people between the ages of 40 and 70.

■ Permits discrimination where age is a necessary qualification for the job.

(Enforced by the U.S. Equal Employment Opportunity Commission or similar state agency)

Title IX of the Education Act Amendments of 1972

■ Prohibits discrimination against students and others on the basis of sex in educational institutions receiving federal funding.

■ Prohibits sex discrimination in a number of areas, including student and faculty recruitment, admissions, financial aid, facilities, and employment.

■ Requires that school athletic programs effectively accommodate the interest and abilities of members of both sexes; equal total expenditure on men's and women's sports is not required.

■ Does not cover sex stereotyping in textbooks and other curricular materials.

(Enforced by the U.S. Department of Education's Office of Civil Rights)

Rehabilitation Act of 1973

■ Prohibits private and government employers from discrimination on the basis of physical handicap.

■ Requires companies that do business with the government to undertake affirmative action to provide jobs for the handicapped.

■ Prohibits activities and programs receiving federal funds from excluding otherwise qualified handicapped people from participation or benefits.

(Enforced by lawsuit in federal court or, in some cases, state or local human rights or fair employment practices commissions)

Education for All Handicapped Children Act of 1975, Public Law 92–142

■ Guarantees a "free appropriate public education" for all handicapped children.

■ Entitles each handicapped child to free special services, including medical services necessary to secure an appropriate education.

■ Requires schools to develop an "individualized education program" for each handicapped child.

■ Requires parental approval of "individualized education programs" and of all changes in plan or placement.

■ Includes learning disabilities, behavioral disorders, and mental and physical impairments within definition of "handicap."

(Enforced by private lawsuit and by state and federal departments of education)

Discrimination Because of Race, National Origin, and Alienage

Most Americans believe that racial discrimination is both morally and legally wrong. Today, almost no one defends segregated public facilities or the operation of separate public school systems for black and white children. Nevertheless, discrimination is still a problem.

Americans are still coming to grips with their history of race discrimination in light of the Constitution's guarantee of equal protection. Today, the government faces the dilemma of helping those exposed to racial injustice while avoiding discrimination against others. The following questions focus our attention on the troubling issue of how to use just means to rid society of injustice.

In 1954, the U.S. Supreme Court ruled that racially segregated schools were unconstitutional.

A school bus arrives under police escort at a big city high school.

Does providing greater opportunities for some who have historically been denied equal protection result in fewer opportunities for others? Do discrimination laws originally passed to protect minorities protect the majority as well? Must the disadvantaged be treated differently in order to be treated equally?

Today, discrimination is more subtle and less blatant. Moreover, reasonable people sometimes disagree as to what constitutes discrimination. For example, a town denied a request to rezone land to build townhouses for low- and medium-income tenants. The town had mostly detached single-family houses, and almost all the town's residents were white. The Supreme Court upheld the zoning law because the Court found no *intent* to discriminate. However, when a school system redrew school attendance lines to keep black and white children from attending the same schools, the Court found that this action violated the Fourteenth Amendment.

To rid society of the lingering effects of discrimination courts have used a number of remedies. These include court-ordered busing to achieve integrated schools and **affirmative action** programs to recruit the disadvantaged for jobs and higher education. Controversy and opposition have surrounded the use of some of these remedies.

Public school segregation was declared unconstitutional in the *Brown* case. In theory, the schools were opened to students of all races. But in many instances, segregation continued. Many methods were used to desegregate the schools, including allowing students to attend any school they desired, redrawing neighborhood school boundary lines, transferring teachers, and developing magnet schools with special programs to attract a racially mixed student population.

Perhaps the most controversial method of school desegregation is busing. Busing as a means of transporting children to school has a long history. Today, almost 20 million children ride buses to and from school. However, controversy arose in 1971 when the Supreme Court required busing as a means of achieving school integration.

Supporters of busing claim that requiring racially balanced schools can help provide equal educational opportunity and quality education for both black and white children. They also argue that busing, which was once used to support segregation by transporting students to separate black and white schools, is an appropriate remedy. Opponents of busing contend that neighborhood schools are better because children will be in school with their friends and will be closer to home in case of an emergency. Critics also maintain that court-ordered busing has caused whites to flee city schools, resulting in even more segregation.

PROBLEM 26

a. What are the arguments in favor of busing? Against busing?

b. How do you feel about busing? If you favor it, which antibusing arguments trouble you most? If you oppose it, which probusing arguments trouble you most?

c. Is there a difference between saying that segregation is illegal and requiring schools to have specific percentages of black and white students? Explain.

Affirmative action is another remedy for dealing with the effects of discrimination. Affirmative action means taking positive steps to remedy past discrimination in employment and education. It goes beyond merely stopping or avoiding discrimination. For example, a business might take affirmative action by starting a program to recruit and hire more blacks and women.

Affirmative action plans can be either voluntary or mandatory. Voluntary plans are those freely adopted by an employer or university. Mandatory plans are imposed by the federal government as a condition of government funding or as a court-imposed remedy in discrimination cases.

Affirmative action programs are sometimes controversial. Supporters of affirmative action say that preferential admissions and hiring policies are needed to overcome the effects of past discrimination. Opponents of affirmative action say that it is a form of reverse discrimination. They argue that race and sex should not be used as a basis for classification, because special treatment for some means discrimination against others.

The affirmative action issue was presented to the Supreme Court in the case of *Bakke* v. *The University of California* (1978). In this case the medical school of the University of California at Davis had decided that the best way to increase minority enrollment was to give certain advantages to minority applicants. Each entering class reserved 16 of 100 places for minority applicants. Alan Bakke,

WHERE YOU LIVE

What is the racial makeup of schools in your area? How has this changed over the past few years? Have there been court decisions where you live regarding school desegregation? Has busing been ordered? Has it worked?

a 33-year-old white engineer, was twice denied admission to the medical school. He claimed that without the special admissions program, he would have been admitted because his grades and test scores were higher than those of the minority students. Bakke sued the university saying that the affirmative action program denied him equal protection of the laws.

The Supreme Court held the special admissions program unconstitutional and ordered Bakke admitted to the university. However, the decision left many questions unanswered. The Court seemed to say that racial quotas were illegal but that race could be considered as one of the factors in the admissions decision as long as schools seek to obtain a diverse student body. Before long, the issue of affirmative action was again before the Court.

THE WEBER CASE

Brian Weber was a white employee at the Kaiser Aluminum factory in a small Louisiana town. After five years at the plant, Weber applied for a position in a training program for skilled workers. He was turned down even though he had more seniority (i.e., more years of experience) than some of those selected.

He was not selected because Kaiser Aluminum had an affirmative action program designed to increase the number of blacks in skilled positions. To do this, Kaiser and the local union had agreed to give 50 percent of the training positions to blacks and 50 percent to whites. The company believed that this was necessary because although nearly 40 percent of the local work force was black, fewer than 2 percent of their skilled employees were blacks.

Weber believed this plan was unfair. He said it discriminated against him because of his race. Weber sued the company, relying on Title VII of the Civil Rights Act of 1964, which makes it illegal for employers to discriminate on the basis of race.

PROBLEM 27

a. What happened in this case? Why was Brian Weber denied admission to the training program?

b. Should schools or businesses ever be allowed to use race as a factor in decision making? If so, when and why? If not, why not?

c. What values are in conflict in this case? In the *Bakke* case?

d. What is the purpose of affirmative action programs? How do these programs affect society?

e. Do you think statistical underrepresentation of a group in school or business proves discrimination?

f. If you are discriminated against because of your race, what can you do? At school? At work?

In 1979 Brian Weber lost his case. The Supreme Court found that Title VII had been passed to improve employment opportunities for minorities and that it did not prohibit a voluntary affirmative action plan designed to end racial imbalance.

In a 1984 decision, the Supreme Court held that federal courts may not force a city employer to adopt an affirmative action plan to protect minority employees during layoffs. More senior white fire fighters had argued that they should not be laid off before more recently hired blacks. The Court held that a bona fide seniority system must be respected during layoffs. The Court explained that minorities were not entitled to special treatment at layoff time, except where individuals could prove that they had been victims of actual discrimination.

PROBLEM 28

Moose Lodge was a private club. Only members and their guests could eat or drink at the club. One day, a state representative who was a club member brought a black state representative as a guest. The club refused to serve the guest in the dining room or bar.

a. Does this action violate either the Fourteenth Amendment or the Civil Rights Act of 1964?

b. Should the law prohibit discrimination in private clubs? Why or why not?

Like race, classifications based on national origin and alienage are considered "suspect." The problem with such classifications is that they treat people as members of a group rather than consider their individual abilities and needs.

WHERE YOU LIVE

Is discrimination based on race, national origin, or alienage a problem in your community? What steps are being taken, or should be taken, to eliminate such discrimination?

In the past, courts have struck down laws that prohibited resident aliens from becoming lawyers or engineers. State laws excluding aliens from all government jobs are also unconstitutional, although citizenship may be required for certain jobs.

In distributing government benefits, state laws that deny welfare benefits to all aliens are unconstitutional. However, Congress's power to exclude some aliens (those living here less than five years) from Medicare has been upheld.

CASE OF KOREMATSU v. UNITED STATES

In 1942 the United States was at war with Japan. Following the surprise attack on Pearl Harbor, many Americans feared that the Japanese might invade the West Coast. Reacting to public fear, President Roosevelt, with congressional approval, ordered military authorities to relocate all 112,000 Japanese-Americans then living on the West Coast.

Among the Japanese-Americans ordered to leave their homes was Fred Korematsu. An American citizen, born in the United States, Korematsu refused to go when ordered to appear at a relocation center. Arrested and convicted for violating the relocation order, Korematsu appealed his case to the U.S. Supreme Court. He argued that the president's order and the act of Congress authorizing his removal were unconstitutional because they discriminated against Japanese-Americans solely on the basis of ancestry and without any evidence of disloyalty.

PROBLEM 29

a. Why did President Roosevelt order Japanese-Americans removed from the West Coast? Should the loyalty of Japanese-Americans have been a consideration in this case?

b. America was also at war with Italy and Germany. Why do you think Italian-Americans and German-Americans were not treated in the same manner as Japanese-Americans?

c. Should the government be able to exercise greater power or suspend the Bill of Rights during a time of war? Should the government have greater power even when not at war if acting in the interest of national security? Explain your answer.

d. How would you decide this case? Why?

PROBLEM 30

In the early 1970s, the San Francisco public schools enrolled several thousand Chinese students who spoke no English. The schools had relatively few Chinese-speaking teachers. Non-English-speaking Chinese students sued the school system, alleging they had been deprived of equal educational opportunity.

a. How should this situation be decided? Does any law guarantee students instruction in their native language?

b. A large suburban school district near Washington, D.C., enrolls students who collectively speak more than 30 different languages. Must the schools establish separate programs for each language?

WHERE YOU LIVE

Was the Equal Rights Amendment ratified by your state? Does your state have its own laws against sex discrimination?

Sex Discrimination

Equality of Rights shall not be denied or abridged by the United States or by any state on account of sex.

—Proposed Twenty-seventh Amendment

The movement to secure equal rights for women has a long history. From the nation's earliest days, women protested against unequal treatment. The first women's rights convention was held in 1848. It set out a list of demands for political, social, and economic equality. The most controversial issue to come out of the Seneca Falls convention was women's demand for the right to vote.

In 1900, only four states allowed women to vote. After a long series of protests, women finally won full voting rights in 1920 with passage of the Nineteenth Amendment. Earlier in the 19th century, all states had passed laws giving married women the right to own property.

Although women made many gains, the Supreme Court was slow to recognize sex discrimination as a problem. Even after passage of the Nineteenth Amendment, it took another 50 years for the Court to hold a government policy based on sex unconstitutional.

In recent years, however, the Court has considered many cases involving sex discrimination. For example, in 1976, the Court struck down an Oklahoma law that set different drinking ages for men and women. If an 18-year-old woman may buy beer, the Court reasoned, an 18-year-old man must also be allowed to buy it.

Similarly, in a 1984 case involving a large law firm, the Supreme Court ruled federal antidiscrimination laws apply when law firms decide who becomes a partner. Public debate, however, focused less on Supreme Court decisions than it did on the **Equal Rights Amendment** (ERA).

First proposed in 1923, the Equal Rights Amendment was approved by Congress and submitted to the states in March 1972. Congress set a deadline for ratification of seven years from this date. In July 1978, Congress extended the deadline for three years. However, the amendment died on June 30, 1982 — three states short of the 38 needed for ratification. If passed, the ERA would have controlled actions by federal, state, and local government. Government would have been prevented from passing discriminatory laws or from enforcing laws in an unequal way.

Opponents of the ERA say it would hurt women. Laws that now favor or protect women would have to be changed. They argue, for example, that women would be subject to the military draft. They also say that the ERA would force women out of the home and into the workplace. Finally, opponents claim the ERA is unnecessary. They say that numerous laws already protect women in employment, education, credit, and other areas.

Supporters say the ERA is necessary to end gender-based discrimination. They say the ERA would give women greater opportunities and choices. They also say it would help men by ending all forms of sex discrimination. Finally, ERA supporters argue that many laws designed to protect woman — such as those limiting the number of hours a women may work — have deprived women of economic benefits.

Although the drive to ratify the ERA has stalled, at least 15 states have equal rights provisions in their state constitutions.

PROBLEM 31

a. Do you favor or oppose the Equal Rights Amendment? Explain.

b. If you favor the Equal Rights Amendment, what arguments against the amendment trouble you the most? If you are against the amendment, what arguments for it trouble you the most?

c. In what ways have society's attitudes changed since the Supreme Court made the following statement in 1873: "The paramount destiny and mission of women is to fulfill the noble and high office of wife and mother." In what ways, if any, do you think these attitudes will continue to change?

For many years, a woman's place was considered to be in the home, not the job market. Today, however, more than half of all married women hold jobs outside the home. In 1963, Congress passed the *Equal Pay Act*, which made it illegal to pay women less money than men for doing the same job.

One year later, Congress passed the *Civil Rights Act of 1964* (see page 350 for a summary of these laws). Title VII of this law prohibits discrimination against women and minorities in all forms of employment: hiring, firing, working conditions, and promotion. Women or men who think they've been discriminated against because of their sex can contact the U.S. Equal Employment Opportunity Commission.

Pro-ERA demonstrators.

Despite the *Equal Pay Act,* women as a group still earn less money than men. Many reasons have been suggested to explain the difference: Some women take time off to raise young children, some work fewer hours, some have less seniority. Although these reasons may explain part of the difference, civil rights groups say sex discrimination is the real cause.

As a result, legal efforts to narrow the pay gap now center on the concept of **comparable worth.** This means that women in traditionally female jobs (such as secretaries and nurses) would be paid the same as men in traditionally male jobs (such as truck drivers and construction workers) when the two kinds of work are deemed to require comparable skill, effort, and responsibility.

PROBLEM 32

a. What does comparable worth mean? Should occupations dominated by women pay the same as occupations dominated by men? Can totally different jobs — such as secretaries and construction workers — really be compared?

b. Should men and women ever be treated differently in employment or education? Explain your answer.

c. Have you ever been the victim of sex discrimination? If so, what happened? What can you do if you are discriminated against because of your sex? At school? At work?

In 1972 Congress acted to end sex discrimination in education. *Title IX of the Education Act of 1972* prohibits sex discrimination in most school activities including curriculum, faculty hiring and student athletic programs.

Title IX's impact on school athletes has been particularly controversial. The law requires equal opportunity in athletic programs. This means that sports programs must effectively accommodate the interests and abilities of *both* sexes. For example, assume a school has a men's basketball team and that it also has a number of women interested in playing basketball. The law requires the school to either establish a women's basketball team or allow women to try out for the men's team. Moreover, if a separate women's team is established the school cannot discriminate against the woman by providing inferior facilities or equipment.

If only one woman is interested in basketball (or any other *noncontact* sport where a men's team exists), the school would have to allow her to try out for the men's team. In *contact* sports, such as football or wrestling, schools can limit teams to members of one sex. Although athletic opportunities must be equal, the law does not require that total expenditures on men's and women's sports be equal.

Title VII of the Civil Rights Act of 1964 prohibits sex discrimination in employment.

If a school violates *Title IX*, the government or the person discriminated against can go to court. *Title IX* also allows the federal government to cut off financial aid to schools that discriminate on the basis of sex.

PROBLEM 33

Title IX states: "No person in the United States shall, on the basis of sex, be excluded from participation in, be denied the benefits of, or be subjected to discrimination under any education program or activity receiving federal financial assistance . . ."

Which, if any, of the following situations do you believe are in violation of *Title IX*? Assume each school receives federal funds.

Title IX was passed to eliminate sex discrimination in public education, including school athletics.

a. A college sponsors one glee club, with membership open only to women.

b. A school establishes a women's baseball team, which receives used equipment from the men's team.

c. A high school grooming code requires that men's hair length not reach the shirt collar, but women's hair length is not regulated.

d. A U.S. history textbook does not include important contributions made by American women.

e. Female students who want to play football are denied the opportunity to try out for the male team and are not provided a separate team.

f. An eighth grade curriculum offers shop for boys and home economics for girls.

PROBLEM 34

Mrs. Weeks, a telephone company employee, applies for the job of electrician. This position sometimes requires lifting items weighing about 30 pounds. The company gives the job to a man with less seniority. In her rejection letter Mrs. Weeks is told that the company has decided not to assign women to the electrician's job.

a. Why did the company decide not to assign women to this job?

b. Was the company's decision fair?

c. Is Mrs. Weeks protected by the law? If so, what law?

d. Are there any jobs women should not have? Are there any jobs men should not have? Explain your answers.

Age Discrimination

Mario Campisi, age 55, had worked for the same company for 20 years. His boss said that Mario was an excellent worker but that he wanted to bring in someone younger. According to his boss, Mario had two choices: take a new, lower-paying job or quit.

Can older workers be fired or given a lower-paying position because of age? No! Age discrimination is against the law.

The *Age Discrimination in Employment Act* protects workers aged 40 to 70. It forbids discrimination in hiring, firing, pay, promotion, and other aspects of employment. The law applies to private employers of 20 or more persons, labor unions, government agencies, and employment agencies.

The law has several important exceptions. It does not apply if age is a *bona fide* job qualification. This means there must be a real and valid reason to consider age. For example, an older person could be refused a youthful role in a movie. The law also does not apply if an employment decision is made for a good reason other than age. For example, an older employee could be fired for misconduct. If you think you've been discriminated against because of age, you can file a complaint with the Equal Employment Opportunity Commission.

Age discrimination is not limited to older people. Many laws and practices discriminate against youth. For example, restric-

---

THE CASE OF THE FORCED RETIREMENT

Massachusetts required state police officers to retire at age 50. The law was designed to ensure that police officers were physically fit. The state police required complete physical examinations every two years until an officer reached age 40. Then it required exams every year until the officer reached age 50, the mandatory retirement age. Officer Murgia passed all examinations and was in excellent health when the state police retired him on his 50th birthday. Murgia sued the state police, arguing that the mandatory retirement age denied him equal protection. Should the Fourteenth Amendment protect Officer Murgia in this case?

In deciding Officer Murgia's case, the Supreme Court said, "drawing lines that create distinctions is . . . a legislative task and an unavoidable one. Perfection in making the classification is neither possible or necessary. Such action by a legislature is presumed to be valid." Although Officer Murgia was in good health, the Court accepted the fact that physical fitness generally declines with age. Therefore, it was rational to draw a line at some age, and the Court upheld this law.

PERSONS 40-70*YEARS NOTE!
Age Discrimination is Against the Law

The Federal Age Discrimination in Employment Act prohibits arbitrary age discrimination in employment by:

- Private Employers of 20 or more persons

- Federal, State and Local Governments, without regard to the number of employees in the employing unit

* There is no upper age limit for Federal employment.

- Employment Agencies serving such employers

- Labor Organizations with 25 or more members

FILING COMPLAINTS

If you feel you have been discriminated against because of age, contact the nearest office of the Equal Employment Opportunity Commission (EEOC). It is important to contact the EEOC promptly.

FILING SUITS

If you wish to bring court action yourself, you must first file a written charge alleging unlawful discrimination with the EEOC, and in states which have an age discrimination law, with the state agency. This charge should be filed promptly, but in no event later than 180 days after the alleged unlawful practice occurred.

The U.S. Equal Employment Opportunity Commission
2401 E Street, N.W., Washington, D.C. 20506

tions on voting, running for public office, making a will, driving, and drinking are generally upheld by the courts.

Although the courts have not used the equal protection clause to protect the rights of youth, some state and local legislatures have passed laws or regulations forbidding age discrimination. In addition, the Twenty-sixth Amendment gives 18-year-olds the right to vote in federal and state elections.

PROBLEM 35

The following laws and practices discriminate against youth in some way. Should any of them be changed? If so, what changes would you make?

a. Because of a high rate of shoplifting, a store owner will not allow anyone under 18 into the store unless accompanied by an adult.

b. Youths between the ages of 6 and 18 are required to attend school.

c. A state law prohibits 17-year-olds from working in factories and from working on any job for more than 40 hours a week.

Discrimination Because of Handicap

No otherwise qualified handicapped individual . . . shall, solely by reason of his handicap, be excluded from participation in, be denied the benefit of, or be subjected to discrimination under any program or activity receiving Federal financial assistance.

—Rehabilitation Act of 1973

Today, a number of laws prohibit unnecessary discrimination against handicapped people and require consideration of their special needs. These laws involve employment, education, building design, and transportation.

The *Rehabilitation Act of 1973* bars discrimination against the handicapped in a variety of federal programs. It bans discrimination in employment and requires employers who receive federal benefits to set up programs to assist handicapped workers. It requires employers to use job application procedures that do not unfairly screen out handicapped people. For instance, a deaf person applying for a job as a typist could not be required to take an oral test on office procedures. The law prohibits prospective employers from asking whether a person has a handicap. However, employers can ask whether a person can handle a job. The law also requires employers to make reasonable efforts to accommodate workers with **disabilities** — for example, making slight architectural changes to make offices accessible to people using wheelchairs or crutches.

Education is another area in which law helps the handicapped. Until recently, millions of children were excluded from public school because of mental or physical disabilities. However,

THIS FACILITY DOES NOT DISCRIMINATE ON THE BASIS OF HANDICAP REGARDING EMPLOYMENT AND ACCESSIBILITY.

Federal law requires that public facilities be made accessible to the handicapped.

in 1975 Congress passed the *Education for All Handicapped Children Act*. This law requires states to provide a free and adequate education to handicapped children. The law also provides money to the states to pay for the extra costs involved.

Handicapped children must be educated in the least restrictive environment possible. This means that a regular school classroom is better than a separate class, and special education is better than no education at all. Overall, this law has done much to move handicapped people into the mainstream of American life.

Other federal, state, and local laws also assist handicapped people. *The Architectural Barriers Act of 1968* requires that all public buildings be made accessible to the handicapped. Rest rooms, elevators, drinking fountains, meeting rooms, and public telephones must be designed to accommodate handicapped people. Similarly, many local laws require wheelchair ramps, braille signs, special parking spaces, and other special accommodations for the handicapped.

Handicapped people now have many rights. However, some problems and conflicts still remain. For example, people who use wheelchairs need curb cuts, but blind people who use canes need curbs to warn them where sidewalks end. Moreover, some mental and physical conditions make people unsuitable for certain jobs or professions. Reasonable efforts to accommodate handicapped people are required, but people sometimes disagree over what is reasonable.

THE CASE OF THE HEARING-IMPAIRED NURSING SCHOOL APPLICANT

Frances Davis, who had a serious hearing disability, applied for a program that would train her as a registered nurse. The program was offered by a state college that received federal funds. With a hearing aid she could hear various sounds, but she could not understand speech unless she was able to see the speaker and lip-read.

After applying to the school, she was interviewed by a faculty member. Her hearing difficulty became apparent in the interview, and her application was rejected.

The school believed that she could neither participate safely in clinical training nor later care safely for patients. Ms. Davis argued that federal law required the school to change its program to accommodate a handicapped person otherwise qualified to be admitted. She sued to have the school's decision reversed.

PROBLEM 36

a. What happened in this case? Why was Ms. Davis denied admission to nursing school?

b. Do you think the school's decision was fair or unfair? Explain your answer.

c. Read the section of the *Rehabilitation Act of 1973* quoted on page 366. Then decide whether the school's action is legal or illegal. Explain your answer.

d. Assume a person confined to a wheelchair applied to a law school receiving federal money. Assume further that he was rejected because the faculty believed that he would not be able to complete research assignments, since the library was accessible only by stairs. How is his case the same as Ms. Davis's? How is it different? How should his case be decided?

Discrimination Because of Income

In some major cases, poor people have been successful in having courts rule that discrimination against them was illegal. However, these decisions have been based on reasons other than equal protection. For example, the Supreme Court has ruled that any person being tried for a criminal offense in which there is a possibility of a jail term has the right to a free lawyer if the person cannot afford one. This decision was based on the Sixth Amendment's right to assistance of counsel.

PROBLEM 37

Many government laws and practices discriminate against the poor. For each of the following statements, decide whether the law or practice should be continued or abolished. Explain your answer.

a. To finance the cost of running an election, people must pay a poll tax to vote.

b. Any person unable to pay a traffic fine must spend time in jail to work off the fine.

c. To sue for divorce, the parties must pay $75 in court costs and filing fees.

d. Before any housing for low-income people can be built, the developer must have the local voters' approval.

e. A federal law states that no abortions can be performed with Medicaid funds except to save the life of the mother.

f. To get on the ballot, a political candidate has to pay a filing fee of 2 percent of the annual salary of the position she is seeking.

g. School systems are financed from local property tax revenues (along with funds from the state and federal governments). Schools in poor neighborhoods have far less money to spend on education than schools in wealthy areas.

State and Local Laws Against Discrimination

When the Supreme Court makes a decision regarding the Constitution, it determines the *minimum* amount of rights that governments must extend to their citizens. Governments may offer greater protection than what the Court says the Constitution requires.

For example, the *Civil Rights Act of 1968* prohibits discrimination in the rental or sale of property on the basis of race, color, religion, or national origin. Although this law provides important protections, it does not forbid discrimination against homosexuals, single people, people with young children, or those whose income is from alimony or welfare. To protect these and other individuals, some state and local governments have passed their own discrimination laws. These laws extend the protections offered by federal law. These laws may cover discrimination based on one or more of the following characteristics:

■ age (young or old)

■ marital status

**WHERE
YOU
LIVE**

Does your state or local government have any laws against discrimination? What state and local agencies are responsible for enforcing these laws?

■ personal appearance

■ source of income

■ sexual orientation

■ family responsibility (having children)

■ physical handicap

■ matriculation (status of being a student)

■ political affiliation

Some places have commissions that receive, investigate, and resolve complaints based on violations of these laws.

THE CASE OF NO WOMEN ALLOWED

The *Minnesota Human Rights Act* makes it illegal for businesses and organizations to discriminate based on "race, color, creed, religion, disability, national origin or sex." At one time, the United States Jaycees, a private organization, limited its membership to "young men between the ages of 18 and 35." In 1974, the Jaycees' Minneapolis chapter ignored the national bylaws and admitted women. The St. Paul chapter admitted women the following year. The U.S. Jaycees imposed sanctions on its two Minnesota chapters for violating the national rules. The Minnesota chapters in turn filed a sex discrimination complaint with the Minnesota Department of Human Rights.

Eventually, the case reached the United States Supreme Court. At issue was the constitutionality of the *Minnesota Human Rights Act*. The U.S. Jaycees argued that the law denied the national Jaycees their First Amendment freedom to associate with people of their choice.

The Supreme Court upheld the human rights law. It said that the Jaycees' desire to limit their membership must give way to the state's interest in preventing discrimination. The Court acknowledged that the law limited the Jaycees' freedom to associate with the people of their choice but held that the limitation was reasonable. The Court noted that the Jaycees are "neither small nor selective." It concluded that membership in the Jaycees was less like the intimate relationship of a family and more like the personal relationship in a business. As such, the right to associate — and discriminate — was less important than the human rights law, "which plainly serves a compelling state interest."

ADVICE ON ACTIONS TO TAKE IF YOUR RIGHTS ARE VIOLATED

No single procedure can be followed for all situations in which your rights have been violated. You should know that civil rights are protected by laws at both the state and federal level. Federal law sometimes requires that you first try to solve your problem on a state or local level. Also, some civil rights laws have specific time limits for filing a case. Don't delay if you believe that some action should be taken. If you decide to act, you may wish to consider the following options:

■ Protest in some way, either verbally, by letter, or by demonstration.

■ Contact an attorney who may be able to negotiate a settlement or file a case for you.

■ Contact a private organization with an interest in your type of problem (e.g., the ACLU for First Amendment problems or the NAACP for race discrimination). See Appendix B for a list of other organizations.

■ Contact a state or local agency with the legal authority to help (e.g., a state fair employment commission or a local human rights agency).

■ Contact a federal agency with the legal authority to help. Although federal agencies are based in Washintgon, D.C., most have regional offices and field offices in larger cities throughout the country. Look in the white pages of the phone directory under "U.S. Government."

■ Contact the U.S. Commission on Civil Rights (see Appendix B for address) for general information on where to look for help, or if your complaint goes unanswered.

PROBLEM 38

Review the civil rights laws summarized earlier in this chapter. For each of the following situations decide which law, if any, could help the person discriminated against. Which agency (or agencies) could be of assistance?

a. A 28-year-old married man applies for a job as a flight attendant for a major airline. The airline's policy is to hire only single men and women between the ages of 19 and 26.

b. Dan is a clerk earning $4.20 an hour; Diane earns $3.75 per hour at the same company. Dan spends 25 percent of his time typing and the rest of his time filing and running errands. Diane spends 60 percent of her time typing and the rest of her time filing and running errands.

c. A 47-year-old adminstrative assistant is told by her boss that because of a slowdown in business, she is being let go. When she returns to pick up her final paycheck several weeks later, she discovers that a 20-year-old woman has been hired to take her place.

d. A college professor from a university in Spain moves to this country. He applies for a job teaching high school Spanish but is refused because he is not yet a U.S. citizen.

e. A high school senior with good grades speaks with the college counselor at her school. The counselor provides her with information on college programs in nursing, elementary education, and home economics.

f. A woman applies for a correctional officer position at the state prison. She is told that state law prohibits the hiring of women prison guards to supervise male inmates at the maximum security prison.

appendix A
THE CONSTITUTION OF THE UNITED STATES OF AMERICA*

We the people of the United States, in Order to form a more perfect Union, establish Justice, insure domestic Tranquility, provide for the common defence, promote the general Welfare, and secure the Blessings of Liberty to ourselves and our Posterity, do ordain and establish this Constitution for the United States of America.

ARTICLE I

Section 1. All legislative Powers herein granted shall be vested in a Congress of the United States, which shall consist of a Senate and House of Representatives.

Section 2. The House of Representatives shall be composed of Members chosen every second Year by the People of the several States, and the Electors in each State shall have the Qualifications requisite for Electors of the most numerous Branch of the State Legislature.

No Person shall be a Representative who shall not have attained to the Age of twenty-five Years, and been seven Years a Citizen of the United States, and who shall not, when elected, be an Inhabitant of that state in which he shall be chosen.

[Representatives and direct Taxes shall be apportioned among the several States which may be included within this Union, ac-

---

* The Constitution and all amendments are shown in their original form. Parts that have been amended or superseded are bracketed and explained in the footnotes.

cording to their respective Numbers, which shall be determined by adding to the whole Number of free Persons, including those bound to Service for a Term of Years, and excluding Indians not taxed, three fifths of all other Persons.][1] The actual Enumeration shall be made within three Years after the first Meeting of the Congress of the United States, and within every subsequent Term of ten Years, in such Manner as they shall by Law direct. The Number of Representatives shall not exceed one for every thirty Thousand, but each State shall have at Least one Representative; and until such enumeration shall be made, the State of New Hampshire shall be entitled to choose three, Massachusetts eight, Rhode-Island and Providence Plantations one, Connecticut five, New-York six, New Jersey four, Pennsylvania eight, Delaware one, Maryland six, Virginia ten, North Carolina five, South Carolina five, and Georgia three.

When vacancies happen in the Representation from any State, the Executive Authority thereof shall issue Writs of Election to fill such Vacancies.

The House of Representatives shall choose their Speaker and other Officers; and shall have the sole Power of Impeachment.

Section 3. The Senate of the United States shall be composed of two Senators from each State, [chosen by the Legislature thereof,][2] for six Years; and each Senator shall have one Vote.

Immediately after they shall be assembled in Consequence of the first Election, they shall be divided as equally as may be into three Classes. The Seats of the Senators of the first Class shall be vacated at the Expiration of the second Year, of the second Class at the Expiration of the fourth Year, and of the third Class at the Expiration of the sixth Year, so that one-third may be chosen every second Year; [and if Vacancies happen by Resignation, or otherwise, during the Recess of the Legislature of any State, the Executive thereof may make temporary Appointments until the next Meeting of the Legislature, which shall then fill such Vacancies].[3]

No Person shall be a Senator who shall not have attained to the Age of thirty Years, and been nine Years a Citizen of the United States, and who shall not, when elected, be an Inhabitant of that State in which he shall be chosen.

The Vice-President of the United States shall be President of the Senate, but shall have no vote, unless they be equally divided.

The Senate shall choose their other Officers, and also a President pro tempore, in the absence of the Vice-President, or when he shall exercise the Office of the President of the United States.

The Senate shall have the sole Power to try all Impeachments. When sitting for that purpose, they shall be an Oath or Affirma-

[1] Modified by the Fourteenth and Sixteenth amendments.
[2] Superseded by the Seventeenth Amendment.
[3] Modified by the Seventeenth Amendment.

tion. When the President of the United States is tried, the Chief Justice shall preside: And no person shall be convicted without the Concurrence of two thirds of the Members present.

Judgment in Cases of Impeachment shall not extend further than to removal from Office, and disqualification to hold and enjoy any Office of honor, Trust, or Profit under the United States: but the Party convicted shall nevertheless be liable and subject to Indictment, Trial, Judgment, and Punishment, according to Law.

Section 4. The Times, Places and Manner of holding Elections for Senators and Representatives, shall be prescribed in each state by the Legislature thereof; but the Congress may at any time by Law make or alter such Regulations, except as to the Places of Choosing Senators.

The Congress shall assemble at least once in every Year, and such Meeting shall [be on the first Monday in December,]⁴ unless they shall by Law appoint a different Day.

Section 5. Each House shall be the Judge of the Elections, Returns and Qualifications of its own Members, and a Majority of each shall constitute a Quorum to do Business; but a smaller number may adjourn from day to day, and may be authorized to compel the Attendance of absent Members, in such Manner, and under such Penalties, as each House may provide.

Each House may determine the Rules of its Proceedings, punish its Members for disorderly Behavior, and, with the Concurrence of two thirds, expel a Member.

Each House shall keep a Journal of its Proceedings, and from time to time publish the same, excepting such Parts as may in their Judgment require Secrecy; and the Yeas and Nays of the Members of either House on any question shall, at the Desire of one fifth of those Present, be entered on the Journal.

Neither House, during the Session of Congress, shall, without the Consent of the other, adjourn for more than three days, nor to any other Place than that in which the two Houses shall be sitting.

Section 6. The Senators and Representatives shall receive a Compensation for their Services, to be ascertained by Law, and paid out of the Treasury of the United States. They shall in all Cases, except Treason, Felony, and Breach of the Peace, be privileged from Arrest during their Attendance at the Session of their respective Houses, and in going to and returning from the same; and for any Speech or Debate in either House, they shall not be questioned in any other Place.

No Senator or Representative shall, during the Time for which he was elected, be appointed to any civil Office under the Authority of the United States, which shall have been created, or the Emoluments whereof shall have been increased, during such time;

---

⁴ Superseded by the Twentieth Amendment.

and no Person holding any Office under the United States shall be a Member of either House during his continuance in Office.

Section 7. All Bills for raising Revenue shall originate in the House of Representatives; but the Senate may propose or concur with Amendments as on other bills.

Every Bill which shall have passed the House of Representatives and the Senate, shall, before it becomes a Law, be presented to the President of the United States; If he approves he shall sign it, but if not he shall return it, with his Objections, to that House in which it shall have originated, who shall enter the Objections at large on their Journal, and proceed to reconsider it. If after such Reconsideration two thirds of that House shall agree to pass the bill, it shall be sent, together with the objections, to the other House, by which it shall likewise be reconsidered, and if approved by two thirds of that House, it shall become a Law. But in all such Cases the Votes of both Houses shall be determined by Yeas and Nays, and the Names of the Persons voting for and against the Bill shall be entered on the Journal of each House respectively. If any Bill shall not be returned by the President within ten Days (Sundays excepted) after it shall have been presented to him, the Same shall be a Law, in like Manner as if he had signed it, unless the Congress by their Adjournment prevent its Return, in which Case it shall not be a Law.

Every Order, Resolution, or Vote to Concurrence of the Senate and House of Representatives may be necessary (except on a question of Adjournment) shall be presented to the President of the United States; and before the Same shall take Effect, shall be approved by him, or being disapproved by him, shall be repassed by two thirds of the Senate and House of Representatives, according to the Rules and Limitations prescribed in the Case of a Bill.

Section 8. The Congress shall have Power To lay and collect Taxes, Duties, Imposts and Excises, to pay the Debts and provide for the common Defence and general Welfare of the United States; but all Duties, Imposts and Excises shall be uniform throughout the United States;

To borrow money on the credit of the United States;

To regulate Commerce with foreign Nations, and among the several States, and with the Indian Tribes;

To establish an uniform Rule of Naturalization, and uniform Laws on the subject of Bankruptcies throughout the United States;

To coin Money, regulate the Value thereof, and of foreign Coin, and fix the Standard of Weights and Measures;

To provide for the Punishment of counterfeiting the Securities and current Coin of the United States;

To establish Post Offices and post Roads;

To promote the Progress of Science and useful Arts, by securing for limited Times to Authors and Inventors the exclusive Right to their respective Writings and Discoveries;

To constitute Tribunals inferior to the Supreme Court;

To define and punish Piracies and Felonies committed on the high Seas, and Offenses against the Law of Nations;

To declare War, grant Letters of Marque and Reprisal, and make Rules concerning Captures on Land and Water;

To raise and support Armies, but no Appropriation of Money to that Use shall be for a longer Term than two Years;

To provide and maintain a Navy;

To make Rules for the Government and Regulation of the land and naval forces;

To provide for calling forth the Militia to execute the Laws of the Union, suppress Insurrections and repel Invasions;

To provide for organizing, arming, and disciplining the Militia, and for governing such Part of them as may be employed in the Service of the United States, reserving to the States respectively, the Appointment of the Officers, and the Authority of training the Militia according to the discipline prescribed by Congress;

To exercise exclusive Legislation in all Cases whatsoever, over such District (not exceeding ten Miles sqaure) as may, by Cession of particular States, and the acceptance of Congress, become the Seat of the Government of the United States, and to exercise like Authority over all Places purchased by the Consent of the Legislature of the State in which the Same shall be, for the Erection of Forts, Magazines, Arsenals, dock-Yards, and other needful Buildings; — And

To make all Laws which shall be necessary and proper for carrying into Execution the foregoing Powers, and all other Powers vested by this Constitution in the Government of the United States, or in any Department or Officer thereof.

Section 9. The Migration or Importation of such Persons as any of the States now existing shall think proper to admit shall not be prohibited by the Congress prior to the Year one thousand eight hundred and eight, but a tax or duty may be imposed on such Importation, not exceeding ten dollars for each Person.

The privilege of the Writ of Habeas Corpus shall not be suspended, unless when in Cases of Rebellion or Invasion the public Safety may require it.

No Bill of Attainder or ex post facto Law shall be passed.

[No capitation, or other direct, Tax shall be laid unless in Proportion to the Census or Enumeration herein before directed to be taken.][5]

No Tax or Duty shall be laid on Articles exported from any State.

No Preference shall be given by any Regulation of Revenue to the Ports of one State over those of another: nor shall Vessels

---

[5] Modified by the Sixteenth Amendment.

bound to, or from, one State, be obliged to enter, clear, or pay Duties in another.

No Money shall be drawn from the Treasury, but in Consequence of Appropriations made by Law; and a regular Statement and Account of the Receipts and Expenditures of all public Money shall be published from time to time.

No Title of Nobility shall be granted by the United States: And no Person holding any Office of Profit or Trust under them, shall, without the Consent of the Congress, accept of any present, Emolument, Office, or Title, of any kind whatever, from any King, Prince, or foreign State.

Section 10. No State shall enter into any Treaty, Alliance, or Confederation; grant Letters of Marque and Reprisal; coin Money; emit Bills of Credit; make any Thing but gold and silver Coin a Tender in Payment of Debts; pass any Bill of Attainder, ex post facto Law, or Law impairing the Obligation of Contracts, or grant any Title of Nobility.

No State shall, without the Consent of the Congress, lay any Imposts or Duties on Imports or Exports, except what may be absolutely necessary for executing its inspection Laws: and the net Produce of all Duties and Imposts, laid by any State on Imports or Exports, shall be for the Use of the Treasury of the United States; and all such Laws shall be subject to the Revision and Control of the Congress.

No State shall, without the Consent of Congress, lay any duty of Tonnage, keep Troops, or Ships of War in time of Peace, enter into any Agreement or Compact with another State, or with a foreign Power, or engage in War, unless actually invaded, or in such imminent Danger as will not admit of delay.

ARTICLE II

Section 1. The executive Power shall be vested in a President of the United States of America. He shall hold his Office during the Term of four years, and, together with the Vice-President, chosen for the same Term, be elected, as follows:

Each State shall appoint, in such Manner as the Legislature thereof may direct, a Number of Electors, equal to the whole Number of Senators and Representatives to which the State may be entitled in the Congress: but no Senator or Representative, or Person holding an Office of Trust or Profit under the United States, shall be appointed an Elector.

[The Electors shall meet in their respective States, and vote by Ballot for two persons, of whom one at least shall not be an Inhabitant of the same State with themselves. And they shall make a List of all the Persons voted for, and of the Number of Votes for each; which List they shall sign and certify, and transmit sealed to the Seat of the Government of the United States, directed to the President of the Senate. The President of the Senate shall, in the Presence of the Senate and House of Representatives, open all the Certificates, and the Votes shall then be counted. The Person having the greatest Number of Votes shall be the President, if such Number be a Majority of the whole Number of Electors appointed; and if there be more than one who have such Majority, and have an equal Number of Votes, then the House of Representatives shall immediately chuse by Ballot one of them for President; and if no Person have a Majority, then from the five highest on the List the said House shall in like Manner chuse the President. But in chusing the President, the Votes shall be taken by States, the Representation from each State having one Vote; a quorum for this Purpose shall consist of a Member or Members from two-thirds of the States, and a Majority of all the States shall be necessary to a Choice. In every Case, after the Choice of the President, the Person having the greatest Number of Votes of the Electors shall be the Vice-President. But if there should remain two or more who have equal votes, the Senate shall chuse from them by Ballot the Vice-President.][6]

The Congress may determine the Time of chusing the Electors, and the Day on which they shall give their Votes; which Day shall be the same throughout the United States.

No person except a natural-born Citizen, or a Citizen of the United States, at the time of the Adoption of this Constitution, shall be eligible to the Office of President; neither shall any Person be eligible to that Office who shall not have attained to the Age of thirty-five years, and been fourteen Years a Resident within the United States.

[In Case of the Removal of the President from Office, or of his Death, Resignation, or Inability to discharge the Powers and Duties of the said Office, the same shall devolve on the Vice-President, and the Congress may by Law provide for the Case of Removal, Death, Resignation, or Inability, both of the President and Vice-President, declaring what Officer shall then act as President, and such Officer shall act accordingly, until the disability be removed, or a President shall be elected.][7]

The President shall, at stated Times, receive for his Services a Compensation, which shall neither be increased nor diminished during the Period for which he shall have been elected, and he shall not receive within that Period any other Emolument from the United States, or any of them.

Before he enter on the execution of his Office, he shall take the following Oath or Affirmation: — "I do solemnly swear (or affirm) that I will faithfully execute the Office of President of the United States, and will, to the best of my Ability, preserve, protect, and defend the Constitution of the United States."

---

[6] Superseded by the Twelfth Amendment.

[7] Modified by the Twenty-fifth Amendment.

Section 2. The President shall be Commander in Chief of the Army and Navy of the United States, and of the Militia of the several States, when called into the actual Service of the United States; he may require the Opinion, in writing, of the principal Officer in each of the executive Departments, upon any subject relating to the Duties of their respective Offices, and he shall have Power to Grant Reprieves and Pardons for Offenses against the United States, except in Cases of Impeachment.

He shall have Power, by and with the Advice and Consent of the Senate, to make Treaties, provided two thirds of the Senators present concur; and he shall nominate, and by and with the Advice and Consent of the Senate, shall appoint Ambassadors, other public Ministers and Consuls, Judges of the supreme Court, and all other Officers of the United States, whose Appointments are not herein otherwise provided for, and which shall be established by Law: but the Congress may by Law vest the Appointment of such inferior Offices, as they think proper, in the President alone, in the Courts of Law, or in the Heads of Departments.

The President shall have Power to fill up all Vacancies that may happen during the Recess of the Senate, by granting Commissions which shall expire at the End of their next Session.

Section 3. He shall from time to time give to the Congress Information of the State of the Union, and recommend to their Consideration such Measures as he shall judge necessary and expedient; he may, on extraordinary occasions, convene both Houses, or either of them, and in Case of Disagreement between them, with respect to the Time of Adjournment, he may adjourn them to such Time as he shall think proper; he shall receive Ambassadors and other public Ministers; he shall take Care that the Laws be faithfully executed, and shall Commmission all the Officers of the United States.

Section 4. The President, Vice-President and all civil Officers of the United States, shall be removed from Office on Impeachment for, and Conviction of, Treason, Bribery, or other high Crimes and Misdemeanors.

ARTICLE III

Section 1. The judicial Power of the United States, shall be vested in one supreme Court, and in such inferior Courts as the Congress may from time to time ordain and establish. The Judges, both of the supreme and inferior Courts, shall hold their Offices during good Behaviour, and shall, at stated Times, receive for their Services, a Compensation, which shall not be diminished during their Continuance in Office.

Section 2. The judicial Power shall extend to all Cases, in Law and Equity, arising under this Constitution, the Laws of the United States, and treaties made, or which shall be made, under their Authority; — to all Cases affecting ambassadors, other public min-

isters and consuls; — to all cases of admiralty and maritime Jurisdiction; — to Controversies to which the United States shall be a
Party; — to Controversies between two or more States; — [be-
tween a State and Citizens of another State;]⁸ — between Citizens
of different States, — between Citizens of the same State claiming
Lands under Grants of different States, and between a State, or the
Citizens thereof, and foreign States, Citizens or Subjects.

In all Cases affecting Ambassadors, other public Ministers and
Consuls, and those in which a State shall be Party, the supreme
Court shall have original Jurisdiction. In all the other Cases before
mentioned, the supreme Court shall have appellate Jurisdiction,
both as to Law and Fact, with such Exceptions, and under such
Regulations as the Congress shall make.

The trial of all Crimes, except in Cases of Impeachment, shall
be by Jury; and such Trial shall be held in the State where the said
Crimes shall have been committed; but when not committed
within any State, the Trial shall be at such Place or Places as the
Congress may by Law have directed.

Section 3. Treason against the United States, shall consist
only in levying War against them, or in adhering to their Enemies,
giving them Aid and Comfort. No Person shall be convicted of
Treason unless on the Testimony of two Witnesses to the same
overt Act, or on Confession in open Court.

The Congress shall have power to declare the Punishment of
Treason, but no Attainder of Treason shall work Corruption of
Blood, or Forfeiture except during the Life of the Person attainted.

ARTICLE IV
Section 1. Full Faith and Credit shall be given in each State to
the public Acts, Records, and judicial Proceedings of every other
State. And the Congress may by general Laws prescribe the Manner in which such Acts, Records and Proceedings shall be proved,
and the Effect thereof.

Section 2. The Citizens of each State shall be entitled to all
Privileges and Immunities of Citizens in the several States.

A Person charged in any State with Treason, Felony, or other
Crime, who shall flee from Justice, and be found in another State,
shall on demand of the executive Authority of the State from which
he fled, be delivered up, to be removed to the State having Jurisdiction of the crime.

[No Person held to Service or Labour in one State, under the
Laws thereof, escaping into another, shall, in Consequence of any
Law or Regulation therein, be discharged from such Service or
Labour, but shall be delivered up on Claim of the Party to whom
such Service or Labour may be due.]⁹

⁸ Modified by the Eleventh Amendment.
⁹ Superseded by the Thirteenth Amendment.

Section 3. New States may be admitted by the Congress into this Union; but no new State shall be formed or erected within the Jurisdiction of any other State; nor any State be formed by the Junction of two or more States, or parts of States, without the Consent of the Legislatures of the States concerned as well as of the Congress.

The Congress shall have Power to dispose of and make all needful Rules and Regulations respecting the Territory or other Property belonging to the United States; and nothing in this Constitution shall be so construed as to Prejudice any Claims of the United States, or of any particular State.

Section 4. The United States shall guarantee to every State in this Union a Republican Form of Government, and shall protect each of them against Invasion; and on Application of the Legislature, or of the Executive (when the Legislature cannot be convened) against domestic Violence.

ARTICLE V

The Congress, whenever two-thirds of both Houses shall deem it necessary, shall propose Amendments to this Constitution, or, on the Application of the Legislatures of two-thirds of the several States, shall call a Convention for the proposing Amendments, which, in either Case, shall be valid to all Intents and Purposes, as part of this Constitution, when ratified by the Legislatures of three-fourths of the several States, or by Conventions in three-fourths thereof, as the one or the other Mode of Ratification may be proposed by the Congress; Provided that No Amendment which may be made prior to the Year One thousand eight hundred and eight shall in any Manner affect the first and fourth Clauses in the Ninth Section of the first Article; and that no State, without its Consent, shall be deprived of its equal Suffrage in the Senate.

ARTICLE VI

All Debts contracted and Engagements entered into, before the Adoption of this Constitution, shall be as valid against the United States under this Constitution, as under the Confederation.

This Constitution, and the Laws of the United States which shall be made in Pursuance thereof; and all Treaties made, or which shall be made, under the Authority of the United States, shall be the supreme Law of the Land; and the Judges in every State shall be bound thereby, any Thing in the Constitution or Laws of any State to the Contrary notwithstanding.

The Senators and Representatives before mentioned, and the Members of the several State Legislatures, and all executive and judicial Officers, both of the United States and of the several States, shall be bound by Oath or Affirmation to support this Constitution; but no religious Test shall ever be required as a qualification to any Office or public Trust under the United States.

ARTICLE VII

The Ratification of the Conventions of nine States shall be sufficient for the Establishment of this Constitution between the States so ratifying the same.

Done in Convention by the Unanimous Consent of the States present the Seventeenth Day of September in the Year of our Lord one thousand seven hundred and Eighty seven, and of the Independence of the United States of America the Twelfth. In Witness whereof We have hereunto subscribed our Names.

AMENDMENTS TO THE CONSTITUTION

Articles in Addition to, and Amendment of, the Constitution of the United States of America, Proposed by Congress, and Ratified by the Legislatures of the Several States, Pursuant to the Fifth Article of the Original Constitution.

AMENDMENT I[10]

Congress shall make no law respecting an establishment of religion, or prohibiting the free exercise thereof; or abridging the freedom of speech, or of the press; or the right of the people peaceably to assemble, and to petition the Government for a redress of grievances.

AMENDMENT II

A well regulated Militia, being necessary to the security of a free State, the right of the people to keep and bear Arms shall not be infringed.

AMENDMENT III

No Soldier shall, in time of peace, be quartered in any house, without the consent of the Owner, nor in time of war, but in a manner to be prescribed by law.

AMENDMENT IV

The right of the people to be secure in their persons, houses, papers, and effects, against unreasonable searches and seizures, shall not be violated, and no Warrants shall issue, but upon probable cause, supported by Oath or affirmation, and particularly describing the place to be searched, and the persons or things to be seized.

AMENDMENT V

No person shall be held to answer for a capital or otherwise infamous crime, unless on a presentment or indictment of a Grand

---

[10]The first ten amendments were passed by Congress September 25, 1789. They were ratified by three-fourths of the states December 15, 1791.

Jury, except in cases arising in the land of naval forces, or in the Militia, when in actual service in time of War or public danger; nor shall any person be subject for the same offence to be twice put in jeopardy of life or limb; nor shall be compelled in any criminal case to be a witness against himself, nor be deprived of life, liberty, or property, without due process of law; nor shall private property be taken for public use, without just compensation.

AMENDMENT VI

In all criminal prosecutions, the accused shall enjoy the right to a speedy and public trial, by an impartial jury of the State and district wherein the crime shall have been committed, which district shall have been previously ascertained by law, and to be informed of the nature and cause of the accusation; to be confronted with the witnesses against him; to have compulsory process for obtaining witnesses in his favor, and to have the Assistance of Counsel for his defence.

AMENDMENT VII

In suits at common law, where the value in controversy shall exceed twenty dollars, the right of trial by jury shall be preserved, and no fact tried by a jury, shall be otherwise reexamined in any Court of the United States, than according to the rules of the common law.

AMENDMENT VIII

Excessive bail shall not be required, nor excessive fines imposed, nor cruel and unusual punishments inflicted.

AMENDMENT IX

The enumeration in the Constitution, of certain rights, shall not be construed to deny or disparage others retained by the people.

AMENDMENT X

The powers not delegated to the United States by the Constitution, nor prohibited by it to the States, are reserved to the States respectively, or to the people.

AMENDMENT XI (1795)[11]

The Judicial power of the United States shall not be construed to extend to any suit in law or equity, commenced or prosecuted against one of the United States by Citizens of another State, or by Citizens or Subjects of any Foreign State.

AMENDMENT XII (1804)

The Electors shall meet in their respective States and vote by ballot for President and Vice-President, one of whom, at least, shall

---

[11]Date of ratification.

not be an inhabitant of the same State with themselves; they shall name in their ballots the person voted for as President, and in distinct ballots the person voted for as Vice-President, and they shall make distinct lists of all persons voted for as President, and of all persons voted for as Vice-President, and of the number of votes for each, which lists they shall sign and certify, and transmit sealed to the seat of the government of the United States, directed to the President of the Senate; — The President of the Senate shall, in the presence of the Senate and House of Representatives, open all the certificates and the votes shall then be counted; — The person having the greatest number of votes for President, shall be the President, if such number be a majority of the whole number of Electors appointed; and if no person have such majority, then from the persons having the highest numbers not exceeding three on the list of those voted for as President, the House of Representatives shall choose immediately, by ballot, the President. But in choosing the President, the votes shall be taken by states, the representation from each state having one vote; a quorum for this purpose shall consist of a member or members from two-thirds of the states, and a majority of all the states shall be necessary to a choice. [And if the House of Representatives shall not choose a President whenever the right of choice shall devolve upon them, before the fourth day of March next following, then the Vice-President shall act as President, as in the case of the death or other constitutional disability of the President.][12] — The person having the greatest number of votes as Vice-President, shall be the Vice-President, if such number be a majority of the whole number of Electors appointed, and if no person have a majority, then from the two highest numbers on the list, the Senate shall choose the Vice-President; a quorum for the purpose shall consist of two-thirds of the whole number of Senators, and a majority of the whole number shall be necessary to a choice. But no person constitutionally ineligible to the office of President shall be eligible to that of Vice-President of the United States.

AMENDMENT XIII (1865)

Section 1. Neither slavery nor involuntary servitude, except as a punishment for crime whereof the party shall have been duly convicted, shall exist within the United States, or any place subject to their jurisdiction.

Section 2. Congress shall have power to enforce this article by appropriate legislation.

AMENDMENT XIV (1868)

Section 1. All persons born or naturalized in the United States, and subject to the jurisdiction thereof, are citizens of the

---

[12] Superseded by the Twentieth Amendment.

United States and of the State wherein they reside. No State shall make or enforce any law which shall abridge the privileges or immunities of citizens of the United States; nor shall any State deprive any person of life, liberty, or property, without due process of law; nor deny to any person within its jurisdiction the equal protection of the laws.

Section 2. Representatives shall be apportioned among the several States according to their respective numbers, counting the whole number of persons in each State, excluding Indians not taxed. But when the right to vote at any election for the choice of electors for President and Vice-President of the United States, Representatives in Congress, the Executive and Judicial officers of a State, or the members of the Legislature thereof, is denied to any of the male inhabitants of such State, being twenty-one years of age, and citizens of the United States, or in any way abridged, except for participation in rebellion, or other crime, the basis of representation therein shall be reduced in the proportioin which the number of such male citizens shall bear to the whole number of male citizens twenty-one years of age in such State.

Section 3. No person shall be a Senator or Representative in Congress, or elector of President and Vice-President, or hold any office, civil or military, under the United States, or under any State, who, having previously taken an oath, as a member of Congress, or as an officer of the United States, or as a member of any State legislature, or as an executive or judicial officer of any State, to support the Constitution of the United States, shall have engaged in insurrection or rebellion against the same, or given aid or comfort to the enemies thereof. But Congress may by a vote of two-thirds of each House, remove such disability.

Section 4. The validity of the public debt of the United States, authorized by law, including debts incurred for payment of pensions and bounties for services in suppressing insurrection or rebellion, shall not be questioned. But neither the United States nor any State shall assume or pay any debt or obligation incurred in aid of insurrection or rebellion against the United States, or any claim for the loss or emancipation of any slave; but all such debts, obligations, and claims shall be held illegal and void.

Section 5. The Congress shall have the power to enforce, by appropriate legislation, the provisions of this article.

AMENDMENT XV (1870)

Section 1. The right of citizens of the United States to vote shall not be denied or abridged by the United States or by any State on account of race, color, or previous condition of servitude.

Section 2. The Congress shall have power to enforce this article by appropriate legislation.

AMENDMENT XVI (1913)

The Congress shall have power to lay and collect taxes on incomes, from whatever source derived, without apportionment among the several States, and without regard to any census or enumeration.

AMENDMENT XVII (1913)

The Senate of the United States shall be composed of two Senators from each State, elected by the people thereof, for six years; and each Senator shall have one vote. The electors in each State shall have the qualifications requisite for electors of the most numerous branch of the State legislatures.

When vacancies happen in the representation of any State in the Senate, the executive authority of such State shall issue writs of election to fill such vacancies: *Provided*, That the legislature of any State may empower the executive thereof to make temporary appointments until the people fill the vacancies by election as the legislature may direct.

This amendment shall not be so construed as to affect the election or term of any Senator chosen before it becomes valid as part of the Constitution.

AMENDMENT XVIII (1919) [13]

Section 1. After one year from the ratification of this article the manufacture, sale, or transportation of intoxicating liquors within, the importation thereof into, or the exportation thereof from the United States and all territory subject to the jurisdiction thereof for beverage purposes is hereby prohibited.

Section 2. The Congress and the several States shall have concurrent power to enforce this article by appropriate legislation.

Section 3. This article shall be inoperative unless it shall have been ratified as an amendment to the Constitution by the legislatures of the several States, as provided in the Constitution, within seven years from the date of the submission hereof to the States by the Congress.

AMENDMENT XIX (1920)

The right of citizens of the United States to vote shall not be denied or abridged by the United States or by any State on account of sex.

Congress shall have power to enforce this article by appropriate legislation.

AMENDMENT XX (1933)

Section 1. The terms of the President and Vice-President shall end at noon on the 20th day of January, and the terms of Senators

---

[13]Repealed by the Twenty-first Amendment.

and Representatives at noon on the 3d day of January, of the years in which such terms would have ended if this article had not been ratified; and the terms of their successors shall then begin.

Section 2. The Congress shall assemble at least once in every year, and such meeting shall begin at noon on the 3d day of January, unless they shall by law appoint a different day.

Section 3. If, at the time fixed for the beginning of the term of the President, the President elect shall have died, the Vice-President elect shall become President. If a President shall not have been chosen before the time fixed for the beginning of his term, or if the President elect shall have failed to qualify, then the Vice-President elect shall act as President until a President shall have qualified; and the Congress may by law provide for the case wherein neither a President elect nor a Vice-President elect shall have qualified, declaring who shall then act as President, or the manner in which one who is to act shall be selected, and such person shall act accordingly until a President or Vice-President shall have qualified.

Section 4. The Congress may by law provide for the case of the death of any of the persons from whom the House of Representatives may choose a President whenever the right of choice shall have devolved upon them, and for the case of the death of any of the persons from whom the Senate may choose a Vice-President whenever the right of choice shall have devolved upon them.

Section 5. Sections 1 and 2 shall take effect on the 13th day of October following the ratification of this article.

Section 6. This article shall be inoperative unless it shall have been ratified as an amendment to the Constitution by the legislatures of three-fourths of the several States within seven years from the date of its submission.

AMENDMENT XXI (1933)

Section 1. The eighteenth article of amendment to the Constitution of the United States is hereby repealed.

Section 2. The transportation or importation into any State, Territory, or possession of the United States for delivery or use therein of intoxicating liquors, in violation of the laws thereof, is hereby prohibited.

Section 3. This article shall be inoperative unless it shall have been ratified as an amendment to the Constitution by conventions in the several States, as provided in the Constitution, within seven years from the date of the submission hereof to the States by the Congress.

AMENDMENT XXII (1951)

No person shall be elected to the office of the President more than twice, and no person who has held the office of President, or acted as President for more than two years of a term to which some

other person was elected President shall be elected to the office of
the President more than once.

But this Article shall not apply to any person holding the office
of President when this Article was proposed by the Congress, and
shall not prevent any person who may be holding the office of
President, or acting as President, during the term within which
this Article becomes operative from holding the office of President
or acting as President during the remainder of such term.

AMENDMENT XXIII (1961)

Section 1. The District constituting the seat of Government of
the United States shall appoint in such manner as the Congress
may direct:

A number of electors of President and Vice-President equal to the
whole number of Senators and Representatives in Congress to
which the District would be entitled if it were a State, but in no
event more than the least populous State; they shall be in addition
to those appointed by the States, but they shall be considered, for
the purposes of the election of President and Vice-President, to be
electors appointed by the State; and they shall meet in the District
and perform such duties as provided by the twelfth article of
amendment.

Section 2. The Congress shall have power to enforce this article
by appropriate legislation.

AMENDMENT XXIV (1964)

Section 1. The right of citizens of the United States to vote in
any primary or other election for President or Vice-President, for
electors for President or Vice-President, or for Senator or Representative in Congress, shall not be denied or abridged by the
United States or any State by reason of failure to pay any poll tax
or other tax.

Section 2. The Congress shall have power to enforce this article
by appropriate legislation.

AMENDMENT XXV (1967)

Section 1. In case of the removal of the President from office or
of his death or resignation, the Vice-President shall become
President.

Section 2. Whenever there is a vacancy in the office of the Vice-
President, the President shall nominate a Vice-President who shall
take office upon confirmation by a majority vote of both Houses of
Congress.

Section 3. Whenever the President transmits to the President
pro tempore of the Senate and the Speaker of the House of Representatives his written declaration that he is unable to discharge
the powers and duties of his office, and until he transmits to them

a written declaration to the contrary, such powers and duties shall be discharged by the Vice-President as Acting President.

Section 4. Whenever the Vice-President and a majority of either the principal officers of the executive department or of such other body as Congress may by law provide, transmit to the President pro tempore of the Senate and the Speaker of the House of Representatives their written declaration that the President is unable to discharge the powers and duties of his office, the Vice-President shall immediately assume the powers and duties of the office as Acting President.

Thereafter, when the President transmits to the President pro tempore of the Senate and the Speaker of the House of Representatives his written declaration that no inability exists, he shall resume the powers and duties of his office unless the Vice-President and a majority of either the principal officers of the executive department or of such other body as Congress may by law provide, transmit within four days to the President pro tempore of the Senate and the Speaker of the House of Representatives their written declaration that the President is unable to discharge the powers and duties of his office. Thereupon Congress shall decide the issue, assembling within forty-eight hours for that purpose if not in session. If the Congress, within twenty-one days after receipt of the latter written declaration, or, if Congress is required to assemble, determines by two-thirds vote of both Houses that the President is unable to discharge the powers and duties of his office, the Vice-President shall continue to discharge the same as Acting President; otherwise, the President shall resume the powers and duties of his office.

AMENDMENT XXVI (1971)

Section 1. The right of citizens of the United States, who are eighteen years of age or older, to vote shall not be denied or abridged by the United States or by any State on account of age.

Section 2. The Congress shall have power to enforce this article by appropriate legislation.

appendix B
ORGANIZATIONS
TO KNOW

I. U.S. GOVERNMENT

Executive Branch

Executive Office of the President
The White House
Washington, D.C. 20500
(202) 456-1414

Office of the Vice President
Executive Office Building
Washington, D.C. 20501
(202) 456-1414

Executive Departments

Department of Agriculture
14th Street & Independence Avenue, S.W.
Washington, D.C.   20250
(202) 655-4000
  Responsible for U.S. argicultural policy. Regulates and expands
  markets for agricultural products. Directs food and nutrition
  services. Inspects, grades, and safeguards quality of food products. Involved in rural development, forest management, and
  water and soil conservation.

Department of Commerce
14th Street & Constitution Avenue, N.W.
Washington, D.C.   20230
(202) 377-2000
  Concerned with economic development and technological advancement. Provides assistance and information to business and industry. Assists development of the U.S. merchant marine and the growth of minority businesses. Provides social, economic, and scientific data to business and government. Conducts the U.S. census. Promotes travel to the United States by foreign tourists, and assists development of economically deprived areas throughout the country.

Department of Defense
The Pentagon
Washington, D.C.   20301
(202) 545-6700
  Develops national security and military defense policies and has overall responsibility for administration of the armed forces and the national defense.

Department of Education
400 Maryland Avenue, S.W.
Washington, D.C.   20202
(202) 426-6420
  Administers federal aid programs for all aspects of education, including preschool through college; adult, vocational, and bilingual education; public libraries; and education for the handicapped.

Department of Energy
1000 Independence Avenue, S.W.
Washington, D.C. 20504
(202) 252-5000
  Has responsibility for energy development and conservation policies. Conducts research on new energy sources and advises the government on energy matters.

Department of Health and Human Services
200 Independence Avenue, S.W.
Washington, D.C.   20201
(202) 245-6296
  Administers federal programs involving all aspects of public health and human services, including medical research, health care financing, mental health and disease control, alcohol and drug abuse, health services, social security, and public welfare.

Department of Housing and Urban Development
451 7th Street, S.W.
Washington, D.C.   20410
(202) 755-6422

Has responsibility for programs concerned with housing and community development. Administers programs involving urban planning, mortgage insurance, rent subsidies, home building, and neighborhood rehabilitation and preservation.

Department of Interior
18th & C Streets, N.W.
Washington, D.C.   20240
(202) 343-1100

Has responsibility for management and conservation of most publicly owned lands and natural resources. Operates and preserves national parks and historical places, protects fish and wildlife, conserves and develops mineral resources, and is responsible for outdoor recreation and Indian and territorial affairs.

Department of Justice
10th Street & Constitution Avenue, N.W.
Washington, D.C.   20530
(202) 633-2000

Has responsibility of enforcing federal laws, representing the government in federal cases, and interpreting laws under which other departments act. Has divisions involved in antitrust, civil rights, natural resources, and tax law. Special bureaus include the FBI, Bureau of Prisons, Immigration and Naturalization Service, U.S. Marshalls, and Law Enforcement Assistance Administration.

Department of Labor
200 Constitution Avenue, N.W.
Washington, D.C.   20210
(202) 523-8271

Has responsibility for all aspects of labor and employment, including wages, hours, safety and health conditions, job training, pensions and benefits, collective bargaining, and union/management relations.

Department of State
2201 C Street, N.W.
Washington, D.C.   20520
(202) 655-4000

Has responsibility to supervise and direct U.S. foreign affairs. Responsible for relations with other countries. Speaks for the United States in the United Nations and other international organizations. Represents the United States in negotiations, treaties, and agreements with other nations.

Department of Transportation
400 7th Street, S.W.
Washington, D.C.   20590
(202) 426-4000

Responsible for U.S. transportation policy. Provides funds for highway planning and construction and urban mass transit. Assists and regulates railroads, airlines, ports, waterways, and highway safety.

Department of Treasury
15th Street & Pennsylvania Avenue, N.W.
Washington, D.C.   20220
(202) 566-2000
Responsible for U.S. tax and money policies. Designs and prints coins, stamps, and currency. Collects federal taxes via the Internal Revenue Service. Oversees the Secret Service, the Customs Service, and the Bureau of Alcohol, Firearms, and Tobacco.

Legislative Branch

U.S. Senate
The Capitol
Washington, D.C.   20510
(202) 224-3121
To contact a member of the Senate, write to the address provided.

U.S. House of Representatives
The Capitol
Washington, D.C.   20510
(202) 224-3121
To contact a member of the House of Representatives, write to the address provided.

Judicial Branch

Supreme Court of the United States
#1 First Street, N.E.
Washington, D.C.   20543
(202) 479-3000
Copies of recently decided cases can be obtained by contacting the clerk of the court at the address provided.

Federal Agencies and Officers

ACTION
806 Connecticut Avenue, N.W.
Washington, D.C.   20525
(202) 634-9135
Administers volunteer programs (including VISTA and the Peace Corps) sponsored by the federal government and provides services to developing nations, minorities, and the disadvantaged.

Commission on Civil Rights
1121 Vermont Avenue, N.W.
Washington, D.C.   20425
(202) 376-8312
 Encourages equal opportunity for minority groups and women.
 Conducts studies and makes recommendations regarding discrimination. Serves as a clearinghouse for civil rights information. Investigates complaints of denial of voting rights.

Consumer Product Safety Commission
5401 Westbard Avenue
Bethesda, MD   20207
(800) 638-2772 Consumer Hotline
(800) 492-6600 in Maryland
 Establishes and enforces product safety standards, studies
 causes and prevention of product-related injuries, and conducts
 surveillance and enforcement programs.

Environmental Protection Agency
401 M Street, S.W.
Washington, D.C.   20460
(202) 829-3535
 Responsible for policies and laws that protect the environment,
 including regulations aimed at land, water, air, and noise pollution, solid waste disposal, pesticides, and other hazardous
 materials.

Equal Employment Opportunity Commission
2401 E Street, N.W.
Washington, D.C.   20506
(202) 634-6922
 Handles complaints regarding job discrimination based on race,
 color, religion, sex, or national origin. Has power to conduct
 investigations and bring court actions where necessary.

Federal Communications Commission
1919 M Street, N.W.
Washington, D.C.   20554
(202) 632-7000
 Regulates communications media, including radio, television,
 cable, and satellite. Investigates complaints regarding radio or
 television broadcasting.

Federal Election Commission
1325 K Street, N.W.
Washington, D.C.   20463
(202) 523-4089
 Administers and enforces provisions of the Federal Election
 Campaign Act. The act requires the disclosure of sources and
 uses of campaign money for any federal office, limits the amount
 of individual contributions, and provides for public financing of
 presidential elections.

Federal Information Center
18th & F Streets, N.W.
Washington, D.C.   20405
(202) 655-4000
  Provides assistance to citizens lost in the maze of federal programs and services by directing them to the proper office for help with their problem.

Federal Mediation and Conciliation Service
2100 K Street, N.W.
Washington, D.C.   20427
(202) 653-5300
  Provides mediation assistance and arbitration referrals in labor disputes. Also provides mediation training in other areas.

Federal Reserve System
20th Street & Constitution Avenue, N.W.
Washington, D.C.   20551
(202) 452-3000
  Serves as the central bank of the United States. Sets banking policies and regulates the availability of money.

Federal Trade Commission
6th Street & Pennsylvania Avenue, N.W.
Washington, D.C.   20580
(202) 523-3598
  Responsible for keeping competition among U.S. business both free and fair. Will investigate complaints of deceptive or unfair practices involving price fixing, advertising, packaging, labeling, or credit.

Interstate Commerce Commission
12th Street & Constitution Avenue, N.W.
Washington, D.C.   20423
(202) 275-7511
  Regulates interstate commerce. The Office of Consumer Affairs, which appears in this listing, handles consumer complaints involving interstate moving companies, buses, trains, and small shipments.

National Labor Relations Board
1717 Pennsylvania Avenue, N.W.
Washington, D.C.   20570
(202) 254-8064
  Prevents and remedies unfair labor practices by employers and labor unions. Conducts elections among workers to determine whether they wish to be represented by a labor union.

National Transportation Safety Board
800 Independence Avenue, S.W.
Washington, D.C.   20591
(202) 382-6500

Reviews adequacy of federal standards for vehicle safety and highway design and maintenance. Studies and makes recommendations on matters of surface transportation safety and accident prevention.

Nuclear Regulatory Commission
1717 H Street, N.W.
Washington, D.C.   20555
(202) 492-7000

Regulates commercial uses of nuclear energy. Responsibilities include licensing, inspection, and enforcement.

Occupational Safety and Health Administration
200 Constitution Avenue, N.W.
Washington, D.C.   20210
(202) 523-9361

Part of the Department of Labor. Sets policy, develops programs, and investigates complaints regarding occupational safety and health hazards.

Office of Consumer Affairs
330 Independence Avenue, S.W.
Washington, D.C.   20024
(202) 245-6158

Set up by the president to be the consumer's "voice" in Washington. Provides consumer information, advises on consumer policies and programs, conducts consumer education, and will advise citizens where and how to file consumer complaints.

Postal Service
475 L'Enfant Plaza West, S.W.
Washington, D.C.   20260
(202) 245-4000

Provides mail processing and delivery services to individuals and businesses throughout the United States. (The Consumer Protection Office handles consumer complaints, enforces law to prevent receipt of unwanted mail, and investigates postal fraud and lost mail.)

Small Business Administration
1441 L Street, N.W.
Washington, D.C.   20416
(202) 653-7557

Provides information and assistance to small businesses on problems of marketing, accounting, product analysis, production methods, and research and development.

Veterans Administration
810 Vermont Avenue, N.W.
Washington, D.C.   20420
(202) 393-4120

Administers veteran benefit programs, including disability compensation, pensions, education, home loans, insurance, vocational rehabilitation, medical care, and burial benefits.

II. NATIONAL ASSOCIATIONS

American Arbitration Association
140 West 51st Street
New York, NY   10020
(212) 484-4000
   Provides dispute resolution services, training, and technical assistance through its headquarters and 25 regional offices.

American Bar Association
750 N. Lakeshore Drive
Chicago, IL   60611
(312) 988-5000
   Professional organization of lawyers that provides services and
   information to state and local bar associations. Serves as a resource on most law-related topics.

American Conservation Union
38 Ivey Street, S.E.
Washington, D.C.   20003
(202) 546-6555
   A conservative lobbying and educational group that supports a
   wide range of programs.

Chamber of Commerce of the United States
1615 H Street, N.W.
Washington, D.C.   20062
(202) 659-6000
   Federation of individuals, corporations, trade associations, and
   local chambers of commerce. Represents the business community's views on economic and other national issues.

Council of Better Business Bureaus
1515 Wilson Boulevard, Suite 300
Arlington, VA   22209
(703) 276-0100
   National headquarters for a network of local Better Business
   Bureaus. Local offices handle consumer complaints and provide
   mediation and arbitration services.

Family Mediation Association
10605 Concord Street, Suite 207
Kensington, MD   20895
(301) 946-3400
   Provides training for family mediators and produces a newsletter on family mediation services.

Foundation for Cooperative Housing
2501 M Street, N.W., Suite 450
Washington, D.C.   20037
(202) 887-0700

Interested in improving the quality of housing and urban development, especially for people of modest income, through the encouragement of cooperative housing.

Institute for Local Self-Reliance
2425 18th Street, N.W.
Washington, D.C.   20009
(202) 232-4105
Tries to teach people the tools of self-reliance. Provides technical assistance to those concerned with issues of local initiations and independence.

National Abortion Rights Action League
1424 K Street, N.W.
Washington, D.C.   20005
(202) 347-7774
Initiates and coordinates political, social, and legal action of individuals and groups concerned with maintaining abortion rights. Conducts research and maintains speakers bureau.

National Association of Attorneys General
444 N. Capital Street, Suite 403
Washington, D.C.   20001
(202) 628-0435
Has committees on many legal issues. Publishes a newsletter and a quarterly.

National Association for Mediation in Education
University of Massachusetts
Amherst, MA   01003
(413) 545-2462
Provides a clearinghouse of information on mediation in education. Helps develop school mediation programs.

National Center of State Courts
300 Newport Avenue
Williamsburg, VA   23187
(804) 253-2000
Provides assistance to state courts in improving their structure and administration. Publishes newsletters, journals, pamphlets, and reports.

National Council of Family Relations
1910 W. County Road B, Suite 147
St. Paul, MN   55113
(612) 633-6933
Provides opportunities for the advancement of marriage and family life.

National Crime Prevention Council
805 15th Street, N.W.
Washington, D.C.   20005
(202) 393-7141

Provides a clearinghouse of information on crime prevention activities and programs.

National Homeowners Association
2021 K Street, N.W.
Washington, D.C.   20006
(202) 243-1453
  National membership organization that promotes consumer interest in housing, including condominiums. Publishes a home-buyer checklist and a monthly newsletter.

National Right to Life Committee
419 7th Street, N.W.
Washington, D.C.   20004
(202) 626-8800
  Lobbies for constitutional amendments against abortion. Operates an information clearinghouse and speakers bureau.

National Rural Development Corporation
1718 Connecticut Avenue, N.W., Suite 400
Washington, D.C.   20009
(202) 747-8820
  A nonprofit charitable organization created to develop and advocate rural development policies and to provide information that can help rural people.

III.   LEGAL SERVICES

Legal Services Corporation
733 15th Street, N.W.
Washington, D.C.   20005
(202) 272-4000
  Makes grants to local agencies that provide legal services to the poor.

Migrant Legal Action Program
2001 S Street, N.W.
Washington, D.C.   20009
(202) 462-7744
(800) 424-9425
  Provides civil legal representation for migrant and seasonal farmworkers. Farmworker clients must meet federal poverty income levels to be eligible. Staff has both English and Spanish language capabilities.

Puerto Rico Legal Defense and Education Fund
99 Hudson Street
New York, NY   10013
(212) 219-3360
  Provides legal services and educational assistance for Puerto Ricans, especially in New York.

National Center of Law and the Deaf
Galludet College
800 Florida Avenue, N.E.
Washington, D.C.   20002
(202) 651-5454
  Provides legal assistance to deaf and hearing-impaired individuals in various civil matters, including landlord/tenant disputes, public benefits, consumer problems, and wills. Does not
  handle personal injury, bankruptcy, or domestic relations cases.

National Clients Council
1050 Connecticut Avenue, N.W., Suite 500
Washington, D.C.   20536
(202) 429-6584
  Provides advocacy of client's interests and concerns in legal
  services programs and trains clients to participate in the planning and execution of these programs.

National Legal Aid and Defender Association
1625 K Street, N.W.
Washington, D.C.   20006
(202) 452-0620
  Association of local organizations and individuals that provides
  legal services to the poor. Publishes a directory of legal aid and
  defender facilities.

National Resource Center for Consumers of Legal Services
3254 Jones Court, N.W.
Washington, D.C.   20007
(202) 338-0714
  Publishes *New Directions*, a review of developments in the field
  of legal services. Serves as a clearinghouse for information on
  legal services.

Native American Rights Fund
1506 Broadway
Boulder, CO   80302
(303) 447-8760
  Represents Indian individuals and tribes in legal matters of
  national significance and publishes a quarterly account of activities.

Pacific Legal Foundation
1990 M Street, N.W.   555 Capitol Mall, Suite 350
Suite 550   or   Sacramento, CA   95814
Washington, D.C.   20036   (916) 444-0154
(202) 466-2686
  Engages in litigation on a nationwide basis, focusing on environment, land use, energy, international relations, national defense, and welfare reform to protect the free enterprise system.

IV. PUBLIC INTEREST GROUPS

American Civil Liberties Union
132 W. 43rd Street
New York, NY   10016
(212) 944-9300
   Nonprofit organization supporting civil liberties through lobbying and test court cases.

Call for Action, Inc.
575 Lexington Avenue
New York, NY   10022
(212) 355-5965
   National office for a group of over 30 local media projects which
   investigate and try to resolve consumer complaints.

Center for Community Justice
918 16th Street, N.W.
Washington, D.C.   20036
(202) 296-2565
   National leader in mediation in a variety of settings.

Center for Law and Social Policy
1751 N Street, N.W.
Washington, D.C.   20036
(202) 872-0670
   Represents the interests of previously unrepresented citizens
   before agencies and courts, primarily in the areas of environmental and consumer protection and health problems of the
   poor.

Children's Defense Fund
122 C Street, N.W.
Washington, D.C.   20001
(202) 628-8787
   Concerned with long-range and systematic advocacy on behalf
   of the nation's children in the areas of education, child health,
   child welfare, juvenile justice, child care, and family support
   services.

Common Cause
2030 M Street, N.W.
Washington, D.C.   20036
(202) 833-1200
   A national citizens lobby devoted to making government at
   national and state levels more open and accountable to citizens.

Consumers Union
2001 S Street, N.W.
Washington, D.C.   20009
(202) 462-6262

Nonprofit organization providing information, education, and counseling about consumer goods and services and the management of a family income. Tests, rates, and reports on competing brands of products, and publishes reports in monthly *Consumer Reports* magazine.

Consumer Federation of America
1424 16th Street, N.W.
Washington, D.C.   20036
(202) 387-6121
Federation of national, regional, state, and local consumer groups. Helps consumer groups organize and act; lobbies on proposed consumer legislation and publicizes important issues.

Consumer Information Center
Pueblo, CO   81002
(303) 948-3334
Publishes a catalog of free federal publications for consumers.

Environmental Defense Fund
444 Park Avenue South
New York, NY   10016
(212) 686-4191
Citizens interest group staffed by lawyers and scientists. Takes legal action on environmental issues.

Federal Women's Program
% U.S. Civil Rights Commission
Washington, D.C.   20415
(202) 376-8554
Organized to assure the recruitment and selection of qualified women for employment in the federal government. Works with agencies and community groups, and develops continuing education and training programs.

Institute for Public Interest Representation
600 New Jersey Avenue, N.W.
Washington, D.C.   20001
(202) 624-8390
Engages in federal administrative practice, encouraging the federal government to consider and be responsive to the views of otherwise unrepresented or underrepresented groups and individuals.

Lawyers Committee for Civil Rights Under Law
1400 I Street, N.W.
Washington, D.C.   20005
(202) 371-1212
Operates through local committees of private lawyers in 10 cities to provide legal assistance to poor and minority groups.

League of Women Voters
1730 M Street, N.W.
Washington, D.C.   20036
(202) 429-1965
  Organization promoting citizen participation in the political
  process. Distributes information on candidates, and works for
  voters registration and turnout.

Major Appliance Consumer Action Panel
Complaint Exchange
20 North Wacker Drive
Chicago, IL   60606
(312) 984-5858 (Call collect)
  Helps resolve consumer complaints with major applicances.
  Several manufacturers have toll-free lines for consumers.
  Admiral   (800) 447-8371
  Westinghouse   (800) 245-0600
  Whirlpool   (800) 253-1301

Mexican American Legal Defense and Educational Fund
28 Geary Street
San Francisco, CA   94108
(415) 981-5800
  Concerned with protecting the constitutional rights of Hispanics
  and supporting the education of Mexican-American lawyers.

Mothers Against Drunk Drivers (MADD)
669 Airport Freeway, Suite 310
Hurst, TX   76053
(202) 328-6233
  National organization with over 200 local chapters. Advocates
  tougher laws against drunken driving. Provides information on
  ways to curb drunken driving.

National Association for the Advancement of Colored People
186 Remsen Street
Brooklyn, NY   11201
(718) 858-0800
  Citizens' interest group seeking elimination of racial segregation
  and discrimination through legal, legislative, citizen action, and
  educational programs.

National Association of Housing and Redevelopment Officials
2600 Virginia Avenue, N.W.
Washington, D.C.   20037
(202) 333-2020
  Engaged in community rebuilding by slum clearance, public
  housing, large-scale private or cooperative housing rehabilitation, and conservation of existing neighborhoods
  through housing code enforcement and voluntary citizen action.

National Center for Youth Law
1663 Mission Street, 5th Floor
San Francisco, CA   94103
(415) 543-3307
   Litigates youth-related issues and publishes a report of
   activities.

National Foundation for Consumer Credit
8701 Georgia Avenue, Suite 601
Silver Spring, MD   20910
(301) 589-5600
   Sponsors nationwide free counseling program to consumers in
   credit difficulty and provides an educational program for low-
   income families.

National Housing and Economic Development Law Project
1950 Addison Street
Berkeley, CA   94604
(415) 548-9400
   Publishes information on housing.

National Institute for Dispute Resolution
1901 L Street, N.W., Suite 600
Washington, D.C.   20036
(202) 466-4764
   Private, nonprofit organization that examines and promotes
   ways of settling disputes without litigation.

National Organization for Victim Assistance
717 D Street, N.W.
Washington, D.C.   20004
(202) 393-6682
   National clearinghouse of information on victim assistance programs. Lobbies for legislation to help victims of crime.

National Organization for Women
425 13th St., N.W., Suite 1048
Washington, D.C.   20004
(202) 347-2279
   Takes action to bring women into full participation in the mainstream of American society so they can assume all its privileges
   and responsibilities in full, equal partnership with men.

National Runaway Switchboard
2210 N. Halsted
Chicago, IL   60614
(800) 621-4000
   A 24-hour, toll-free national switchboard for runaways and their
   families. Provides information on shelters and counseling services. Offers to relay messages confidentially.

National Trust for Historic Preservation
1785 Massachusetts Avenue, N.W.
Washington, D.C.   20036
(202) 673-4000
  Nonprofit organization created to help protect the built environment and our cultural heritage. Offers advice on preservation
  problems; works with individuals, preservation groups, and
  public agencies to help them plan and carry out preservation
  programs; sponsors educational programs; issues publications;
  and owns and operates historical museums.

National Urban League
425 13th Street, N.W.
Washington, D.C.   20004
(202) 393-4332
  Nonprofit charitable and educational social services organization working to secure equal opportunity for black Americans
  and other minorities. Concerned with all issues that affect their
  constituency. Publishes information booklets supplying research
  data on the economic gap between black and white Americans.

Public Citizen Organization
2000 P Street, N.W.
Washington, D.C.   20036
(202) 293-9142
  Various public interest groups organized by Ralph Nader, including: (1) Congress Watch — lobbying organization that puts
  out newsletters regarding current issues in Congress; (2) Critical
  Mass Energy Project — concerned with education regarding nuclear and solar energy and other energy issues; (3) Health Research Group — concerned with research and occupational safety, food, health, and health care delivery, and handles individual complaints; (4) Tax Reform Research Group — puts out
  newsletter and does research on taxes; (5) Center for Auto Safety
  — will refer complaints on auto problems and is interested in
  class action work; (6) Aviation Consumer Action Project —
  handles individual complaints on airlines, buses, and railroads,
  and deals with safety issues and lower fares.

Southern Poverty Law Center
P.O. Box 548
Montgomery, AL   36195
(205) 264-0286
  Seeks, through legal precedents it helps to establish, to protect
  and guarantee the legal and civil rights of the poor population in
  the United States. Publishes bimonthly annual reports.

Women's Legal Defense Fund, Incorporated
2000 P Street, N.W.
Washington, D.C.   20036
(202) 887-0344

Established for the purpose of fighting sex discrimination. Has phone counseling dealing with domestic relations, employment discrimination, credit, and name change.

appendix C
GLOSSARY

a

Abandonment desertion of people or things.

Abortion a premature end to a pregnancy. Can result from a medical procedure performed in the early stages of pregnancy or from the premature expulsion of the human fetus as in a miscarriage.

Acceleration Clause a provision in a contract that makes the entire debt due if a payment is not made on time or if some other condition is not met.

Acceptance agreeing to an offer and becoming bound to the terms of a contract.

Accessory or Accomplice a person who helps commit a crime. An accesssory before the fact is one who encourages, orders, or helps plan a crime. An accessory after the fact is someone who, knowing a crime has been committed, helps conceal the crime or the person who committed the crime.

Act (1) something done voluntarily that may have legal consequences; (2) written law that has been passed by Congress.

Adjustable Rate Mortgages mortgages that allow buyers to adjust their payments as the interest rates in an area rise or fall over time.

Administrator a person appointed by the court to supervise the distribution of a person's property after his or her death.

Admissible evidence that can be used or introduced in a trial or other court proceeding.

Adoption legal process of taking a child of other parents as one's own.

Adultery voluntary sexual intercourse between a married person and someone other than his or her spouse.

Advocacy   supporting or arguing for a cause.

Advocate   a person who speaks for the cause of another or on behalf of someone.

Affidavit   a written statement sworn to or made under oath before someone authorized to administer an oath.

Affirmative Action   steps taken by an organization to remedy past discrimination in hiring, promotion, education, etc.; for example, by recruiting minorities and women.

Aftercare   the equivalent of parole in the juvenile justice system. It involves a juvenile being supervised and assisted by a parole officer or social worker.

Age of Majority   the age (usually 18 or 21) when a person becomes an adult as specified by state law. It gives the individual both the rights and the responsibilities of adulthood.

Agency   an administrative division of a government set up to carry out certain laws.

Aggravating Factors   factors that might raise the seriousness of an offense; the presence of this factor may be considered by the judge and jury.

Alibi   a Latin word meaning "elsewhere." An excuse or plea that a person was somewhere else at the time a crime was committed.

Alienage   the status of being a person born in a foreign country who has not qualified for citizenship.

Alimony   payments ordered by a court that are made by a person to a divorced spouse for personal support.

Allegation   an accusation that has not been proved.

Amendment   one of the provisions of the U.S. Constitution enacted since the original constitution became law.

Annual Percentage Rate   the interest rate paid per year on borrowed money.

Annulment   a court order that sets aside a marriage, declaring that it never existed.

Answer   a defendant's response to a complaint made in a written statement and filed with the court.

Appeal   taking a case to a higher court for a rehearing.

Appeals Court   a court in which appeals from trial court decisions are heard.

Appraisal   a determination of the value of something, such as a house.

Arbitration   a means of settling a dispute by submitting the dispute to a neutral party whose decision is binding.

Arraignment   the time at which a defendant enters a plea. For a misdemeanor, this is also the defendant's initial appearance where the judge informs the defendant of the charges and sets the bail.

Arrest   taking a person suspected of a crime into custody.

Arson   the deliberate and malicious burning of property.

Assault   an intentional physical attack, or a threat of attack with the apparent ability to carry out the threat so that the victim feels in danger of physical attack or harm.

Assumption of a Mortgage   occurs when the seller and whoever holds the mortgage on a building allow the buyer to take over the mortgage and make payments at the existing interest rate.

Attachment   taking a debtor's property or money to satisfy a debt, by court approval.

Attempt   an effort to commit a crime that goes beyond mere preparation but that does not result in the commission of the crime.

Bail money or property put up by the accused or his or her agent to allow release from jail before trial. The purpose of bail is to assure the court that the defendant will return for trial.

Bait and Switch a deceptive sales technique in which customers are "baited" into a store by an ad promising an item at a low price and then "switched" to a more expensive item.

Balloon Payment the last payment of a loan which is much higher than any of the regular monthly payments.

Bankruptcy the procedure under the Federal Bankruptcy Act by which a person is relieved of all debts once the person has placed all property and money in a court's care.

Bar Association an organization of lawyers.

Battery any intentional, unlawful, or unconsented to physical contact by one upon another.

Bequeathal act of giving anything by will; for example, giving your body to a medical institution.

Beyond a Reasonable Doubt the level of proof required to convict a person of a crime. It does not mean "convinced 100 percent," but does mean there are no reasonable doubts as to guilt.

Bigamy the crime of being married to more than one person at a time.

Bill (1) a draft of a proposed law being considered by a legislature; (2) a written statement of money owed.

Bill Consolidation a form of credit in which the lender combines all of a person's debts into a single monthly payment. In effect, this is a refinancing of a person's existing debts, often with an additional interest charge.

Binder a buyer's offer to purchase something that is written up and presented to the seller.

Black Market Adoptions a form of adoption, illegal in many states, that bypasses licensed adoption agencies by using a go-between to negotiate between the expectant mother and the adopting parent(s).

Bond a mandatory insurance or obligation. A bail bond is the money a defendant pays to secure release from jail before the trial.

Booking the formal process of making a police record of an arrest.

Breach failure to keep a promise or perform a duty. A breach of contract is a failure to carry out the terms of a contract.

Burglary breaking and entering a building with the intention of committing a felony.

Burial the act of placing the dead in a grave, underground or above ground.

Capital Offense an offense that may be punishable by death or life imprisonment.

Capital Punishment the death penalty.

Caveat Emptor Latin phrase meaning "let the buyer beware."

Cease and Desist Order an order given by an administrative agency or a judge to stop some illegal or deceptive activity.

Censorship (1) the denial of freedom of speech or freedom of the press; (2) the process of examining publications or films for material that is considered harmful or objectionable to the government.

Charge (1) the formal accusation of a crime; (2) a type of credit in which payment is made over a period of time.

Child Abuse neglect or mistreatment of children.

Child Snatching the act by a divorced or separated parent of taking his or her child away from the parent with custody and fleeing to another state.

Civil Action a lawsuit brought by one or more individuals against another person, a business, or the government.

Civil Law all areas of law that do not involve criminal matters. Civil law usually deals with private rights of individuals, groups, or businesses.

Class Action a lawsuit brought by one or more persons on behalf of a larger group.

Clause a paragraph, sentence, or phrase in a legal document, such as a contract, lease, or will.

Closing the final meeting for sale of land when property is formally transferred and all payments are made.

Closing Costs charges for finishing a real estate deal, which include taxes, mortgage fees, credit reports, and insurance.

Codicil an addition to a will made after the will is drawn up.

Coercion forcing a person to act against his or her free will.

Collateral money or property given to back up a person's promise to pay a debt.

Commercial Speech speech that is directed at buying or selling of goods and services. The law treats commercial speech differently from political speech and other forms of expression.

Common Law judge-made law (as opposed to law made by a legislature). Our common law is based on the legal customs and court decisions of England that were followed in the U.S. judicial system when it was established.

Common Law Marriage a marriage created without legal ceremony by a couple living together and publicly presenting themselves as husband and wife.

Community Property property acquired during a marriage that is owned commonly by husband and wife, no matter who earned it or paid for it.

Comparable Worth a legal theory that women in traditional female jobs should be paid the same as men in traditional male jobs when the two kinds of work involve comparable skill, effort, and responsibility.

Complaint the first legal document filed in a civil lawsuit. It includes a statement of the wrong or harm done to the plaintiff by the defendant and a request for a specific remedy from the court. A complaint in a criminal case is a sworn statement regarding the defendant's actions that constitute the crime charged.

Condominium a building in which residents own individual units or apartments as well as a share of the building's common property, such as elevators, laundry rooms, and garages.

Confession of Judgment a provision in a lease in which the tenant agrees in advance to let the landlord decide without challenge if a tenant has been at fault in any disagreement.

Consent Order a voluntary agreement to stop a practice that is claimed to be illegal.

Consideration something of value offered or received, constituting the main reason for making a contract.

Conspiracy an agreement or plan between two or more persons to commit a crime.

Constituents those entitled to vote for a representative from a district.

Constructive Eviction a situation in which a tenant may be able to leave before the lease expires without owing rent if a landlord fails to maintain housing in a livable condition.

Consumer anyone who buys or uses a product or service.

Contempt of Court any act to embarrass, hinder, or obstruct the court in the administration of justice.

Contested Divorce a divorce in which the parties disagree over the ending of the marriage itself or over issues such as custody or the division of property.

Contraband any items that are illegal to possess.

Contraceptives any of a number of devices that reduce the chance of conceiving a baby.

Contract a legally enforceable agreement between two or more people to do a certain thing in exchange for payment in some form.

Convict (1) a person who has been found guilty of a crime and is now in prison; (2) to find a person guilty of a crime or a wrongdoing.

Cooperative a building in which the individual owners buy stock in the building as a whole and each owner has the right to occupy a specific unit.

Corrective Advertising a remedy imposed by the Federal Trade Commission requiring that any false claim in an advertisement be corrected in future ads.

Cosign an act in which a person, other than one of the original two parties, signs a legal document guaranteeing to pay off the debt or contract if the signer defaults.

Counterclaim a claim made by a defendant against the plaintiff in a civil lawsuit.

Credit (1) a deduction from what is owed; (2) purchasing goods with delayed payment, as with a credit card; (3) money that is loaned.

Creditor a person who provides credit or who loans money or delivers goods or services before payment is made.

Cremation the act of reducing a dead body to ashes with fire.

Criminal a person who is judged guilty of commiting a crime.

Cross-examination the questioning during a hearing or trial of witnesses for the opposing side.

Custody the care and keeping of something or someone, such as a child.

Damages (1) the injuries or losses suffered by one person because of the fault of another; (2) money asked for or paid by a court order for the injuries or losses suffered.

Death Certificate a legal document that certifies the date and place of a person's death.

Death Penalty a sentence to death for commission of a serious crime, for example, murder.

Debtor a person who owes money or buys on credit.

Deceased term used to refer to the dead.

Decree an official decision of a court setting out the legal consequences of the facts found in a case. It orders that the court's decision be carried out; for example, a divorce decree.

Defamation written or spoken expression about a person that is false and damages that person's reputation.

Default failure to fulfill a legal obligation, such as failing to make a loan payment or appear in court on a specified time and date.

Default Judgment a ruling against a party to a lawsuit who fails to take a required step; for example, failing to file a paper on time.

Defendant the person against whom a claim is made. In a civil suit the defendant is the person being sued; in a criminal case the defendant is the person charged with committing a crime.

Deliberate   to consider carefully, discuss, and work toward forming an opinion or making a decision.

Delinquent   a child who has committed an act that, if committed by an adult, would be a crime under federal, state, or local law.

Desertion   abandoning one's spouse with no intention of returning or of reassuming the duties of marriage. Desertion is usually a ground for divorce.

Deterrence   a reason for punishment based on the belief that the punishment will discourage the offender from committing another crime in the future and will serve as an example to keep other people from committing crimes.

Direct Examination   the questioning of a witness by the side calling the witness to the stand.

Directed Verdict   a verdict in a criminal case entered by the judge when the prosecution has not presented enough evidence to show that defendant committed the crime.

Disability   a physical or mental handicap.

Disclaimer   a clause or statement that rejects liability for anything not expressly promised.

Discovery   the pretrial process of exchanging information between the opposing sides.

Disposition   the final settlement or result of a case.

Divorce   the ending of a marriage by court order.

Down Payment   the cash that must be paid initially when something is bought by installments.

Due Process of Law   the idea stated in the Fifth and Fourteenth Amendments that every person involved in a legal dispute is entitled to a fair hearing or trial. The requirements of due process vary from situation to situation, but due process basically requires that

no law or government procedure be arbitrary or unfair.

Duress   unlawful pressure on a person to do something that he or she would not otherwise do. Duress may be a defense to a criminal charge.

Elements   the conditions that make an act a crime.

Emancipation   the voluntary surrender by parents of the care, control, and earnings of a minor. A minor becomes emancipated upon reaching legal adulthood, or before that time if legally married or self-supporting.

Embalming   to treat a corpse with chemicals so as to preserve it.

Embezzlement   the taking of money or property by a person who has been entrusted with it, such as a bank teller or a company accountant.

Entrapment   an act by law enforcement officials to induce a person to commit a crime that the person would not have otherwise committed. If proven, entrapment is a valid defense to a criminal charge.

Equal Protection   a constitutional requirement of the Fourteenth Amendment which protects against unlawful discrimination by the states.

Equal Rights Amendment   a proposed amendment to the U.S. Constitution. It would prevent the denial or abridgment of rights on account of sex.

Equitable   just, fair, and right for a particular situation.

Error of Law   a mistake made by a judge in legal procedures or rulings during a trial that may allow the case to be appealed.

Escrow   money or property that a neutral party, such as a bank, holds for someone until that person fulfills some obligation or requirement.

Establishment Clause part of the U.S. Constitution that prohibits government from establishing a church or preferring one religion over another.

Estate an individual's personal property, including money, stocks, and all belongings.

Euthanasia an act of mercy killing in instances where individuals are terminally sick or injured.

Eviction the action by a landlord of removing a tenant from a rental unit.

Ex Post Facto Law law that attempts to make criminal an act that was not a crime at the time the act was committed. These laws are prohibited by the Constitution.

Exclusionary Rule a legal rule that prohibits illegally obtained evidence from being used against a defendant at trial.

Executor, Executrix the person named in a will as responsible for carrying out its terms and paying all debts, taxes, and funeral expenses of the deceased.

Express Warranty a statement of fact or a demonstration concerning the quality or performance of goods offered for sale.

Extortion taking property illegally by force or threats of harm or blackmail.

Family Car Doctrine legal rule that the owner of a car will be liable for damage done by a family member driving the owner's car.

Family Immunity Laws common law doctrine that prevents husbands and wives or children and parents from suing one another for damages.

Family Responsibility Laws laws that require children to care for their parents in their old age.

Felon a person serving a sentence for a felony.

Felony a serious crime punishable by a prison sentence of more than one year.

Fighting Words legal term applying to words that are so abusive that they are likely to cause a fight between the speaker and the person spoken to.

Fixture anything attached to land or a building. Also used to mean those things that once attached may not be removed by a tenant.

Flexible Payment Mortgages mortgages that allow buyers to make smaller payments in the early years of the loan and larger payments in future years.

Foreclosure a proceeding in which a bank or other lender takes a house and sells it if a person fails to make mortgage payments.

Forgery making a fake document or altering a real one with the intent to commit fraud.

Foster Home the residence or home of people who take in a child.

Foster Parents a couple or family who take in and care for a child who is without parents or who has been removed from the custody of his or her parents.

Fraud any deception, lie, or dishonest statement made to cheat someone.

Free Exercise Clause part of the U.S. Constitution that protects individuals' right to worship as they believe.

Funeral Services ceremonies held for a dead person before the burial.

Garnishment the legally authorized means to take a person's money, through payroll deductions or other means in order to pay creditors.

Grand Jury   a group of 12 to 23 people who hear preliminary evidence to decide if there is sufficient reason to formally charge a person with a crime.

Grounds   the basis or foundation for some action; legal reasons for filing a lawsuit.

Guardian Ad Litem   a guardian appointed to prosecute or defend a suit on behalf of a minor or other party unable to represent him- or herself.

Guilty but Mentally Ill   a verdict that allows convicted criminal defendants to be sent to a hospital and later transferred to a prison after recovery from their mental illness.

Heirs   people who inherit property/or money (or both) from a person who dies.

Holdover Tenants   tenants who are allowed to remain on the property after the lease expires.

Homesteading   a program whereby older homes in rundown areas are sold to people for low prices if they promise to live in and repair them.

Homicide   the crime of killing a person.

Homosexuality   an individual's sexual and emotional preference for a person of the same sex.

Housing Codes   the municipal ordinances that regulate standards of safety and upkeep for buildings.

Hung Jury   the situation in which a jury cannot reach a unanimous decision.

Immunity   free from; protected from some action, such as being sued.

Implied Warranty   the unwritten standard of quality required, by law, of a product offered for sale.

Incapacitation   a theory of sentencing that stresses keeping a convicted criminal locked up to protect society.

Incest   sexual relations between people who are closely related to each other.

Indictment   a grand jury's formal charge or accusation of criminal action.

Informal Separation   occurs when a married couple lives apart without a formal legal agreement.

Information   a prosecuting attorney's formal accusation of commission of a crime.

Inheritance   property received from a dead person either by intestacy laws or from a will.

Insanity Defense   defense raised by a criminal defendant stating that because of mental disease or defect, the defendant should not be held responsible for the crime committed.

Insurance   a contract in which one person pays money and the other person promises to reimburse the first person for specified types of losses if they occur.

Intake   the informal process by which court officials or social workers decide if a complaint against a youth should be referred to juvenile court.

Intent   determination to achieve a particular end by a particular means.

Interest   money earned for the use of someone's money; the cost of borrowing money. Money put in a savings account earns interest, while borrowing money costs interest.

Intestate   dying without a will.

Joint Custody   custody arrangement where divorced or separated parents have an equal right to make important decisions concerning their children.

Joint Property property owned by two or more people.

Judgment a court's decision on a case.

Judicial Review the process by which courts decide whether the laws passed by Congress or state legislatures are constitutional.

Jurisprudence the study of law and legal philosophy.

Landlord the owner of property who leases or rents space. The company or person that manages the property for the owner.

Larceny the unlawful taking of another's property with the intent to steal it. Grand larceny, a felony, is the theft of anything above a certain value (often $100). Petty larceny, a misdemeanor, is the theft of anything below a certain value (often $100).

Lease a contract between a landlord and a tenant for the use of property for a specified length of time at a specified cost.

Lease Application a form the landlord uses to determine whether someone qualifies for a rental.

Legal Separation a situation in which the two spouses are separated but still maintain some marital obligations.

Legislation laws or statutes that have been enacted by a legislature.

Legitimate lawful or legal; a child born to a married couple is called legitimate.

Libel a written expression about a person that is false and damages that person's reputation.

Lien a claim on some property made by a creditor until a debt is paid.

Living Will a document that specifies what a person wants done in the event that he or she is being kept alive by artificial means or has become totally unable to func-

tion mentally and physically, with no hope of recovery.

Loan Sharking lending money at high, often illegal, interest rates.

Lobbying influencing or persuading legislators to take action to introduce a bill or vote a certain way on a proposed law.

Malice ill will; intentionally harming someone.

Mandatory Sentencing laws that require courts to sentence convicted criminals to certain prison terms.

Marriage the state of a man and a woman being married.

Marriage Counselor trained person who helps couples settle their marital differences.

Mausoleum Greek word for a large tomb; usually a building with a place for burying the dead above ground.

Mediation the act or process of reconciling a dispute between two or more parties.

Memorial Services services commemorating the life of the deceased after the burial.

Minor a child; a person under the legal age of adulthood (usually 18 or 21).

Misdemeanor a criminal offense, less serious than a felony, punishable by a prison sentence of one year or less.

Mitigating Factors factors that may lower the seriousness of an offense; the presence of these factors may be considered by the judge or jury.

Month-to-Month Lease a lease enabling the tenant to leave with 30 days' notice and the landlord to raise the rent or evict the tenant with 30 days' notice.

Mortgage a loan in which land or buildings are put up as security.

Mortgage Assumption act of a new buyer taking over another person's mortgage at the old interest rate.

Motions   requests made by one party to a lawsuit that a judge take some specific action or make a decision.

Motion to Suppress Evidence   a motion filed by a criminal defense attorney, asking the court to exclude any evidence that was illegally obtained from the attorney's client.

Motive   the reason a person commits a crime.

Mutual Agreement   agreement by the parties to the exact terms of a contract, either by signing the contract or by beginning to carry it out.

National Origin   country where one was born or from where one's ancestors came.

Necessities   those things that parents have a legal obligation to provide their children and which one spouse has the responsibility to provide the other. These usually include food, clothing, housing, and medical care.

Necessity   a possible defense to a crime if the defendant acts in the reasonable belief that he or she had no choice.

Negligence   the failure to exercise a reasonable amount of care in either doing or not doing something, resulting in harm or injury.

Negotiation   the process of discussing an issue to reach a settlement or agreement.

No-fault Divorce   a divorce in which neither party is charged with any wrongdoing but the marriage is ended on the grounds that there are irreconcilable differences causing the marriage to break down.

Nolo Contendere   Latin phrase meaning "no contest." A defendant's plea to criminal charges that does not admit guilt but also does not contest the charges. It is equivalent to a guilty plea, but it cannot be used as evidence in a later civil trial for damages based on the same facts.

Notice   a written statement intended to inform a person of some proceeding in which his or her interests are involved.

Obscenity   a general term applying to anything that is immoral, indecent, or lewd.

Offer   a definite proposal by one person to another to make a deal or contract.

Ordinance   a county or city law.

Overt   open, clear; for example, an overt act in criminal law is more than mere preparation to do something; it is at least the first step of actually attempting the crime.

Palimony   name given to support payment made by one unmarried cohabitant to another after the couple splits up.

Parens Patriae   the doctrine under which the court protects the interests of a juvenile.

Parochial School   a school supported and controlled by a church.

Parole   release from prison before the full sentence has been served, granted at the discretion of a parole board.

Partial Emancipation   the legal doctrine that allows minor to keep and spend their own earnings.

Parties   the people concerned with or taking part in any legal matter.

Paternity Suit   a lawsuit brought by a woman against a man she claims is the father of her child. If a paternity suit is proved, the man is legally responsible for contributing to the support of the child.

Peace Bond   a sum of money deposited with the court to guarantee good behavior for a period of time.

Penal Institution   a prison or jail.

Peremptory Challenge   part of the pretrial jury selection in which each side is given the right to dismiss a certain number of potential jurors without giving any reason.

Personal Recognizance   a release from legal custody based on a defendant's promise to return to court. An alternative to cash bail, this practice is used if the judge decides that the defendant is likely to show up for trial.

Petition   (1) to file charges in a juvenile court proceeding; (2) a request to a court or public official.

Physical Incapacity   the inability of a spouse to engage in sexual intercourse. This may be grounds for annulment.

Plaintiff   the person who brings (starts) a lawsuit against another person.

Plea Bargaining   negotiations in a criminal case between a prosecutor and a defendant and his or her attorney in which a guilty plea is exchanged for a lesser charge or a lesser sentence.

Points   an initial charge made for lending money.

Precedent   court decisions on legal questions that give direction to future cases on similar questions.

Preliminary Hearing   pretrial proceeding at which the prosecutor must prove that a crime was committed and establish the probable guilt of the defendant. If the evidence presented does not show probable guilt, the judge may dismiss the case.

Preponderance of Evidence evidence of greater weight or more convincing to prove one party's version of the disputed issue or event; the amount of evidence that overcomes evidence offered in opposition.

Presentence Report   a written report by a probation officer that gives the sentencing judge information about the defendant's background and prospects for rehabilitation.

Presentment   the initial appearance in felony cases at which time defendants are informed of the charges against them and advised of their rights.

Principal   (1) the person who actually commits a crime; (2) the amount of money borrowed or loaned as opposed to the interest on the money.

Prior Restraint   any effort to censor a publication before it goes to press.

Privacy   the right to let alone.

Privilege   (1) an advantage, a right to preferential treatment; (2) an exemption from a duty that others like you must perform.

Privilege Against Self-incrimination   the rule that suspects have a right to remain silent and cannot be forced to testify against themselves.

Probable Cause   a reasonable belief, known personally or through reliable sources, that a person has committed a crime.

Probate   the process of proving to a court that a will is genuine; giving out the property according to the terms of the will.

Pro se   Latin term meaning "for oneself," "on one's own behalf," typically used to describe a person who represents him- or herself in court.

Prosecutor   the government's attorney in a criminal case.

Prosecution   (1) the process of suing a person in a civil case or of bringing a person to trial on criminal charges; (2) the side bringing a case against another party.

Prostitution   the act of performing sexual acts for money.

Protective Order   in family law, a court order directing one spouse not to abuse the other spouse or children. The penalty for violating a protective order is jail.

Puffing   an exaggerated statement as to the desirability of a product or service.

r

Rape   unlawful sexual intercourse committed by a man with a woman by force and without her consent.

Ratify   to confirm previous act done by you or another person.

Real Estate Agent   representative of seller or buyer in a real estate sale.

Receiving Stolen Property receiving or buying property that is known or reasonably believed to be stolen.

Redlining   a discriminatory procedure in which certain geographical areas in a community are designated by a bank as ineligible for mortgage loans.

Referenda   procedure in which issues are voted on directly by the citizens rather than by their representatives in government.

Regulation   a rule made by a government agency.

Rehabilitate   the attempt to change or reform a convicted person so that he or she will not commit another criminal act.

Rehabilitation   the act of attempting to change or reform a convicted person so that he or she will not commit another criminal act.

Release   the giving up of a claim or right by a person. A landlord's act of excusing a tenant from all duties related to the apartment and the lease.

Remedy   what is done to compensate for an injury or to enforce some right.

Removal for Cause   part of the jury selection process that permits removal of any juror who does not appear capable of rendering a fair and impartial verdict.

Rent Control   a law that limits how much existing rents can be raised.

Repossession   a lender's act of taking back the property of a debtor who has failed to repay a debt.

Rescission   the act of canceling a contract as if it never existed.

Restitution   a court order in which a convicted person is required to pay back or otherwise compensate the victim.

Retaliatory Eviction   the illegal action on the part of a landlord of evicting a tenant because the tenant complained about the building or otherwise took action against the landlord.

Retribution   punishment given as a kind of revenge to pay back the individual for a wrongdoing.

Revoke   to take back or cancel.

Right of Entry or Access   the part of a lease that allows a landlord and his or her agents to enter a tenant's premises to make repairs, collect the rent, or enforce other provisions of the lease.

Right to Quiet Enjoyment   a tenant's right to use and enjoy the property without being disturbed by the landlord or other tenants.

Robbery   the unlawful taking of property from a person's immediate possession by force or threat of force.

s

Sales Contract   a contract that includes all the major terms of a sale and that becomes enforceable when the buyer agrees to and signs the seller's offer.

Search Warrant   an order issued by a magistrate, giving police the power to enter a building to search and seize items related to a crime.

Secured Credit   the act of putting up some kind of property as a protection in the event a debt is not repaid.

Security Deposit money that a landlord requires a tenant to pay before moving in, used to cover any damages, cleaning costs, or unpaid rent, if such fees arise.

Separate Property a system under which property owned by either spouse before the marriage remains that person's property throughout the marriage, and any property acquired during the marriage belongs to the person who acquired it.

Settlement a mutual agreement between two sides in a lawsuit, made before the case goes to trial that settles or ends the dispute.

Slander spoken expression about a person that is false and damages that person's reputation.

Small Claims Court a court that handles civil claims for small amounts of money. People usually represent themselves rather than hire an attorney.

Solicitation the act of requesting or strongly urging someone to do something. If the request is to do something illegal, solicitation is considered a crime.

Specific Performance a remedy available in civil court that orders the breaching party to do exactly what he or she promised under the contract.

Speculation the process of buying property at a low price, holding it for a short period of time, and then selling if for a profit.

Spouse Abuse the criminal act of one spouse beating or physically assaulting the other.

Status Offenders youths who are charged with the status of being beyond the control of their legal guardian, habitually disobedient, truant from school or other acts that would not be crimes if committed by an adult.

Status Offenses illegal acts which can only be committed by juveniles, for example truancy or running away from home.

Statutes laws enacted by legislatures.

Steering a discriminatory practice on the part of real estate agents that directs buyers or renters to particular areas because of their race or for other reasons.

Stop and Frisk to "pat down" or search someone who the police believe is acting suspiciously.

Strict Liability the legal responsibility for damage or injury even if you are not at fault.

Sublease the part of most standard leases that requires the tenant to obtain the landlord's permission before allowing someone else to live on the premises and pay all or part of the rent.

Subpoena a court order to appear in court at a specified date and time.

Suicide the deliberate taking of one's own life.

Suit a lawsuit or civil action in court.

Summons a legal notice informing a person of a lawsuit and telling that person when and where to go to court.

Symbolic Speech conduct that expresses an idea, for example flag-waving.

Tenant a person who rents property.

Tenancy for Years refers to any lease for a fixed period of time. The lease specifies that the tenant may live on the property for a single definite period of time.

Tenancy at Will a situation in which a tenant remains on the rented property beyond the end of the lease. In this situation, either the landlord or the tenant can end the lease with whatever notice the law requires.

Testify to give evidence under oath.

Title   the legal right of property ownership.

Title Insurance   insurance that protects a person's right to his or her property.

Title Search   a search of government records to make sure the seller has the right to convey or give valid title of ownership to this property.

Tort   a breach of some obligation causing harm or injury to someone. A civil wrong, such as negligence or libel.

Treason   the offense whereby a U.S. citizen attempts by overt acts to overthrow or seriously harm the U.S. government.

Trial Courts   courts that listen to testimony, consider evidence, and decide the facts in a disputed situation.

Truant   a pupil who stays away from school without permission.

Unconscionable   (1) unfair, harsh, oppressive, (2) a sales practice or term in a contract that is so unfair that a judge will not permit it.

Uncontested Divorce   a divorce in which the parties agree to the grounds and terms of the settlement.

Undertaking   putting up bond or stocks as security against theft. An executor of an estate is often named in a will and specifically exempted from putting up bond or undertaking.

Unsecured Credit   credit based only on a promise to repay in the future.

Usury   charging interest for various types of credit at rates higher than the state's legal limit.

Uttering   offering to someone as genuine a document known to be a fake.

Vagueness   indefinite, uncertain, imprecise.

Vandalism   the deliberate destruction or defacement of property.

Verdict   a jury's decision on a case.

Void   not valid, canceled, not legally binding.

Voir dire   the process in which opposing lawyers question prospective jurors to try to get as favorable or as impartial a jury as possible.

Voluntary Separation   act of a married couple informally agreeing to live apart.

Waive   to give up some right, privilege, or benefit voluntarily.

Wavier of Tort Liability   a clause in a lease where the tenant agrees to give up the usual right to hold the landlord responsible for personal injuries.

Warrant   a paper signed by a judge authorizing some action, such as an arrest or a search and seizure.

Warranty   a guarantee or promise made by a seller or manufacturer concerning the quality or performance of goods offered for sale.

Warranty of Fitness for Particular Purpose   a seller's implied promise that the item will meet the buyer's stated purpose.

Warranty of Habitability   implied or unwritten obligation of landlord to provide a unit that is fit to live in.

Warranty of Merchantability   an implied promise that the item sold is of at least average quality for that type of item.

Warranty of Title   the seller's promise that he or she owns and may transmit title to the item being offered for sale.

Waste   damages caused by a tenant's misuse or neglect of property for which the landlord can force the tenant to make repairs or can sue for damages.

Will   a legal document that states
what a person wants done with his
or her belongings after death.
Writ   a judge's order, or author-
ization, that something be done.

INDEX

PHOTO CREDITS

Chapter one

p. 3, *bottom center*, H. Armstrong Roberts; **p. 7** National Conference of State Legislatures; **p. 9** Bruce Roberts/Photo Researchers, Inc.; **p. 12** UPI/Bettmann Newsphotos; **p. 14** © Carol Bernson, 1978; **p. 16** Supreme Court of the United States; **p. 24** Bob Sullivan; **p. 25** Jim Davis, The Arizona Daily Star; **p. 28** William Auth/Georgetown University; **p. 29** James L. Shaffer; **p. 32** U.S. Civil Rights Commission; **p. 33** Daniel S. Brody, Stock, Boston

Chapter two

p. 43 Mayor of the District of Columbia, and the Metropolitan Department; **p. 44** © Linda Montano/Jeroboam, Inc.; **p. 47** Cliff Garboden, Stock, Boston; **p. 52** James L. Shaffer; **p. 55** *Corrections* Magazine; **p. 57** George W. Gardner, Stock, Boston; **p. 59** Bob Sullivan; **p. 60**, *top*, Eugene Richards; **p. 60**, *bottom*, Mayor of the District of Columbia, and the Metropolitan Police Department; **p. 62** Mayor of the District of Columbia, and the Metropolitan Police Department; **p. 63** Burt Glinn/Magnum; **p. 69** James L. Shaffer; **p. 72** Bob Sullivan; **p. 73** Leo de Wys, Inc.; **p. 77** Ray Lustig; **p. 80** Charles Harbutt/Archive; **p. 81** UPI/Bettmann Newsphotos; **p. 83** Martin J. Dain/Magnum; **p. 88** Bob Sullivan; **p. 89** Bohdan Hrynewych & Southern Light; **p. 90** Sentinel Star Photo by Bill Phillips; **p. 91** Bob Sullivan; **p. 92** James L. Shaffer; **p. 97** Wayne Miller/Magnum; **p. 101** Rhoda Sidney/Leo de Wys, Inc.; **p. 102** Cornell Capa/Magnum; **p. 103** *Corrections* Magazine; **p. 105** UPI/Bettmann Newsphotos; **p. 109** James L. Shaffer; **p. 113** Ray Lustig; **p. 117** *Corrections* Magazine

Chapter three

p. 118, *left*, © Carol Bernson, 1978; **p. 123** Charles L. Farrow; **p. 124** Eugene Richards; **p. 125** Bob Sullivan; **p. 126** James L. Shaffer; **p. 127** Bob Sullivan; **p. 129** National Auto Dealers Association; **p. 131** Bob Sullivan; **p. 137** © Carol Bernson, 1978; **p. 139** © 1984 Donna Jernigan; **p. 144** Library of Congress; **p. 145** J. Berndt, Stock, Boston; **p. 147** U.S. Postal Service; **p. 149** Bob Sullivan; **p. 150** Legal Services Corporation; **p. 154** Charles L. Farrow; **p. 155** Bob Sullivan; **p. 157** Bob Sullivan; **p. 159** Charles L. Farrow; **p. 161** Bohdan Hrynewych; **p. 162** Charles L. Farrow; **p. 163** James L. Shaffer; **p. 170** Paolo Koch/Photo Researchers, Inc.; **p. 173** © Carol Bernson, 1978; **p. 175** Charles L. Farrow; **p. 177** Bob Sullivan; **p. 179** Charles L. Farrow; **p. 181** UPI/Bettmann Newsphotos; **p. 183** © Carol Bernson, 1978; **p. 188** UPI/Bettmann Newsphotos; **p. 189** Charles L. Farrow

Chapter four

p. 192, *bottom left*, James Carroll; **pp. 192-193**, *top center*, Robert Kingman; **pp. 192-193**, *bottom center*, Thomas Hopker, Woodfin Camp & Associates; **p. 193**, *center*, Dick Swift; **p. 193**, *top right*, John Veltri/Photo Researchers, Inc.; **p. 202** J. Berndt, Stock, Boston; **p. 203** © Susan Ylvisaker/Jeroboam, Inc.; **p. 204** Chester Higgins/Photo Researchers, Inc.; **p. 208** Mimi Forsyth/Monkmeyer Press Photo Service, Inc.; **p. 211** Rape and Sexual Assault Center, Minneapolis; **p. 215** James L. Shaffer; **p. 217**, *top*, UPI/Bettmann Newsphotos; **p. 217**, *bottom*, National Abortion Rights Action League; **p. 218** Bill Owens/Archive; **p. 222** Bob Sullivan; **p. 224** Ray Lustig; **p. 225** Steve Hansen, Stock, Boston; **p. 229** U.S. Department of Labor; **p. 230** Owen Franken, Stock, Boston; **p. 234** Legal Services Organization of Indiana; **p. 235** Paul Zakoian; **p. 239** U.S. Civil Rights Commission; **p. 240** Ray Lustig; **p. 242** Bob Sullivan; **p. 243** Bonnie Freer/Photo Researchers, Inc.; **p. 244** Alice Kandell/Photo Researchers, Inc.; **p. 245** Bob Sullivan; **p. 249** Fredrik D. Bodin; **p. 252** Dan and Mark Jury/Photo Researchers, Inc.

Chapter five

p. 258 Charles Harbutt/Archive; **p. 259** U.S. Department of Housing and Urban Development; **p. 260** Miriam Harmatz; **p. 262** James L. Shaffer; **p. 266** U.S. Department of Housing and Urban Development; **p. 268** Charles Harbutt/Archive; **p. 270** Everett C. Johnson/Leo de Wys, Inc.; **p. 274** Paul Zakoian; **p. 276** UPI/Bettmann Newsphotos; **p. 278** Ray Ellis/Photo Researchers, Inc.; **p. 283** U.S. Department of Housing and Urban Development; **p. 286** Institute of Life Insurance; **p. 287** UPI/Bettmann Newsphotos; **p. 290** UPI/Bettmann Newsphotos; **p. 292** Bob Sullivan; **p. 297** UPI/Bettmann Newsphotos; **p. 298** Ed McMahon; **p. 299** Fredrik D. Bodin; **p. 300** © Carol Bernson, 1978; **p. 304** Ed McMahon; **p. 305** © Carol Bernson, 1978; **p. 307** Hube Henry

Chapter six

p. 311 Bob Sullivan; **p. 313** Hiroji Kubota/Magnum; **p. 315** UPI/Bettmann Newsphotos; **p. 317** Edward McMahon; **p. 321** UPI/Bettmann Newsphotos; **p. 326** James L. Shaffer; **p. 328** Danny Lyon/Magnum; **p. 332** © Emilio A. Mercado/Jeroboam, Inc.; **p. 334** Library of Congress; **p. 339** Bob Sullivan; **p. 341** U.S. Department of Labor; **p. 343** Bob Sullivan; **p. 348** U.S. Equal Employment Opportunity Commission; **p. 350** U.S. Department of Labor; **p. 352** UPI/Bettmann Newsphotos; **p. 353** Copyright Washington Post; reprinted by permission of the D.C. Public Library; **p. 354** Alon Reininger/Leo de Wys, Inc.; **p. 357** U.S. Department of Labor; **p. 361** UPI/Bettmann Newsphotos; **p. 362** Copyright Washington Post; reprinted by permission of the D.C. Public Library; **p. 363** UPI/Bettmann Newsphotos; **p. 368** U.S. Department of Labor; **p. 369** U.S. Department of Labor

Note: Unless listed separately above, photos on each chapter-opening spread also appear within the corresponding chapter text. Please refer to text page numbers for credits of photos shown on chapter-opening spreads.

NATIONAL ADVISORY COMMITTEE

Chairperson:
David R. Brink
Dorsey & Whitney
2200 First Bank Place East
Minneapolis, MN 55402
  (612) 340–2600

Grace Baisinger
Past President
National PTA
2870 Arizona Terrace, N.W.
Washington, D.C. 20016
  (202) 537–0811

Richard Bastiani
Vice President for Marketing
Syva Company
900 Arastradero Road
Palo Alto, CA 94303
  (415) 493–2200

Lowell R. Beck
President
National Association of
  Independent Insurers
2600 River Road
Des Plaines, IL 60018
  (312) 297–7800

Jane A. Couch
Vice President for Development
National Public Radio
2025 M Street, N.W.
Washington, D.C. 20036
  (202) 822–2070

Richard Crane
Vice President/Legal Affairs
Corrections Corporation of
  America
28 White Bridge Road
Nashville, TN 37205
  (800) 624–2931

Lawrence J. Dark
Corporate Initiative Associate
American Red Cross
National Headquarters
17th & D Streets, N.W.
Washington, D.C. 20006
  (202) 639–3254

Elisabeth T. Dreyfuss
Professor
Cleveland-Marshall College
  of Law
Cleveland State University
1801 Euclid Avenue
Cleveland, OH 44115
  (216) 687–2352

Thomas W. Evans
Mudge Rose Guthrie
  Alexander & Ferdon
180 Maiden Lane
New York, NY 10038
  (212) 510–7000

C. Hugh Friedman
Professor of Law
University of San Diego
  School of Law
Alcala Park
San Diego, CA 92110
  (619) 260–4600

Frances Haley
Executive Director
National Council for the
  Social Studies
3501 Newark Street, N.W.
Washington, D.C. 20016
  (202) 966–7840

Ruth J. Hinerfeld
Past President
League of Women Voters
  of the U.S.
11 Oak Lane
Larchmont, NY 10538
  (914) 834–7799

Michael J. Lenaghan
Health Services Management
  Group
American Red Cross
1730 E Street, N.W.
Attention: EIP Unions Bldg.
2nd Floor
Washington, D.C. 20006
  (202) 639–3116

Robert A. Leonard
Vice President
Bank of Boulder
1335A Bear Mountain Drive
Boulder, CO 80303
  (303) 499–9686
  (303) 443–9090 (O)

Thomas A. Nazario
Director
Community Legal Education
University of San Francisco
  School of Law
San Francisco, CA 94117
  (415) 666–6832

Robert Pitofsky
Dean and Executive Vice
    President for Law Center
    Affairs
Georgetown University Law
    Center
600 New Jersey Avenue, N.W.
Room 404
Washington, D.C. 20001
    (202) 624–8200

Marion K. Poynter
Director
Times Publishing Company
(St. Petersburg, Florida)
629 A Street, S.E.
Washington, D.C. 20003
    (202) 547–5588

E. Barrett Prettyman, Jr.
Hogan & Hartson
815 Connecticut Avenue, N.W.
Washington, D.C. 20006
    (202) 331–4500

Thomas F. Railsback
Blum, Nash and Railsback
1133 Fifteenth Street, N.W.
Washington, D.C. 20005
    (202) 857–0220

Bernard Rapoport
Chairman of the Board
American Income Life
    Insurance Company
P.O. Box 2608
Waco, TX 76797
    (817) 772–1875

Melinda Smith
Director, New Mexico Law-
    Related Education Project
State Bar of New Mexico
P.O. Box 25883
Albuquerque, NM 87125
    (505) 842–6269

Jerrol M. Tostrud
Vice President and
    Assistant to the
    President
West Publishing Company
50 W. Kellogg Blvd.
P.O. Box 64526
St. Paul, MN 55164
    (612) 228–2641

Patrick W. Wallace
Vice President
Loss Prevention
Montgomery Ward & Co., Inc.
One Montgomery Plaza (13–S)
Chicago, IL 60671
    (312) 467–3479

Kenneth G. Walsh
Vice President & General
    Counsel
U.S. Trust Company
45 Wall Street
New York, NY 10005
    (212) 806–4990

Judge Reggie Walton
Superior Court of the
    District of Columbia
500 Indiana Avenue, N.W.
Room 1630
Washington, D.C. 20001
    (202) 879–1200

Rev. John P. Whalen
Executive Director
Consortium of Universities
    of the Washington
    Metropolitan Area
1717 Massachusetts Avenue, N.W.
Washington, D.C. 20035
    (202) 265–1313

Fay Williams
Attorney at Law
156 East Market Street
Suite 600
Indianapolis, IN 46204
    (317) 639–4126

NEW YORK STATE SUPPLEMENT TO

STREET LAW

A COURSE IN PRACTICAL LAW

third edition

Developed by the NEW YORK STATE BAR ASSOCIATION'S Committee on Citizenship Education, Lisa H. Blitman, Editor.

Harold I. Abramson, Esq.

Edward B. Alderman, Esq.
Syracuse, New York

Lisa H. Blitman, Esq.
New York, New York

Hon. Albert M. Rosenblatt
Supreme Court Judge
Poughkeepsie, New York

David A. Smith, Esq.
Assistant Attorney General
State of New York

John A. Williamson, Jr.
Associate Executive Director
New York State Bar Association

West Publishing Company
St. Paul   New York   Los Angeles   San Francisco

NOTICE TO READERS

The information contained in this supplement is not intended to be legal advice. Before taking any legal action, be sure to check with an attorney. Also note that since the law is constantly changing, readers should attempt to keep abreast of recent changes in New York state law.

CONTENTS

three

CONSUMER LAW • 481
David A. Smith, Esq.
Harold I. Abramson, Esq.

four

FAMILY LAW • 493
Edward B. Alderman, Esq.

five

HOUSING LAW • 507
Lisa H. Blitman, Esq.

six

INDIVIDUAL RIGHTS AND LIBERTIES • 513
John A. Williamson, Jr.

appendix
NEW YORK STATE ORGANIZATIONS TO KNOW · 525

PREFACE AND ACKNOWLEDGMENTS

This supplement, written by the attorneys listed on the title page, is part of a project of the Committee on Citizenship Education of the New York State Bar Association. This group was organized and coordinated through the generous efforts of Dan Goldstein, past Director of Public Relations, New York State Bar Association. Credit should also be given to the Law, Youth and Citizenship Program, a joint project of the New York State Bar Association and the New York State Department of Education, directed by Eric Mondschein, which has helped so much to spread the teaching of law throughout New York State. The completion and final editing of this supplement was the work of Lisa Blitman, New York City attorney.

It is the belief of NICEL that if education in law is to be most beneficial, the law of the state where one lives must be taught. This supplement goes far towards helping students in New York State achieve that goal.

Edward L. O'Brien
Co-Director
National Institute for Citizen Education in the Law

453

one
INTRODUCTION TO LAW AND THE LEGAL SYSTEM

WHO MAKES LAWS?

Legislatures

The New York State Legislature The New York State Legislature has the power to enact laws that affect all aspects of the lives of New York residents—matters like income and sales taxes, welfare, transportation, and education.

The New York State Legislature consists of two houses: the senate, with sixty-one members, and the assembly, with one hundred fifty members. The state has been divided into senate and assembly districts in which these representatives are elected. The geographic borders of the districts may be changed by reapportionment to ensure fair and equal representation for everyone in the state. Senators and members of the assembly serve two-year terms and are chosen at the biennial November general election. Both houses meet at the state capital in Albany each year; the sessions begin in January and continue until late spring or early summer. These sessions are open to all unless the legislature de-cides that the public welfare requires secrecy.

Proposed laws, called *bills*, may originate in either house, and if they are passed by one house, may be amended by the other. For a bill to become a law, it must first be passed by a majority of both houses. Certain finance bills require a two-thirds majority for passage. Enacted bills are then sent to the governor for approval and signature. They then become law. If the governor disapproves, or vetoes, a bill, the legislature has the power to override this veto by passing the bill again; but this time a two-thirds majority is required in each house.

Local and City Legislatures   Local governments, cities, towns, and villages may also have legislative bodies called councils, boards, assemblies, or legislatures, which have the power to pass laws affecting localities. Examples of these are the New York City Council, the Westchester County Council, and the Albany County Legislature.

Voting   To qualify as a voter in New York State, a person must be a citizen of the United States, at least eighteen years of age on or before election day, and a resident of the state and of the county, city, or village where he or she wishes to vote for a minimum of thirty days before the election. A person with these qualifications must then register. Provision is made by law for voters to register centrally at the main office of the Board of Elections or at any branch office during regular business hours. Voters may also register in their local election districts, usually on a Saturday no earlier than the sixth Saturday nor later than the fourth Saturday before the general election. An additional day is provided for registration in densely populated counties or in a presidential election year. The day and hours of registration must be uniform throughout a county, and advance notice must be published in local newspapers.

Voting by absentee ballot is available to people who will not be in their residences because of service in the armed forces, attendance at an educational institution, or travel for business or vacation, or to those who cannot vote in person because of illness or physical disability. An absentee ballot may be obtained either in person or by mail from the Board of Elections in your city. The completed ballot must be returned to the Board of Elections, either in person or by mail, by election day.

Should the eligibility of a person to register and vote be questioned, the Board of Elections, when deciding, may consider factors such as the individual's residence for income tax purposes, home of family members, location of real property, or place of motor vehicle registration.

Certain categories of people are ineligible to vote. Among them are persons who have been convicted of a felony and who have not been pardoned or had their right to vote restored. In addition, those who have been judged incompetent or who have been committed to a mental institution are not eligible to vote while under disability.

Lobbying   To assure the integrity of the governmental decision-making process in New York State and at the same time allow the people to petition their government and freely express their opinions on legislation and government operations to appropriate officials, the legislature passed the Regulation of Lobbying Act. The New York Temporary State Commission on Regulation of Lobbying was created to carry out this law. Lobbyists who are active above certain minimal levels are required to register annually with the Temporary State Commission and to file with that body annually (or in some instances to periodically report) lobbying activities and expenditures. Registration statements and reports are required to be kept on file for a period of three years and are open to public inspection.

The Temporary State Commission has the power to enforce these requirements by conducting investigations and holding public and private hearings. The commission may subpoena witnesses and compel relevant books and records to be produced for inspection.

It is illegal for a lobbyist to accept compensation contingent upon the passage or defeat of any legislative bill or the approval or veto of legislation by the governor.

Thus the Regulation of Lobbying Act is designed to encourage the orderly expression of opinions and wishes to legislators and government officials, and to allow easy identification of lobbyists who represent interest groups or specific organizations.

Agencies

In New York State numerous agencies serve the various needs of the people. Some affect your daily life.

Office for the Aging   This agency develops and sponsors various nutrition, recreation, and information programs to meet the needs of the elderly, and cooperates with local governments in promoting public interest and education about aging.

Office of Drug Abuse Services   This agency develops plans to administer laws controlling drug abuse and treating and rehabilitating drug addicts. It also educates people about the drug problem.

Department of Education   This agency manages and supervises all public education in the state, including the state university, its Board of Regents, the commissioner of education, and the children on Indian reservations. The chief executive officer of the state system of education is the commissioner of education, who is elected by a majority of the Board of Regents. The commissioner must advise and judge the duties and general management of school officers of all districts and cities of the state, including industrial, trade, agriculture, and homemaking schools.

Board of Regents   The Board of Regents governs the state university and functions as the head of the state's Department of Education. In its first role, it acts much like a board of directors for any corporation. The fifteen members decide how money will be spent for the state's public universities. They determine regulations for school employees and are responsible for the basic organization of each campus. The Board of Regents must make rules carrying out any laws on education made by the state legislature. The board can also make specific policies. Every higher-education institution in New York State submits long-range development plans to the Board of Regents. Using this material the board develops a master plan for the state. By law, a new master plan must be created by the board every four years.

Department of Environmental Conservation   In keeping with our increasing concern for the quality of our environment, this agency has the responsibility for encouraging conservation of resources, proper disposal and recycling of waste products, pollution control, preservation of scenic beauty, and development of plans to preserve the environment for the benefit of future generations.

Department of Health   This department administers the Public Health Law and State Sanitary Code and supervises local health agencies. It deals with all aspects of the health field, from standards for hospitals and nursing homes to disease control and emergency medical services.

State Division of Human Rights   This agency was created to help eliminate racial, religious, age, and sex discrimination in employment, housing, and public accommodations. It has the power to investigate complaints, hold hearings, subpoena witnesses, and in some instances, grant compensatory damages to victims of discrimination.

Department of Labor   By enforcing the State Labor Law, this agency helps protect the safety of employees, improve their working conditions, and ensure the payment of full minimum wages and the maintenance of proper employee benefit programs.

Department of Social Services   This department provides a variety of services to the needy and assists local social service agencies in programs that include income maintenance, food stamps, medical assistance through Medicaid, day care, foster care, and family planning.

Division for Youth   Through research and education programs, this division works to prevent delinquency and crime among young people. It controls the facilities to which young people have been committed by the courts as juvenile delinquents. It helps maintain youth centers and works with local government to develop youth programs.

Courts

Three levels of courts exist in the New York State court system: the trial courts, the appellate division, and the Court of Appeals.

The New York Court of Appeals   The Court of Appeals, which consists of seven judges, is New York's highest court. Located in Albany, it hears appeals in both civil and criminal cases and decides whether errors of law have been committed by lower courts. The circumstances in which a person may appeal a case to the Court of Appeals are governed by the state constitution and laws enacted by the legislature.

The Appellate Division   The appellate division is the court directly below the New York Court of Appeals. New York State is divided into four judicial departments. Each judicial department contains one appellate division and one or more districts. These districts may in turn be made up of one or more counties. For example, the first department of New York City contains the first and twelfth districts, which include the counties of New York and the Bronx. The appellate divisions in each department can create appellate terms for the districts or counties in the department. The appellate term courts hear appeals from county and city courts.

The appellate division handles appeals from lower court decisions in both civil and criminal cases. In most instances, five judges hear and decide each case. In certain cases a dissatisfied party may appeal to the Court of Appeals from a decision of the appellate division.

The New York Supreme Court   A New York State Supreme Court, located in each district, is known as the court of general original jurisdiction; this court can hear all types of cases. It is a trial-level court in which a civil or criminal case is initiated. There is no maximum limit to the amount of money that a person can sue for when filing a civil case in the supreme court.

Local and City Courts New York State also has lower courts where a civil or criminal case can begin. For instance, it has city and town courts where a person can file a civil suit or where the state can file criminal charges. Only limited types of civil or criminal cases are handled by these lower city-level courts. For example, if a person sues someone for breach of contract and requests recovery of five thousand dollars, that case can be filed in the city-level court, where the limit of recovery may not exceed that fixed for the district courts. (An exception exists for the Civil Court of the City of New York, which has a jurisdictional limit of twenty-five thousand dollars.) If the same person wants to sue for fifty thousand dollars, the case will be filed in the New York Supreme Court.

The court of claims hears civil claims brought by or against the state. For example, if the state wants to build a highway, it may take the necessary land and pay the owners for the property taken. If an owner thinks the compensation offered by the state is insufficient, he or she may bring an action against the state in the court of claims to obtain an award of additional money.

County courts, which have criminal and limited civil jurisdiction, can hear summary proceedings to recover possession of real property and to remove tenants. They may also hear appeals from certain lower courts, like town or city courts, within the county.

The surrogate's court has jurisdiction over all proceedings relating to the affairs of those who have died, including the probate of wills and the administration of estates.

The Family Court The family court deals with the treatment of juvenile delinquents, the custody of children, the support of dependents, the paternity of children, adoptions, proceedings for the conciliation of husbands and wives, and other family matters.

United States Federal Courts in New York State In addition to the state courts, there are federal courts in New York. For the purposes of the federal court system, the United States is divided into thirteen geographical sections called *circuits*. New York, Connecticut, and Vermont form the Second Circuit. The Second Circuit Court of Appeals is located in New York City; it hears appeals from the lower federal courts, called United States district courts. New York State has four district courts: Southern, Eastern, Northern, and Western. The jurisdiction of these courts, which is set by the United States Constitution and federal law, includes the power

FIGURE 1   **Diagram of New York State Court System**

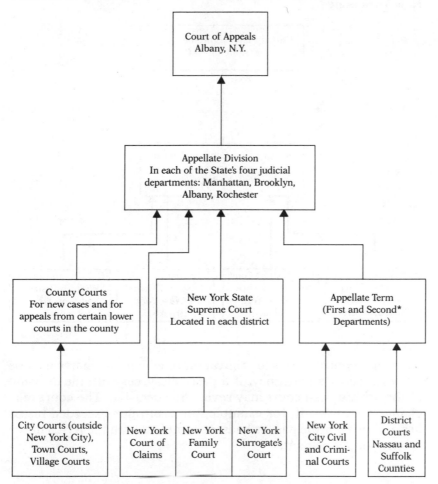

* The appellate term in the second department is also empowered to hear appeals from certain of
  the town, city, and village courts within the department.

to hear cases involving violation of federal civil rights, cases between citizens of different states, and violations of federal criminal laws, including mail fraud and federal income tax evasion.

SETTLING DISPUTES OUT OF COURT

Arbitration

Arbitration is becoming more widespread in New York State as a
way to settle civil disputes. In labor or corporate matters, for
example, each party may agree before beginning a suit to submit

FIGURE 2   Diagram of Supreme Court and Federal Courts located in New York State

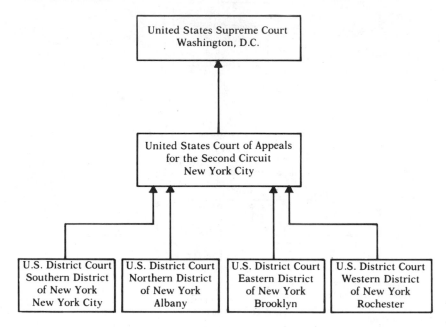

particular controversies to arbitration in which each party may be represented by an attorney. If a party disagrees with the decision of the arbitrator, a court may review the decision. The court may change the award if, for example, the arbitrator exceeded his or her authority or the parties had not complied with the terms of the arbitration agreement.

Mediation

New York has a Community Dispute Resolution Centers Program functioning in approximately one-third of the counties in the state. The program utilizes a mediation-type approach to resolve disputes arising among neighbors, families, or friends. Difficulties such as noise, trespass, or uncontrolled pets typify the matters the program is intended to address. The program is capable of handling minor criminal matters, and may provide first offenders with an opportunity to make restitution or perform public service instead of being subjected to criminal prosecution. Minor criminal cases are sometimes referred to the dispute resolution centers by the courts.

THE ADVERSARY SYSTEM

Order of a Trial

Generally the section "Steps in a Trial" on page 27 of this text applies to trials in New York State; however, in civil cases the party having the burden of proof (making a claim and so being obliged to prove that claim), usually the plaintiff, has the right to make the initial opening statement. The other party, the defendant, then makes an opening statement. The closing statements are made in reverse order so that the party having the burden of proof will address the jury last. However, neither party in New York State has the right to a rebuttal, or an additional closing argument, as page 28 in part one suggests.

A similar procedure is followed in criminal cases. The prosecution, which has the burden of proof, is first given the chance to make an opening statement, followed by the defense. Closing summations are delivered in reverse order, with the defense going first and the prosecution giving its closing statement last. As in civil cases, the prosecution does not have the opportunity to make a second closing statement in New York State.

Certain civil cases will be transferred to arbitrators by some courts to end the cases quickly where money in question does not exceed six thousand dollars. Under these circumstances, a party dissatisfied with the decision of an arbitrator may request rehearing by a jury trial.

Juries

Jury selection is similar in both civil and criminal cases. To qualify as trial jurors, individuals must be United States citizens and residents of the county where the trial is to be held, between the ages of eighteen and seventy-six, in possession of their natural faculties (jurors must be competent to see, hear, and understand proceedings), and not incapable of giving satisfactory service because of physical or mental infirmity. Prospective jurors also must be of good character, intelligent, and able to speak, read, and write English well enough to complete the juror qualification questionnaire satisfactorily. In addition, jurors must never have been convicted of a felony.

The trial jury in New York is known as the *petit jury*. Jurors for each term of court are drawn at random by the commissioner of jurors, or sometimes by the county clerk, from names obtained from voter registration lists and from other available lists of county residents (for example, utility subscribers, state and local taxpayers, or licensed drivers).

Some persons, such as federal, state, or city officers, are disqualified from serving as jurors; others, including lawyers, doctors, nurses, members of the clergy, police officers, and firefighters, may be *exempted* (excused) from jury duty because of their occupations.

Occasionally, an attorney may object to the entire panel of prospective trial jurors, making a *challenge to the panel.* The reason given is usually that members of a particular group, such as blacks or women, have been intentionally excluded from jury service.

In criminal cases a jury of twelve is required for felonies, while six is the number fixed for misdemeanor trials. Alternate jurors are selected to replace a regular juror who may become ill or disabled during trial. From one to four alternates may be selected for a felony trial and one or two for a misdemeanor case. In civil trials, the jury is composed of six people, with provision for the selection of one or two alternates.

The process of questioning the prospective jurors to determine whether they will be selected is called a *voir dire,* and it is conducted in a courtroom by the lawyers for both parties. The six or twelve jurors for a trial will be selected from the panel or pool of prospective jurors. The names of six or twelve people are called, and they enter the jury box. As is described on page 29 of part one, the voir dire is then conducted. The judge and the attorneys tell the prospective jurors the facts of the case and question the jurors to determine whether they will be fair. For example, if a juror were found to be related to one of the parties or had personal knowledge of the case, he or she might not be able to consider the evidence impartially.

If during the voir dire a lawyer for either party decides that someone should not be selected, the lawyer may exercise a challenge to remove that person from the jury. A *challenge* is the term used for a lawyer's objection to a prospective juror. A challenge for cause and a peremptory challenge are the two kinds of challenges a lawyer may make.

A challenge for cause is made when questioning during the voir dire has demonstrated a clear reason why the prospective juror should not be selected. It may become apparent that a particular juror has a bias, prejudice, or opinion affecting his or her judgment. For example, if a juror in a criminal case involving the sale of drugs felt that the statute making such sale a crime should not be enforced, a basis would exist to make a challenge for cause.

An attorney may exercise a peremptory challenge and need not state a reason. When a peremptory challenge is made, a prospective juror will automatically be excused. The number of peremptory challenges permitted is fixed by law and varies according to the type of case.

　　　Questioning continues until the attorneys for both parties are satisfied with the composition of the jury or have exhausted all challenges allowed them by law. Once all jurors and alternates have been chosen, an oath will be administered to them, and the trial can proceed.

　　　Upon completion of proof and after being instructed concerning the law in the case by the judge, the jury deliberates and returns a verdict. A unanimous verdict is required in criminal cases, while a five-sixths verdict is permitted in civil trials.

Lawyers and the Legal System

As pages 30 and 31 state, the services of an attorney may be needed in a variety of situations. Since many lawyers limit their practice to specific areas such as tax or matrimonial problems, some people may need help in locating an attorney who specializes in the kind of legal situations in which they are involved.

　　　Many county and city bar associations operate lawyer reference services to assist individuals in obtaining legal counsel. In counties whose county or local bar associations do not have a lawyer referral service, this service is provided through the New York State Bar Association. Bar associations generally will suggest several lawyers, allowing the inquirer to make the final selection. In many instances the attorney will charge a relatively low, preset fee for the first consultation.

　　　Persons without the money to hire an attorney may qualify for the services of a legal aid or similar agency designed to help them. When in doubt concerning the financial qualifications or the type of cases handled by a legal assistance office, persons should contact the office directly for this information. Some agencies, usually called legal services offices, handle only civil cases, while others, usually called legal aid or public defenders, may be limited to criminal matters. A given agency may not accept certain types of cases as a matter of policy. In criminal cases, most counties have either a public defender or an assigned counsel plan to provide adequate representation for someone charged with a crime who lacks funds to hire an attorney. When a person qualifies for such assistance, the court in which the case is to be tried will appoint legal counsel.

　　　In New York, the conduct of attorneys is supervised by the appellate division. In each judicial department the appellate division has appointed grievance committees to investigate complaints of improper activities by lawyers. In situations in which professional misconduct is found, the appellate division has the power to censure (rebuke), suspend, or disbar the lawyer.

The following list sets forth the grievance committees in New York State as appointed by the appellate division in each judicial department.

FIRST DEPARTMENT
Michael Gentile, Chief Counsel
Departmental Disciplinary
    Committee—1st Department
41 Madison Avenue, 39th
    Floor
New York, NY 10010

SECOND DEPARTMENT
Frank Finnerty, Chief Counsel
Grievance Committee—
    2nd and 11th Districts
Municipal Building, 6th Floor
210 Joralemon Street
Brooklyn, NY 11201

Gary J. Casella, Chief Counsel
Grievance Committee for
    9th District
200 Bloomingdale Road
White Plains, NY 10606

Frank A. Finnerty, Jr., Chief
    Counsel
Grievance Committee for
    10th District
900 Ellison Avenue, Room 304
Westbury, NY 11590

THIRD DEPARTMENT
George B. Burke, Chief
    Attorney
Committee on Professional
    Standards—3rd Department
Governor Alfred E. Smith
    Office Building
P.O. Box 7013
Capital Station Annex, 22nd
    Floor
Albany, NY 12225

FOURTH DEPARTMENT
David E. Brennan, Chief
    Attorney
Grievance Committee for 8th
    District
Ellicott Square Building
Buffalo, NY 14203

Gerard M. LaRusso, Staff
    Attorney
Grievance Committee for 7th
    District
19 W. Main Street, Room 1002
Rochester, NY 14614

Paul J. Gennelly, Staff
    Attorney
Grievance Committee for 5th
    District
Syracuse Square
465 S. Salina Street
Syracuse, NY 13202

two
CRIMINAL AND JUVENILE JUSTICE

CLASSES OF CRIMES

In New York State, as in other states, the legislature grades crimes according to severity. There are three types of crimes in New York State: a felony, a misdemeanor, and a violation or infraction. The greatest distinction is that between a felony and a misdemeanor. While these terms generally differentiate more serious crimes from less serious crimes, they have distinct legal definitions.

Felony

A felony is an offense for which the court *may* impose a sentence of imprisonment of more than one year, regardless of whether the court decides to impose a longer or shorter sentence. Thus a burglary, with a potential punishment of more than one year's imprisonment, is a felony even though the sentence of the judge in one particular case is only that of six months.

Felonies are divided into subcategories ranging from class E, the least serious variety, to class A–1, the most serious variety. Examples of class A–1 felonies are intentional murder, kidnaping in the first degree, and arson in the first degree. The next grade is a class B felony, which includes first degree manslaughter (killing someone without intending to do so, but while intending to cause serious physical injury), forcible rape, and armed robbery. An example of a class C felony is manslaughter in the second degree, in which a person causes the death of another by recklessness, without the intent either to kill or to do serious physical injury. Another example is second degree burglary, or illegal entry with intent to commit a crime. An example of a class D felony is the theft of property worth more than one thousand five hundred dollars. An example of a class E felony is third degree criminal mischief, in which a person purposely damages property of another when the property is valued at more than two hundred fifty dollars.

There are also categories of felonies, such as armed felonies and violent felonies, that raise the level of a crime. In addition, statutes provide for, and in some cases require, increased sentence terms for repeat felons. The most aggravated category of repeat felons is a persistent felony offender, punishable by a maximum sentence of life imprisonment.

Misdemeanor

A misdemeanor is an offense punishable by not more than one year of imprisonment. Misdemeanors are divided into class A and class B varieties. Class A is punishable by the maximum sentence of one year, and class B is punishable by not more than three months in jail.

Violation or Infraction

The third variety of offense in New York is a violation, generally defined as an offense less serious than a misdemeanor, for which a prison sentence of not more than fifteen days may be imposed. Loitering, using obscene language in public places, and the unlawful posting of advertisements are examples of violations. Infractions usually involve violations of law within the Penal Laws, Traffic Laws and Fish and Wildlife Laws to name a few, and the punishments usually do not involve prison sentences.

THE FACTS DETERMINE THE LEVEL OF THE CRIME

You may be able to understand the structure of criminal grada-tions in New York State better by imagining a particular crime and then adding or subtracting certain aggravating or mitigating facts which can expand or lessen the degree of the crime. If, for example, a person trespasses upon the property of another with-out permission and does nothing more, he or she would be guilty of a violation. If the trespass occurs on fenced-in property, the offense is more serious and is labeled a class B misdemeanor. If, however, the trespass occurs in a dwelling, the crime is still more serious and becomes a class A misdemeanor, punishable by up to a year of imprisonment. If a person trespasses while intending to commit another crime, like theft, the matter becomes still more serious. If the trespass consists of knowingly entering or unlaw-fully remaining in a building for the purpose of committing a crime inside, the act is elevated to the status of a class D felony.

An analysis of the facts is made in weighing criminal conduct, and the facts determine the level of the crime.

In keeping with our Constitution as described on pages 7 and 8 of part one, the state legislature examines the seriousness of different kinds of conduct and defines the conduct that constitutes a felony and a misdemeanor. These statutes are subject to inter-pretation and implementation by the courts.

DEFENSES

In a criminal trial the prosecution has the responsibility to prove the defendant guilty beyond a reasonable doubt. The defense need not introduce any proof, and a defendant need not testify. A defen-dant may, of course, testify on his or her own behalf, and failure to testify may not be held against him or her. Some specific de-fenses may be claimed:

Self-Defense

Self-defense is defined as acting in defense of an immediate threat to one's own life or limb. The person threatened is justified in using whatever force necessary and equal to the threat to repel the attack. This amount of force may in certain circumstances even justify killing the initial assailant. Whether such conduct is justi-fied in one case and not in another is determined by juries accord-ing to the legal standards governing the plea of self-defense. Deadly physical force may be used to repel deadly physical force so long as those who used such force were not the initial aggressors, and so long as they had reasonable belief that assailants were using or were about to use deadly physical force against them. In New York people may not use deadly physical force in self-defense if they are able to retreat to complete safety, unless they are already in their own homes, where the plea of self-defense demands no such duty to retreat.

Intoxication

Sometimes evidence will show that an accused person was intoxicated at the time of the act. This is not always a defense because it is not an excuse or a justification for criminal conduct; however, when a specific intent must be proved in order to define an act as a particular crime, it may be found that the defendant could not have been able to form that intent. For example, the definition of the crime of murder includes proof of a specific intent to kill. If the killer was too intoxicated to be capable of forming this intent, there is no basis for a murder conviction. A killer in this situation may be guilty of other homicidal acts not requiring a specific intent to kill but defined as disregard of a substantial risk in a manner varying widely from reasonable standards of care.

Insanity

A legal insanity defense is used when an accused offers evidence that he or she should not be responsible for an act because of a mental disability. If the accused proves the defense by a "preponderance of the evidence" (the better part of the evidence), he or she may not be punished by imprisonment even though he or she committed the act. Under former law, the prosecution had to disprove legal insanity, beyond a reasonable doubt. However, the legislature, changed the law in 1984, and it now requires the defense to prove legal insanity. In New York a person is not criminally responsible for conduct if as a result of mental disease or defect the person lacks substantial capacity to know or appreciate either the nature or consequence of such conduct, or that such conduct was wrong. If this defense is upheld, the verdict or the guilty plea will be "not responsible by reason of mental disease or defect."

The defense of insanity differs from the defense of incompetency, which concerns the mental condition of the defendant *at the time of the trial.* The court must consider whether the defendant is competent to understand the charges and to confer with his or her attorney, and whether he or she is able to undergo trial.

Duress

The prosecution must prove guilt beyond a reasonable doubt if the defendant is to be convicted, but the defendant will be relieved of criminal responsibility if the jury can be convinced that the crime was committed because the defendant was forced by another person to act and was not reasonably able to resist. This is the defense of *duress*.

Entrapment

Entrapment occurs when a police officer or agent, while trying to incriminate someone, actively induces the defendant to commit a crime that the defendant would not have committed without the inducement. The defendant will be relieved of criminal responsibility if the jury believes that the police methods created a substantial risk and that the person was not otherwise prone to criminal behavior and would not have committed the crime without police persuasion.

Renunciation

A defendant can also claim renunciation as a defense. Renunciation occurs when a person abandons a criminal scheme genuinely, voluntarily, and completely before it has been committed, and tries to stop it from taking place.

THE CRIMINAL JUSTICE PROCESS

Arrest

The criminal proceeding frequently begins with an arrest, which may be made by a police officer with a warrant or without a warrant, depending on the circumstances. A great many technical rules govern the need for warrants by police, peace officers, and others. Generally speaking, police officers have greater latitude in making warrantless arrests for felonies than they do for lesser crimes, for which warrants may be needed. Police need an arrest warrant to arrest a person in his or her home, except in "exigent (critical) circumstances."

Under New York law a police officer may arrest a person for any offense, felony, misdemeanor, or violation when the officer has reasonable cause to believe that the person has committed the offense in the officer's presence. A police officer may arrest a person for a crime (a felony or a misdemeanor) when the officer has reasonable cause to believe that the person has committed the crime, whether in the officer's presence or not.

Private citizens in New York may also make arrests, but the standards for them are far stricter than they are for police officers.

A *warrant of arrest* is a command in writing issued by a judge to arrest a person or persons. The judge, who may first have ordered a hearing, must have found a sufficient basis for believing that the person had committed the offense for which he or she is charged in the warrant.

All criminal prosecutions need not begin with arrest. A police officer may issue and serve an "appearance ticket" upon a person for certain less serious offenses. The appearance ticket requires the suspect to appear in court at a particular time. Appearance tickets are frequently used for traffic violations. If the person fails to appear in court in response to an appearance ticket, the judge may issue a summons or an arrest warrant. Appearance tickets may be issued by police officers without judicial approval. A *summons*, on the other hand, is issued by a judge to command a defendant to appear in court at a definite time.

Proceedings Before Trial

After an arrest has been made, the police officer should, without delay, perform the necessary police procedures, like booking and fingerprinting, and immediately bring the arrested person before a local criminal court. In court, the officer must file papers charging the individual in writing and in specific terms with the offense, and must also file other factual information explaining the basis for the criminal charge. When a person under sixteen is arrested, the police must inform the parents of the charges and of where the youth is being held.

When a person is brought before the court in response to an appearance ticket, a summons, or an arrest, with or without a warrant, the judge *arraigns* the defendant. At the arraignment the court informs the accused of the charges and furnishes him or her with a written copy of these charges. After an arraignment, the accused has a right to an attorney and certain other rights, including an adjournment to get an attorney, communication with others for the purpose of obtaining an attorney, and free services of an attorney if he or she cannot afford one (except in minor infractions of the law, like traffic violations).

Bail and Pretrial Release

After arrest, the subject of bail arises. Bail is the mechanism by which money or property is offered as security for the accused to guarantee his or her future appearances in court. The type and amount of bail required varies from case to case. In New York bail decisions depend on the severity of the crime, the prior record or background of the accused, the accused's community ties and employment record, and other information that indicates whether the accused is likely to return to court in the future. Often a defendant is *released on his or her own recognizance* or in the custody of friends or parents, which means that instead of money or property, a personal guarantee for the future appearance of the defendant in court is given. Bail jumping is a prosecutable crime.

Role of the District Attorney, Grand Jury, and Indictment

Traffic infraction cases are prosecuted less formally, but in criminal cases (felonies and misdemeanors), the police will remit a case file to the county prosecutor or district attorney, who will then assume responsibility. The district attorney has wide discretion in deciding whether to prosecute and, if so, to what extent. He or she may drop, compromise (adjust), or prosecute the charges to the full extent.

The Grand Jury

Felony cases are handled by the New York Supreme Court and, in some counties, the county court. Misdemeanor cases are handled by lower courts, often called local criminal courts, which have the authority to accept guilty pleas to misdemeanors even though the cases were originally charged as felonies. These local criminal courts may not accept guilty pleas to felonies, nor may they conduct felony trials.

   If the district attorney decides to prosecute a case, he or she will present it to a grand jury, which decides whether the evidence is sufficient to indict the accused. This decision is made by a majority of twenty-three grand jurors who have heard proof presented by witnesses summoned by the district attorney. If the grand jury finds legally sufficient evidence to establish that the defendant committed such offense, it will render an indictment, a written accusation describing the offense. Otherwise, the accused will not be charged.

Indictment

In New York, a new procedure has arisen in which a felony can be prosecuted without an indictment. Under this arrangement an accused may elect to waive or bypass the grand jury and choose instead to be prosecuted by a "superior court information."

After the indictment has been rendered or the information has been drawn up, the defendant then appears in the county or supreme court, where arraignment takes place on the charge. At this point the defendant will again be informed of his or her rights. The attorneys for the defendant will undertake certain pretrial procedures to protect their client's statutory and constitutional rights. These procedures include applications addressed to the court to review the adequacy of proof before the grand jury, applications to test the voluntariness and constitutionality of any claimed statement or confession, applications to examine any lineup or identification procedure used, and a host of other pretrial forms of relief, including motions to suppress evidence or hold separate trials for codefendants, or to discover evidence.

Plea Bargaining

Not all cases go to trial; indeed, the great majority do not. Many are settled by negotiated pleas or *plea bargaining*, a practice in which the prosecution and defense agree on a guilty plea that is less than the original charge or that involves a lesser sentence than the one corresponding to the charge. Other cases are dropped by the prosecutor for many reasons. For instance, important evidence may have been ruled inadmissible at a pretrial suppression hearing. Another form of plea bargaining is an agreement between prosecution and defense attorneys that a particular recommendation be made to the court, which is then free to act as it sees fit.

There is no uniform practice in New York State regarding plea bargaining; its use depends on the practices and personalities of the defense attorney, the district attorney, and the judge. In New York State, district attorneys and judges are elected and have freedom and discretion to follow their own policies and philosophies about plea bargaining. While policies on plea bargaining throughout the United States may change along with regional attitudes to some extent, plea bargaining occurs in virtually every jurisdiction. The legislative trend in New York State is to place limitations on plea bargaining, particularly in violent and armed felony cases. Under current conditions the New York State criminal justice system could not function if plea bargaining were eliminated and all cases came to trial.

Interrogations and Confessions

Both statutory and constitutional issues are involved in the use of a confession or statement (that is, the admissibility at trial of any statement made by a person to a law enforcement official, whether the statement incriminates or clears from blame).

Most of the rules concerning interrogation stem from the Fifth Amendment to the United States Constitution, which guarantees against self-incrimination. The Fifth Amendment restrains law enforcement officials in questioning about alleged criminal activities. The Constitution, state law, and common sense do not prohibit the use of confessions at trials. The law is, however, designed to protect individuals from encroachment by law enforcement officials and to guarantee that confessions or statements are the result of choices made by individuals voluntarily, with due regard to their own constitutional rights. The Fifth Amendment emphasizes *voluntariness,* a term that now has more than one legal meaning. Under the state criminal procedure law, for example, evidence of a written or oral statement made by a defendant is inadmissible if the statement is involuntary in the traditional sense; that is, if it was made after the use or threatened use of physical force or other improper conduct or undue pressure which undermined the person's ability to make the free choice whether or not to give a statement. This is involuntariness in its most commonly understood form. Other forms of involuntariness, such as statements obtained by promises, create a substantial risk that defendants might falsely incriminate themselves.

Other conditions besides threats or promises influence voluntariness. Before a person in police custody is questioned by law enforcement officials, he or she must receive and understand the *Miranda warnings* and then indicate a willingness to speak. These warnings include the right to remain silent, the knowledge that anything said will be used against him or her in court, the right to have an attorney present before questioning, and the right to have an attorney appointed if he or she has no money to hire one. Moreover, it must be made plain to the person that he or she has the right to stop the questioning at any point, and that the person questioned understands these rights and has freely decided to speak.

If law enforcement officials obtain a statement from a defendant in violation of these rules, the statement, and in most cases evidence that is derived from the statement, will be inadmissible at the trial against the defendant.

If an attorney contacts the police and forbids them to question his or her client, the police must desist, and may not question the defendant later when the attorney is absent. Recent case law has decided that once an arrest warrant has been issued against a defendant, judicial proceedings are held to have begun; and the police may not question the defendant in the absence of an attorney. Nor may they question an accused if they know he or she has an attorney in a pending criminal case.

There is a mistaken impression that failure to warn a person in custody of Miranda rights will result in a dismissal of charges.

Any statement taken in violation of a person's rights will result in the exclusion of that statement from a trial; but if there is other proof upon which to base a prosecution, the trial will take place. It is important to bear in mind that the police must give Miranda warnings only to persons *who are in custody*. A person not under police restraint may be questioned without having first been given the Miranda warnings. Whether the warnings are necessary in a particular case, and whether they have been given, understood, and waived, as well as other issues concerning voluntariness, are all determined by judges in pretrial proceedings called *Huntley hearings*, where the court hears proof. Then the court determines whether the statement or confession is admissible at trial. The jury decides at trial whether voluntariness has been established.

In May 1980 the United States Supreme Court defined an *interrogation* as occurring when the police subject a person in custody either to definite questioning or to words and actions that the police should know are reasonably likely to result in an incriminating response.

Bearing in mind that the Miranda warnings must be given when a person is *in custody*, debate has arisen over the definition of custody. The courts have held that the standard to be applied is whether a reasonable person, innocent of any crime, would have felt free to leave the place where the police were holding him or her.

The Trial

Juries are selected by the attorneys for both sides under strict control by the judge. There now is a trend toward swifter jury selection in New York, and greater judicial participation in the selection.

At the trial itself the jury will see and hear only admissible evidence. Questions regarding the admissibility of evidence or the means by which the defendant was identified are resolved by the judge away from the jury and normally before the trial. In New York a felony trial verdict is reached only after all twelve jurors agree. If the jury is not unanimous, there is no verdict; and a "hung jury" may be declared, resulting either in a new trial or in the case being dropped.

The court will appoint a free lawyer to indigent defendants, those who cannot afford to hire an attorney. There are no differences in the standards applied to lawyers who are hired and lawyers who are assigned to indigent defendants. They are treated exactly the same by the court, except that assigned lawyers may petition the court for funds for investigative purposes or for expert testimony and witnesses.

　　　The speedy trial laws require that a felony case be tried within six months of arrest, except for delays caused by the defendant.

Sentencing

Under the current state of the law, jail sentences for misdemeanors must be imposed as "flat" or "definite" sentences. The court must state that the defendant is sentenced to a definite period of incarceration. The period of imprisonment for a misdemeanor cannot exceed one year.

　　　In the felony category, however, courts are empowered to impose sentences of imprisonment in state institutions. Whenever a sentence of this kind is pronounced, the judge must state that the defendant is remanded to the custody of the New York State Department of Corrections. The period of imprisonment for a felony must be "indeterminate." The judge sets a "minimum" term, the least time a convicted person will have to serve, and a "maximum" term, the most time he or she may have to serve. These periods must fall within the range of sentences that correspond to the level of the crime involved. For example, the maximum period of imprisonment for a class E felony is four years.

　　　A person is eligible for parole after the minimum term of an indeterminate sentence has been served. For example, if the indeterminate sentence is three to ten years' imprisonment, the person may be paroled after serving the three-year minimum. Parole, however, is not automatic. The parole board may grant parole or deny it. If after serving the minimum period of imprisonment the person is denied parole, he or she has the right to a review by the parole board at least once every two years. The parole board has the right to continue to deny parole for justifiable reasons and to require the person to serve the maximum period of imprisonment.

　　　The sentencing structure in New York has been heavily influenced by legislative definition and categorization of new types of felonies.

　　　The number of crimes for which there is a mandatory or required prison sentence has been increased. While murder and certain first degree crimes, including arson, conspiracy, certain drug crimes, and kidnaping, have carried mandatory maximum life imprisonment terms with minimum terms of between fifteen and twenty-five years, the legislature has also provided for mandatory prison terms with varying minimum and maximum provisions for a host of other offenses in class B felony grade and in certain class C violent felonies. There is now a mandatory prison sentence of at least one year for anyone found guilty of possessing a loaded handgun on the street, and plea bargaining has been curtailed for these cases in order to assure mandatory sentencing. Thus a judge's discretion in some sentencing has been replaced by mandatory imprisonment provisions, even for first offenders. In the case of repeaters, mandatory sentencing provisions exist, with even more severe punishment contemplated by the legislature.

The legislature has also increased penalties for offenses involving the unlawful sale of handguns and has provided for increased mandatory prison sentences for persons who commit felonies by using handguns.

Justice for Juveniles

Under new provisions in the law, the adult criminal courts now conduct *juvenile offender* trials of cases against serious offenders thirteen to sixteen years of age. Formerly, cases for offenders in this age group were handled exclusively in family court, where sentencing provisions are far more lenient. But under new laws anyone over thirteen may be tried in an adult criminal court for intentional murder, and anyone over fourteen may be tried for attempted murder, first degree manslaughter, first degree kidnaping or attempted kidnaping, first degree arson and assault, first degree rape and sodomy, and first and second degree burglary and robbery. Such crimes are aggravated in degree when weapons or serious injury is involved.

For murder committed by a person thirteen to sixteen years old, there is a mandatory maximum term of life imprisonment, but the minimum term, the range for which is five to nine years, is considerably less than it is for those over sixteen. Thus, if anyone between the ages of thirteen and sixteen is convicted of intentional murder, the required minimum sentence is anywhere between five and nine years, at the judge's discretion; and the maximum must be life. The parole board will determine the date of release with provision for time off for good behavior.

There are provisions for removal (transfer) of such juvenile offender cases from adult court to family court, but removal to family court becomes less likely as the severity of the criminal charge increases.

Juvenile offenders of thirteen to sixteen who are tried in adult criminal court, are differentiated from the *youthful offenders*, who are age sixteen to nineteen. The *juvenile delinquent* classification is a family court term that applies to youths under sixteen.

If a juvenile offender is tried in adult criminal court, and the jury finds that he or she committed only the lesser crimes of the type to be tried in family court, the case will be transferred to family court for sentencing.

The judge may also order a transfer from adult court to family court under certain circumstances; but in the most serious cases, the judge may not remove a juvenile offender case to family court without the consent of the prosecution. The manner in which the crime was committed, the degree of participation of the minor in the crime, and difficulties in proving the crime are some of the factors in the decision.

three

CONSUMER

LAW

HOW NEW YORK LAWS PROTECT
THE CONSUMER

Public Agencies

Many *federal government agencies* that protect consumers have
regional offices in New York City, including the Federal Trade
Commission, the Food and Drug Administration, and the Consumer Product Safety Commission.

The state attorney general's office handles consumer complaints, and the state Consumer Protection Board helps people
find agencies for specific complaints (for example, the Public Service Commission for utility problems). Many of the larger localities in New York State also have *local agencies* like the New York
City Bureau of Consumer Affairs, which handles particular kinds
of consumer complaints.

The Courts

In New York State a person under eighteen years of age is considered a minor and can sue in court only through a guardian, a parent who has legal custody of the minor, or the minor's adult spouse.

In New York State, a consumer may bring a small claims suit in justice, city, district, or civil court if the case involves one thousand five hundred dollars or less. A consumer can recover only *money damages* in small claims court and cannot obtain any other relief such as the cancellation of a contract there. Corporations, partnerships, and associations must sue in a city or county civil court; however, attorneys may appear in small claims court.

New York State law also provides criminal penalties for various kinds of consumer frauds, including the following:

1. Falsely advertising a product by intentionally or recklessly making a false or misleading statement to a large number of people to induce them to buy the product

2. Knowingly charging an interest rate greater than twenty-five percent per year on any loan

3. Knowingly sending a person an imitation of a court document in an attempt to get that person to pay a debt

4. Understating or failing to state the interest rate on a loan when such a rate must be disclosed under the federal Truth in Lending Act, or making a false, inaccurate, or incomplete statement of any other credit term of the loan in violation of the Truth in Lending Act

5. Obtaining property from at least one person as the result of a scheme to defraud several people or as the result of making false representations or promises

DECEPTIVE SALES PRACTICES

All deceptive acts and practices by a business are unlawful. This law is very broad, leaving the courts to decide what specific acts and practices are *deceptive and unlawful.*

New York laws also prohibit some specific business practices. For instance, *false advertising*, any advertising that is misleading, is illegal. In determining whether advertising is misleading, the court considers both what the seller told the consumer and what the seller concealed from the consumer about the goods or services involved.

It is also unlawful to label goods falsely; to sell falsely labeled goods with knowledge of such falsity or with intent to defraud; or to represent goods as made by one manufacturer when in fact they are made by another and the goods do not show the identity of the real manufacturer.

Bait and Switch

It is unlawful in New York State for a seller to advertise goods or services for a price he or she does not intend to accept.

State law gives the New York State attorney general wide-ranging authority to investigate and forbid consumer fraud and to obtain restitution for defrauded consumers.

Door-to-Door Sales

When a purchase takes place away from the seller's place of business, a buyer of goods worth more than twenty-five dollars has three days from the date of purchase to inform the seller that he or she does not want to keep the goods. Written notice of the right to cancel must be provided to the consumer at the time of sale. A right to cancel protects the buyer from purchases resulting from high-pressured, door-to-door sales tactics. If the buyer cancels the sale, he or she must return the purchased goods to the seller.

Repair and Estimate Fraud

The general New York law on repair and estimate fraud regulates automobile repairs. All automobile repair shops must register with the New York State Department of Motor Vehicles. Upon the consumer's specific request, the shop must furnish a written estimate of parts and labor and may not charge for any other work without the consumer's consent. All labor performed and parts supplied must be recorded on an invoice which is then given to the consumer. If there is a request, the shop must return to the consumer all parts replaced.

Mail-Order Sales

No mail-order business may advertise merchandise or accept orders for merchandise that the business does not reasonably expect to have available within thirty days of advertising. If payment has already been received and a delay in delivery beyond thirty days occurs, the mail-order business must issue a refund, give the consumer credit, or send notice of the delay to the consumer. Such notice must give the option of returning the merchandise, when it finally arrives, for a refund of the purchase price and return postage if the delay has destroyed the consumer's wish for the merchandise.

Educational Contracts

Vocational schools in New York State may not seek to enroll students by assuring or seeming to assure employment after graduation; by making claims about potential earnings unless the claims reflect current information and can be documented; or by misrepresenting the experience or abilities required to complete a course of training successfully.

A student may cancel enrollment in a private vocational or business school and receive compensation. Compensation is dependent on when the cancellation occurs. All other fees and charges that have already been paid for goods and services not received must also be refunded.

If a student cancels enrollment in a correspondence course the school may retain five percent of the cash price of the course, at most fifty dollars; and a *pro rata* portion of the total price, representing the portion of goods and services already used or completed. The school may retain the cost of goods and services already used or completed and the cost of goods the consumer wishes to retain after cancellation. The school cannot collect more than the full contract price of the course as payment for goods and services already used or retained for personal use.

Utility Problems

Because most utilities that supply such basic services as telephone lines, gas, and electricity are monopolies, they are subject to state regulation of many of their business affairs, including the rates they charge customers. In New York State public utilities are regulated by the Public Service Commission, which has a consumer assistance unit to help consumers with problems with any commission-regulated utility.

Insurance

The insurance industry in the United States offers such a wide-ranging choice of insurance coverage that it is very difficult for consumers to protect themselves adequately against fraud. The State Insurance Department regulates the insurance industry in New York, and any complaints consumers may have about the practices of an insurance company or agent should be directed there.

Charity Fraud

There is increasing public concern that people who operate some charities spend a disproportionate amount of the money raised from contributions on salaries and other internal expenses, instead of directly on the causes. Sometimes the public may believe itself to be supporting charitable activities when only a small fraction of the funds collected are used for the solicited purposes. In even more severe cases, an entire "charity" may be only a fraudulent scheme to make money for the fund raiser.

The secretary of state and the state attorney general's office monitor and regulate the activities of charitable organizations in New York State.

Health Spa Regulation

In recent years the number of consumer complaints made against health spas has increased dramatically. As more people try to stay physically fit, fraudulent advertising and sales tactics enticing consumers into spending money on health spa services have also increased.

New York now has a series of laws enforced by the attorney general that regulate the practices of all health clubs, tennis clubs, figure salons, weight control centers, martial arts schools, and self-defense schools. Important features of the law include the establishment of an escrow account for funds paid by a consumer to a spa before it opens for business and a three-day "cooling off period" which allows a consumer to cancel a health spa contract within three days of signing.

TYPES OF CONTRACTS

Minors and Contracts

In New York the age of majority is eighteen. In most circumstances a contract entered into by a person under eighteen may be voided by the minor and is unenforceable while the person is under eighteen.

The law that a minor cannot be forced to carry out a contract has an important exception: a minor must pay the reasonable value of "necessaries" supplied to him or her if the parents are financially unable to pay. "Necessaries" are defined as food, shelter, and clothing.

Written and Oral Contracts

A contract that cannot be completely performed within one year or before someone dies, like a life insurance policy, is not valid unless the contract is in writing. Furthermore, all written consumer agreements must be drafted clearly and coherently, using words with common, everyday meanings rather than hard-to-understand legal language. Contracts with consumers cannot be written in small print.

If a buyer receives goods that have been ordered and the goods are not exactly as ordered, the buyer may accept all of the goods; reject all of the goods; or accept part and reject part of the goods. All rejections must be made within a reasonable time after delivery. If a buyer takes physical possession of the goods before rejecting them, he or she must care for them long enough for the seller to be able to collect them.

CONSUMER CREDIT

New York Consumer Credit Laws

Because credit buying is increasingly important in our economy, credit abuse by some lenders is a large problem. Various provisions of New York State law deal with the many problems of consumer credit, from a first establishment of credit to a last debt collection attempt.

Sources of Credit

The lending business is very competitive, and many moneylenders specialize in specific types of loans. Therefore, it is wise for those seeking credit to hunt for the source offering the best bargain in price, service, and convenience. Borrowers of money should check with commercial banks, savings and loans, industrial loan corporations (thrift institutions), credit unions, and finance companies. A dealer or retail store from whom a debtor's goods are being purchased may sell on credit or installment contracts. Pawnbrokers and loan sharks should be avoided because of the high interest they demand.

Disclosing Costs of Credit

In New York the federal Truth in Lending Act determines that costs and terms of credit are to be fully disclosed. It also controls these subcategories:

Interest Rates

Due to fairly recent changes in New York State law, the only remaining ceiling on interest rates relating to consumer credit transactions is the usury rate. Any person who charges more than usuary rate of interest is guilty of a felony.

Security Interests

Usually, only goods in the process of being bought can be used as collateral for a consumer transaction. For example, if a consumer is buying a car, the car can be put up as collateral; but the buyer's television set, which is already his or her property, may not be so used.

If a consumer fails to pay a loan or fails to pay the full price of goods bought on an installment payment plan, the lender or seller can take the collateral and sell it. The money from the sale is then used to pay the debt. If sale of the collateral results in more money than is needed to pay off the debt and the expenses of the sale, the surplus amount must be returned to the debtor. Sometimes the lender or seller is allowed to keep the collateral as payment for the debt. However, if the debtor has paid at least sixty percent of the loan, or at least sixty percent of the price of the goods purchased, if the goods are being used as collateral, the creditor cannot use the collateral to satisfy the debt without written permission from the debtor after default. If the debtor does not give written permission, the collateral must be sold and the money received from the sale used to pay the debt. In this case, too, any surplus from the sale is paid to the debtor.

What to Do if Credit Is Denied

In granting credit, it is unlawful under New York State law to discriminate on the basis of race, creed, color, national origin, sex, marital status, age, or disability. Complaints are filed with either the superintendent of banking or the New York State Division of Human Rights.

A New York State fair credit reporting law provides consumers with protection in addition to the protections of the federal Fair Credit Reporting Act.

A consumer applying for credit must be told that a credit report may be requested along with the application. A consumer may ask to learn whether a report has been requested from a credit bureau and the name and address of the agency that furnished the report. The consumer shall also be told that he or she may receive a copy of the credit report by contacting the credit bureau.

Anyone wishing to interview friends and neighbors of a consumer in order to gather information for a credit report must first obtain from the consumer written permission to conduct the interviews. If the consumer refuses to give permission, he or she may be denied credit.

Credit Insurance

Credit insurance is sold along with loans and credit sales. Credit life insurance, for example, will pay a loan if the borrower dies, and credit accident and disability insurance will make payments if a borrower is sick or disabled for an extended period. Although it is not required for many transactions, borrowers sometimes unwittingly purchase the insurance as part of a loan. Credit insurance is rarely a prudent purchase and should be avoided.

DEFAULT AND COLLECTION PRACTICES

Consumers who fail to make payments on credit transactions will eventually find that creditors will try to collect from them. Although collecting a legitimate debt by proper means is perfectly legal, consumers are given some significant protection against improper debt collection practices. In New York the State Debt Collection Procedures Law applies to the activities of original creditors as well as to the debt collecting agencies, while the federal law applies only to the activities of debt collection agencies.

Harassment

New York law prohibits creditors from using certain methods in collecting debts from debtors. A creditor cannot claim to be a law enforcement officer or a representative of any governmental agency; attempt to collect or assert a right to any fees unless the fees are legally due; disclose or threaten to disclose any information affecting the debtor's reputation for creditworthiness while knowing that the information is false; communicate or threaten to communicate the nature of a consumer claim to the debtor's employer before obtaining final judgment against the debtor; disclose or threaten to disclose information concerning the existence of a debt known to be disputed without disclosing the dispute; threaten any action that the creditor does not perform in the usual course of business; claim or threaten to enforce a right with knowledge that the right does not exist; or communicate or attempt to communicate with a debtor or his or her family with such frequency or at such unusual hours or in such a way that would seem abusive and harassing to a reasonable person.

Violation of any of these provisions constitutes a misdemeanor, and either the attorney general or the local district attorney handles complaints.

Court Action

Corporations, partnerships, and associations cannot sue their debtors in small claims court. These creditors may, however, file in local civil courts.

A summons is the legal document that informs a person he or she is being sued. To be sure the defendant understands why he or she is being sued, a summons used in an action arising out of a consumer credit transaction must display prominently at the top the words "consumer credit transaction" and must state the county, if it is within the state of New York, where the transaction took place. Further, such a suit may be brought only in the county where the contract was signed or in the county where the consumer resides.

Enforcement of Money Judgments

After a creditor has obtained a money judgment against a consumer who has not repaid a debt, the creditor can file an income execution with the debtor's employer. The creditor will then receive up to ten percent of the debtor's income. A creditor cannot file an income execution if the income is less than eighty-five dollars per week, and an employer cannot discharge an employee simply because an income execution is on file against him or her.

CARS AND THE CONSUMER

The New Car Lemon Law

New York State recently became one of the first states in the country to enact a law that requires a car dealer to buy back defective, unrepairable cars. This so-called "lemon law" covers new cars that are sold and registered in New York State and are normally used for personal, family, or household purposes. Motorcycles, motor homes, and off-road vehicles are not covered by the law. The law became effective September 1, 1983, applying to new cars purchased after that date.

The law imposes a duty of repair upon the manufacturer and its agent or authorized dealer. If a new car experiences a malfunction or defect within the first eighteen thousand miles or two years, whichever comes first, the dealer must repair the car free of charge. If the problem cannot be repaired in four attempts, or if the car is out of service for repairs for a total of thirty days or more during the first eighteen thousand miles or two years, and the problem "substantially impairs the value of the car," the buyer can begin a process of mediation that may lead to a full refund of the purchase price or a comparable replacement car. If the buyer is dissatisfied with the results of the mediation proceeding, or if the manufacturer does not participate in a mediation program that complies with Federal Trade Commission regulations, the buyer may file a lawsuit to attempt to get a full refund or a replacement car.

The Used Car Lemon Law

Even more recently, New York became the first state to pass a used car lemon law. The law covers any passenger car sold for one thousand five hundred dollars or more by a dealer in New York State. The law mandates that a written warranty with specific terms be given to the consumer at the time of sale. This warranty requires that repairs to components of the car covered by the warranty be made free of charge to the buyer during the warranty period. If the used car has thirty-six thousand miles or less, the warranty must last for at least sixty days or three thousand miles, whichever comes first. If the used car has more than thirty-six thousand miles, the warranty must last for at least thirty days or one thousand miles, whichever comes first. The warranty must cover all major parts of the engine, transmission, drive axle, brakes, radiator, steering, alternator, generator, starter, and ignition system. Furthermore, the law provides this warranty to the buyer even if the dealer fails to provide the warranty in writing.

If the dealer is unable to repair any problem after a reasonable number of attempts, and if the problem "substantially impairs the value of the used car," the dealer must accept the return of the car and make a full refund, including sales tax paid. Under the used car law, the dealer is limited to three attempts to repair the problem during the warranty period. Further, the car may not be out of service for more than a total of fifteen days for repairs during the warranty period. If these limits are exceeded, the consumer may avail himself or herself of the refund provision of the law.

As with the new car lemon law, if the dealer and consumer cannot agree on a resolution of a complaint, mediation will usually have to be undertaken as a first step to resolving the complaint. If the customer is not satisfied with the result of the mediation, or if the dealer does not participate in a mediation program that conforms with Federal Trade Commission regulations, the customer may file a lawsuit against the dealer to enforce his or her rights under the law.

Consumers buying used cars priced at less than one thousand five hundred dollars from dealers in New York do not receive the protections of the lemon law. However, another provision of New York law provides that no dealer in used automobiles may sell a used car that is not in the condition and repair necessary to render satisfactory and adequate service. The dealer must give the buyer a written certificate verifying that the car is in proper condition. The dealer can lose his or her license to sell used vehicles for failing to deliver a minimally serviceable car, or even for failing to give the required certificate. This law does not apply when a used car is bought from someone who is not a dealer.

four
FAMILY
LAW

MARRIAGE

Formal (Legal) Marriage

The right to marry is fundamental and is regulated by the state in the public interest. To prevent marriage between immature persons, the New York legislature has ruled that a couple must be eighteen years of age or older to be married without parental permission. A man or woman between the ages of sixteen and eighteen must obtain the written consent of both parents or of the surviving parent or guardian. If the parents are divorced then the custodial parent must give the required consent. When either person is under sixteen years of age, the written consent of the family or the supreme court is also necessary. No one under fourteen years of age can marry in New York State. A person on parole may marry only with the consent of the parole officer.

A marriage license can be issued without any tests for syphilis and gonorrhea. Any applicant who is not Caucasian, Indian, or Oriental must be tested for sickle-cell anemia, but a license may be issued even if this test is positive. An applicant may refuse to take this test because of religious beliefs.

Applications for marriage licenses are made before a town or city clerk. If the clerk is in doubt, proof of age must accompany the application. Divorce papers may also be necessary if there has been a previous marriage. Once all the documents have been presented, the fee paid, and the license issued, a twenty-four-hour waiting period is required before the marriage can take place. No marriage can be solemnized after sixty days from the date the license was issued. A court can waive this waiting period if an applicant is in danger of imminent death, or if an emergency exists or great hardship will occur.

Marriages may be performed by a priest, member of the clergy, rabbi, mayor, or judge, or by a police justice within the geographical jurisdiction to which the justice was elected.

The New York State Penal Law prohibits incestuous marriages between brothers and sisters, uncles and nieces, or nephews and aunts.

Common-Law Marriage

Common-law marriages occurring in New York State after 1933 are not valid. Common-law marriages occurring in other states, where such marriages are still allowed, will be recognized in New York State if there is sufficient evidence of a present agreement to live together as husband and wife while the couple is in the other state.

When a man and woman live together without a civil marriage license or without a common-law marriage, there is no obligation for one person to support the other, but an obligation to support may be legally enforceable when one person expressly agrees, orally or in writing, to support or maintain the other. Unlike the *Marvin* case from California, a support obligation cannot be based upon an *implied* agreement in New York.

Name Change

A wife may adopt the last name of her husband upon marriage, but she has no *legal obligation* to do so. Either spouse may continue to use her or his prior name either alone or combined with her or his spouse's name. Every person has a right to adopt any name he or she desires if the name is used consistently and without the intent to defraud.

HUSBANDS AND WIVES

Spouse Abuse

An abused spouse, in addition to seeking help from the police, the State Department of Social Services, the family court, or the hospital, can call without cost the Volunteer Center, Salvation Army, or Rescue Mission. Free legal services are also available. Counseling services for spouses and families include the Catholic Charities, the Al-Anon Family Group, hospital clinics, and the Women's Information Center.

PARENTS AND CHILDREN

Abortion

Under the Penal Law of New York, an act of abortion is defined as an act committed (1) upon a female, (2) by another person or by the female herself, (3) whether the female is pregnant or not, (4) either directly on the body of the female or by administering drugs or other manner, (5) with the intention to cause a miscarriage. An abortion is legal if it is performed with the female's consent, by a licensed physician believing that the abortion is necessary to save her life, or within twenty-four weeks from the commencement of her pregnancy. An abortion performed after the twelfth week of pregnancy can be performed only in a hospital, and the female must stay in the hospital until she has been discharged by a doctor.

Basic Rule of Parental Support

Children reach majority at age eighteen and are then legally responsible for themselves. Their parents, however, must continue to support them until age twenty-one unless the children do not require support because they have married, found gainful employment, or entered military service.

Duty to Support

Both parents are responsible for child support; the amount each contributes depends upon financial ability. Child support includes food, clothing, shelter, and medical and dental expenses, and may include other items like piano lessons, travel, and transportation expenses, depending on the family's prior standard of living and the parents' ability to pay for these expenses. Parents are not normally obligated to provide a college education for their children unless special circumstances exist, such as the ability to pay for college. A parent may not be obligated to support a minor child if the child has left the parental home without a good reason. A mere argument or parental disapproval of the child's conduct does not constitute good reason for a child to leave home. When a child unreasonably refuses to obey parental rules, the parents have no legal duty to support the child. If the child's parents are divorced and the child unreasonably refuses to maintain a relationship with his or her parents, the child may not be entitled to support.

Enforcing Family Court Support Order

Family court orders can be enforced in the following ways:

1. Directing the person to post a bond guaranteeing payment of the support

2. Authorizing an income execution through which support money will be deducted from the employee's pay by the employer

3. Placing the person in jail

4. Seizing the person's property and selling it to help pay for support

Parental Responsibility for Injury to the Child

A parent may use a reasonable amount of physical force in disciplining a child. What is legally "reasonable" depends upon the circumstances. A parent whose carelessness causes an accident that injures a child may be sued by the injured child for money damages, but a child may not sue a parent for injuries resulting from a lack of parental supervision. For example, a child may sue his or her father for driving an automobile negligently if the father caused an accident that injured the child, but not for failing to supervise the child if the child crossed the street and was hit by a car.

Child Abuse

A child who suffers substantial physical or emotional harm, including sexual abuse, from a parent is considered an *abused child*.

An example is a sick daughter neglected by an alcoholic mother. An abused child must be under eighteen years of age. Accidents resulting in a child's harm are not considered abuse.

Generally, the family court has jurisdiction in cases of abuse, and may, without a hearing, temporarily remove a child thought to be abused from his or her home to avoid an imminent danger to the child's life or health. The court must then notify the parents to appear in court and present a defense or explanation of their conduct. The court may issue an order protecting the child from any further harm before a hearing takes place.

The family court conducts two hearings in a child abuse case. The first hearing is fact-finding, in which the important facts are determined by a judge. The second hearing is dispositional, conducted after the family court has ruled that the facts prove the crime of child abuse. In the dispositional hearing the judge considers appropriate protection of the child from future harm, perhaps placing the abused child in a foster home or returning him or her to one parent or both under supervision of a child protection agency. These hearings are not public.

Child Neglect

A neglected child is one whose health is impaired by a lack of proper food, clothing, shelter, parental supervision, education, or medical care. A neglected child might be one whose parent refused to consent to a blood transfusion needed to save the life of the child or one whose parent suffers from drug addiction. In a neglect case the family court holds a fact-finding hearing and a dispositional hearing, as it does for child abuse. Child abuse ordinarily involves a more serious harm than neglect.

Doctors, police officers, hospital personnel, and social workers are required to report child abuse or neglect. Other people can call a toll-free number at the state capital, or the local department of social services hot line, to report child abuse or neglect. An investigation will begin within twenty-four hours after a child abuse call has been received. A police officer may remove a child from his or her home if an imminent danger to life or health exists.

Family Court Order of Protection

Abusive behavior by one spouse to the other spouse or to the children may result in the court issuing an order of protection. An order of protection directs the offending spouse to stop harassment or abuse or risk contempt of court, which could result in a jail term. The offending spouse can also be ordered out of the family home. The abused spouse or child can choose either the criminal court or the family court to handle the charges. A spouse need not be planning a divorce or separation action to obtain an order of protection. An order of protection may also be granted as part of a divorce or separation action.

FOSTER CARE AND ADOPTION

Guardians

A person under eighteen years of age is unable to make a legal claim in his or her own name. He or she must have a legal guardian act for him or her. Unless the court appoints a specific person, the parent having custody or, if there is no available parent, the person or agency having custody will act as guardian. In a lawsuit, any money realized on behalf of the minor is controlled by the court. It can be given to the guardian for the minor; or if the amount is more than three thousand dollars, the money is placed in a bank account for the minor until he or she is eighteen years of age. The money cannot be withdrawn without the consent of the court until the child is age eighteen.

Foster Care

Foster homes are under the jurisdiction of the Department of Social Services, which may place a child in a certified, licensed foster home under the supervision of the family court if the child is abused, neglected, abandoned, or destitute. Other alternatives can be placement with a parent or relative, placement in a local group home operated by a charity like the Salvation Army or the New York State Division for Youth, or placement in a home or an orphanage operated by a nonprofit private organization, like Boys Town.

The family court will continue to monitor placement of a foster child. After the child has been in foster care for eighteen months, the family court will review the placement and decide whether to return the foster child to the parent, continue foster care, or make the child eligible for adoption.

Illegitimate Children

An illegitimate child can inherit from his or her mother's estate without qualification. Only if an order has established the paternity of the child during the lifetime of the father or if the father has written an acknowledgement that the child is his can the child inherit from his or her father's estate. If the father is killed in an accident, an illegitimate child can share in the proceeds of a wrongful death claim without an order establishing paternity, because when a father dies, the illegitimate child suffers a loss of support just as a legitimate child does.

Illegitimate children are entitled to support by both fathers and mothers. To compel the father to support his illegitimate children, the family court must issue an order establishing that a particular person is the father of a child or children. The mother has twenty-one years after the birth of her child to establish the child's paternity. Blood tests may be used to prove or disprove the paternity of the father. A parent of an illegitimate child has visitation rights, which can be enforced by a court unless a parent has abandoned a child.

Adoption

An adoption is not valid unless it is approved by order of the family court or the surrogate's court. A person to be adopted may be of any age, even over twenty-one years. Usually the natural parents of the child, whether the child is legitimate or illegitimate, must consent to the adoption unless they have abandoned the child. Whenever practicable, the adopting parents will be of the same religion as the child. The court will decide whether it will allow an adoption between a child and parents of different religious backgrounds. The race of the child is not determinative; for example, a white parent may adopt a black child. Once the adoption is approved by the court, the natural parents have no more rights to the child, and the child can no longer inherit from his or her natural parents. The adopted child has the same support and inheritance rights from his or her adoptive parents as a natural child.

Stepchildren

A stepparent has no obligation to support a stepchild unless the stepchild is likely to need welfare assistance. A stepchild cannot inherit from a stepparent unless a will gives the stepchild a bequest, and a stepparent cannot inherit from a stepchild without bequest.

ENDING MARRIAGE

Void and Voidable Marriages

A void marriage is a marriage the law does not recognize. An example might be an incestuous marriage or one in which a prior marriage had not been dissolved by law or death. Although a void marriage does not require a court declaration to make it void, a man or woman may ask the court to declare formally that the marriage is invalid.

A voidable marriage is treated as invalid from the time the court decides it is not legal, but a void marriage never existed.

Annulment

An annulment action can be started to determine whether a marriage is void or to invalidate a voidable marriage. The grounds for an annulment are as follows:

1. Nonage—One spouse was not of legal age and could not legally consent to the marriage. However, the minor, upon reaching legal age, may ratify the marriage by continuing to live with the spouse, thus preventing an annulment of the marriage. When the spouse is under eighteen years of age, a parent or guardian may start an annulment action on behalf of the minor; or with permission of the court, any person may begin annulment proceedings as an interested friend of the minor. A parent of an underage spouse may or may not be able to bring an annulment action based on nonage against the wishes of the underage spouse. A spouse over eighteen cannot start an annulment based upon the nonage of his or her spouse.

2. Idiocy—One of the spouses was an idiot or a lunatic at the time of marriage and thus was unable to understand and consent freely. If restored to a sound mind, the former lunatic may ratify the marriage by continuing to live with the other spouse.

3. Fraud—The spouse's consent to marry was obtained through force, fraud, or duress. For example, one spouse had promised before the marriage to convert to the innocent spouse's religion but never had intended to carry out that promise.

4. Physical incapacity—One spouse was unable to have sexual relations with the other spouse.

5. Incurable insanity—Either spouse had been incurably insane for more than five years of married life.

Separation

Many spouses will resolve their differences when they separate by signing a separation agreement. This agreement is usually made part of a divorce decree because it contains their decisions regarding their property, children, and finances. A court can later increase the support provisions made for children in a separation agreement only if important and unanticipated reasons for a change have developed or if the support is inadequate. However, maintenance for a spouse stated in a separation agreement can be changed by court order when the paying spouse experiences extreme financial hardship such as loss of employment. A spouse may waive the right to receive present or future maintenance in a separation agreement. If so, only extreme financial hardship such as becoming eligible for welfare assistance or loss of employment would enable a spouse to receive future maintenance.

Every separation agreement presented to the court must be fair and reasonable when made and not grossly unfair when the court reviews it. If a separation agreement is unfair or not voluntarily made by both spouses, or if one spouse has forced or tricked the other spouse into signing, the court can invalidate all or parts of the separation agreement.

Furthermore, the court has the right to make its own inquiry concerning custody of the children, although the custody agreement of the parties will carry much weight.

Legal Separation

The fault grounds for a divorce are the grounds for a separation judgment granted by the court. Under certain circumstances an additional ground for a separation judgment is nonsupport by a spouse.

Sometimes one spouse will ask for a legal separation because it does not dissolve the marriage and allows the spouses to reconsider their problems and perhaps to be reconciled. A separation judgment will provide for child support, maintenance for either spouse, custody of the children, right to live in the family home, visitation rights to the children, and lawyers' fees.

Most religious organizations provide marriage counseling services, and some family courts offer *reconciliation services.* Private counseling centers will charge based upon your ability to pay. Most private counselors will charge fifty to ninety-five dollars an hour, depending on the location. Public or religious counseling is free or costs less per hour.

Many cities have mediation centers where husbands and wives go to resolve their differences over custody, support, property, and financial issues. These centers usually do not reconcile parties but instead resolve their problems regarding the separation or divorce.

Divorce

In New York a divorce may be granted on one of these grounds:

1. Adultery

2. Cruel and inhuman treatment

3. Abandonment or desertion for one year or more

4. Imprisonment for a period of three years or more

5. Living separately and apart according to a separation decree or separation agreement for a period of one year or more

A divorce action may begin in New York State if at least one spouse has been a continuous resident of the state for one year. An uncontested divorce takes several months; a contested divorce takes one to two years. Once the divorce has been granted and the divorce decree has been filed in the clerk's office of the county where the action was started, the divorce is final. Either spouse may remarry thereafter without a waiting period.

Child Custody

By law each parent has an equal right to child custody, but children are usually awarded to the mother. The premise is that mothers can give children, especially young children, more time and affection than can fathers, who are usually working. Today fathers are arguing to change this traditional arrangement, and courts are realizing the importance of ties between fathers and children. As a child grows older, he or she may express a preference to live with one of the parents, but the judge makes the final decision, considering the best interests of the child. Sometimes the court will award joint custody, but only if the parents will cooperate peacefully for the good of the child. If the child has been living for a long time with a nonparent and has become emotionally attached to that person, the judge might not force the child to return to either parent, leaving the child in the environment best suited to his or her emotional and physical stability and growth. However, parents usually will be given a priority over other people in custody matters.

Once custody has been determined by agreement of the parents or the judge, the provisions of custody can be changed only by a substantial change in the circumstances. For example, the parent might become a drug addict and would no longer be fit to supervise the child.

Once the court has awarded custody of a child, a noncustodial parent cannot interfere with the arrangements. Any interference is a crime. A parent has to apply to the court to make changes in custody.

Courts have recognized that visitation by the noncustodial parent, usually the father, is extremely important to the child. If the mother interferes with this relationship by *intentionally* denying the father visitation rights, the judge may remove the child from the custody of the mother and place him or her with the father. The court can also excuse a parent from paying alimony and/or child support until his or her visitation rights are restored.

Child Support, Maintenance, and Property Division

Both parents must support their children. The amount of support depends upon the financial needs of the child and each parent's ability to pay the support. There are no fixed formulas determining the amount of child support or maintenance a spouse must make. The spouses agree on the amount of child support or maintenance, or the court determines the amount. Either spouse may be ordered to pay maintenance to the other, depending on a number of factors: the length of the marriage, the ability of the spouse to support herself or himself, the health and ages of the spouses, and the income and resources of the spouses. Before 1980, if the court granted a divorce because one of the spouses had been at fault, that spouse could not receive alimony. A new law states that after July 19, 1980, the fault of the spouse seeking maintenance for himself or herself is not a bar to receiving maintenance. Now even a spouse who commits adultery may receive maintenance. In its order, the court may change the amount of child support or maintenance for a spouse when there have been changes in circumstances. Maintenance for a spouse can be limited to a fixed period of time or may be for an unlimited period of time.

Before July 19, 1980, a husband or wife in New York State did not share property that the other spouse acquired before, during, or after the marriage. After July 19, 1980, the property acquired by the husband and/or wife during the marriage and before divorce is equitably divided at the time of divorce. Property acquired during the marriage is thus divided between husband and wife regardless of ownership. The new law recognizes marriage as a partnership, with each spouse contributing toward their joint acquisition of property in different ways. Usually the court will not consider fault when it divides the property. The court can give to either spouse the exclusive right to live in the family home for a certain period of time, and it usually gives this right to the parent having custody of the children. When dividing property, the court will consider factors similar to those it considers when awarding maintenance. In addition, it will consider special factors such as the loss of inheritance and pension rights and the contributions made by one spouse to the career of the other spouse. The division of property between the spouses need not be equal; it must only be equitable.

Not all property acquired during marriage is subject to an equitable division when a divorce takes place. If property is acquired during the marriage through an inheritance or gift from someone besides the other spouse, it can be considered separate, and not subject to equitable division. Property owned by one spouse before the marriage is separate and is not divided between the spouses. But if the property appreciates in value, as real estate may, the value of the appreciation may be divided between the spouses. The husband and wife can, by agreement, decide the property to be equitably divided and the property to be left separate from equitable division. If they cannot agree, the court will make the equitable division of the property.

Even when no divorce or separation action has begun, a spouse, usually the husband, may be considered legally responsible for the basic living expenses of the family. The law implies an obligation upon the husband to provide necessities for the family based upon his income and financial resources.

GOVERNMENT SUPPORT FOR NEEDY FAMILIES

The rules governing eligibility for state programs are very complex. Several categories are as follows:

1. A person receiving Social Security benefits can also receive supplemental welfare assistance, depending to a large degree on the size of the family. A person receiving supplemental assistance is eligible for Medicaid and food stamps.

2. A person receiving Supplemental Security Income (SSI) is entitled to Medicaid and food stamps.

3. A poor person or family not receiving any federal benefits is eligible for public assistance as well as Medicaid and food stamps.

A person receiving public assistance is eligible for the Work Incentive Program, which offers vocational training for jobs like nurse's aide, welder, or secretary, and which provides day care services for children. The program also trains the mentally retarded for jobs like guard and janitor.

Applications for Social Security and Medicaid benefits are made to the local Social Security office. In each county, applications for Medicaid and public assistance are made to the office of the Department of Social Services.

Applications for unemployment insurance benefits are made to the local New York State Department of Labor, Unemployment Insurance Division. In 1982, the minimum unemployment insurance benefit was twenty-five dollars per week, and the maximum was one hundred twenty-five dollars per week.

Handicapped children are guaranteed special teachers paid by the school district to give special instruction. Deaf children have special teachers provided by the state.

The Mental Health Department operates foster and group homes for adults and children who need special supervision. Emotionally retarded children in institutions within the state can be supported by the school district in which the children originally lived.

Parents eligible to receive Aid to Families with Dependent Children (AFDC) from the New York State Department of Social Services receive allowances for basic support and shelter. Generally, AFDC recipients are eligible for Medicaid and food stamps.

In New York, public assistance is available to families when one or both parents are unable to work because of illness; when one or both parents have died and the child is living with a relative or stepparent; when one or both parents have deserted the child; or when one or both parents have been unemployed for over thirty days.

DEATH, WILLS, AND INHERITANCE

Any competent person eighteen years old or older can make a will. When someone dies *without* a will, all his or her property is distributed according to the laws of *intestacy*. In New York, these laws can be summarized as follows:

1. Surviving spouse, no surviving children, and no surviving parent—The spouse takes all.

2. Surviving spouse and one surviving child—The surviving spouse takes four thousand dollars and one-half of the balance. The child receives the balance.

3. Surviving spouse and more than one surviving child—The surviving spouse takes four thousand dollars and one-third of the balance. The children divide the balance equally.

4. Surviving spouse, no surviving child, and one or both surviving parents—The surviving spouse takes twenty-five thousand dollars and one-half of the balance. The parent or parents receive the balance.

5. No surviving spouse, children, or parents—The brothers and sisters receive equal shares of everything.

A will must be written, and two witnesses to the signing of a valid will are required.

five
HOUSING
LAW

The rights and obligations of New York landlords and tenants are governed by both state law and local city and county laws.

ANTIDISCRIMINATION IN HOUSING AND ENFORCEMENT

In New York both state law and local city and county laws forbid a landlord from discriminating on the basis of race, creed, color, religion, sex, or national origin. A landlord may not refuse to rent on those bases, and some city or county laws also forbid discrimination in housing against homosexuals and families with children. However, the law does not prevent some kinds of discrimination; for instance, in one case the court allowed a landlord to decide that he would not rent to a lawyer. An owner of a two-family residence may rent the second unit as he or she pleases while the owner or members of the owner's family occupy one unit.

Complaints of unlawful discrimination in housing transactions should be filed with the New York State Division of Human Rights. (See address in Appendix.)

RENTING A HOME

The Lease

A lease is a contract between landlord and tenant on the terms of rental. The agreement may be either written or oral, but if it is a valid agreement to rent for a year or more it must be in writing and must be in plain English so that the terms are clearly understandable, with all rights and duties set forth. A lease usually contains the names and addresses of the parties; the dates on which the occupancy will begin and end; the address of the premises and a brief description of the property; the amount of rent and the date on which it is due; the number and identities of occupants who will reside in the premises; whether pets are allowed; and other terms regarding the conditions of tenancy. In New York many leases are printed on a standard form which can be bought in a stationery store that carries legal documents.

Landlord-Tenant Negotiations

In many areas of New York housing is severely limited, and often a tenant must accept any available apartment on the terms proposed by the landlord. A prospective tenant should, however, try to include his or her particular needs in the lease. A certain amount of negotiation—on dates of payment, for example—is possible.

RIGHTS AND DUTIES OF LANDLORDS AND TENANTS

Duties of the Landlord

The landlords' duties and obligations are specified in various state and city laws as well as in the provisions of the lease. Essentially, landlords are required to maintain the premises in good repair and in a safe, livable condition in compliance with state and local housing laws. For instance, in New York City the Multiple Dwelling Law requires specifically that in cold weather an apartment must be provided with at least sixty-eight degrees of heat each day between 6 A.M. and 10 P.M.

In some instances landlords are held liable for injuries occurring on their property. For example, if landlords fail to comply with laws requiring security measures, courts may hold them responsible for robberies resulting from the lack of security.

Duties of Tenants

The basic duties and obligations of tenants are recognized in the provisions of a lease. In general, tenants are required to maintain the premises in good condition, to comply with the terms of lease, to refrain from making any structural changes, and to pay the rent at the required time. The tenants are also required to permit landlords to enter the premises for repairs, emergencies, and other valid purposes at reasonable times and upon advance notice. Failure to fulfill these duties can result in tenants being "evicted," or forced to move out of the rented property.

Warranty of Habitability

The New York Real Property Law recognizes an *implied warranty of habitability* in every lease for residential purposes. Under this section of the law landlords have the duty to maintain residential premises in a safe and habitable condition. If a landlord fails in this duty, a tenant may charge the landlord in court with a breach of the warranty of habitability. If the proof submitted convinces the court that the premises are unsafe or hazardous, the court may order the rent to be reduced. The amount of rent reduction depends upon the severity of the problem as shown by the evidence; for instance, if a tenant proves that the bathroom cannot be used and that the tenant must go elsewhere to bathe, the court may greatly reduce the rent, perhaps by fifty percent. If the court finds that a landlord fails to provide heat between 12 P.M. and 2 P.M. each day, it would probably award a smaller reduction in rent.

Security Deposit

At the time of renting, a tenant may be required to deposit a month's rent with the landlord as security against damage to the property. The landlord may not mingle the money collected as security in an account with other money. He or she must place the money in a separate bank account. The law requires that the landlord deposit this security in an interest-bearing account, that the landlord tell the tenant what bank the security is deposited in, and that the landlord annually pay the tenant the interest the security deposit earns. The landlord is entitled to keep one percent of the annual interest earned by the security deposit as a fee for administering the bank account.

Sublease of a House
or an Apartment

The law prohibits the landlord from unreasonably withholding the right to sublet. For instance, a landlord may be held to be acting unreasonably if he or she does not give the tenant permission to sublet to a colleague for four months while the tenant must be out of town if the colleague who wants to sublet is responsible, can afford the rent, and is willing to assume the obligations established in the lease. If the landlord refuses to allow the sublet, the tenant may break the lease and move out. The landlord would then have no right to hold the tenant liable for rent.

Raising the Rent

A lease will state the amount of rent to be charged. City laws in some cases determine and control the amount of rent a landlord may charge. In New York City and in certain other cities in the state, two laws govern rent: the Rent Control Law and the Rent Stabilization Law. These laws control the maximum amount of rent a landlord may charge and the terms of a lease. If a lease covers two years, the rent charged may not be increased during that two-year period. After the lease has expired, the rent may be increased; but if the property is covered by either the Rent Control Law or the Rent Stabilization Law, any rent increase will be limited by those laws. If there is a rent increase, the lease should be checked to see whether the property is covered by any state or local law governing rent increases. Questions regarding apartment rentals may also be raised with the New York State Division of Housing and Community Renewal.

Tenants who are sixty-two years of age or older, who have a certain minimum annual income, and who pay more than one-third of their income for rent may be eligible for a *senior citizen rent increase exemption.* A local rental or housing office will give information about this rent increase exemption. In New York City a tenant should check with the New York City Housing and Preservation Department. After a tenant has obtained a senior citizen rent increase exemption, a landlord may not raise the rent.

Eviction

A landlord cannot evict a tenant unless there is a court proceeding in which the tenant is given notice and an opportunity to appear in court, and the court issues an order of eviction. Only a sheriff or marshal can carry out an eviction—remove a tenant's belongings from the premises. A landlord may not go into the premises and remove the tenant's belongings. Nor may a landlord lock a tenant out unless a court first grants the landlord an order of eviction. A tenant who is evicted without a court order may sue the landlord, and if the tenant wins in court the landlord may be required to pay treble damages.

Apartment Sharing

The law entitles a tenant named on the lease to share the apartment with immediate family and with one additional occupant, who need not be related to the tenant, and with the occupant's dependent children. Tenants are required to tell the landlord about this additional occupant within thirty days.

six
INDIVIDUAL RIGHTS AND LIBERTIES

THE FEDERAL AND NEW YORK STATE CONSTITUTIONS

The United States Constitution guarantees, primarily through the Bill of Rights, certain basic liberties to all citizens of the United States. The Constitution of the State of New York also assures fundamental rights to the residents of the state.

Comparison of certain provisions of the two constitutions demonstrates the similarity in rights granted by both. For example, the First Amendment to the United States Constitution provides for freedom of speech, press, and religion, and for the right of the people to assemble and petition the government to correct injustices. The New York State Constitution also protects free speech and press in Article Eight, guarantees freedom of worship in Article One, Section Three, and ensures the rights of the people to peaceably assemble and to petition the government in Article Nine.

The Fourth Amendment to the federal Constitution prohibits unreasonable searches. The Fifth Amendment protects against self-incrimination and double jeopardy. The Sixth Amendment recognizes the rights to counsel and speedy trial in criminal cases. Article One, Sections Five and Six of the state constitution provide similar guarantees, including the rights to grand jury indictment, due process, counsel, confrontation of adverse witnesses, freedom from self-incrimination, protection against double jeopardy, and prohibitions against excessive bail, fines, or cruel and unusual punishments.

The basic rights of New York citizens are thus protected by both the state and federal constitutions. If these freedoms are violated, relief is available through the courts, or in some instances through government agencies.

FREEDOM OF SPEECH

Obscenity

Following the guidelines established by the United States Supreme Court, the New York State Legislature has formulated a definition of obscenity similar to the one outlined on page 314 of this text. The New York Penal Law has defined obscenity in the following language:

Any material or performance is "obscene" if (a) the average person, applying contemporary community standards, would find that considered as a whole, its predominant appeal is to the prurient interest in sex, and (b) it depicts or describes in a patently offensive manner, actual or simulated: sexual intercourse, sodomy, sexual bestiality, masturbation, sadism, masochism, excretion or lewd exhibition of the genitals, and (c) considered as a whole, it lacks serious literary, artistic, political, and scientific value. Predominant appeal shall be judged with reference to ordinary adults unless it appears from the character of the material or the circumstances of its dissemination to be designed for children or other specially susceptible audience.

The latter part of this definition refers to the special status of minors as a susceptible audience needing protection. The Penal Law lists separate provisions making it a felony to disseminate indecent material, including photographs, movies, books, pamphlets, and magazines, to minors. This statute defines a minor as any person less than seventeen years of age; and the rules for testing what constitutes "harmful material" are phrased in terms similar to those used in defining obscenity.

FREEDOM OF THE PRESS

Court Proceedings

As indicated in the text, a defendant's request to exclude the public and news media from pretrial hearings in criminal cases may be allowed under certain circumstances. The court must balance the right of the accused to a fair trial against the right of the public to attend the proceedings. Seemingly slight variations in the facts may cause different decisions. For example, the New York State Court of Appeals upheld a lower court decision excluding the public from a pretrial suppression hearing in a murder case in which the admissibility of the defendant's confession was at issue. The Court of Appeals decided that closing a hearing to the public might be necessary to protect the defendant's right to a fair trial and to ensure that prospective jurors not hear matters that might prejudice them. In another decision, the Court of Appeals determined that the public should not have been excluded from a pretrial hearing in a criminal case in which the defendant's competency to stand trial was in question. Because the question of competency dealt with the defendant's mental state at the time of trial and not at the time when the crime was alleged to have taken place, news accounts would not have created a danger of prejudicing the opinions of potential jurors.

The right of the public to attend court proceedings is not absolute; and when the accused's right to a fair trial is jeopardized, competing interests must be balanced by a judgment based on circumstances.

FREEDOM OF INFORMATION LAW

Public access to information is not limited to attendance at court proceedings. In New York, a related question concerning the degree to which the records and proceedings of government agencies should be open to public inspection is addressed by the Freedom of Information Law and the Open Meetings Law. In enacting these statutes the legislature recognized that the maintenance of a free society depends on a government responsive to the public, and that the public should be aware of government actions and should be able to observe the deliberations of public bodies. The legislature further recognized that the more open a government is with its citizens, the greater will be public participation in its processes.

The federal Freedom of Information Law requires state and municipal agencies to issue rules governing the availability of records and the procedures to be followed by those who want to examine documents. The rules cover items such as the times and places records are available, the persons from whom records may be obtained, and the fees for procuring copies.

Every record need not be disclosed to the public; the statute notes certain exclusions such as exemption of records from disclosure by law, or a situation where disclosure would constitute an unwarranted invasion of personal privacy, or a situation where revelation would endanger the life or safety of any person. Information compiled for law enforcement purposes is exempted if disclosure would interfere with law enforcement investigations or judicial proceedings, deprive a person of a fair trial, identify confidential sources of information, or reveal nonroutine criminal investigative techniques.

The Freedom of Information Law outlines the functions of the Committee on Open Government, which has the power to furnish advisory guidelines and establish rules to carry out the provisions of the statute. The law also lists general review procedures which may be followed by individuals who have been denied access to records.

The Open Meetings Law states that meetings of a public body shall be open to the general public with advance notice, but that certain items, such as matters relating to litigation or the discipline of particular employees, may be discussed in executive session. The Open Meetings Law also contains provision for enforcement, including the power of the courts under certain circumstances to declare invalid actions taken at meetings that have not been conducted in conformity with the statute.

REQUIRING THE PRESS TO DISCLOSE INFORMATION

The New York Civil Rights Law provides protection for reporters' sources of information. By its provisions, professional journalists and newscasters may not be held in contempt by any court, legislature, or other body possessing contempt powers. Nor may a grand jury seek to have reporters held in contempt for refusing to disclose any news or news source coming into their possession while they are gathering news for publication by newspapers, magazines, radio, or television stations with which they are associated, even though the information is not relevant to the investigation, and regardless of whether it was solicited or volunteered.

Courts have interpreted this law as the protection only of information that has been received by the reporter under *cloak of confidentiality*. For example, in one case an attempt was made to declare invalid a subpoena issued by a district attorney because the subpoena had sought the production of outtakes from a televised interview with an individual charged with the sale of arms to foreign terrorists. The court refused to invalidate the subpoena because it found that there could be no expectation of confidentiality in this situation, since the defendant had agreed to the interview with the understanding that any or all of it could be televised.

FREEDOM OF EXPRESSION IN SCHOOLS

As described in chapter six of part one, the First Amendment applies to schools; but because educational institutions are unique in nature, the freedom of expression allowed there is more limited than that afforded the general public. School authorities have the right to establish reasonable regulations governing student publications based on their responsibility to supervise the development and education of young people. Thus when First Amendment freedoms clash with school regulations, courts have to balance the two interests in making a decision.

An example is a case in which a high school principal refused to allow publication of an anti–Vietnam War advertisement in a student newspaper. He argued that the newspaper should be limited to school activities, while the students contended that his decision prevented the free expression of their ideas. Because the newspaper had previously been allowed to publish material dealing with controversial, extracurricular topics, the right of students to express their views in the school newspaper was upheld by the court.

FREEDOM OF RELIGION

Establishment Clause

An area of delicate balance is found when religious freedom and public education meet. Under the United States Constitution, church and state must be kept separate. Pupils may not receive religious instruction in public schools. In recognizing the right to religious freedom, however, New York State permits parents to educate their children outside the public schools if the religious or other private schools meet the state's minimum educational requirements. Parents who desire their children to be educated in public schools but want to have them withdrawn for a certain period of time each week to receive religious instruction elsewhere under a "released time program" may receive permission to do so.

Free Exercise Clause

The balancing of the claims of religious freedom and public education may be seen in immunization rules for school children. The law requires that children attending public school be immunized against certain diseases such as polio and smallpox; however, immunization is not required if the parents are members of a religious sect whose teachings disapprove of this practice.

Laws regulating Sunday sales in New York developed over many years, while there was a general prohibition against public selling of merchandise on Sunday, a religious holiday. However, many exceptions to this general ban were created. Milk, eggs, ice, fruit, souvenirs, antiques, newspapers, magazines, cemetery monuments, drugs, gasoline, tires, and thoroughbred racehorses, by auction, could all be sold publicly on Sunday. This partial listing gives some idea of the extent and variety of the exceptions. The Sunday sales law was challenged and was declared unconstitutional by the Court of Appeals, which found the mixture of exceptions to the general closing law to be without reason or order. The court noted that lack of enforcement and public disregard for the law showed how irrational it had become. In finding the law unconstitutional, however, the court suggested that new legislation be drafted that would be both acceptable to the public and enforceable.

THE RIGHT TO PRIVACY

Privacy in the Home

The extent to which a person may expect the right to privacy will vary with the place, circumstances, and activity. In one case a person was permitted to possess obscene materials at home for private use. However, if that same person had opened a theater to show movies publicly, he or she might have been subjected to criminal prosecution in New York State. In similar fashion people may smoke cigarettes at home or in their automobiles but are subject to restrictions in public places or on public transportation. Certain criminal activities, however, including possession of dangerous drugs such as heroin, are prohibited in either a public place or the privacy of a home.

The protection of privacy of New York residents against *wiretapping* or "bugging" by police agencies is also strictly safeguarded by law. A warrant based on probable cause is required before a wiretap is begun, and the warrant must particularly describe the types of conversation to be intercepted and the crimes involved. A time limit is placed on the wiretapping warrant, and the issuing judge may require progress reports to be made. After the wiretapping has ended, the judge orders the recordings to be sealed to prevent any tampering, and notice that wiretapping has taken place is given to the individuals named in the warrant.

Privacy at School

Students enjoy certain constitutional safeguards of their privacy, although not to the same degree as adults. High school students are protected from unreasonable searches in school by employees of the state, whether the employees are police officers or teachers.

New York courts have recognized that public school teachers are responsible for the discipline and security of students, but teachers are forbidden from conducting random, causeless searches. In determining whether a reasonable basis exists to search a student, New York's highest court has provided some factors to be considered, including the pupil's age, history, and record in school; the prevalence and seriousness of the school problem for which the search is being conducted; and the need to make the search without a delay.

The United States Supreme Court has indicated that searches of students will be upheld if reasonable grounds exist for suspecting that the search will turn up evidence of a violation of the law or of school rules, and when the measures used are reasonably related to the purpose of the search and are not excessively intrusive when measured against the age and sex of the student and the nature of the violation involved.

A different situation is presented by the police search of a high school student's locker upon consent of school authorities who have a master key and a copy of the lock combination. Under such circumstances a student may have exclusive possession of the locker against other pupils, but not against the school administration. A student cannot reasonably expect privacy in a locker over which the school authorities have retained control.

Privacy on the Job

In New York it is unlawful for employers or their agents to require, request, or even suggest that employees or prospective employees submit to a lie detector test, called a "psychological stress evaluator" by the statute. Should an employer attempt to administer such a test, the law declares that no employee may be discharged, disciplined, or discriminated against for filing a complaint or testifying against the violation.

Information Gathering and Privacy

Administrative agencies, such as the State Liquor Authority, are bound to observe the constitutional protection of privacy. While the constitution may not limit certain narrowly defined and reasonable inspection procedures, the state may not require as a condition of doing business that a person give what is really blanket permission to a state agency to conduct warrantless searches at any time and for any purpose. When a state agency has exceeded constitutional limits in conducting a search, it will not be permitted to use the results of the unlawful search to impose sanctions on the person whose rights have been violated.

New York also has enacted the personal privacy Protection Law, which governs the disclosure of personal information and records by state agencies. This statute requires state agencies to establish procedures whereby individuals may have access to records pertaining to them and may obtain correction of inaccurate information. Certain data, such as investigatory material compiled by the state police, are exempt from access for reasons of security and confidentiality.

DUE PROCESS

Criminal Proceedings

Due process requirements apply to criminal proceedings in New York. Statutes that define crimes must give fair notice to people of ordinary intelligence that certain actions are forbidden. A person charged with a felony or a misdemeanor has a *right to counsel* and must be advised that a lawyer will be appointed by the court if he or she cannot afford one. A defendant has the right to assistance of a lawyer before pleading guilty. Like all constitutional rights, the right to counsel may be knowingly and voluntarily waived by an individual charged with a crime. However, no right to a lawyer exists in prosecutions for traffic violations.

Under the due process clause, a parolee has a right to counsel at a parole revocation hearing. Because a parolee's freedom or imprisonment depends on the board of parole's decision, the revocation hearing involves a possible deprivation of liberty just as the original criminal prosecution did, and the guarantee of legal representation at a revocation hearing is thus warranted.

Civil Proceedings

Due process protection may also be applicable in certain civil and administrative proceedings, such as disciplinary actions against public employees; however, these rights can be waived if the employee wishes.

Due Process in Schools

Due process rights attach to administrative proceedings involving high school students. A pupil may be suspended for insubordinate or disorderly conduct; but if the suspension is to exceed five days, the student and his or her parent or guardian must be given, upon reasonable notice, the opportunity for a fair hearing at which the student may be represented by counsel and may question the witnesses.

Teachers in many circumstances will be held to a standard of reasonableness. For example, they are permitted to use physical force to discipline students, but the use and degree of such force must be reasonable.

Dress codes in public schools have been challenged by students. In one instance a board of education regulation prohibited girls from wearing slacks to school except by special permission of the principal due to cold weather. In striking down the regulation, a court found that while the board of education had the duty to protect students from injury and thus had the power to regulate the students' dress for reasons of safety, the regulation in question bore no relation to protecting the pupils' safety or controlling a disturbance interfering with the education of other students.

DISCRIMINATION

What Is Discrimination?

Many laws in the state distinguish among classes of people, but these laws do not create unconstitutional denials of equal protection. If the differentiation rests on a rational basis there has been no denial of equal protection. For example, juvenile offenders may be treated differently than adults in some ways because there is a reasonable distinction between the two classes.

The equal protection clause is generally applicable to actions by the state, which may also forbid certain acts of private discrimination. State and federal law prohibit racial discrimination in the rental of residential or commercial property. All persons in New York are entitled to admission to places of public accommodation, resort, or amusement. People cannot be excluded from hotels, motels, restaurants, theaters, amusement parks, or other similar facilities because of race, creed, color, or national origin.

There are certain limited exceptions to this general antidiscrimination requirement. New York courts have recognized that private organizations or clubs are not subject to the constitutional standards of the equal protection clause.

Sex Discrimination

In light of changing views on women's rights to equality, New York courts are now broadening constitutional interpretation and examining laws that discriminate on the basis of sex. At one time, for example, women were exempted by statute from jury service, and were underrepresented on juries in proportion to their numbers in the general population. Therefore, the statutory exemption has been abolished.

Other court decisions have made it illegal to distinguish between men and women in publishing help-wanted advertisements, or have required that worker's compensation death benefits be awarded to widows and widowers on the same basis. In addition, the same laws that forbid racial discrimination in employment or housing also specifically prohibit such discrimination based on sex or marital status.

Matrimonial law also reflects changing attitudes toward the roles of men and women in society. Many statutes assumed the traditional image of the husband as provider for the family and the wife as mother and homemaker; as a consequence, under law only women were entitled to receive alimony. As the family law chapter shows, a New York equitable distribution statute has now been enacted requiring that as part of a divorce settlement, women receive a fair share of the property acquired during a marriage.

All the provisions of the equitable distribution law are neutral in gender, providing equal protection for both spouses, depending on the facts of each case. Courts now recognize the ever-increasing role of women as wage earners and providers. Under the new law, courts must show the factors considered and the reasons supporting determinations involving distribution of property, child support, or "maintenance," the statutory term now used in place of alimony.

Age Discrimination

As already shown, in certain instances young people may be treated differently than adults because they are still maturing and have yet to assume full adult responsibilities and attitudes. Age requirements must be met before many responsibilities and rights are assumed by young people. One must be at least eighteen years of age to vote or to enter into a binding contract. To purchase alcoholic beverages an individual must be at least age twenty-one. An adult driver's license may be obtained at eighteen, or at seventeen if the individual has completed an approved driver education course; a restricted license may be issued at age sixteen. Males under the age of sixteen and females under fourteen are prohibited from marrying, and it is possible for a marriage to be voided under certain circumstances if either party is under eighteen. The Labor Law places restrictions on the employment of minors, especially if dangerous machinery or explosives are involved. With certain exceptions such as child entertainers or newspaper carriers, children under fourteen may not be employed.

It is unlawful for an employer to refuse to hire someone solely because that individual is eighteen years or older. Similarly, it is unlawful to terminate people eighteen years or older because of age or to discriminate against them in compensation, promotion, or conditions of employment. Employers or employment agencies may not advertise jobs or make inquiries about prospective employees in a way that indicates any discrimination concerning individuals between the ages of eighteen and sixty-five. Employers are, however, permitted to terminate employees who are physically unable to perform their duties.

Discrimination Because of Disability

New York has recognized the special difficulties of the disabled and has taken steps to help them reach their full potential as members of society. It is now unlawful for employers to refuse to hire persons because of disability, or to discharge or otherwise discriminate against them in wages or conditions of employment. The disabled are also protected against discrimination in purchasing or renting a residence.

The New York Civil Rights Law specifically states that the blind or deaf, even when accompanied by guide dogs, shall not be denied admittance to or equal use of any public facility solely because of their handicaps. In addition, unless it can be demonstrated that an individual's blindness or deafness would prevent that person from performing a particular job, no one who is otherwise qualified may be denied equal opportunity to obtain or advance in a position solely because he or she is blind or deaf.

Newly constructed or rehabilitated public buildings are required to provide for access and use by the physically handicapped. The statute has defined handicaps as wheelchair confinement, impairment causing difficulty or insecurity in walking or climbing stairs, semiambulatory conditions, impairment of hearing or sight, and impairment caused by aging and uncoordination.

State aid has been used to assist school districts in furnishing the costly educational programs and related services essential to help handicapped children under age twenty-one realize their full potential.

appendix
NEW YORK STATE ORGANIZATIONS TO KNOW

Aging

New York State Office for the
  Aging
Agency Building 2
Empire State Plaza
Albany, New York 12223
1–800–342–9871 (hotline)

Banking

New York State Banking
  Department
Consumer Affairs Division of
  Two Rector St.
New York, New York 10006
212–618–6445

Regional Office of the
  Comptroller of the Currency
1211 Avenue of Americas,
  Suite 4250
New York, New York
212–944–3491

Business Permits

Office of Business Permits
Alfred E. Smith Office
  Building
17th Floor
Albany, New York 12225
518–474–8275
1–800–342–3464

Cable TV

New York State Commission
on Cable TV
Tower Building, 21st Floor
Empire State Plaza
Albany, New York 12223
518–474–4992
1–800–342–3330

Charities

New York State Department
of State
Office of Charities Registration
162 Washington Avenue
Albany, New York 12231
518–474–3720

Child Abuse and Maltreatment Reporting Center

Child Abuse and Maltreatment
Reporting Center
40 North Pearl Street
Albany, New York 12243
1–800–342–3700

Committee on Child Welfare

Committee on Child Welfare
2 World Trade Center
New York, New York 10047
212–488–4843

Consumer Complaints (General)

New York State Attorney
General's Office,
Consumer Frauds and
Protection Bureau
State Capitol
Albany, New York 12224
518–474–5481 (also check local
telephone listings)

Consumer Protection

New York State Consumer
Protection Board
99 Washington Avenue
Albany, New York 12210
518–474–8583

Crime Victims Compensation
Board
97 Central Avenue
Albany, New York 12206
518–473–9649

Dentists

Dental Society of the State of
New York
30 East 42nd Street, Room
1606
New York, New York 10017
212–986–3937

Disabled

New York State Office of the
Advocate for the Disabled
Agency Building 1, 10th Floor
Empire State Plaza
Albany, New York 12223
518–474–2825

Workers' Compensation Board
100 Broadway
Albany, New York 12204–9990
518–474–6681

Discrimination

New York State Division of
Human Rights
Twin Towers
99 Washington Avenue
Albany, New York 12210
518–474–2705

Education

Department of Education
89 Washington Avenue
Albany, New York 12234
518–474–3852

Higher Education Services
 Corporation
99 Washington Avenue
Albany, New York 12255
518–473–1574

Energy

New York State Energy
 Office—Hotline
Agency Building 2
Empire State Plaza
Albany, New York 12223
518–474–2121
1–800–342–3722

Energy Audits

New York State Public Service
 Commission
HEICA Hotline
Agency Building 3
Empire State Plaza
Albany, New York 12223
1–800–342–3237

Energy Weatherization

New York State Department of
 State, Division of Economic
 Opportunity
162 Washington Avenue
Albany, New York 12231
518–474–5700

Food Consumers Complaint

Department of Health
Corn Tower Building
Albany, New York 12237
518–474–2121

Food Consumers Complaints
2 World Trade Center
New York, New York 10047
212–498–4820

Funerals

Bureau of Funeral Directing
Corn Tower Building
Empire State Plaza
Albany, New York 12237
518–457–6708

Hospitals

New York State Health
 Department, Bureau of
 Hospital Services
Room 2038
Tower Building
Empire State Plaza
Albany, New York 12237
518–474–4447

Insurance

New York State Insurance
 Department, Consumer
 Services Bureau
Agency Building 1
Empire State Plaza
Albany, New York 12257
518–474–6600
1–800–342–3736

Judges

Office of Court Administration
Empire State Plaza
Agency Building 4
Albany, New York 12223
518–474–3603

Division of Minority Business
 Development, New York
 State Department of
 Commerce
230 Park Avenue
New York, New York 10169
212–309–0400

Department of Social Services
40 North Pearl Street
Albany, New York 12243
1–800–342–3720

Lawyers

New York State Bar
  Association
1 Elk Street
Albany, New York 12207
518–463–3200

Licensing (of Barbers, Beauticians, Hearing Aid Dealers, Apartment Referral Agents, Real Estate Brokers)

New York State Department of
  State Division of Licensing
  Services
162 Washington Avenue
Albany, New York 12231
518–474–2643

Motor Vehicles Recalls

National Highway Traffic
  Safety Administration,
  Department of
  Transportation
460 7th Street Southwest
Washington, DC 20591
202–366–4000
1–800–424–9393

Movers Within New York State

New York State Department of
  Transportation
Regulation Division Building
  4, Room G–16
1220 Washington Avenue
Albany, New York 12232
518–457–6503
212–488–4396

Movers Between States

United States Interstate
  Commerce Commission
12th & Constitution Avenue,
  Northwest
Washington, DC 20423
202–275–0885

Physicians

New York State Department of
  Health, Office of
  Professional Medical
  Conduct
Tower Building
Empire State Plaza
Albany, New York 12237
518–474–8357
212–696–2616

Product Safety

United States Consumer
  Product Safety Commission
6 World Trade Center
New York, New York 10048
212–264–1125

Professional Conduct

New York State Department of
  Education, Division of
  Professional Discipline
622 Third Avenue, 37th Floor
New York, New York 10017
212–557–2100
1–800–442–8106

Public Utilities

New York State Public Service
  Commission
Empire State Plaza
Agency Building 3
Albany, New York 12223
Gas: 518–474–8665
Electric: 518–474–1373
Telephone: 518–474–4504

Youth Division Administration

Youth Division Administration
163 West 125th Street
New York, New York 10027
212–870–4117

Repairs and Used Car Dealers

New York State Department of
    Motor Vehicles, Division of
    Vehicle Safety
Empire State Plaza
Swan Street Building
Albany, New York 12228
518–474–2121
1–800–324–3842

Travel

Amtrak Office of Consumer
    Relations
400 North Capital Northwest
Washington, DC 20001
202–383–2121

American Society of Travel
    Agents
666 5th Avenue, 12th Floor
New York, New York 10103
212–974–0640

Vocational Schools

New York State Educational
    Department, Bureau for
    Proprietory Vocational
    Schools
99 Washington Avenue, Room
    1613
Albany, New York 12234
518–474–3969
212–488–3252